344.0

D1587767

SOCIAL WELFARE LAW

UNITED KINGDOM
Sweet & Maxwell Ltd
London

AUSTRALIA
Law Book Co. Ltd
Sydney

CANADA AND THE USA
Carswell
Toronto

NEW ZEALAND
Brookers
Wellington

SINGAPORE AND MALAYSIA
Sweet and Maxwell
Singapore and Kuala Lumpur

Social Welfare Law

MEL COUSINS

Thomson Round Hall
2002

Published in 2002 by
Round Hall Sweet & Maxwell
43 Fitzwilliam Place,
Dublin 2, Ireland

Typeset by
Gough Typesetting Services, Dublin

Printed by
ColourBooks Ltd, Dublin

ISBN 1-85800-289-3

A catalogue record for this book
is available from the British Library.

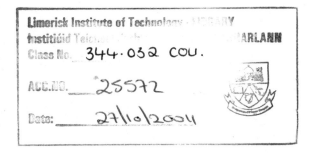

Preface

This book provides a detailed outline of statutory social welfare payments and related issues. It examines, in particular, key issues of relevance to legal practitioners. This is a complex area. In addition to the lengthy primary legislation – the Social Welfare (Consolidation) Act 1993 – there are one or two amending Acts each year. There is also a considerable body of secondary legislation, some of it – despite the consolidation of the main regulations in the 1990s – dating back to the 1950s.

There is, however, a paucity of Irish case law in the social welfare area. And given the fairly rapid rate of legal change in this area, many of the decisions which are given soon become of little relevance.[1] There is, in contrast, extensive U.K. case law in this area — both court decisions and decisions of the specialist Social Security Commissioners.[2] It would be tempting to deluge the reader with references to U.K. authority. I have, however, attempted to resist this temptation and to confine references to those which are clearly relevant. There are, of course, significant differences between the legal and social policy contexts in which social welfare law is interpreted in both countries. More importantly, although the basic principles underpinning our respective systems remain quite similar, there has been a growing difference in the detail of the legislation – particularly since the 1970s – which makes much of the U.K. case law of limited value in many areas.[3]

In view of the pending "incorporation" of the European Convention on Human Rights into Irish law, I have referred to the case law of the European Commission and Court of Human Rights in the social welfare area.[4] I have also made reference to relevant case law from Australia, Canada, New Zealand and the United States of America.

I have, in a number of areas, included details from departmental guidelines

---

[1] See G. Whyte, *Social Inclusion and the Legal System* (IPA, Dublin, 2002), chap. 4 for a concise summary of recent litigation in this area.

[2] For the most recent summary of U.K. law see Wikely, Ogus and Barendt, *The Law of Social Security* (5th ed., Butterworths, London, 2002). This edition was not to hand at the time of writing this book.

[3] It is for that reason that I refer to the older editions of Ogus and Barendt – the leading U.K. text book.

[4] It is striking how many social security cases in the U.K. now involve an ECHR point (albeit usually an unsuccessful one).

as to how particular aspects of the legislation are interpreted. While the departmental interpretation obviously does not have the status of a court decision, it seemed useful that readers should be aware of how an issue is interpreted in practice.

I would like to thank a very wide range of people for their assistance in the preparation of this book. In particular, I must thank Gerry Whyte. Gerry not only commented on a number of chapters but several of the chapters in this book draw on work which we have done jointly over the past decade. I would also like to thank Les Allamby, Geraldine Gleeson, Cyril Havelin, John Hynes, Gerry Mangan, Deirdre McDonough, Michael Murphy and Mike Sullivan, all of whom assisted in one way or another. The usual disclaimers apply. I should emphasise that all views expressed are purely personal.

For access to U.K. court and Social Security Commissioner decisions, to the case law of the European Court of Justice, the European Court of Human Rights, and the case law of Australia, Canada, New Zealand and the United States of America, I would like to thank the Internet. For access to a number of decisions which have, as yet, escaped free Internet access and to other legal materials, I would like to thank the libraries of the Department of Social and Family Affairs and the Honourable Society of the King's Inns.

Catherine Dolan and Elina Talvitie of Round Hall were extremely helpful both in giving direction to the shape of the book and in finalising the text.

The law is stated as I understand it to be on October 1, 2002.

Mel Cousins

Table of Contents

Part II: Old Age, Disability and Unemployment

Table of Cases

Table of Statutes

Social Welfare (Consolidation) Act 1993—*contd.*

Social Welfare (Consolidation) Act 1993—*contd.*

Table of Statutory Instruments

Table of European Legislation

EUROPEAN TREATIES AND CONVENTIONS

E.C. REGULATIONS

CHAPTER 1

The Development of the Social Welfare System in Ireland

1–01 In this chapter we look at the main developments in the Irish social welfare system from its earliest stages to date. We go on, in subsequent chapters, to look at the development of specific schemes and the detailed legal provisions. We first summarise briefly the main features of the current system and some of the main trends in its development.

1–02 The Irish social welfare system currently includes three types of benefits: social insurance (or contributory) schemes; social assistance (or means-tested) schemes; and a universal child benefit. Almost all benefits are paid at a flat (subsistence) rate with increases for adult and child dependants. Most social welfare schemes are administered by the Department of Social and Family Affairs (hereafter the Department), although the residual means-tested supplementary welfare allowance is administered by the regional health boards/authorities on behalf of the Department. In addition there are a number of minor health and disability related payments administered by the Department of Health and Children and the regional health boards.

1–03 The first statutory system of social welfare in Ireland was the means-tested Poor Law (1838). Subsequently a range of social welfare schemes introduced in the United Kingdom at the end of the nineteenth and in the early twentieth century also applied to Ireland.[1] These included the first social insurance scheme introduced in 1911.[2] Thus, at the time of Independence in 1921–22, the basis of the current social insurance and social assistance system already existed in Ireland. Developments since then have consolidated and expanded the social insurance system and introduced new social assistance schemes in order to take people off the unpopular Poor Law. In 1975, the old Poor Law (by then renamed "home assistance") was abolished and replaced by supplementary welfare allowance. Economic recession in the 1980s saw a

---

[1] See M. Cousins, *The Birth of Social Welfare* (Four Courts Press, Dublin, 2002), Chap. 1.

[2] Readers should note that there is often a one or two-year difference between the year in which a measure was enacted by the legislature and that in which it came into effect. The dates given in this book are generally those of the legal adoption.

renewed emphasis on the importance of means-tested payments, although the social insurance scheme continued to expand with its extension to cover the self-employed (1988) and part-time workers (1991). The recent economic boom has seen significant changes in the operation of the social welfare system with a sharp fall in the proportion of individuals of working age on welfare payments.

1. The Development of the System to the Twentieth Century

A. Early Developments (600–1838)

1–04   Early Irish law (Brehon Law) did not provide for any collective system of social welfare.[3] However, it did impose a legal responsibility on the kin group to care for its members who were insane, aged or suffering from physical disability.[4] The kin group consisted of the descendants through the male line of the same great-grandfather. Early Irish law also included provisions imposing liability on individuals to provide support to persons incapacitated by them as a result of an unlawful attack. This was known as sick-maintenance. The original Irish laws were suppressed as the English gained control over an increasing proportion of Ireland, and after about 1600 the Brehon Laws largely disappeared and were replaced by English legislation. In 1634, summoned by the then Viceroy (appointed by the King of England), the Irish Parliament passed an Act for the erecting of Houses of Correction and for the Punishment of Rogues, Vagabonds, Sturdy Beggars and other Lewd and Idle Persons.[5] This provided that houses of correction were to be built in each county where persons could be set to work. The groups to which this Act applied included mendicant scholars, gypsies and labourers unwilling to work for reasonable wages. This Act also provided that "an able bodied rogue" who had deserted his family would be sent to a house of correction until support had been provided. Thus, the onus of support had shifted from the Celtic kin group to the common law concept of the more immediate family. The houses of correction soon fell into disuse and the Government sought other means of controlling the poor. In 1701, vagrancy was made a transportable offence in Ireland. As a vagrant was not allowed to contest the charge of vagrancy, this meant that any poor homeless person could be transported. However, it appears that this draconian measure was also not implemented strictly. In 1771–72,

---

[3]   It should be borne in mind that the Brehon laws were not a formal legal system but rather "a highly idealized picture ... of what popular practices and habits would be like (or might be like) in terms of law ..."; O'Faolain, *The Irish* (Penguin, Harmondsworth, 1969), p. 47.

[4]   Kelly, *A Guide to Early Irish Law* (Dublin Institute for Advanced Studies, 1988).

[5]   Powell, *The Politics of Irish Social Policy 1600–1990* (Edwin Mellen, Lewiston, 1992).

the Irish Parliament enacted legislation to set up houses of industry. These were intended to provide shelter for the "aged, infirm and industrious" and to provide a prison for the "profligate, idle and refractory". This was in effect a model for the workhouses which later appeared under the Poor Law. However, unlike the situation in the United Kingdom, no Poor Law existed in Ireland prior to 1838 and the relief of the poor was the sole responsibility of charitable organisations, including church bodies.

B. The Introduction of the Poor Law (1838–97)

1–05 In England, the Poor Law had existed since the sixteenth century. In 1834, the English Poor Law system was extensively revised and, following the establishment of several Commissions and Inquiries to investigate the matter, it was decided to establish a broadly similar system of Poor Law in Ireland.[6] The Poor Law system was based on the principle of "less eligibility", *i.e.* the conditions for those in receipt of Poor Law must be worse than those of the poorest labourer. As a result of the very impoverished conditions of Irish workers in the early nineteenth century, it was insisted that support would only be provided to those prepared to enter a workhouse and it was intended that "outdoor relief" would not be provided. One of the arguments put forward by those who objected to the extension of the English system of Poor Law to Ireland was that the conditions of Irish workers were so bad that it would be impossible to achieve the principle of "less eligibility". Thus, it was feared that the Poor Law would undermine the Irish economy as it would be at least as attractive to exist on the Poor Law as to work. Powell[7] argues that the introduction of the Poor Law was a response to a recognition that the agricultural system was incapable of supporting the increasing population and that a transformation of the Irish peasantry into wage labour was ultimately necessary. The Poor Law was to support this period of transition. In the event, the introduction of the Poor Law in Ireland was followed almost immediately by a series of famines in the 1840s culminating in the Great Famine of 1846–49. The Poor Law was not intended to cope with the extent of poverty caused by the famine and it is estimated that a million people died and a million others emigrated during the famine years. The famine was followed by a long-term pattern of emigration such that the population dropped from over 6.5 million people in 1841 (in the part of Ireland which now constitutes the Republic) to below three million in the 1920s. However, one consequence of the famine was that, in 1847, the Poor Law was amended to allow outdoor relief to be paid. This remained a feature of poor law relief in Ireland.

---

[6] In addition to providing support in cash or in kind, the Poor Law also provided a range of medical and other social services; Powell, above, n.5.

[7] Powell, above, n.5, p. 52.

2. Developments in the Twentieth Century

A. U.K. Laws Applied to Ireland (1897–1921)

1–06 In the period until Ireland became independent of the United Kingdom in 1921–22, the developing United Kindgom social welfare system generally applied to Ireland.[8] Thus, the Workmen's Compensation Act[9] of 1897 applied as did the non-contributory old age pension established in 1908.[10] The majority of benefits under the National Insurance Act 1911 (including unemployment, sickness and maternity benefit) also applied, although medical benefit (*i.e.* treatment by a general practitioner and other medical expenses) was not extended to this country as a result of the opposition of the Catholic Church and sections of the Irish medical profession.[11] The Church argued that the national insurance system as a whole was not appropriate to Irish conditions, which were agricultural rather than industrial. The opposition of the medical profession appears to have been largely based on a claim for higher remuneration. Barrington argues that this outcome favoured doctors with large private practices who feared a loss of paying patients. She also points out that the approach of the Catholic Church "illustrates the way in which the bishops viewed the issues raised by the Bill through predominantly rural and capitalist eyes and from the standpoint of the farmer and the small trader".[12] The failure to extend medical benefit to Ireland began a trend whereby primary health care did not develop as an insurance-based scheme, unlike in most other countries in Europe.

1–07 Although much U.K. legislation was applied to Ireland, it must be remembered that circumstances in Ireland were quite different to those which applied in England and Wales. Ireland as a whole had not experienced large-scale industrialisation and a large proportion of the population was engaged in agriculture. In 1926, 44 per cent of the male working population was engaged in farming other than in an employed capacity (*i.e.* as employers, self-employed or assisting relatives), compared to only 32.5 per cent manual employees.[13] Friendly societies developed relatively slowly and it has been estimated that in the early twentieth century there were only about 40,000 members of such

---

[8] Cousins, above, n.1, Chap. 1.

[9] The workmen's compensation scheme was not a state-funded system of social welfare but provided for a system of compensation for injured workers by their employers.

[10] Carney, "A Case Study in Social Policy: The Non-Contributory Old Age Pension" (1985) 33 *Administration* 483.

[11] Barrington, *Health, Medicine and Politics in Ireland 1900–1970* (IPA, Dublin, 1987).

[12] *ibid.*, p. 50.

[13] This heavy dependence on farming persisted into the 1960s. In 1961, 36% of the male working population still fell into this category.

societies.[14] Thus, the social welfare schemes which applied to employees only, such as the workmen's compensation scheme and the national insurance system, had a significantly different impact in Ireland than in England.

B. Independence and After (1922–44)

1–08 Following Independence, Ireland was governed by a conservative Cumann na nGaedheal Government until 1932. During this period there was little development in social welfare and, in fact, the amount of the old age pension was reduced by 10 per cent in 1924.[15] The Democratic Programme of the First Dáil had called for the abolition of the "odious, degrading and foreign poor law system", but the Poor Law system was retained, although indoor relief was largely abolished and outdoor relief was renamed "home assistance".[16] In addition the administrative structure of the Poor Law was extensively reformed. The National Insurance Act 1911 had been based on the assumption of a male breadwinner supporting his dependent wife and children. Reflecting the generally lower rates of women's earnings, different rates of unemployment and sickness benefit were paid to men and women. The earnings of married women were assumed to be of secondary importance and even lower rates of benefit were generally paid to such women. In 1929, the government reinforced this assumption of women's dependency by providing that a woman's membership of the insurance scheme terminated on marriage. In return women received a once-off marriage benefit.

1–09 It was not until the Fianna Fáil Government came to power in 1932 that significant developments occurred in the area of social welfare.[17] First, in response to the unemployment crisis in the 1930s, an unemployment assistance scheme was introduced in 1933. This meant that one group of people (unemployed people without entitlement to unemployment benefit or whose entitlement had expired) no longer had to rely on the Poor Law for support. Secondly, a widow's and orphan's pension scheme was introduced in 1935. This followed the introduction of a similar scheme in the United Kingdom in 1925 and the report of a Committee on Widows and Orphans Pensions (1933). The Irish scheme provided for a mainly insurance-based pension but a parallel means-tested pension was subsequently introduced, because of the narrow scope of the social insurance scheme (with only 32 per cent of the male population of insurable age actually covered by social insurance). Thus, a further group of people were removed from the scope of the Poor Law.

---

[14] Barrington, above, n.11.
[15] Cousins, above, n.1, Chap. 2.
[16] Ó Cinnéide, *A Law for the Poor* (IPA, Dublin, 1970).
[17] Cousins, above, n.1, Chap. 3.

1–10 The benefits provided under the national insurance scheme were administered by a range of non-profit making organisations, including friendly societies which had already been involved in the provision of such benefits. The operation of these bodies was overseen by the government-appointed Irish Insurance Commissioners. Only bodies approved by the Commissioners were allowed to administer the benefits. In 1933 there were about 474,000 insured persons affiliated to 65 approved societies. The societies enjoyed a large degree of autonomy in financial matters and, while there were common rates of contributions, benefits varied from one society to another. The solvency of the individual societies varied greatly due both to variations in type of membership and to variations in administrative efficiency. By the early 1930s, although the system overall was solvent, many individual societies were threatened with insolvency. These problems together with variations in benefits and the administrative difficulties and costs generated by the multiplicity of societies subsequently led to their amalgamation into the National Health Insurance Society in 1933. This approach had been recommended by the Committee of Inquiry into Health Insurance and Medical Services (1925). In 1936, the Catholic Bishop of Clonfert, Bishop Dignan, was appointed Chairman of the Society. In 1939, the Poor Law was further revised and renamed "public assistance". However, it remained a locally administered discretionary payment, and the rates of assistance and administrative practices varied greatly from one area to another.

1–11 In 1944, following the report of an interdepartmental committee in 1942, a children's allowance for families with three or more children was introduced.[18] This led to a significant increase in the level of social welfare spending. The introduction of children's allowance followed a trend evident in other European countries to provide a family allowance in the post-war period. In total, 11 European countries introduced family allowances in the period between 1921 and 1944, including Austria (1921), Belgium (1930), France (1932), Italy (1937), Spain and Hungary (1938), Netherlands (1939) and Portugal (1942). The purpose of the payment was declared to be to assist in the "alleviation of want in large families" rather than any pro-natalist policy.[19] The interdepartmental committee had recommended that, as in several other countries, the payments should be means-tested. Subsequently, Seán Lemass T.D., Minister for Industry and Commerce, had proposed an insurance-based payment. However, the Government decided to opt for a universal payment in respect of all children (although the income tax child dependent allowances were reduced where children's allowance was payable).[20] Seán

---

[18] Cousins, above, n.1, Chap. 5.
[19] 92 *Dáil Debates*, Cols 23 *et seq.*
[20] The clawback was dropped in 1954, although a similar arrangement was introduced between 1969 and 1974.

Lemass, the Minister responsible, explained that the decision not to have an insurance-based scheme was based on the fact that it would be impossible to collect contributions from self-employed persons and other non-employees and that, as a result, these groups would not benefit from an insurance-type scheme. The debate on children's allowances was influenced by the publication in the United Kingdom of the Beveridge report (1942), which was cited in the Dáil debates during the discussion of the new payment. In fact, in this case Ireland anticipated the United Kingdom, which did not introduce such a payment until the following year.

1–12 Expenditure on social welfare increased sharply in the mid-1930s following the introduction of the unemployment assistance and widow's and orphan's pensions schemes, and again in the early 1940s with the establishment of children's allowances. Expenditure as a proportion of national income was about 3 per cent in the second half of the 1920s and the early 1930s.[21] It subsequently rose to almost 5 per cent by the late 1930s, reflecting the increased spending by the Fianna Fáil Government. This subsequently declined to about 3.5 per cent by 1945 as social welfare spending failed to keep pace with the sharp increase in national income. As can be seen from Table 1, means-tested payments dominated the system in its early years, with over two-thirds of social welfare expenditure being means-tested as opposed to one-third by way of social insurance payments. However, by 1945 this had been reduced to about 60 per cent, although the shift was towards the universal children's allowance (14 per cent) rather than to social insurance payments.

1–13 In summary, following an initial period of austerity up to 1932, there was a development in social welfare either in response to a crisis situation (unemployment) or for particular categories of claimant who were seen as deserving (widows, orphans and large families). The commitment to the "deserving" poor can be seen in the new Constitution adopted in 1937, Article 45 of which sets out non-binding principles of social policy including a commitment by the State to contribute, where necessary, "to the support of the infirm, the widow, the orphan, and the aged". The structure of the Irish welfare system began to diverge from the United Kingdom system during this period, although where schemes were introduced in Ireland, United Kingdom provisions tended to be used as a guide.

C. Post-War Expansion (1945–54)

1–14 This period began with the publication of several Irish responses to

---

[21] These figures must be treated with some caution as no official estimates were produced before 1938.

the Beveridge report and proposals for expansion of the Irish system. These included an article by a prominent Catholic theologian and future bishop, Revd Cornelius Lucey, who, while commenting favourably on the report's proposals for the United Kingdom, did not support its application in Ireland.[22] While accepting the necessity to plan for a more comprehensive social welfare system in the near future, he argued that Ireland should not turn to an industrialised country such as Great Britain for inspiration but rather to countries with a more similar economic position and to Catholic social teaching. Revd Lucey argued that the majority of the Irish population were property owners – not employees – and therefore in a position to support themselves without compulsory state insurance. Somewhat in contradiction to this point, he went on to argue that many were so poor that compulsory insurance contributions would lead to bankruptcy. He supported the retention of a (modified) means-tested system, the introduction of pay-related contributions and benefits and the administration of the scheme by a vocational body (*i.e.* consisting of representatives of the various interested parties) such as the National Health Insurance Society.

1–15 Shortly after this, Dr Dignan, in his capacity as Chairman of the Society, published a plan for Social Security.[23] He argued for the extension of social insurance to all employees (including public servants) and, on a voluntary basis, to the self-employed. Like Revd Lucey, he supported earnings-related contributions and benefits. All schemes were to be amalgamated under the control of one vocational body responsible to a Minister for Social Security but with a wide degree of autonomy. This proposal was influenced by Catholic social teaching (including the principle of subsidiarity) and by the experience of Catholic European countries rather than the British experience. The vocational aspects of the proposals were also in line with the proposals of the Government-appointed Commission on Vocational Organisation (1943). However, the government did not respond favourably either to the proposals or to the fact that Dr Dignan had taken it upon himself to make them and, when his period as Chairman of the National Health Insurance Society ended in 1945, he was replaced by a civil servant.[24]

1–16 Up to 1947, the administration of the social welfare system was the responsibility of a range of different departments, including the Departments of Local Government and Public Health (old age pensions), Industry and Commerce (unemployment insurance and workmen's compensation), the

---

[22] Lucey, "The Beveridge Report and Éire" (1943) XXXII *Studies* 36.
[23] Dignan, *Social Security: Outlines of a Scheme of National Health Insurance* (Sligo, 1945).
[24] Whyte, *Church and State in Modern Ireland, 1923–1979* (Gill & Macmillan, Dublin, 1980).

Revenue Commissioners (old age pensions) and the National Health Insurance Society (sickness and maternity benefits). In 1947 a unified Department of Social Welfare was established, which took over responsibility for the majority of social welfare schemes.[25] Following the establishment of the Department, a White Paper on *Social Security* was published in 1949.[26] This proposed the extension of social insurance to all employees and the establishment of a range of new benefits, including a retirement pension.[27] While it followed the recommendation of the Dignan proposals on several issues, it differed in opting for a centralised system of control through the Department of Social Welfare and for flat-rate benefits and contributions. Thus, it followed the solutions proposed by the Beveridge report in these areas. The White Paper discussed the possibility of relating benefits to wages but, echoing the Beveridge report, it argued that flat-rate benefits were preferable. This was based on the argument that the State should only insist on a basic standard of protection, that earnings-related benefits might provide a "moral danger" and could impose intolerable financial pressures on contribution levels, that earnings-related benefits would be complicated and, finally, that it was desirable to leave room for voluntary private insurance. The White Paper also argued against extending social insurance to the self-employed as many farmers were too poor to afford the contributions and the collection of contributions would create great administrative difficulties.

1–17 The proposals contained in the White Paper were introduced by the then inter-party Government (made up of a very wide spectrum of parties) in the Social Welfare Bill 1950.[28] However, the Government fell before the Bill was passed. Many of the proposals were accepted by the new Fianna Fáil Government in the Social Welfare Act 1952.[29] This unified the various existing schemes and introduced a new maternity allowance. Equal rates of benefit for single men and women were also introduced, but married women still received lower rates and many other areas of gender discrimination remained. At this time, children's allowance became payable for the second child in the family (although this was largely to compensate for the reduction in food subsidisation). However, the proposal to extend social insurance to all employees was not accepted and employees earning above a set amount were excluded from insurance. Although civil and public servants were insured under the general social insurance scheme, they paid reduced contributions and were entitled to limited benefits on the grounds that they had general

---

[25] Cousins, above, n.1, Chap. 6.
[26] See Lavan, ed., *50 Years of Social Welfare Policy* (Department of Social, Community and Family Affairs, 2000).
[27] Cousins, above, n.1, Chap. 7.
[28] 124 *Dáil Debates*, Cols 1069 *et seq.*
[29] 130 *Dáil Debates*, Cols 616 *et seq.*

security of employment and had occupational pension schemes. The retirement pension was not introduced at that time, although a contributory old age pension payable at age 70 was subsequently introduced in 1961.

1–18 Thus, in terms of the scope of the social insurance scheme, the Irish scheme, unlike that in the United Kingdom, excluded (or substantially excluded) the higher paid non-manual workers (the middle class), the self-employed and civil servants from coverage and from liability to pay contributions. The exclusion of the self-employed can be seen as recognising the interests of the better-off members of that group in that they did not have to pay contributions while the poorer members received tax-funded social assistance payments. The exclusion of the non-manual workers recognised their lower exposure to insurable risks, while the partial inclusion of civil servants (with their low level of exposure to insurable risks and separate occupational schemes) emphasises both the extent to which the scheme recognised the interests of specific advantaged groups by excluding them from liability to pay social insurance contributions and the *étatist* policy of the Irish State in providing generous welfare benefits to its civil servants. In his speech on the second stage of the 1952 Bill, the Minister for Social Welfare, James Ryan, T.D. accepted that the scope of the Irish social insurance scheme was not comprehensive and stated: "I cannot see either the justice or necessity for the inclusion of classes that can never benefit"; he could not approve of what he described as "hidden" taxation on such classes by the imposition of social insurance contributions.[30] Thus, in contrast to the relative universality of the U.K. system post-Beveridge, the Irish system remained essentially fragmented and showed little commitment to inter-class solidarity.

1–19 Not surprisingly, given the different proposals put forward by prominent Catholic churchmen, exponents of Catholic social teaching did not welcome the White Paper or the subsequent Bill.[31] There was opposition in particular to the proposed abolition of the National Health Insurance Society and the centralisation of control within the Department of Social Welfare and to the fact that the scheme did not apply to the self-employed. However, the hierarchy as a body did not come out against the proposals and by 1952 the Fianna Fáil Government encountered little opposition in introducing the legislation.

1–20 Thus, the 1952 Act integrated and improved the existing social insurance scheme and provided a national social welfare system under the central administration of the Department of Social Welfare (although at a

---

[30] 130 *Dáil Debates*, Col. 633.
[31] Dignan, "The Government Proposals for Social Security" (1950) IV *Christus Rex* 103; Whyte, above, n.24, p. 179.

time when services were being unified in one department, the Department of Health established two "health-related" income maintenance payments under its own auspices: infectious diseases maintenance allowance (1947) and disabled persons maintenance allowance (1954)). The influence of the Beveridge report can clearly be seen in the adoption of flat-rate contributions and benefits and, again, U.K. provisions tended to be used as a model for the introduction of schemes in Ireland, *e.g.* maternity allowance. In the period between 1947 and 1954, social welfare expenditure as a percentage of GDP grew from 4.5 per cent to 5.9 per cent, with a "growth pause" in 1950 and 1951 followed by rapid growth to the mid-1950s. The expansion of social insurance and the extension of children's allowance resulted in a shift away from assistance payments; by 1955 less than half of expenditure was on means-tested payments (Table 1). In 1953, 59 per cent of those in employment were insured under the social welfare scheme (52 per cent for all benefits). However, no national means-tested payment was established during this period; the old Poor Law (now home assistance) remaining in force.

D. Consolidation (1954–64)

1–21 Following the activity of the previous decade, the period from the mid-1950s to the mid-1960s was one of consolidation. The mid to late-1950s saw a period of economic depression in Ireland which did not begin to change until after the publication of the Programme for Economic Expansion (1958). The only major developments during this period were the introduction of a contributory old age pension in 1961 and the extension of children's allowance to the first child in 1963. The policy during this period is perhaps best described in the Second Programme for Economic Expansion (1964), which stated: "the policy adopted in the first and second programmes is to improve social welfare services in line with improvements in national production and prosperity". The Programme declared that such increases must have regard to the extent to which national resources make "such increases possible and desirable". During this period, expenditure as a percentage of GDP remained fairly static, with a increase from 5.9 per cent in 1954 to 6.2 per cent in 1965. This conceals a drop in expenditure both in real terms and as a proportion of GDP in 1958 and 1959, with spending as a proportion of GDP not returning to 1957 levels until the early 1960s. The introduction of the contributory old age pension marked a sharp increase in the importance of social insurance payments, with expenditure on social insurance growing from 28 per cent of spending in 1955 to 46 per cent in 1965. Social assistance now accounted for less than 30 per cent of all spending. The importance of state funding declined from 76 per cent in 1955 to 68 per cent in 1965, with a consequent rise in the level of employers' and employees' contributions arising from the shift to insurance payments (Tables 2 and 3).

E. Economic Development (1965–79)

1–22   The Irish economy improved substantially in the period from the early 1960s until the 1970s. This period corresponded with a significant expansion in the social welfare scheme. The change in government policy can be seen in the Third Programme for Economic and Social Development published in 1969. In contrast to the cautious approach of the Second Programme, this set out an extensive list of promised reforms including the introduction of pay-related benefits, and of retirement and invalidity pensions. In the same period, the emphasis of the Catholic social movement shifted away from concern about excessive state intervention towards calling for increased state action in many poverty-related areas.[32] However, this did not mean that there was unanimous support in the Catholic hierarchy for an expanded welfare state, and several eminent Catholic theologians remained firmly opposed to "excessive" state intervention in social welfare.[33]

1–23   In 1966, the workmen's compensation scheme was finally abolished and, following the report of a Commission on Workmen's Compensation (1962), an occupational injuries scheme was adopted which was largely similar to the industrial injuries scheme in the United Kingdom. A range of new social insurance payments was also established, including a retirement pension payable at age 65 (1970), an invalidity pension for persons with a long-term incapacity (1970), a death grant (1970) and a deserted wife's benefit (1973). In 1974, social insurance was extended to all private-sector employees (except part-time workers). This resulted in an increase in the numbers insured as a proportion of those in employment from 73 per cent (66 per cent insured for all benefits) in 1973 to 85 per cent (73 per cent for all benefits) in 1975. The eligibility age for the old age pension was reduced from 70 to 66 years between 1973 and 1977. A pay-related benefit scheme was introduced in 1974 payable with unemployment, maternity and disability benefits. This followed the introduction of earnings-related supplements in the United Kingdom in 1966. However, the earnings related pension for long-term pensions introduced in the United Kingdom in 1975 was never followed in Ireland, although a Green Paper on a National Income Related Pension scheme was published in 1976.

1–24   In the area of social assistance or means-tested payments, several new payments were introduced, particularly in the area of payments to lone mothers (1970–74). Many of these payments had been recommended by the government-appointed Commission on the Status of Women (1972). A limited payment towards the costs of caring for older and disabled persons was also

---

[32] Whyte, above, n.24, Chap. XI.
[33] Newman, *Puppets of Utopia* (Four Courts Press, Dublin, 1987).

established (1968). In 1975, the remnants of the old Poor Law were finally abolished and a new national means-tested scheme (supplementary welfare allowance) was established. This supplemented rather than replaced the existing categorical payments to the unemployed, widows, etc. While the legislation established a legal right to benefit in some cases, the administration of the payment remained at a local level and much of the old discretionary approach to this payment remained.

1–25 As we have seen, the self-employed were generally not covered for contingencies such as unemployment and disability under the social welfare system. However, some self-employed persons on low incomes were allowed to claim unemployment assistance if their income was below the relevant threshold. In rural areas, occupiers of land over a certain value were automatically disqualified for unemployment assistance, regardless of means, from March to October; as were all men without dependants in rural areas from June to October (when it was assumed that seasonal farm work would be available). In 1965, following an Inter-departmental Committee Report which indicated that the means test acted as a disincentive to increased output by small holders, a scheme of notional assessment was introduced in the poorest farming areas. The farmer's entitlement was assessed not on the actual income but on a notional basis according to the value of the farmland owned. Thus, a farmer could increase income without a decrease in assistance. The numbers in receipt of "smallholders assistance" increased to over 30,000 by 1976. Concern at the increase in numbers led to restrictions on the scheme in the late 1970s.

1–26 Over this period, the emphasis continued to shift towards social insurance payments which accounted for over half of spending by 1975 and over 55 per cent by 1980 (see Table 1). This was due in part to a decline in the importance of children's allowance (8.5 per cent of expenditure in 1980), the real rate of which had been allowed to decline so that it did not keep pace with the growth in GDP nor with the growth in relative prices. Social assistance payments increased slightly to over 30 per cent of total spending. The proportion of funding from employers increased substantially from 15 per cent in 1965 to 31.5 per cent in 1980. This allowed a decrease in state funding from 68 per cent in 1965 to 56 per cent in 1980, while employee funding declined slightly to 12 per cent (Table 2). As a proportion of GDP, social welfare spending increased sharply from 6.2 per cent in 1965 to 7.6 per cent in 1970 and 10.7 per cent by 1980. There was a steady growth in the period to 1976 followed by a drop in spending as a proportion of GDP between 1977 and 1979 before a further increase in 1980.

1–27 The end of the 1970s probably marked the high point in the expansionist phase of the scheme. As we have seen, a Green Paper on earnings-related pensions was published in 1976. This was followed by a Green Paper on the expansion of social insurance to the self-employed in 1978. In 1974, a limited pay-related contribution had been introduced to finance pay-related benefit and, in 1979, the contribution system was altered from a flat-rate system to a pay-related system (PRSI). Thus, at the end of the 1970s, the Irish system looked as though it might develop in the same way as the U.K. system, with an expansion of social insurance to the self-employed and a move towards earnings-related contributions and benefits. The U.K. system had itself been moving more towards the Continental system of earnings-related benefits in the 1970s. However, the move towards a pay-related system in Ireland did not develop further, and the marked change in the U.K. system was already under way with the election of the Conservative Government in 1979.

F. Crisis and Consolidation (1980–96)

(1) Growth in social welfare spending and cost containment

1–28   The sustained economic boom of the 1960s and early 1970s was not repeated in this period and there was a sharp rise in unemployment over the period in question, with the numbers in receipt of unemployment payments rising from 109,000 at the start of 1980 to 290,000 at the end of 1993. These difficulties were reflected in cuts introduced in some areas of social welfare. However, unlike the situation in the United Kingdom, there was no large-scale assault on social welfare spending and in many areas the social welfare scheme expanded. Social welfare expenditure continued to grow sharply in the early 1980s, reaching 13 per cent of GDP in 1985. It subsequently declined to 9.6 per cent by 1996. In 1996, the State financed 57 per cent of expenditure, with 30 per cent coming from employers, 10 per cent from employees and 3 per cent from the self-employed. The trend towards increased expenditure on social insurance payments has been reversed, and in 1996 only 41 per cent of expenditure was in this area, with 45 per cent on social assistance, 9 per cent on child benefit and 5 per cent on administration. The shift towards assistance appears to arise largely from the sharp increase in the numbers in receipt of means-tested unemployment payments.

1–29   The Coalition Government (1982–87) had found it impossible to halt the rise in the proportion of GDP spent on social welfare in the light of the continuing economic crisis and the opposition to social welfare cuts from the Labour Party – the smaller coalition partner. However, the Fianna Fáil Government, on its return to office in 1987, made determined efforts to control costs. These policies broadly continued under successive administrations and, indeed, Fianna Fáil Minister Dr Michael Woods T.D. was in charge of the Department for much of this period. In particular, these policies centred on controlling the cost to the State of the Social Insurance Fund. This involved increasing the contribution requirements for several benefits, thereby tightening the link between benefit entitlement and participation in the paid labour force. This in turn had the effect of forcing people with inadequate contribution records to rely on means-tested benefits and of increasing the importance of social assistance as a proportion of spending. The level of the state subvention to the Social Insurance Fund dropped from 31 per cent in 1986 to a mere 5 per cent by 1996. The extension of social insurance to the self-employed in 1988 can also be seen as a part of this trend (albeit a short-term measure) as funding from the self-employed (4 per cent of the Social Insurance Fund by 1993) greatly exceeded expenditure in the early years. The reduction and eventual abolition of pay-related benefit (1994) formed part of this policy of making the Social Insurance Fund self-sufficient and also reduced the notional replacement ratio for short-term benefits. This shift away from social insurance payments towards social assistance echoed developments in the United Kingdom, where it was argued that means testing allowed payments to be concentrated on those most in need.

1–30 In 1992, the newly appointed Minister for Social Welfare, Charlie McCreevy T.D., introduced a range of social welfare cuts – immortalised in the 1992 election campaign as the "dirty dozen". Some of these cuts were quite minor, but widespread concern about the future of the social welfare system was caused by the manner of their introduction, combined with claims that the cost of the social welfare system was almost out of control (at a time when spending as a percentage of GDP was significantly lower than it had been in 1986) and warnings that "in the years to come we will not have the resources to pay those in need, for example, the old, the sick and people on pensions".[34] It is commonly believed that this had a negative impact on Fianna Fáil's performance in the subsequent election: 1993 saw the return to the Department of Michael Woods and the partial reversal of some of the cuts. The issue of the taxation of short-term social welfare benefits was addressed with disability benefit and unemployment benefit becoming taxable in 1993.

(2) Commission on Social Welfare

1–31 One of the main features of this period was the report of the government-appointed Commission on Social Welfare (1986) The Commission, which had undertaken the first comprehensive review of the social welfare code since the 1949 White Paper, made a total of 65 recommendations. It generally recommended a consolidation and expansion of the existing scheme rather than any radically new approach. Its priority recommendations were for increased rates of benefits; improvements in child income support; the extension of the social insurance base; and improved

---

[34] Quoted in Council for Social Welfare, *Emerging Trends in the Social Welfare System* (CSU, Dublin, 1992).

delivery of services. Although there has been no clear government commitment to the full implementation of the report, in practice the thrust of many of its recommendations has been followed. The Commission played an important role at a time of financial difficulties for the social welfare system both in expressing and confirming a consensus on continued support for the Irish welfare system and in setting targets for "adequate" welfare rates. In 1991, the Government and the social partners agreed to raise benefit levels to the "priority" rates set by the Commission by 1993. This commitment was achieved in 1994.

(3) Social insurance and social assistance

1–32   The major initiatives in the period were the extension of social insurance to the self-employed in 1988 and to part-time workers in 1991. The former extended social insurance to about 130,000 persons, although they were only entitled to a very limited range of benefits, primarily old age and widow's pensions. This allowed an initial increase in insurance revenue through the extra contributions. In 1991, social insurance was extended to all workers earning over £25 (now €38) per week; this meant that a further 25,000 workers (predominantly women) became entitled to pro-rata short-term benefits.

1–33   Several means-tested schemes were introduced in the period 1988–96. These included a pre-retirement allowance, which was largely a measure to get unemployed persons approaching retirement age who were in receipt of unemployment assistance to "pre-retire", whereby they received the same rate of payment without having to be available for and seeking employment. As a result, there was a reduction in the recorded unemployment figures. A lone parent's allowance was introduced in 1990, which amalgamated and extended the existing lone parent's schemes. In 1996, this was expanded into a one-parent family payment to replace the existing deserted wife's benefit scheme (for new claimants). A carer's allowance was also introduced, although take-up was initially much lower than expected. These two payments recognised the caring responsibilities of women (96 per cent of lone parent claimants and 77 per cent of carers are women). In 1986, the responsibility for funding the supplementary welfare allowance scheme was transferred entirely to central government and local authority funding was abolished. This represented the final stage in a long process of transferring responsibility for such funding from local authorities (as under the Poor Law) to central government, a process which can also be seen in relation to health services. The special scheme of unemployment assistance for farmers was abolished in 1983, but about 12,000 smallholders continued to claim unemployment assistance. In 1996, the means-tested disabled person's maintenance allowance was transferred from the Department of Health to the Department of Social

Welfare and renamed disability allowance. This meant that the vast majority of contingencies were now catered for by means-tested schemes under the auspices of the Department of Social Welfare.

(4) Child income support

1–34 Income support for children was restructured in the mid-1980s with the introduction of a means-tested family income supplement (FIS) (1984), the general abolition of child dependant allowances under the tax code and the renaming of children's allowance as "child benefit" (1986). The original intention was that the child benefit would be increased significantly and would be taxable, eventually replacing FIS. However, the amount of child benefit was not increased significantly when the tax allowances were abolished in 1986. Family income supplement is a payment to low-income families in employment and is largely based on the similar U.K. payment. It encountered similar difficulties to the U.K. scheme in terms of low take-up of benefit. In 1995, the new Rainbow Government provided significant increases in child benefit payments and froze the level of allowances for child dependants. However, it did not provide any further significant increases in the remainder of its term of office.

(5) E.U. Equality Directive

1–35 The implementation of the E.U. Directive on equal treatment for men and women in matters of social security[35] created major difficulties for the Irish scheme as it required considerable amendment of the welfare code (see Chapter 9). This led to a delay in implementation of the Directive between 1984 and 1986, during which period many married women continued to receive lower rates of benefits than their male counterparts. This delay led to considerable litigation which, in turn, led to a government decision to pay arrears of benefit to over 40,000 married women amounting to over £60 million. Subsequently, a further £250 million was paid to 77,500 women in settlement of their claims. The legislation, which came into effect in 1986, removed direct discrimination against women in those areas within its scope, and in 1994 the widow's pension scheme was extended to widowers. Directly discriminatory provisions remain in relation to some family payments but this is allowed under the Directive.

1–36 Over the period from 1980, there were a number of distinct trends in the social welfare system. The rise in unemployment led to greatly increased numbers of claimants relying on social welfare support. This, in turn, led to a

---

[35] Directive 79/7 [1979] O.J. L6/24.

growth in the level of cost and attempts to limit spending. The level of total spending as a percentage of GDP was at an historically high level over the entire period, fluctuating with the performance of the economy and employment levels. In relation to the social insurance scheme, the State attempted to cut its subvention to the fund. While there was an increased reliance on means-tested payments over the period, the real value of many payments increased. Moreover, a sustained attack on the level of social welfare payments, particularly from employers' organisations and economists, was not reflected in government policies, and the same employers' organisations have agreed to substantial rises in social welfare rates in the three National Programmes from 1987.

G. "Opportunity and Incentive" (1997–   )[36]

1–37 The Irish economy began to grow dramatically from the early 1990s, although it took some time for this to feed though to the social welfare system. Economic growth in recent years has been exceptional in comparative and historical terms, with Ireland now exceeding the E.U. average in terms of GDP per capita. The rapid economic growth has had major implications for the social welfare system, although there have been relatively few changes in the structure of the system in the recent period. There has been a dramatic increase in the numbers insured under the social insurance scheme (an increase of two-thirds over the decade of the 1990s (Table 4). As a result of the significant growth in social insurance contributions, the Social Insurance Fund has become self-financing for the first time since it was established.

1–38 The level of unemployment fell dramatically to under 140,000 in early 2001 (before the world economic downturn). Also, the proportion of the working-age population dependent on welfare fell rapidly from one in four in 1997 to one-in-five by 2000. There was a much greater emphasis on an active role for social welfare policy in relation to people of working age. This was particularly apparent in relation to those on unemployment payments, where the Employment Action Plan (1998) required that unemployed people passing a certain duration of employment be referred to FÁS, the state employment and training agency, for an assessment of their labour market status. Related measures were also gradually introduced on a trial basis in relation to lone parents and people with disabilities. In the early years of the Government led by Fianna Fáil from 1997, welfare rates for those of working age increased less rapidly than take-home pay (although well ahead of inflation), leading to

---

[36] The reference is to the Government's Action Programme (1997), which seeks to establish a society "where all citizens have the opportunity and the incentive to participate fully in the social and economic life of the country".

a fall in replacement ratios. Thus, the emphasis for those of working age was heavily on incentivisation. More recently, given the significant fall in unemployment levels and in the context of the recommendations of the Social Welfare Benchmarking and Indexation (2001) group established under the Programme for Prosperity and Fairness, the Government has given a commitment to raise social welfare levels to a benchmark of €150 in 2002 terms to be met by 2007 in conjunction with a continued active social policy.[37] One of the challenges for the coming years will be to ensure that policy does not return to the old passive approach of compensation rather than activation.

1–39 In relation to pensions, significantly higher increases have been given to pensioners in the period from 1997, with the old age pension increasing as a percentage of gross average industrial earnings towards the target of 34 per cent set in 1998 by the National Pensions Policy Initiative.[38] In addition, the population has been further incentivised to build on the base of the social welfare pension by providing personal pension cover with the introduction in 2002 of the new personal retirement savings account (PRSA) to which increased tax incentives apply. A National Pensions Reserve Fund has been established to fund future pensions with a legal commitment to put aside 1 per cent of GNP per annum.

1–40 In the area of child support, the policy of the Rainbow Government of freezing child dependant allowances and putting any available resources into child benefit increases was continued by the coalition led by Fianna Fáil; but, in the early years of that Government, the level of resources invested was low. However, in 1999, the Government decided to embark on a three-year programme of investment which will see £1 billion being invested in the child benefit scheme by 2003 and the rates of payment almost tripled. In addition, the Government has given a commitment to set basic child income support (*i.e.* child benefit and allowances for child dependants) at 33–35 per cent of the minimum adult social welfare payment rate.[39]

1–41 One other area in which there has been significant development in recent years has been in support for carers. The carer's allowance scheme has been broadened out, with take-up of the scheme more than doubling in the period from 1997. In addition, a new carer's leave and (insurance-based)

---

[37] *Building an Inclusive Society* (Department of Social, Community and Family Law Affairs, Dublin, 2002), p. 10. Based on current estimates, the commitment to a payment of the €150 would imply a figure of between 25 and 30% of gross average industrial earnings by 2007 (depending on the manner in which it is uprated), significantly ahead of the current level of about 23%.

[38] Pensions Board, *Securing Retirement Income* (Pensions Board, Dublin, 1998).

[39] *Building an Inclusive Society*, above, n.37, p. 10.

benefit was introduced to allow workers to take up to 15 months off work to care for a person in need of full-time care and attention while receiving a social welfare payment. The Health Strategy, published in 2001, has proposed the establishment of a new home care subvention, although no details of this scheme have been published at the time of writing. There were also a range of other improvements in schemes, including the extension of the period of maternity leave and benefit, the introduction of a newly increased bereavement grant, the establishment of a widowed parent's grant to benefit widow(er)s with children on bereavement, and the transformation of the smallholders' unemployment assistance scheme into a reformed farm assist scheme.

1–42 In summary, there have been fairly significant changes in the social welfare system in the period from the mid-1990s relating primarily to the impact of the economic changes. The dramatic employment growth has led to a reduction in dependence on social welfare, while the improved budgetary position has meant that much more resources are available for social welfare spending, although spending has fallen sharply as a percentage of GDP as economic growth raced away. It may still be too soon to evaluate these policy trends in detail and several of the trends towards increased incentivisation had already begun under the Rainbow Government of the mid-1990s. However, in general terms there has been an emphasis on providing "adequate" social welfare support for those of working age combined with a much greater emphasis on incentivising people to take up available work. For people over pension age, there has been a commitment to higher levels of social welfare support, in the absence of employment opportunities, and for the future steps have been taken to fund future pension costs both by setting aside exchequer funds in the National Pensions Reserve Fund and by encouraging the uptake of private pensions. Finally, there has been significantly increased support for children though the child benefit system and for carers.

3. Conclusion

1–43 In this chapter we have looked at some of the main developments in the Irish social welfare system. These are summarised in schematic form in Table 5 for ease of reference. In the coming chapters we look in detail at the main individual schemes.

Table 1: Structure of Social Welfare Spending (% of spending)

Year	Social insurance	Social assistance	Children's* allowance	Administration	Other
1924	33	67	—	+	—
1935	28	72	—	+	—
1945	26	60	14	+	0
1955	28	46	20	7	0
1965	46	28	20	6	0
1975	51	32	12	4	0
1980	56	32	9	4	0
1985	53	36	8	4	0
1990	47	41	8	5	0
2000	45	41	10	5	0

* Children's allowance was introduced in 1945. From 1986, it became known as child benefit.
+ Administration costs recorded under individual headings.

Sources: Department of Social Welfare, *Social Security* (1924–1945), *Reports* (1955–1980), *Statistical Information on Social Welfare Services* (1985–2000).

Note: The data for the period from 1955 to 1993 do not include expenditure by local authorities on home assistance/supplementary welfare allowance nor by the Department of Health. The inclusion of these figures would increase slightly the proportion of spending on social assistance.

Table 2: Funding of Social Welfare Spending

Year	State	Employees	Employers	Self-E	Income from Investments and receipts	Local Authorities
1956	76	9	10	—	3	1
1965	68	14	15	—	1	1
1975	57	16	26	—	1	1
1980	56	12	32	—	0	0
1985	60	13	27	—	0	0
1990	53	13	32	2	0	—
2000	53	9	35	2	0	—

Sources: Department of Social Welfare, *Reports* (1955–1980), *Statistical Information on Social Welfare Services* (1985–2000).

Note: This table relates only to spending by the Department of Social Welfare and so does not include spending by local authorities in relation to home assistance/supplementary welfare allowance nor spending by the Department of Health.

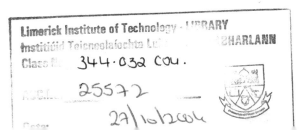

Table 3: Funding of Social Insurance Fund (%)

Year	State	Employees	Employers	Self-Employed	Other
1955	26	30	34	—	10
1965	40	28	30	—	3
1975	22	29	47	—	1
1980	24	21	55	—	0
1985	28	23	49	—	0
1990	6	26	64	4	0
2000	0	20	75	5	1

Sources: Department of Social Welfare, *Reports* (1955–1980), *Statistical Information on Social Welfare Services* (1985–2000).

Table 4: Social Insurance Coverage (000)

Year	Total Numbers Insured*	Numbers fully insured (% of total insured)
1923	418	241+
1935	538	400+
1945	608	410+
1955	726	639 (88%)
1965	744	671 (90%)
1975	969	832 (86%)
1980	1034	864 (84%)
1985	1174	949 (81%)
1990	1343	937 (70%)
2000	2255	1695 (75%)

* Excluding Class K, which does not provide cover for any social insurance benefits. Figures for 1923–1945 are for those insured under the national health insurance scheme.
+ Prior to the amalgamation of the social insurance schemes in 1952, there were three schemes (national health insurance, unemployment insurance and widow's and orphan's pensions) which operated separately. Figures for the numbers covered under all three schemes are not published. The figure shown here is for the number insured under the smallest scheme, *i.e.* the unemployment insurance scheme.

Sources: Department of Social Welfare, *Social Security* (1923–1945), *Reports* (1955–1980), *Statistical Information on Social Welfare Services* (1985–2000).

Table 5: The Development of the Social Welfare System

Year	General	Older people	Unemployed	Disability	Family, Survivor and Lone Parents
1838	Poor Law				
1847	Outdoor Relief				
1897	Workmen's Compensation				
1908		Old age Pension			
1911	National Insurance		Unemployment benefit	Sickness benefit	
1924	Poor Law reform	Cut in pensions			
1929	Married women excluded from insurance				
1933			Unemployment assistance		
1935	Amalgamation of insurance societies				Widow's Pension
1939	Public assistance				
1944					Children's allowance
1947	Establishment of Department of Social Welfare			Infectious diseases maintenance allowance	
1949	White Paper				
1952	Social Welfare Act				
1954				Disabled persons maintenance allowance	
1961		Contributory pension			
1967				Occupational injuries	
1970		Retirement pension		Invalidity pension	Deserted wife's allowance
1973		Pension age reduced from 70 to 66 by 1977			Deserted wife's benefit Unmarried mother's allowance

Table 5—*contd.*

Year	General	Older people	Unemployed	Disability	Family, Survivor and Lone Parents
1974	Social insurance extended to higher earners Pay related benefit				
1975	Supplementary welfare allowance				
1979	PRSI system EU directive on equal treatment				
1984			Social employment scheme		
1986	Commission on Social Welfare EU Directive implemented				Family income supplement Child benefit
1988	Social insurance for self-employed		Pre-retirement allowance		
1990					Lone parent's allowance Carer's allowance
1991	Social insurance for part-time workers				
1992				Abolition of pay-related benefit	
1994			Abolition of pay-related benefit		Survivor's pension
1998			Employment Action Plan		
1999	Farm assist-Bereavement grant				
2000		National Pensions Reserve Fund		Carer's benefit	Child benefit increases
2002		Personal Retirement Savings Accounts			

CHAPTER 2

The Legal Status of Social Welfare Payments

2–01 This chapter considers the legal status of social welfare payments. It looks at the extent to which such payments have a basis other than in statute. For example, is there any contractual element in entitlement to social insurance payments on the basis of contributions paid? It goes on to look at the extent to which welfare payments give rise to any "property right" under the Irish Constitution, under the European Convention on Human Rights or in E.U. law.

Although most social welfare payments are based on a statutory entitlement, some are provided for in administrative schemes and, even in relation to statutory entitlements, many aspects of payments are covered by administrative guidelines. The legal status of such administrative rules is considered.

Finally, the chapter looks at the broader issues arising in relation to the meaning of "the law" from a sociological point of view in the area of social welfare payments.

1. Statutory Entitlement

2–02 The vast majority of social welfare payments are based on statutory entitlement as set out in the Social Welfare Acts and Regulations. The current primary legislation is the Social Welfare (Consolidation) Act 1993, which is amended on at least an annual basis. In general, the Act sets out the main features of the particular payment. Further details in relation to expanding on specific definitions, transitional provisions and so on are set out in Social Welfare Regulations. Obviously, these Regulations must be constitutional, must be *intra vires* the Minister in terms of the powers given in primary legislation and, in particular, must not be so unreasonable as to be *ultra vires* the Minister.[1]

2–03 In addition, as we will see throughout this book, the Department issues a very large numbers of guidelines to its staff (most of which are available on

---

[1] See *McHugh v. Minister for Social Welfare* [1994] 2 I.R. 139; *State (McLoughlin v. Eastern Health Board* [1998] I.R. 416. The general power to make Regulations is contained in the Social Welfare (Consolidation) Act 1993 (SW(C)A 1993), s. 4.

the departmental website).[2] These largely explain the Acts and Regulations in non-legalistic terms. However, in a number of cases, issues which have not been addressed in legislation are provided for in guidelines. Obviously, again, such guidelines must be consistent with the primary and secondary legislation.[3] In addition, in a number of cases – including the Household Benefit schemes and the Back to Work and Back to Education Allowance – entitlement is not provided for in the Social Welfare Acts and the details of the schemes are entirely set out in administrative guidelines. The legal status of such guidelines is considered in more detail below.

2. A Contractual Right to Benefits?

2–04 The notion of social insurance is, to some extent, presented as being analogous with commercial insurance. Contributions are paid in relation to a specific risk and, on the occurrence of that risk, compensation is payable to the insured person. However, as Freud wrote, analogies "decide nothing but they can make one feel more at home".[4] In the case of the introduction of social insurance, this was clearly the intended purpose of the analogy with commercial insurance. It helped to portray a new type of "social welfare" payment in a manner with which the general public and legislators were familiar. However, there are very significant differences between social and commercial insurance. Unlike commercial insurance, social insurance is generally made compulsory by law; there is no actuarial relationship between the level of contribution and likely risk nor between contribution and benefits. It is submitted that it is clear that entitlements to social insurance payments are entirely on a statutory basis and that there is no element of contractual relationship between the citizen and the State in this regard.[5] Thus, there is no

---

[2] www.welfare.ie.

[3] See, for example, *State (Kershaw) v. Eastern Health Board* [1985] I.L.R.M. 235.

[4] "The Dissection of the Psychical Personality" in *The Essentials of Psychoanalysis* (Harmondsworth, Penguin, 1986).

[5] *Flemming v. Nestor* 363 U.S. 603; *Richardson v. Belcher* 404 U.S. 78. Although see *contra* Marshall J. dissenting in *Belcher* (with whom Brennan J. joined), who opined that "surely a worker who is forced to pay a social security tax on his earnings has a clearly cognizable contract interest in the benefits that justify the tax. The characterization of this interest as 'noncontractual' in *Flemming v. Nestor*, 363 U.S. 603, 611 (1960), is, in my view, incorrect. The analogy to an annuity or insurance contract, rejected there, seems apt. ... Of course, as the Court says, Congress may 'fix the levels of benefits under the Act or the conditions upon which they may be paid'. But once Congress has fixed that level and those conditions, and a worker has contributed his tax in accord with the law, may Congress unilaterally modify the benefits in a way that defeats the expectations of beneficiaries and prospective beneficiaries? At the least, it would seem that after a worker has contributed ... and his interest in the benefits has fully accrued, Congress may not unilaterally qualify that interest by introducing an offset provision

contractual reason why the Oireachtas cannot modify (or even abolish) entitlement by legislation – as has been done, for example, in relation to pay-related benefit.

3. Legitimate Expectation

2–05 If an insured person cannot rely on any contractual right to benefit, is there any situation in which he or she could rely on a legitimate expectation of entitlement against the State? Legitimate expectation is a developing area in Irish administrative law and its boundaries are as yet ill defined.[6] Its operation has to date received only limited judicial consideration in the area of social welfare law. In the words of Hogan and Morgan: "legitimate expectations are protected in the interests of safeguarding the citizen against haphazard and unfair changes in administrative policy and practice."[7] However, how does this principle fit in with the important principle of administrative law that a public body cannot act *ultra vires, i.e.* outside its legal powers? Traditionally, it has been held that a statutory authority cannot extend its powers by creating an estoppel – a concept similar to but not the same as legitimate expectation.[8]

2–06 In *Galvin v. Minister for Social Welfare*[9] Costello P. considered a claim that the applicant was entitled to a pension based either on the doctrine of estoppel or legitimate expectation. It was alleged that he had been assured both verbally and in writing by an official of the Department that his social insurance record was such that he would qualify for a contributory pension at retirement. However, the Department, while accepting that the applicant was given incorrect information, argued that the doctrine of estoppel did not apply because the applicant suffered no detriment as a result (as he could not have improved his contribution record in any case) and as the doctrine of estoppel could not confer a right on the applicant to which he was not statutorily entitled. Costello P. accepted these submissions and held that the doctrine of estoppel had no application where the applicant was not entitled by statute to the benefit claimed. He also held, albeit without detailed discussion, that the doctrine of legitimate expectation could not be relied on to support a claim that the Department could not be heard to submit that the law does not permit the payment of the benefit claimed.

---

not previously contemplated by the parties": *Richardson v. Belcher* 404 U.S. 78 at 97, n.10.

[6] For an extensive discussion, see Hogan and Morgan, *Administrative Law in Ireland* (3rd ed., Round Hall Sweet & Maxwell, 1998).

[7] *ibid.*, p. 860.

[8] *Power v. Minister for Social Welfare* [1987] I.R. 307 at 308; *Davies v. Social Security Commissioner*, reported in R(SB) 4/91.

[9] [1997] 3 I.R. 240.

2–07   In *Wiley v. Revenue Commissions*[10] the Supreme Court considered a claim of legitimate expectation on an issue analogous to welfare entitlements. The applicant, who was a driver with a disability, had received repayments of excise duty under the Disabled Drivers scheme on two previous occasions (although he had not in fact been strictly eligible to do so). In 1986, the Revenue Commissioners, in effect, tightened up the criteria for the operation of the scheme and rejected the applicant's claim. Mr Wylie had not been aware of this change in the administration of the scheme at the time when he purchased a new vehicle and, when his claim was rejected, he claimed that he had acquired a legitimate expectation that the pre-1986 approach would be continued in his case or that he should have been told in advance of his purchase of the change in administration. His application was rejected by the Supreme Court. The Court held that to accept this argument would be to state that the administration was not entitled to set more stringent standards in order to discharge its statutory obligations without giving notice to anybody who had benefited under the scheme in the past. In addition, Blayney J. questioned whether, in the circumstances of the case, the applicant's expectations could be described as "legitimate" given that he had not in fact been eligible under the scheme at any stage.

2–08   Hogan and Morgan have argued that while the doctrine of legitimate expectation cannot be relied on to prevent a change in the law, it can be invoked to require the observance of procedural rights, and it may be that this and the issue of the creation of legitimate expectation by administrative circulars are the main areas in which it may have implications in relation to social welfare law.[11] The status of administrative guidelines is considered in more detail below.

4. A Constitutional Right to Social Welfare[12]

2–09   The Irish Constitution contains no explicit reference to social welfare payments. Article 45 might be considered to be relevant in so far as it states:

> "The State pledges itself to safeguard with especial care the economic interests of the weaker sections of the community, and, where necessary, to contribute to the support of the infirm, the widow, the orphan, and the aged."

---

[10] [1993] I.L.R.M. 482.

[11] Hogan and Morgan, above, n.6, p. 889; see also pp. 890 *et seq.*

[12] On the broader issue of whether the courts *should* provide judicial recognition of socio-economic rights, see G. Whyte, *Social Inclusion and the Law: Public Interest Litigation in Ireland* (IPA, Dublin, 2002) and *Report of the Constitutional Review Group* (Stationery Office, Dublin, 1996). Issues relating to fair procedures are discussed in Chap. 18.

However, Article 45 itself specifically provides that the "directive principles of social policy" which it sets out are not cognisable by the courts.

2–10 It might be argued that entitlement to social welfare could constitute a "property right" under Article 43.1, which provides:

> "1° The State acknowledges that man, in virtue of his rational being, has the natural right, antecedent to positive law, to the private ownership of external goods.
>
> 2° The State accordingly guarantees to pass no law attempting to abolish the right of private ownership or the general right to transfer, bequeath, and inherit property."

Given the status which has been attached to property rights in Irish constitutional jurisprudence, this could provide important additional weight to the rights of social welfare claimants. However, the very wording of the Article and the philosophical approach underlying it would argue against a statutory right to a welfare payment being elevated to a "natural right antecedent to positive law". In so far as this issue has been considered by the Supreme Court, it would appear that the Court does not see entitlement to social welfare as being a property right within the meaning of Article 43.

2–11 The case of *Minister for Social, Community and Family Affairs v. Scanlon* involved the retrospective application of legislation concerning recovery of overpaid benefits.[13] It was argued that the claimant enjoyed a property right in the benefits he had received and that accordingly a retrospective reading of the legislation should not be adopted. However, Fennelly J. (with whom the other Judges agreed) stated that the entitlement was created by statute and that he could not identify any constitutional right to retain benefits which had been wrongly paid.

2–12 It is worth digressing to consider the position under U.S. constitutional law – albeit that the approach to property rights is substantially different to that in Irish law. The Due Process clause of the Fifth Amendment to the U.S. Constitution provides:

> "No person shall … be deprived of life, liberty, or property, without due process of law; nor shall private property be taken for public use, without just compensation. "

The U.S. Supreme Court has held:

> "Procedural due process imposes constraints on governmental decisions which

---

[13] [2001] 1 I.R. 64. See Chap. 15.

deprive individuals of 'liberty' or 'property' interests within the meaning of the Due Process Clause of the Fifth or Fourteenth Amendment. "[14]

The Court held the interest of an individual in continued receipt of social security benefits is a statutorily created "property" interest protected by the Fifth Amendment so as to bring into play the right to procedural due process and protection against "arbitrary governmental action".[15] The Court has *not* gone further to hold that an interest in social security gave rise to strong substantive constitutional property rights. In *Flemming v. Nestor*[16] – a case involving the termination of old-age benefits payable to a person who was deported from the United States – the Court held that a person covered by the Social Security Act did not have such a right in old-age benefit payments as would make every defeasance of "accrued" interests violative of the Due Process Clause of the Fifth Amendment. The Court took the view that the non-contractual interest of an employee covered by the Social Security Act could not be soundly analogised to that of the holder of an annuity, whose right to benefits was based on his contractual premium payments and that "to engraft upon the Social Security System a concept of 'accrued property rights' would deprive it of the flexibility and boldness in adjustment to ever-changing conditions which it demands and which Congress probably had in mind when it expressly reserved the right to alter, amend or repeal any provision of the Act".[17]

5. Social Welfare under European Law

2–13   Article 1 of the First Protocol to the European Convention on Human Rights provides:

> "Every natural or legal person is entitled to the peaceful enjoyment of his possessions. No one shall be deprived of his possessions except in the public interest and subject to the conditions provided for by the law and by the general principles of international law.
>
> The preceding provisions shall not, however, in any way impair the right of a state to enforce such laws as it deems necessary to control the use of property in accordance with the general interest or to secure the payment of taxes or other contributions or penalties."

---

[14] *Mathews v. Eldridge* 424 U.S. 319.
[15] *ibid.*
[16] 363 U.S. 603. Affirmed in *Richardson v. Belcher* 404 U.S. 78.
[17] *Fleming v. Nestor* 363 U.S. 603 at 608–611. Although the decision was by a 5–4 majority, only Black J. dissented on the question of accrued property rights. The case concerned a Bulgarian who had lived in the USA for 43 years and was deported in 1956 for having been a member of the Communist party between 1933 and 1939 at a time when this was neither illegal nor grounds for deportation.

2–14 In a number of recent cases, the European Court of Human Rights has considered whether social welfare payments constitute "possessions within the meaning of Article 1. In *Gaygusuz v. Austria*[18] the applicant claimed that an "emergency assistance" payment – payable after the expiry of entitlement to unemployment benefit was a "possession" with the meaning of Article 1. Emergency assistance was payable to a person who had exhausted entitlement to contributory benefit where he or she was, *inter alia*, capable of and available for work and in urgent need. Austria argued that the payment did not fall within the scope of Article 1 as entitlement did not result automatically from the payment of contributions but was payable in case of need. However, the Court noted that emergency assistance was "linked to the payment of contributions to the unemployment insurance fund" and that it followed that there was "no entitlement to emergency assistance where such contributions ha[d] not been made".[19] The Court, therefore, considered that the right to emergency assistance was a pecuniary right within the meaning of Article 1 of Protocol 1. The Court, somewhat obscurely, went on to say that that provision was applicable "without it being necessary to rely solely on the link between entitlement to emergency assistance and the obligation to pay taxes or contributions".[20] It is unclear whether the Court was suggesting that the scope of Article 1 may, in fact, extend beyond contributory benefits.

2–15 This decision indicates that any social insurance benefits where there is a clear link between payment of contributions and receipt of benefits would be considered to be a possession within the scope of Article 1 (which thereby brings into play the non-discrimination provisions set out in Article 14 of the ECHR). The Court has subsequently held a man's claim to be entitled to a widower's pension to be within the scope of Article 1 and did not consider it significant that the statutory condition requiring payment of contributions required the contributions to have been made, not by the applicant, but by his late wife. The Court went on to state that it was not, therefore, necessary for it to address the issue of whether a social security benefit must be contributory in nature in order that it can constitute a possession for the purposes of Article 1.[21] The Court has also held that payment of social insurance contributions

---

[18] (1997) 23 E.H.R.R. 364.

[19] *ibid.* at para. 39.

[20] *ibid.*

[21] *Willis v. United Kingdom* (2002) 35 E.H.R.R. 21 at para. 35. The European Commission on Human Rights had previously held that a right of a Dutch disability benefit did not constitute a property right because the relevant social security legislation was set up as a general insurance system based on the principle of social solidarity and there was no direct link between the level of contributions and the benefits awarded; *De Kleine Staarman v. Netherlands*, May 16, 1985, DR 42, p. 166. Whether this is still good law must now be open to question in the light of the recent decisions of the Court.

falls within Article 1.[22] However, the Court has stated that even assuming Article 1 guarantees benefits to persons who have contributed to a social insurance system, it cannot be interpreted as entitling the person to a pension of a particular amount.[23]

2–16 The European Commission of Human Rights has held that the State Earning Related Pension (SERPS) in the United Kingdom is also be to considered to be a possession for the purposes of Article 1.[24] The Commission has recently considered the question as to whether a disablement benefit payable under the U.K. industrial injuries scheme is within the scope of Article 1.[25] This payment is very similar to disablement benefit under the Irish occupational injuries code. The Commission noted that – as in the Irish case – while disablement benefit was not a benefit for which the claimant made direct contributions, it was payable only to qualifying workers who are subject to the national insurance regime. However, the Commission found it unnecessary, on the facts of the case, to decide whether this indirect connection between contributions and benefit was sufficient to bring the benefit within Article 1.

2–17 In the case of E.U. law, in *Testa*[26] the European Court of Justice considered an argument that a provision of Regulation 1408/71 which deprived a person of entitlement to unemployment benefit under national law might be regarded as being incompatible with the German constitutional protection of the right to property. The Court held that:

> "... the question of a possible infringement of fundamental rights by a measure of the Community institutions can only be judged in the light of Community law itself, since fundamental rights form an integral part of the general principles of the law, the observance of which it ensures. One of the fundamental rights which is accordingly protected under Community law in accordance with the constitutional concepts common to the member states and in the light of international treaties for the protection of human rights on which member states have collaborated or to which they are signatories is the right to property, as the Court has recognised, notably in its judgement of 13 December 1979 in case 44/79 Hauer."[27]

However, on the facts of the case, the Court concluded that it was not necessary

---

[22] *Van Raalte v. Netherlands* (1997) 24 E.H.R.R. 503.
[23] *Skórkiewicz v. Poland*, June 1, 1999 following *Müller v. Austria* (1975) 3 D.R. 25.
[24] *Szrabjer v. United Kingdom* [1998] P.L.R. 281.
[25] *Carlin v. United Kingdom* (1998) 25 E.H.R.R. CD 73.
[26] Joined Cases 41 & 121 and 796/79 *Testa v. Bundesanstalt für Arbeit* [1980] E.C.R. 1979.
[27] *ibid.* at para. 18.

to decide whether or not the entitlement to the social security benefits in question might be held to be covered by the protection of the right to property, as guaranteed by Community law.

6. The Legal Status of Administrative Guidelines[28]

2–18   As has been outlined above, the Department relies heavily on the issue of administrative guidelines to its staff. These are used both to explain statutory provisions to its staff (including deciding officers) in readable English and to fill in lacunae which are not covered by legislation (*e.g.* the precise operation of the "benefit and privilege" rule)[29] or to expand on statutory provisions (*e.g.* to discuss in more detail the definition of farmer).[30] In addition, administrative guidelines are utilised to suggest how discretion might be exercised in the limited number of areas in which discretionary social welfare payments arise (*e.g.* in relation to exceptional needs payments under the supplementary welfare allowance code).[31] Administrative guidelines are also used to set out the detailed rules of non-statutory schemes such as the Household Benefits, Back to Work and Back to Education schemes. The High Court has held that the issue of administrative guidelines concerning the operation of a particular social welfare scheme was, in itself, "clearly a proper and valid administrative act."[32]

   In so far as they purport to explain or interpret legislation or indicate in what manner discretion might be exercised, guidelines must be consistent with the relevant primary and secondary legislation (and, of course, with the Constitution and E.U. law) and, in particular, they must not fetter the discretion of adjudicating officers.

2–19   Hogan and Morgan state that the fundamental principles of common law indicate that administrative guidelines "are not law".[33] Indeed, if they were, this would raise the issue of the compatibility of the use of circulars with Article 15.2 of the Constitution, which provides:

   "1°   The sole and exclusive power of making laws for the State is hereby vested

---

[28] See Hogan and Morgan, above, n.6, pp. 41–57 and G. Hogan, "The Legal Status of Administrative Rules and Circulars" (1987) *Ir. Jur.* 194.

[29] See Chap. 6.

[30] See Chap. 6.

[31] See Chap. 7.

[32] *State (Kershaw) v. Eastern Health Board* [1985] I.L.R.M. 235 at 239. The case involved the operation of the fuel scheme under the Social Welfare (Consolidation) Act 1981. In the particular circumstances, Finlay P. held that the guidelines could not operate to bind the discretion of the adjudicating authorities.

[33] See Hogan and Morgan, above, n.6, p. 48.

in the Oireachtas: no other legislative authority has power to make laws for the State.[34]

Thus a public body cannot rely on guidelines as against an individual to affect or prejudice his or her legal rights. However, the Irish courts have held that an administrative guideline can create legally binding entitlements as against a public body and may be subject to judicial review.[35]

7. What is the Law?

2–20   Finally, this chapter considers the broader question as to the definition of "the law". From a legal positivist point of view "law consists of data – primarily rules – which can be recognised by relatively simple tests or 'rules of recognition' ".[36] The principal test is that the rules have gone through the formal stages of a legislative procedure, *i.e.* they have been properly adopted by Parliament or by a subordinate authority. Thus, for example, one frequently reads it said that social welfare law "is an exclusively twentieth century phenomenon and as such is almost exclusively derived from Acts of the Oireachtas and delegated legislation".[37]

2–21   Others, however, have put forward a much broader view of the law. Ehrlich,[38] for example, sees the law as involving not just the norms created and applied by the State but also including what he calls "social order", *i.e.* the rules which are actually followed in social life – the real "living law". Cotterrell,[39] for the purposes of his study of the sociology of the law, steers a path between these two approaches and refers to law as:

> "The social rules and related doctrine created, adopted, interpreted and enforced by state agencies as a framework of general regulation within a politically organised society."

Studies show that bureaucracies – from time to time – have adopted official practices which are not fully in line with the legal rules. Sometimes, these "official practices" operate to the advantage of individuals; on other occasions

---

[34] See Hogan, above, n.28, p. 211.

[35] *Latchford v. Minister for Industry and Commerce* [1950] I.R. 33 . As Hogan and Morgan point out, this result could be arrived at on the basis of the doctrine of legitimate expectations although *Latchford* long predates this concept.

[36] R. Cotterrell, *Sociology of the Law* (Butterworths, 1992), p. 9.

[37] G. Whyte, *et al.*, *Social Welfare Law: Materials for the Professional Course* (Law Society of Ireland, 1994), p. 1.

[38] Ehrlich, "The Sociology of Law" (1922) 36 *Harv. L. Rev.* 130.

[39] R. Cotterrell, above, n.36, p. 9.

to their disadvantage.[40] The legal positivist viewpoint would see the law as consisting solely of the legal rules and any discordant "official practice" would be seen as in breach of the law. However, in the broader sense, discussed above, the "official practice" could certainly be seen as being "the law" in a situation where sections of the State create and adopt a practice which is implemented by a state agency which is also able to enforce its decisions by awarding or failing to award welfare payments to those affected.

2–22 The usefulness of definitions depends, of course, on the purpose for which the definitions are required. For the purposes of this legal study of the operation of the social welfare system, we will, in general, confine ourselves to the narrower "legal" understanding of the law. However, for those who wish to understand the practical operation of the social welfare system, it may be that a broader definition of the law is more helpful to a practical and theoretical understanding. For example, if one wishes to consider the development of public interest litigation to establish socio-economic rights, it is as well to be aware that welfare law involves much more than the legal rules contained in the relevant statutes and statutory instruments.[41]

---

[40] In the area of social welfare, see M. Cousins, *The Irish Social Welfare System* (Round Hall Press, Dublin, 1995), Chap. 10.

[41] On public interest litigation, see G. Whyte, *Social Inclusion and the Law: Public Interest Law in Ireland* (IPA, Dublin, 2002).

CHAPTER 3

Old Age, Retirement and Survivor's Pensions

3–01 This chapter looks at the main social welfare payments available for older people (aged 65 and over). The chapter also looks at the widow's and widower's pension, as the majority of claimants are over the age of 65/66.

1. Background

3–02 Old age pensions constituted the first major "New Liberal" welfare reform being introduced by the Asquith Government in 1908. There had been considerable debate in the United Kingdom in the previous decades about the need for a state pension and different options had been canvassed.[1] These included both universal and contributory social insurance based approaches. However, ultimately the Government opted for a means-tested pension of 5 shillings per week funded out of taxation and paid at the age of 70, the relatively high age being chosen to reduce the cost of the pensions. Macnicol has pointed out that the non-contributory and tax-funded nature of the payment meant that it was both highly redistributive and that the majority of pensioners were women.[2]

3–03 The Old Age Pensions Act was particularly advantageous to Ireland, given that the rates were set at a uniform basis for the entire United Kingdom (although wages and the cost of living were significantly lower in Ireland than in parts of Great Britain). The decision to opt for a means-tested approach also benefited poorer Ireland. Also, the massive outflow of younger people since the Famine meant that Ireland had a greater proportion of older people in the population. The proportion of pensioners to the total population was much higher in Ireland than in England and Wales.[3] One largely unanticipated reason why Ireland benefited disproportionately was the fact that civil

---

[1] See J. Macnicol, *The Politics of Retirement in Britain, 1978–1948* (Cambridge University Press, Cambridge, 1998), Chaps 2–6; P. Thane, *Old Age in English History* (Oxford University Press, Oxford, 2000), Chaps 10 and 11; C. Carney, "A Case Study in Social Policy: The Non-Contributory Old Age Pension" (1985) 33 *Administration* 483.
[2] Macnicol, above, n.1, p. 162.
[3] *ibid.*, p. 161.

registration became compulsory in Ireland only in 1864, which meant that there was no formal record of the age of many people. It was widely suggested that people overstated their true age in order to qualify for the pension – and there appears to be statistical evidence that this did in fact occur. Arising from the considerable increase in the cost of living during the War years, the pension was increased as a temporary measure during the First World War and then doubled to 10 shillings per week in 1919 following the report of the government appointed Ryland Atkins committee.[4]

3–04 Cumman na nGaedheal infamously cut the pension by 1 shilling in 1924 and made a number of other reductions in entitlements at that time.[5] This had the effect of reducing the percentage of the population entitled to pension from about 75 per cent to about two-thirds. On coming to office in 1932, Fianna Fáil immediately introduced a number of improvements to the pension which had the effect of restoring the proportion of the population receiving a pension to about three quarters of the older population (over 70), although this subsequently fell back somewhat during the Second World War. There were relatively few changes in the structure of the pension scheme for many decades. A contributory retirement pension was proposed in the 1949 White Paper but was not introduced at that time. However, improvements in the means test for the non-contributory pension meant that the proportion of the population receiving a pension increased again to about 75 per cent in the 1950s. A contributory old age pension was finally introduced in 1961 – very much at the behest of the then Taoiseach Séan Lemass.

3–05 A contributory retirement pension was introduced in 1970, with retirement age set at 65. The pension age for the general old age pensions was reduced from 70 to 66 between 1973 and 1977. However, it has not been further reduced, leading to the somewhat anomalous position that Ireland now has a pension with a retirement condition at age 65 and a pension without a retirement condition at age 66 – both with slightly different qualification conditions. The extension of social insurance to the self-employed in 1988 now means that significant numbers of self-employed persons are qualifying for pensions. The old age (non-contributory) pension continues to apply to those with insufficient social insurance contributions to qualify for a contributory pension. The numbers on the means-tested pension are still large but declining.

3–06 A widow's contributory pension was introduced in 1935 with a limited non-contributory pension for existing widows of employees and for the widows of smallholders. However, significant numbers of widows failed to qualify

---

[4] Macnicol, above, n.1, Chap. 7.
[5] M. Cousins, *The Birth of Social Welfare* (Four Courts Press, Dublin, 2002).

under this approach and the non-contributory scheme was broadened out to apply to all qualifying widows who satisfied the means test. When originally introduced, the non-contributory scheme applied only to widows with children or to those without children if aged over 55; but this age requirement was gradually relaxed over the years and eventually abolished. Up to 1961, recipients of widow's pension automatically transferred to the old age pension on reaching pension age (then 70). However, with the introduction of the old age (contributory) pension in that year, widows were allowed to remain on the widow's pension over pension age and the proportion of widows over pension age has gradually increased so that currently the widow's pension is primarily an old age pension.

3–07 Although the proposed E.U. Directive extending equal treatment to survivor's pensions has not been agreed to date, several changes in Irish payments in this area have been influenced by the trend towards equality.[6] In relation to widow's (contributory) pension, the question arose as to whether the pension should be extended to widowers or abolished altogether to be replaced by an alternative system of personal entitlements. The original purpose of the pension had been to provide an income on the death of the husband who was assumed (accurately so in the vast majority of cases in 1935) to be the main breadwinner. This rationale was undermined to some extent by the rising number of married women in the paid labour force. Accordingly, the National Pension Board (1993) proposed that the widow's pension should be extended to all survivors but with an earnings limit being applied to all claimants under 66 after 12 months' payment. This would have maintained the original rationale of supporting the surviving spouse on the death of the main breadwinner. Existing claimants of the widow's pension would not have been affected by this rule. The cost of the extension would have been more than offset by the savings achieved by introducing the earnings limit.[7] In the 1994 Budget, it was announced that such a pension would be introduced in the next Social Welfare Bill, but after some public criticism (particularly from widows' organisations), the Minister for Social Welfare, Dr Woods, announced that the income limit would be dropped and a survivor's benefit introduced from October 1994. Thus, a spouse now receives a pension (possibly for life) on the death of the other spouse, regardless of whether that spouse was a dependant or not.

---

[6]   G. Whyte, "Gender and Equality in the Irish Social Welfare System" in Quinn ed., *Irish Human Rights Yearbook 1995.*
[7]   *Report of the National Pension Board* (Stationery Office, Dublin, 1993), p. 187.

2. Old Age/Retirement Pensions

3–08 There are currently three main "old age" pensions: the contributory old age pension (OACP), the retirement pension (RP) and the non-contributory old age pension (OANCP).[8]

A. Old Age (Contributory) Pension

(1) Qualification conditions

3–09 In order to qualify for the OACP, a person must have attained pensionable age (*i.e.* 66) and satisfy the contribution requirements.[9]

(2) Contribution conditions

3–10 The general contribution requirements are that a person must:

(a) have entered insurable employment before attaining the age of 56;

(b) have a certain number of paid contributions since entry into insurance; and

(c) have a minimum "yearly average" of paid or credited contributions.[10]

3–11 "Entry into insurance" means, subject to section 83(7):

(a) the date on which a person first becomes an insured person by virtue of section 9(1) (as an employed contributor), except where he or she becomes an insured person for occupational injuries purposes only; or

(b) the date on which he or she first becomes an insured person by virtue of section 17 (as a self-employed contributor).[11]

3–12 Section 83(7) provides that where a person became a self-employed contributor on April 6, 1988 (when insurance for self-employment was introduced) and at any time prior to that date was an employed contributor, the date on which the person first entered into insurance or April 6, 1988,

---

[8] In addition to the widow(er)'s pension, in a number of cases, for example invalidity pension, a person may retain the pension over the age of 65/66 if it is to their advantage to do so. The numbers involved are comparatively small.

[9] The main provisions are set out in the Social Welfare (Consolidation) Act 1993 (SW(C)A 1993), ss.83–87 and Social Welfare (Consolidated Payments Provisions) Regulations 1994 (S.I. No. 417 of 1994) (SW(CPP)R 1994), arts 36–43 as amended.

[10] SW(C)A 1993, s. 84. There is a range of variations on these requirements set out in the legislation in transitional cases to take account of the reduction in pensionable age from 70 to 66 during the 1970s: see s. 84(2)–(5).

[11] *ibid.*, s. 83(4).

whichever is the more favourable to him or her, is regarded as the date of entry into insurance.

3–13 The minimum number of paid contributions required had been 156 (*i.e.* three years' insurable employment) but this increased to 260 (five years) in 2002 and will increase further to 520 (10 years) in 2012.[12]

3–14 The issue that gives rise to most disputes in relation to OACP is the operation of the "yearly average" rule. "Yearly average" is defined as:

> "the average per contribution year of contribution weeks in respect of which [the] claimant has qualifying [*i.e.* paid] contributions, voluntary contributions or credited contributions in the period commencing either–
>
> (a) on the 5th day of January, 1953, in case the claimant is a man, or on the 6th day of July, 1953, in case the claimant is a woman, or
> (b) at the beginning of the contribution year in which the claimant's entry into insurance occurred [if after the dates set out in (a)] …"[13]

3–15 A person is required to have a yearly average of 48 contributions (paid or credited) from entering insurable employment (or from 1953, whichever is the later) up to the last complete tax year before reaching pension age in order to qualify for a full pension. Alternatively, a person can satisfy an "alternative yearly average" from 1979 (when the PRSI system was introduced).[14] A yearly average of 20 is sufficient to qualify for a slightly reduced pension and a yearly average of as low as 10 will qualify for a pro-rata pension.[15] The rationale behind the rule is to ensure that a person has a reasonable record of contribution to the social insurance fund over his or her working life. However, the manner in which the rule operates can mean that a person who has paid a large number of contributions may fail to qualify for a pension or may qualify for a lower pension than a person with a lower number of contributions. For example, a person who enters insurable employment late in life (but before age 56) and works reasonably continuously to pension age will qualify for a full pension (because the denominator of years worked is small). In contrast, a person who entered insurable employment at a young age, took a significant number of years out, perhaps due to family responsibilities, and returned to insurable employment may have a lower average (as the denominator is much larger).

---

[12] SW(C)A 1993, s. 84(1)(b) and (1A) as amended and inserted respectively by the Social Welfare Act 1997 (SWA 1997), s.12.

[13] *ibid.*, s. 83(1). The reason for the different dates for men and women is that, for administrative reasons, men and women had different contribution years at that time. "Contribution year" means a year of assessment within the meaning of the Income Tax Acts: SW(C)A 1993, s.2.

[14] *ibid.*, s. 83(2).

[15] *ibid.*, s. 84(7) as substituted by SWA 1997, s.12.

3–16 This issue was considered in the case of *Kinghan v. Minister for Social Welfare*,[16] where a technical argument in relation to the construction of the relevant legislation was rejected by Lynch J., who, however, indicated that he had considerable sympathy with the case being advanced.

3–17 A further issue in relation to the yearly average arises in relation to women (and indeed men) on home duties. Many women have worked at an early age, taken time out of the paid labour force after marriage or childbirth, and returned to paid work later in life. Such women would tend to be adversely affected by the yearly average. In order to address this issue, a "homemakers disregard" was introduced in 1994. This means that complete contribution years spent as a homemaker, commencing on or after April 6, 1994, in which the person does not have any credited or voluntary contributions, can be disregarded for the purposes of calculating the yearly average contributions for the old age (contributory) pension up to a maximum of 20 years.[17] "Homemaker" is defined as a person who:

"(a) is resident in the State and is under pensionable age [66],
(b) is not engaged in remunerative employment, other than employment specified [as being of inconsiderable extent] in paragraph 5 of Part II of the First Schedule,
(c) either—
  (i) resides with and cares for a child under 12 years of age on a full-time basis, or
  (ii) resides with and provides full-time care and attention to a person who is so incapacitated as to require full-time care and attention within the meaning of section 163 (3), and
(d) other than in the case of such class or classes of person as may be prescribed, makes application to be regarded as a homemaker in the prescribed manner and within the prescribed time."[18]

The effect of this is that up to 20 years in which a person does not have social insurance contributions (and during which that person was a homemaker) can be taken away from the denominator in calculating the yearly average, thereby improving the average and that person's chances of qualifying for a (higher) pension.

3 18 A range of special and "pro-rata" old age pensions have been introduced over the years in order to assist certain people who for various reasons did not satisfy the general contribution requirements, including people whose earnings exceeded the then earnings threshold for insurability (before

---

[16] Unreported, High Court, Lynch J., November 25, 1985.
[17] SW(C)A 1993, s. 83(2) as inserted by SWA 1996, s.24.
[18] *ibid.*, s. 83 as inserted by SWA 1996, s.24.

this was abolished in 1974) and therefore had "gaps" in their insurance record,[19] persons who were also employed in the civil or public service and insured at a "modified" rate,[20] people became self-employed contributors for the first time on or after April 6, 1988 and who on or before that date had reached the age of 56,[21] and people who entered insurance prior to 1953.[22]

(3) Payments

3–19 OACP is payable at a flat rate with increases for qualified adults and qualified children as appropriate.[23] Additional payments are made where the person is aged over 80, is living alone or is ordinarily resident on an island. "Secondary benefits" (such as the Household Benefits and Fuel Allowance) are generally payable with OACP subject to a means limit in some cases where the person has additional income.

(4) Disqualifications

3–20 A person is disqualified for payment of OACP while undergoing penal servitude, imprisonment or detention in legal custody.[24] An increase for a qualified adult or qualified child can still be paid.

B. Retirement Pension

(1) Qualification conditions

3–21 The qualification conditions for RP are broadly similar to those outlined above in relation the OACP.[25] In order to qualify for the RP, a person must have attained the age of 65, be in "retirement" and satisfy the contribution requirements.[26] A period of retirement is defined in Regulations as:

> "(i) where the person has attained the age of 65 years and has not yet attained the age of 66 years, any period subsequent to his retirement from employment which is insurable employment or insurable self-employment (other than employment which is insurable only for occupational injuries benefit) during which he does not engage in such employment, or

---

[19] SW(C)A 1993, s. 84(12) and see SW(CPP)R 1994, art. 100 as amended by S.I. No. 293 of 1997 and S.I. No. 82 of 2000.

[20] SW(C)A 1993, s. 84(14).

[21] *ibid.*, s. 84(16).

[22] *ibid.*, s. 87A as inserted by SWA 2000, s.6 and amended by SWA 2001, s.15.

[23] *ibid.*, s. 87.

[24] *ibid.*, s. 211, see Chap. 15.

[25] The main provisions are set out in SW(C)A 1993, ss.88–91 and in SW(CPP)R 1994, arts 44–51 as amended.

[26] SW(C)A 1993, s. 88.

(ii) where the person has attained the age of 66 years, any period subsequent to his attainment of that age whether he is engaged in employment or not."[27]

As a result of this definition, the retirement condition does not apply after the age of 66.[28]

(2) Contribution conditions

3–22 The general contribution requirements are that a person must:

(a) have entered insurable employment before attaining the age of 55;

(b) have a certain number of paid contributions since entry into insurance[29]; and

(c) a minimum yearly average of paid or credited contributions.[30]

3–23 Similar issues arise in relation to the "yearly average" as set out above. In order to qualify for a full RP, a person must have a yearly average of 48 contributions; but a person with an average of at least 24 (rather than 20 in the case of OACP) will qualify for a slightly reduced pension. As in the case of OACP, the number of paid contributions required for RP has risen to 260 from 2002 and will rise further to 520 in 2012.[31] No pro-rata pensions apply in the case of RP and the "homemakers" provisions also do not apply.

(3) Payments

3–24 RP is payable at a flat rate with increases for qualified adults and qualified children as appropriate.[32] Additional payments are made where the person is aged over 80, is living alone or is ordinarily resident on an island. "Secondary benefits" are generally payable with RP subject to a means limit in some cases where the person has additional income.

(4) Disqualifications

3–25 A person is disqualified for payment of RP while undergoing penal

---

[27] SW(CPP)R 1994, art. 46.
[28] It is questionable whether it is possible to define a "period of retirement" as a period in which no retirement condition applies but the issue is unlikely to be challenged.
[29] Self-employed contributions do not qualify for the purpose of RP.
[30] SW(C)A 1993, s. 89. There is a range of variations on these requirements set out in the legislation in specific cases.
[31] *ibid.*, s. 89(1)(b) and (1A) as amended and inserted by SWA 1997, s.12.
[32] *ibid.*, s. 91.

servitude, imprisonment or detention in legal custody.[33] An increase for a qualified adult or qualified child can still be paid.

C. Old Age (Non-Contributory) Pension

(1) Qualification conditions

3–26 In the case of the OANCP, a person must have reached the age of 66 and satisfy a means test which takes account, in general terms, of both actual income and a notional assessment of income derived from capital.[34]

(2) Means test

3–27 The means test[35] includes means from:

- most property owned by the person and/or by his or her spouse (but excluding property personally used or enjoyed by the person);
- all income which the person and/or spouse may reasonably expect to receive in the coming year (which certain exceptions);
- the value of any advantage accruing to the person or spouse from the use of property (other than a domestic dwelling or farm building, owned and occupied, furniture and personal effects) which is personally used or enjoyed by the person or spouse and the value of any advantage from the leasing of a farm of land;
- any property which the person or spouse have deprived themselves of either directly or indirectly in order to qualify for assistance.

The detailed means test provides that in calculating the means of a person for the purposes of the old age (non-contributory) pension, account shall be taken of the following rules.

(a) Rule 1(1)[36]

3–28 Other than in such circumstances and subject to such conditions and for such periods as may be prescribed, the weekly value of any property belonging to the person (not being property personally used or enjoyed by the person or a farm of land leased by him or her) which is invested or is otherwise put to profitable use by the person or which, though capable of investment or profitable use is not invested or put to profitable use by the person is taken

---

[33] SW(C)A 1993, s. 211; see Chap. 15.
[34] *ibid.*, ss.132–140 and Pt II of Third Sched. as amended.
[35] *ibid.*, Pt II of the Third Sched.
[36] *ibid.* as substituted by SWA 2000, s.17. See SW(CPP)R 1994, art. 87A as substituted by S.I. No. 324 of 1999.

into account. The weekly value of the property being calculated as follows:

(i) the first €12,697 of the capital value of the property shall be excluded; and

(ii) the weekly value of so much of the capital value of the property as exceeds €12,697 but does not exceed €25,394.76 shall be assessed at €1.27 per each €1,269.74; and

(iii) the weekly value of so much of the capital value of the property as exceeds €25,394.76 but does not exceed €38,092.14 shall be assessed at €2.54 per each €1,269.74; and

(iv) the weekly value of so much of the capital value of the property as exceeds €38,092.14 shall be assessed at €5.08 per each €1,269.74;

but no account shall be taken under any other provision of these Rules of any appropriation of the property for the purpose of current expenditure.

3–29 Thus Rule 1(1) provides for a system of notional assessment of means from capital. It does not matter whether the actual income from capital is greater or lesser than the notional assessment, as the latter is deemed to constitute the weekly means of a person from such capital. In practice, it would be administratively impossible to operate a system of assessment of actual income, as this would vary constantly with, for example, varying interest rates on deposit accounts or variation in returns from shares, leading to frequent fluctuations in the level of pension payable. In addition, the notional system is designed to favour those with relatively small amounts of capital as can be seen from the exclusion of the first €12,697 from assessment.

<u>(b) Rule 1(4)</u>[37]

3–30 All income[38] in cash which the person may reasonably expect to receive during the year succeeding the date of calculation is taken into account, but excluding:

1(4)(a): any sums arising from the investment or profitable use of property (not being property personally used or enjoyed by the person or a farm of land leased by him or her)[39];

1(4)(b): any sums received by way of benefit, pension, assistance, allowance,

---

[37] Substituted by SWA 1997, s.26. Rule 1(2) was dropped in SWA 1997 and Rules 1(2A) and 3 refer to transitional measures.

[38] On the distinction between capital and income see *Lillystone v. Supplementary Benefits Commission* (1982) 3 F.L.R. 52.

[39] Thus, actual income from capital which is subject to assessment under Rule 1(1) is excluded from the scope of Rule 1(4).

supplement or continued payment under Part II, III, IV, V or VA, or by way of a payment corresponding to child benefit under Part IV from another Member State of the E.U.;

1(4)(c):   any income arising from a bonus under a scheme administered by the Minister for Education for the making of special grants to parents or guardians resident in the Gaeltacht or Breac-Gaeltacht of children attending primary schools;

1(4)(d):   in the case of a qualified applicant under a scheme administered by the Minister for the Gaeltacht and known as Scéim na bhFoghlaimeoirí Gaeilge, any income received under that scheme in respect of a person who is temporarily resident with the qualified applicant, together with any other income received in respect of such temporary resident;

1(4)(e):   any moneys from a charitable organisation, being a body whose activities are carried on otherwise than for profit (but excluding any public or local authority) and one of whose functions is to assist persons in need by making grants of money to them;

1(4)(f):   any income arising by way of:
(i) infectious diseases maintenance allowance to or in respect of the person or the person's dependants,
(ii) payments by a health board in respect of a child who is boarded out,
(iii) payments in respect of not more than two persons boarded out under section 10 of the Health (Nursing Homes) Act 1990 (insofar as the aggregate amount received in respect of each person does not exceed the maximum amount of the old age (non-contributory) pension),[40] or,
(iv) a mobility allowance payable under section 61 of the Health Act 1970, to the person,

1(4)(g):   subject to Rule 5 [this should, in fact, read Rule 6], an amount of an allowance, dependant's allowance, disability pension or wound pension under the Army Pensions Acts 1923 to 1980 (including, for the purposes of this subparagraph, a British war pension) or of a combination of such allowances and such pensions except so far as such amount exceeds €101.60 per year;

[1(4)(h)   relates to blind pension];

1(4)(i):   in the case of a person who is not a blind person or a lone parent (within the meaning of section 157), and who has a qualified child or qualified children who normally resides or reside with him or her, his or her earnings except and in so far as the annual amount of

---

[40] Inserted by SWA 2001, s.13.

such earnings is calculated to exceed €132.08 for each such child of whom account has not already been taken in accordance with this paragraph in calculating the means of another person;

[1(4)(j)   relates to one-parent family payment (OFP)];

1(4)(k):   in the case of a person who is not a blind person, any moneys, except so far as they exceed €66.04 per year, received by the person in respect of employment as an outworker under a scheme that is, in the opinion of the Minister, charitable in character and purpose;

1(4)(l):   such amount as may be prescribed, of income from employment by a health board or by a person approved by a health board as a home help;

1(4)(m):   any moneys received by way of a training allowance from an organisation while undergoing a course of rehabilitative training provided by an organisation approved by the Minister for Health and Children for the provision of such training;

[1(4)(mm) relates to OFP];

[1(4)(n)   relates to blind pension and OFP];

1(4)(o):   such income as may be prescribed, arising from such activities as may be prescribed;

1(4)(p):   payments by a health board in respect of the provision of accommodation for a child under section 5 of the Child Care Act 1991;

1(4)(q):   an amount of €2,540 together with one-half of any amount in excess of €2,540 under the Rural Environment Protection Scheme (REPS) and the Special Areas of Conservation Scheme;

1(4)(r):   in the case of a person who has attained pensionable age, any moneys received under the Early Retirement from Farming Scheme operated under E.U. Council Regulation 2079/92;

[1(4)(s)   relates to OFP];

1(4)(t):   any moneys in respect of rent from a person who resides with the claimant or beneficiary and but for the residence of such person the claimant or beneficiary would reside alone[41];

1(4)(u):   any moneys received by his or her spouse in respect of participation in the Vocational Opportunities Scheme;

1(4)(v):   any moneys received by his or her spouse in respect of participation in the Back to Work Allowances, Back to Education Allowance or Part-Time Job Incentive Schemes;

---

[41] Substituted by SWA 1998, s.10.

1(4)(w): any moneys received by his or her spouse in respect of participation in a FÁS course;

1(4)(x): such other income received by a person or his or her spouse as may be prescribed.[42]

3–31   Income assessed under Rule 1(4) is, in the absence of other means for ascertaining it, taken to be that actually received during the year immediately preceding the date of calculation. However, where such income is attributable to a period prior to the year immediately preceding the date of calculation but is received in a subsequent year, it is regarded as having been received in the year to which it is attributable.

3–32   Thus, Rule 1(4) provides for the assessment of all income in cash but subject to a lengthy list of exceptions. Many of these are now of a largely historical nature and affect relatively few people. Even the more recent exclusions tend to affect relatively few people. Although there are a number of clauses which allow general exclusion of income by regulation,[43] the practice has been to legislative for specific exclusions as these arise.

<u>(c) Rule 1(5)</u>

3–33 The means of a person are deemed to include the yearly value of any advantage accruing to the person from:

(a) the use or enjoyment of property (other than a domestic dwelling or a farm building owned and occupied, furniture and personal effects) which is personally used or enjoyed by the person; and

(b) a farm of land leased by the person.[44]

3–34   For the purposes of this Rule a cottage provided under the Labourers Acts 1883 to 1965, and vested in the person or the spouse of that person under those Acts or the Housing Acts 1966 to 1984, is not treated as property that is personally used or enjoyed by that person or the spouse of that person so long as payment of the purchase annuity has not been completed.

<u>(d) Rule 2</u>

3–35   Notwithstanding the provisions of other Rules, for the purposes of

---

[42] SW(CPP)R 1994, art. 90B (as inserted by S.I. No. 324 of 1999) prescribes income from an award relating to Hepatitis C from the Compensation Tribunal or a court, and compensating arising from thalidomide.

[43] See Rule 1(4) (o) and (x).

[44] Amended by SWA 1996, s.37.

old age (non-contributory) pension, the gross proceeds derived from the sale of the principal residence of the claimant or beneficiary or, in the case of a married couple who are living together, the spouse of the claimant or beneficiary where such spouse has attained pensionable age, is *not*, subject to prescribed limits, conditions, circumstances, and periods, taken into account in calculating the means of the pensioner.

3–36 In this Rule "gross proceeds derived from the sale of the principal residence" means:

(a) the agreed sale price of the residence; or

(b) where the claimant or beneficiary purchases alternative accommodation, the difference between the agreed sale price of the former residence and the agreed purchase price of the replacement residence.

3–37 The exemptions do not apply to any sums arising from the investment or profitable use of the gross proceeds derived from the sale of the principal residence.

3–38 Thus, where a person sells his or her principal residence, the gross proceeds of the sale up to a maximum figure (currently €190,460.71) are exempted from the means test where the residence has been sold so as to enable the person to:

• purchase or rent alternative accommodation, which he or she occupies as his or her only or main residence; or

• move into a private nursing home which has been registered under section 4 of the Health (Nursing Home) Acts 1990.[45]

3–39 From April 5, 2002, this provision is extended to people who:

• move in with a recipient of carer's allowance or benefit, where the recipient is that pensioner's carer; or

• move to sheltered or special housing in the voluntary co-operative, statutory or private sectors that is funded under the Capital Assistance Scheme operated by the Department of the Environment and Local Government.[46]

(e) Rule 3

3–40 If it appears that any person has directly or indirectly deprived him or herself of any income or property in order to qualify him or herself for the receipt of the pension or allowance in question, or for the receipt of the pension

---

[45] SW(CPP)R 1994, art. 90 as amended by S.I. No. 132 of 2001 and S.I. No. 120 of 2002.
[46] S. I. No. 120 of 2002.

at a higher rate than that to which he or she would otherwise be entitled, that income or the yearly value of that property is taken to be part of the means of that person.

3–41 However, Rule 3(2)(a) provides that this does not apply to any assignment:

(i) which is an assignment to a child or children of the assignor; and

(ii) which is an assignment of property consisting of a farm of land (together with or without the stock and chattels thereon) the rateable value of which (including the buildings thereon) does not exceed £30 and of which the assignor is the owner and the occupier or the occupier only.

3–42 But Rule 3(2)(b) goes on to provide that subparagraph (a) does not apply to an assignment by a person who, at any time within the three years ending when the relevant claim for a pension or application for an increase of a pension is made, was the owner and/or occupier of any agricultural lands *exceeding* £30 in rateable value. "Assignment" includes any form of conveyance, transfer or other transaction by which a person parts with the ownership or possession of property.

3–43 A transfer will generally be accepted by the Department where the farm or business is transferred due to advanced age and or failing health of the claimant or where the transfer is considered to be part of a genuine family settlement.[47]

3–44 Where the income or the value of the property taken to be part of the person's means has reduced since the date of calculation, the calculation may be revised, subject to such conditions and in such circumstances as may be prescribed; but Regulations shall not cause the income or the yearly value of the property taken to be part of his or her means to be increased.

(f) Rule 4

3–45 The following provisions apply when calculating the means of a person who is one of a couple living together[48]:

---

[47] See *State (Power) v. Moran* [1976–77] I.L.R.M. 20.

[48] See the appeal officer's decision that the term "living together" "is interpreted in the ordinary way as meaning the existence of the state of marriage or of a marriage-like relationship and not that the couple are residing together in the one place (although co-residence is ordinarily a feature of a marriage or a marriage-like relationship)." However, "there could be exceptional situations in which that test would not yield a reasonable and defensible result." *Social Welfare Appeals Office Report 1996*, p. 20.

(a) the means of the person are taken to be one-half of the total means of the couple;

(b) the person is deemed to be entitled to one-half of all property to which the person or the other member of the couple is entitled or to which the person and the other member of the couple are jointly entitled;

(c) the means of each member of the couple are first determined in accordance with these Rules and the total means are the sum of the means of each member as so determined;

(d) where one member of the couple dies, nothing which was reckoned for the purposes of pension, or would (if such deceased member had been entitled to receive any pension) have been so reckoned, as means of the deceased member is so reckoned as means of the surviving member for the purpose of reducing the pension of the surviving member if any payment in respect of that pension was made before the death of the deceased member or becomes payable in respect of a period previous or part of which was previous to that death.

3–46 "Couple" means a married couple who are living together or a man and woman who are not married to each other but are cohabiting as husband and wife. In calculating the means of a person who is one of a married couple living apart from his spouse, any sum paid by him to his spouse under a separation order is deducted in calculating his means.

(g) Rule 5

3–47 Where:

(a) an old age (non-contributory) pension, blind pension, widow(er)'s (non-contributory) pension, orphan's (non-contributory) pension, one parent family payment or carer's allowance is in course of payment to or in respect of a person or the spouse of the person or both of them; and

(b) a pension or pensions (in this Rule referred to as "the other pension"), not being a pension or pensions mentioned in paragraph (*a*), is in course of payment to or in respect of the person or the spouse of the person or both of them;

in calculating the means of the person or of the spouse or of both of them for the purposes of old age (non-contributory) pension, blind pension, widow(er)'s (non-contributory) pension, orphan's (non-contributory) pension, one parent family payment or carer's allowance (as the case may require), any portion of the amount of an increase in the other pension or the aggregate increase, where more than one increase in the other pension has occurred, which, if it were reckoned as means, would result in a reduction in the amount of the pension or combined pensions (as the case may be) which would be greater than the amount by which the other pension has been increased, shall not be reckoned as means.[49]

The purpose of this Rule is to ensure that an increase in, for example, a British retirement pension does not lead to an overall decrease in the combined pension payable.

(h) Rule 6

3–48   The amount of any allowance, special allowance, dependant's allowance, disability pension or wound pension under the Army Pensions Acts 1923 to 1980, or pension under the Military Service (Pensions) Acts 1924 to 1964, arising out of service in the period commencing on April 23, 1916, and ending on September 30, 1923, or pension under the Connaught Rangers (Pensions) Acts 1936 to 1964, is disregarded in the calculation of means.

(3) Payments

3–49   OANCP is payable at a flat rate, with increases for qualified children as appropriate.[50] The normal "qualified adult" rules do not apply to OANCP. Increases are payable where the claimant is living with, or is wholly or mainly maintaining, his or her spouse and the spouse is not in receipt of a payment.[51] However, where the spouse is aged over 66, he or she will normally qualify for an OANCP in his or her own right. Additional payments are made where the person is aged over 80, is living alone or is ordinarily resident on an island. "Secondary benefits" are generally payable with OANCP.

(4) Disqualifications

3–50   A person is generally disqualified for payment of OANCP where he or she is receiving a contributory pension.[52] A person is also disqualified while undergoing penal servitude, imprisonment or detention in legal custody.[53] An increase for an adult or qualified child can still be paid. OANCP is not normally payable outside the State.[54] Section 140 provides that OANCP payable to a person who is detained in a district or auxiliary mental hospital

---

[49] Amended by SWA 1995, s.23, SWA 1996, s.19 and SWA 1997, s.20.

[50] SW(C)A 1993, s. 136.

[51] *ibid.*, s. 137. Spouse includes a party to a marriage that has been validly dissolved or a man and woman who are not married to each other but are cohabiting as husband and wife: see s. 132 as amended by SWA (No. 2) 1995, s.10(2).

[52] SW(C)A 1993, s. 139 subject to s. 135.

[53] *ibid.*, s. 211. See Chap. 15.

[54] *ibid.*

within the meaning of the Mental Treatment Act 1945, or while he or she is detained in any place as an eligible patient within the meaning of that Act, or in the Central Mental Hospital, shall be appropriated towards the cost of maintenance of the person in that place. However, the person in charge may pay a portion of the pension to the person or make certain payments out of the pension towards rent, insurance premiums, etc.[55]

3. Widow(er)'s Pension

3–51 There are two widow(er)'s pensions – contributory and non-contributory. There are currently 100,000 widow(er)s on the widow(er)'s contributory pension – of whom 9 per cent have children and 70 per cent are over 65. About 10 per cent of those on the contributory pension are men. There are 17,000 people on the non-contributory pension almost all of whom are women and 85 per cent of whom are over 65.[56]

A. Widow(er)'s (Contributory) Pension

(1) Qualification conditions

3–52 In order to qualify for the contributory pension, one must be a widow or widower and satisfy the contribution conditions.[57] Widow is defined as a widow or a woman who would otherwise be a widow but for the fact that her marriage has been dissolved (being a dissolution that is recognised as valid in the State).[58] Widower is defined in the same manner. Thus, in order to qualify for a pension a person must have been validly married and the spouse must be dead.[59] However, in order to ensure that "widows" did not lose out a result of the introduction of divorce, the legislation provides that a person who would be a widow(er) but for the dissolution of his or her marriage, where that is recognised as valid by the State, may qualify for a pension.[60] This provision specifically refers to the "dissolution" of a marriage and would thus not appear to apply to nullity. Therefore, where a marriage is validly annulled it would appear that the person is not entitled to a widow(er)'s pension.

---

[55] SW(C)A 1993, s. 140(2).

[56] There are also about 2,000 women with children on the one parent family payment; see Chap. 11.

[57] See SW(C)A 1993, ss.100–105 (as substituted by SWA 1994, s.11) and SW(CPP)R 1994, arts 55–59 as amended.

[58] SW(C)A 1993, s. 100 as amended by SWA 1996, s.28.

[59] On the law relating to marriage, see A. Shatter, *Family Law* (Butterworths, Dublin 1997), chap. 7. In relation to death, see Chap. 16.

[60] On the recognition of valid divorces, see Shatter, above, n.59, Chap. 10.

(2) Contribution conditions

3–53   The contribution conditions for widow's contributory pension are much easier to satisfy than in the case of the old age or retirement pension. A person can qualify on the basis of her own or her spouse's contributions (but not a combination of both).[61] The person (or spouse) must have at least 156 qualifying contributions and a yearly average of at least 39 paid or credited contributions in the three or five years before the spouse's death or the date when he or she attained pension age or, alternatively a yearly average of at least 48 paid or credited contributions from the entry into insurance to the end of the last complete contribution year. As can be seen the widow(er)'s pension requires a much shorter contribution record in order to qualify for pension than do the old age and retirement pensions.[62]

(3) Payments

3–54   WCP is payable at a flat rate, with increases for qualified children as appropriate.[63] Additional payments are made where the person is aged over 80 or living alone. "Secondary benefits" are generally payable with WCP to persons over 65, subject to a means limit in some cases where the person has additional income. In addition, in the case of a widow(er) aged 60 to 65 where the late spouse was getting the household benefits at the time of his or her death, the person may continue to qualify for these benefits.

(4) Disqualifications

3–55   A pension is not payable to a widow(er) for any period after remarriage and a person is also disqualified for payment of pension where he or she is cohabiting with another person as man and wife.[64] Pension is also not generally payable where the person is imprisoned.[65]

B. Widower's (Non-Contributory) Pension

3–56   In order to qualify for a widow(er)'s (non-contributory) pension, one must be a widow (as defined above in the case of the contributory pension) and one must satisfy a means test.[66] The means test is broadly the same as that

---

[61] SW(C)A 1993, s.101(1). Spouse in relation to a widow(er) who has been married more than once refers only to the last spouse (including where that last marriage has been validly dissolved): s. 100 as amended by SWA 1996, s. 28.

[62] *ibid.*, s. 102. A reduced pension is payable where the person has an average of at least 24 contributions per year.

[63] *ibid.*, ss. 103 and 104.

[64] Issues in relation to cohabitation are discussed in Chap. 11.

[65] SW(C)A 1993, s. 211. See Chap. 15.

[66] *ibid.*, s. 142.

outlined above in relation to the old age (non-contributory) pension.[67] However, income assessed under Rule 1(4) includes, in the case of widow's (non-contributory) pension, the net cash value of such non-cash benefits as may be prescribed, and such income received by a qualified child or qualified children as may be prescribed.

3–57 WNCP is payable at a flat rate, with increases for qualified children as appropriate.[68] Additional payments are made where the person is aged over 80 or living alone. "Secondary benefits" are generally payable with WNCP to persons over 65. In addition, in the case of a widow(er) aged 60 to 65 where the late spouse was getting the household benefits at the time of his or her death, the person may continue to qualify for these benefits. A pension is not payable to a widow(er) for any period after remarriage and a person is also disqualified for payment of pension where he or she is cohabiting with another person as man and wife.[69] Pension is also not generally payable where the person is imprisoned.[70]

4. Legal Issues

3–58 Relatively few legal issues arise in relation to the old age and retirement pensions. The qualifications conditions in relation to age and retirement are straightforward. While the conditions in relation to the contribution requirements have become inordinately confusing due to the range of alternative contribution conditions and special or pro-rata pensions which have been introduced, these generally raise issues of an administrative rather than a legal nature. As outlined above at para. 3–16, the only case that reached the superior courts in relation to pension conditions in recent years – *Kinghan v. Minister for Social Welfare* – involved a narrow technical issue of construction in relation to the "yearly average" rule. A broader argument might be made that the operation of the "yearly average" rule is so unreasonable as to be unconstitutional.[71] However, while the rule can in some cases lead to seemingly anomalous results, the rule has a clear rationale and does not directly discriminate against any particular class of person. It would seem unlikely that a court would strike down this rule on a broad constitutional argument.

3–59 Because of the fact that the pensionable age is the same for both men and women, Ireland has been spared the extensive litigation on this issue

---

[67] SW(C)A 1993, ss. 142–147 and Pt II of Third Sched.
[68] *ibid.*, ss. 144 & 145.
[69] *ibid.*, ss. 143(2) and 146. Issues in relation to cohabitation are discussed in Chap. 11.
[70] *ibid.*, s. 211.
[71] *Morgan v. Park Developments* [1983] I.L.R.M. 156.

under E.U. equality law which has occurred in some other E.U. countries. There are, however, a number of issues which could potentially be challenged under E.U. equality law and, in particular, Directive 79/7 on equal treatment in social security.[72]

3–60 It might be argued that the operation of the yearly average rule (see above) indirectly discriminates against women. As we have seen, the homemakers disregard which goes some way to address this only applies from 1994 and does not apply to retirement pension. This issue was argued before an appeals officer of the Social Welfare Appeals Office.[73] The appellant had worked from 1945 to 1954 and had then given up work on marriage. She returned to work in 1974 when her youngest child finished school. In 1991, having reached the age of 65, she applied for the retirement pension and was refused on the basis that her yearly average of 21 was below the statutory requirement of 24. She argued that the operation of the rule was indirectly discriminatory in that it was more likely to affect women than men and suggested that she should only be required to satisfy the averaging requirement over the period of her working life, excluding those years when she was not available to take up work due to family responsibilities.[74] The appeals officer, however, rejected the appeal. He held that the averaging requirement was justified by the need to protect the Social Insurance Fund and that the averaging requirement affected a number of different categories of persons (not just persons on home duties) and, accordingly, that the averaging condition was not in breach of E.U. law.

3–61 A second issue is the treatment of part-time workers under Irish social welfare law. Prior to 1991, most part-time workers (working less than 18 hours per week) were excluded from social insurance. Since 1991, the vast majority of part-time workers are included in the social insurance scheme. However, as a result of the contribution conditions for pensions, current claimants may not qualify for pension on the basis that they were excluded from insurance in the period before 1991. Prima facie this might appear to be contrary to E.U. law, as the majority of part-time workers are women. At one time, it appeared that the European Court of Justice was of the view that unfavourable treatment of part-time workers was likely to be in breach of the directive.[75] However, in a number of cases appeals officers upheld the Irish position.[76] The more recent jurisprudence of the ECJ now appears to have

---

[72] See generally Chap. 9.

[73] M. Cousins, "Indirect Discrimination in Social Welfare" (1993) 11 I.L.T. 147–151.

[74] This is broadly the approach which was subsequently introduced by way of the homemakers' disregard.

[75] Case C–102/88 *Ruzius-Wilbrink v. Bestuur van de Bedrijfsvereniging voor Overheidsdiensten* [1989] E.C.R. 4311.

[76] M. Cousins, above, n.73.

held that discrimination against part-time workers is not necessarily in breach of E.U. law and to have confirmed the Irish decisions.[77]

3–62 The main legal issues that arise in relation to the old age (non-contributory) pension concern the recovery of overpaid pensions after the death of the pensioner. These issues are considered in Chapter 15.

3–63 In the case of the widow(er)'s pension, legal issues again rarely arise. In the United Kingdom it has been held, on grounds of public policy, that a widow responsible for the manslaughter of her husband was not entitled to widow's pension.[78] It is not clear whether such an approach would be followed in this jurisdiction.

3–64 Some issues have arisen in relation to the period prior to the introduction of divorce in 1996. In a significant number of cases persons obtained a church annulment (which has no legal effect) and subsequently "remarried" in church. However, the second "marriage" is not legally valid and, therefore, the second "spouse" is not entitled to a widow(er)'s pension on the death of the person whereas the original spouse may qualify. It might be suggested that U.K. case law in this area be followed to provide assistance in such cases. In *Chief Adjudication Officer v. Bath*,[79] the Court of Appeal held that the presumption of marriage by virtue of a period of long cohabitation would not be rebutted merely because it was preceded by an irregular marriage ceremony. In that case a lady went though a Sikh marriage ceremony which did not comply with the formal legal requirements, and subsequently lived with the man for 40 years until his death. Her claim for a widow's pension was allowed by the Court of Appeal following a line of U.K. cases in relation to the presumption of marriage based on long cohabitation. However, given the constitutional status attached to marriage in Irish law, this line of case law has not been followed in this country and it would appear unlikely that an Irish court would uphold a claim for a widow's pension where a person had contracted a previous valid marriage which had not been validly dissolved or annulled.[80] Issues in relation to the cohabitation bar are discussed in Chapter 11.[81]

---

[77] Case C 317/1993 *Nolte v. Landesversicherungsansalt Hannover* [1995] E.C.R. I–4625; Case C–444/1993 *Megner v. Innungskranken-Kase Vorderpfalz* [1995] E.C.R. I–4741.

[78] *R. v. Chief National Insurance Commissioner, ex parte Connor* [1981] Q.B. 758; *Burns v. Secretary of State for Social Services* 1985 S.L.T. 351.

[79] [2000] 1 F.L.R. 8, also reported in RG1/00.

[80] In addition, the European Court of Human Rights has held that the failure to provide a "widow's" benefit to a person who was not married was not a breach of the European Convention on Human Rights: *Shackell v. United Kingdom*, unreported, European Court of Human Rights, April 27, 2000.

[81] See *Foley v. Moulton* [1989] I.L.R.M. 169.

3–65 Survivor's pensions are specifically excluded from the ambit of Directive 79/7[82] but, in any case, there is now no differentiation in the treatment of men and women in this area in the Irish social welfare code. The European Court of Human Rights has recently held that the difference in treatment between men and women as regards entitlement to a U.K. widow's benefit is not based on any "objective and reasonable" justification and, accordingly, is in breach of Article 14 of the European Convention on Human Rights taken in conjunction with Article 1 of Protocol 1.[83]

---

[82] [1979] O.J. L6/24.
[83] *Willis v. United Kingdom* (2002) 35 E.H.R.R. 21.

CHAPTER 4

Sickness and Disability Benefits

4–01 This chapter looks at the main payments in respect of sickness and disability with the exception of the occupational injuries scheme, which is discussed in Chapter 5.

1. Background

4–02 The introduction of a sickness benefit was one of the first "New Liberal" reforms in the National Insurance Act 1911. In Great Britain, but to a much lesser extent in Ireland, friendly societies already provided sickness benefits to their members and industrial insurance companies also provided insurance, and in particular, life cover. In England and Wales, it has been estimated that about 50 per cent of workers were members of friendly societies. In contrast friendly society membership in Ireland was "negligible".[1] The evolution of national insurance was a complicated story as the Chancellor of the Exchequer, Lloyd George, steered the proposals though the conflicting interests of the friendly societies, the industrial insurance companies and the medical profession.[2] The scheme as finally adopted provided for sickness benefit for up to 26 weeks, disablement benefit payable after the initial 26 weeks (possibly up to the pension age of 70 when benefit ceased), and maternity benefit administered not by central government but by a range of "approved societies". A complicated system of funding was adopted with a notional reserve fund (to cover the actuarial cost of future benefits) being redeemed from ongoing contributions. In most of the United Kingdom, national health insurance also covered medical benefit, *i.e.* the services of a general practitioner. However, as Barrington has shown, as a result of opposition from various interest groups, medical benefit was not extended to Ireland.[3]

---

[1] Barrington estimates that only about 40,000 people were members of friendly societies, of whom half were in the friendly society section of the Ancient Order of Hibernians; see Barrington, *Health, Medicine and Politics* (Institute of Public Administration, Dublin, 1987), p. 35.

[2] See generally Gilbert, *The Evolution of National Insurance in Great Britain* (Micheal Joseph, London, 1966), Chaps 6 and 7.

[3] See above, n.1.

4–03 A Commission was established to review the operation of the scheme in 1925. But this led to only minor changes in its operation.[4] However, on Fianna Fáil coming to office in 1932, the existing schemes operated by independent societies were amalgamated into one national scheme under the auspices of the National Health Insurance Society (NHIS). The Society was governed by a board consisting of representatives of employers, contributors and the State, and it was chaired by the Catholic Bishop of Clonfert, Dr John Dignan. The NHIS – led by Dr Dignan – was quite an active body, seeking to improve services. This led to a switch from a fully actuarial scheme in 1942 and to the publication of the Dignan Plan, in which his lordship set out proposals for radical reform of the social services. This led to a major clash with the then Minister for Local Government and Public Health, Seán MacEntee T.D., and Dignan was effectively dismissed from his post as chairman.

4–04 The NHIS itself was abolished in 1950, with its functions being taken over by the new Department of Social Welfare. The national insurance scheme was incorporated into the co-ordinated scheme of social insurance established in the Social Welfare Act 1952. The 1952 legislation saw the unification of the various social insurance schemes and the establishment of broadly similar qualification conditions for unemployment and disability benefit. Disability benefit was to be payable for up to a year once a person had at least six months' paid contributions and, at the same level, indefinitely (to pension age) where the person had three years' contributions replacing the existing sickness and disablement benefit. Dependency payments were introduced with disability benefit. At about the same time, the Department of Health set up a number of means-tested health-related payments, including the disabled person's maintenance allowance. Comparative studies show that the percentage of the labour force covered for sickness insurance was initially quite low at just over 30 per cent in 1930 and increased slowly over time reaching about 50 per cent by 1960.[5]

4–05 There were very limited changes in the disability benefit scheme in the period to 1970, although the number in receipt of benefit at year-end rose from 42,000 in the early 1950s to 60,000 by 1969 (of whom about 20,000 were incapacitated for more than one year).[6] While this, in part, reflected an increase in the number of persons in insurable employment, it also reflected

---

[4] M. Cousins, *The Birth of Social Welfare* (Four Courts Press, Dublin, 2002).

[5] W. Korpi, *Welfare State Development in Europe since 1930: Ireland in Comparative Perspective* (Dublin, ESRI, 1992).

[6] These figures relate to the stock of claims at year-end. Given that most DB claims are of short duration, it is important to note that the number of claims in any one year would be a large multiple of the claims in payment at a given time.

an increase in the propensity to claim benefits.[7] Coverage continued to increase to about two-thirds of the labour force by 1970.[8] In 1970, the Fianna Fáil Government introduced an invalidity pension for persons on disability benefit who were long-term incapacitated and in 1974 pay-related benefit was introduced with disability benefit. Sickness benefits had started out at about the European average of 40 per cent of average earnings in the 1930s, but had remained at that level in the period to 1970 while other European countries had increased significantly.[9] The introduction of pay-related benefit led to a significant increase in the replacement rate. Initially invalidity pension was set at the same flat rate as disability benefit, but over time the invalidity benefit rate was increased ahead of the disability benefit flat rate.

4–06 The next decade saw a further increase of 10,000 in the numbers claiming sickness payments at one time and by 1978 nearly as many working days were lost because of sickness as were lost because of unemployment.[10] The rate of sickness-related absence from work was not exceptional in the 1950s and up to the end of the 1960s. However, by the end of the 1970s the rate of absence was nearly double the British rate. Hughes's econometric study suggested that the increased replacement ratio due to the introduction of pay-related benefit contributed to a 20 per cent increase in disability claims. Employers became extremely concerned that the disability benefit system was being abused and called for a range of measures to tighten up access to benefit.[11] Key issues included better claim control and taxation of disability benefits. In 1987, the Fianna Fáil Government announced that it intended to follow the U.K. example and to introduce a new sick pay scheme which would transfer responsibility for the payment of sickness benefit to employers for the first 13 weeks.[12] However, opposition from employers meant that neither this nor a subsequent similar decision in 1992 were implemented. However, disability benefit was made taxable in 1993. In addition, the control measures were progressively tightened up over the 1980s. Studies showed that women were significantly more likely to claim disability benefits than were men and changes in the contribution requirements were introduced in the late 1980s and early 1990s to link more closely the payment of disability benefit to participation in employment.[13] Additionally, pay-related benefit was reduced

---

[7] J. Deeny, *The Irish Worker* (Institute of Public Administration, Dublin, 1971), Chap. 5
[8] W. Korpi, above, n.5.
[9] *ibid.*
[10] G. Hughes, *Social Insurance and Absence from Work in Ireland* (ESRI, Dublin, 1982).
[11] Federated Union of Employers, *Absenteeism Control* (FUE, Dublin, 1980). For a comparative context, see O. Kangas, *The Politics of Social Rights* (Swedish Institute of Social Research, Stockholm, 1991).
[12] G. Hughes, *Disability Benefit Reform* (ESRI, Dublin, 1988).
[13] R. O'Leary, "Female Workers on Long-term Sickness Benefit in the Republic of Ireland" (1998) 32 *Social Policy and Administration* 245.

and eventually abolished in 1994, leading to a significant fall in replacement rates.

4–07 A combination of these measures led to a very significant fall in the number of people in receipt of disability benefit at the year-end, from 80,000 in 1986 to only 42,000 in 1994. Invalidity pension claims rose from 26,000 in 1986 to 40,000 by 1994 as long-term disability cases transferred to disability benefit; but overall the numbers claiming sickness and disability payments fell markedly. Whereas in 1986 there were 233,000 claims for disability benefit, or one claim for every five people in the labour force, by 1994 this had fallen to 169,000, or one for every eight workers. Although the total numbers claiming disability benefit increased somewhat thereafter with the booming labour force, the numbers continued to fall as a proportion of those at work. About 50 per cent of those on disability benefit are short-term. The numbers on invalidity pension have continued to rise slowly to 48,700 in 2000.

4–08 The disabled person's maintenance allowance, introduced by the Minister for Health in 1954, had grown considerably in numbers to about 34,500 by 1996. There was considerable dissatisfaction with the manner in which it was administered by the health boards and a number of bodies had recommended that it be transferred to the Department of Social Welfare. This was done in 1997 with its replacement by a disability allowance payment. The numbers on disability allowance increased rapidly thereafter to 50,400 by 2000.

4–09 In 1997 a sickness allowance payment was introduced to fill one of the few remaining gaps in social assistance coverage by bringing in a means-tested equivalent of disability benefit. However, the payment has not been brought into effect to date.

2. Current Situation

4–10 As outlined above, there are three main sickness and disability benefits: disability benefit, invalidity pension and disability allowance. The main features of these schemes are outlined below. In addition, there is a means-tested blind pension which originated as an old age pension payable to persons under pension age who were unable to work due to blindness.[14] There are also a number of sickness and disability-related payments administered by the Department of Health and Children and the regional health boards/authorities, including infectious diseases maintenance allowance, mobility allowance and blind welfare allowance.

---

[14] Social Welfare (Consolidation) Act 1993 (SW(C)A 1993), s. 141.

A. Disability Benefit

4–11 Disability benefit is a payment for people who are incapable of work due to sickness or disability.[15] Although it is often referred to as a short-term payment, in many cases it may be paid indefinitely (up to the age of 66), and currently about 50 per cent of all claimants have been in receipt of disability benefit for over one year.

(1) Qualification conditions

4–12 Disability benefit is payable to any person under the age of 66 in respect of any day of incapacity for work which forms part of a period of interruption of employment where that person satisfies the contribution conditions (see below).[16]

(a) Day of incapacity for work

4–13 A day of incapacity for work is a day on which a person is "incapable of work".[17] However, disability benefit is not payable for the first three days of any period of incapacity for work.[18] Sunday is not included as a day of incapacity for work and any day on which a person is paid holiday pay by his or her employer is also not generally treated as a day of incapacity.[19] Any day when a person fails to prove that he or she is incapable of work or on which he or she does any work other than that specified in Rule 5 of the Rules of Behaviour (see below) will not be treated as a day of incapacity for work.[20] Any three days of incapacity within a period of six consecutive days will be treated as a period of incapacity for work and any two such periods not separated by more than three days shall be treated as one period of incapacity.[21]

(b) Period of interruption of employment

4–14 Any three days of interruption of employment (*i.e.* a day which is a day of incapacity for work or a day of unemployment),[22] whether consecutive

---

[15] The details of the payment are set out in SW(C)A 1993, ss. 31–36 and in the Social Welfare (Consolidated Payments Provisions) Regulations 1994 (S.I. No. 417 of 1994) (SW(CPP)R 1994), arts 11–19.

[16] SW(C)A 1993, s. 31(1).

[17] *ibid.*, s. 31(3)(a).

[18] *ibid.*, s. 31(2).

[19] *ibid.*, s. 31(3).

[20] SW(CPP)R 1994, art. 12.

[21] SW(C)A 1993, s. 31(3)(d). See also s. 31(3)(dd) as inserted by the Socail Welfare Act 2002 (SWA 2002), s.5.

[22] *ibid.*, s. 31(3)(b).

or not, within a period of six consecutive days will be treated as "a period of interruption of employment" and any two such periods not separated by more than 13 weeks will be treated as one period of interruption of employment.[23] So a person who, having been incapable, returns to work for more than 13 weeks will have to establish a new period of interruption of employment and will not be entitled to benefit for the three-day waiting period. Any day in respect of which a woman is entitled to and in receipt of maternity benefit will be treated as a day of incapacity for work for the purposes of reckoning periods of interruption of employment only.[24] Thus, a woman who has been on maternity benefit and who then claims disability benefit due to incapacity for work can have the days on which she received maternity benefit counted as part of the period of interruption of unemployment. However, a woman who was in receipt of maternity benefit on any of the three days prior to her claim for disability benefit is not entitled to disability benefit for the three-day waiting period.[25] This means that women transferring from maternity benefit to disability benefit will normally have established a period of interruption of unemployment and will be entitled to disability benefit after the three-day waiting period.

Notwithstanding the above, in the case of a person who, on or after April 1, 2002, has been in receipt of disability benefit for not less than 1,560 days in respect of a period of incapacity for work and who, within the same period of interruption of employment, has subsequent periods of incapacity for work, any such two subsequent periods of incapacity within that period of interruption not separated by more than 13 weeks shall be treated as one period of incapacity for work.[26]

(c) Incapable of work

4–15   Incapable of work means incapable by reason of some specific disease or bodily or mental disablement or deemed, in accordance with regulations, to be so incapable.[27] There is no more detailed statutory definition of incapacity, nor does there appear to be any Irish case law on the issue.[28] The departmental guidelines on Medical Certification state that in the case of temporary incapacity:

---

[23] SW(C)A 1993, s. 31(3)(c).

[24] SW(CPP)R 1994, art. 16.

[25] SW(C)A 1993, s. 31(6).

[26] SWA 2002, s. 5.

[27] SW(C)A 1993, s. 2(1). See Clark, *Annotated Guide to Social Welfare Law* (Sweet & Maxwell, London, 1995), pp. 66–8. Thus, incapacity due to pregnancy *per se* does not fall within the statutory definition although a pregnancy-related illness could give rise to incapacity in this sense.

[28] For the U.K. case law, see Ogus and Barendt, *The Law of Social Security* (3rd ed., Butterworths, London, 1988), pp. 150–156.

"If the claimant is unable to follow his usual occupation but could be fit for a less demanding form of work, he may be regarded as incapable of work if it is likely that he will soon be able to return to his former occupation."

However, in the longer term:

"The certifier should consider if the physical and mental condition of the claimant is such that he is capable of performing alternative work, which he could reasonably be expected to undertake after taking into account his training, education, experience and age."

4–16 In some circumstances a person can be deemed to be incapable of work even though he or she is not so incapable.[29] This can happen where a person is under medical care for a disease or disablement and where it is certified by a doctor that because of the disease or disablement he or she should not work and he or she does not work, or where a person is a probable source of infection with a disease specified as an infectious disease (specified under the Health Act 1947) and he or she abstains from work on the written order or advice of a doctor.

(d) Night workers

4–17 Where a person is employed to work continuously from one day until the next (*e.g.* someone on a night shift), such person will be regarded as being employed: (a) only on the first day, where the first day is Monday to Friday and where the employment on the first day is longer than on the second day, or where the first day is Saturday; (b) in any other case, on the second day.[30] Where a person is regarded as being employed on only one of two days and a person is incapable of work on the other day, such person will be deemed to be incapable of work for the other day.

(2) Contribution conditions

4–18 The contribution conditions for disability benefit require that a person must have[31]:

- 39 weeks reckonable paid contributions since he or she first entered insurable employment; and
- 39 paid or credited contributions in the relevant contribution year; and
- 13 paid contributions at the appropriate rate in one of the following years:

---

[29] SW(CPP)R 1994, art. 11.

[30] *ibid.*, art. 13.

[31] SW(C)A 1993, s. 32 as amended by SWA 2001, s. 20, and SW(CPP)R 1994, art. 19 as amended by S.I. No. 106 of 2000. Persons who were receiving certain social welfare payments are exempted from the 13-contribution requirement.

– the relevant contribution year;

– in either of the two previous contribution years;

– the most recent complete contribution year;

– the current contribution year;

or

– 26 weeks paid at the appropriate class in the relevant contribution year and 26 weeks contributions paid at the appropriate class in the contribution year before the contribution year.

The latter alternative is to facilitate persons who are job sharing to qualify for benefit.

4–19   In addition, one must have prescribed reckonable weekly earnings in excess of a prescribed amount in the relevant contribution year.[32] The prescribed amount is currently €88.88 per week.[33] This is calculated by taking the reckonable weekly earnings in the year and dividing by the number of paid contributions in that period. In the case of a person whose reckonable weekly earnings are less than €31.74 per week, he or she shall be deemed to have reckonable earnings of €31.74 per week. Where the reckonable weekly earnings are less than €88.87 but are €31.74 or more, one will be entitled to a reduced rate of benefit.[34]

(3) Payments

4–20   Disability benefit is payable at a flat rate, with increases for qualified adults and qualified children as appropriate.[35] "Secondary benefits" are not generally payable with disability benefit. Any person who satisfies the above contribution conditions may receive disability benefit for up to one year. Any two periods separated by less than one year are counted as one.[36] In order to requalify for benefit, one must have 13 paid contributions begun or ended since the last day for which one was entitled to benefit. A person who has 260 or more paid contributions may receive disability benefit indefinitely up to the age of 66.

(4) Disqualifications

4–21   A person will be disqualified for disability benefit for a period of up to nine weeks if he or she becomes incapable of work through his or her own

---

[32] SW(C)A 1993, s. 32(1)(c) as substituted by SWA (No. 2) 1993, s. 7.

[33] SW(CPP)R 1994, art. 17 as amended.

[34] *ibid.*, art. 18 as amended.

[35] SW(C)A 1993, ss. 33 and 34.

[36] *ibid.*, s. 35.

misconduct, fails without good cause to attend for or submit himself or herself to a medical or other examination required by the Department, or fails, without good cause, to observe the Rules of Behaviour.[37]

4–22 The Rules of Behaviour provide that the person[38]:

(1) must obey any instructions, relating to his or her behaviour or any other matter concerning the incapacity for work, of a doctor attending on the person or of a medical referee;

(2) must refrain from behaviour which is likely to retard recovery;

(3) must not be absent from the place of residence without leaving word where he or she may be found (in practice this rule does not seem to be enforced);

(4) must not unreasonably refuse to see an officer of the Department and must answer any reasonable enquiries by such officer relating to the claim;

(5) must not engage in work unless it is:
 (a) light work for which no remuneration is, or would ordinarily be, payable,
 (b) work undertaken primarily as part of his or her treatment while a person is a patient of a hospital, sanatorium or other similar institution and the weekly earnings from such work do not exceed €42.30, or
 (c) work under a scheme that is charitable and the weekly earnings do not exceed €42.30.

4–23 A person may, with the prior written permission of an officer of the Minister, be exempted from the operation of Rule 5 of the Rules of Behaviour for a specified period in which: (a) having become incapable of following his normal occupation, he or she is undergoing a course of training with a view to taking up some other occupation, or (b) he or she is engaged in part-time work in the nature of rehabilitation or occupational therapy. This is interpreted as being work of less than 20 hours per week. Persons who take up these options can still retain their disability benefit.[39]

4–24 A person will also be disqualified if he or she is absent from the State (subject to certain exceptions) or is undergoing penal servitude, imprisonment or detention in legal custody (again, subject to certain exceptions).[40]

---

[37] SW(C)A 1993, s. 36 and SW(CPP)R 1994, art. 15.
[38] SW(CPP)R 1994, Sched. A.
[39] *ibid.*, art. 15(3).
[40] SW(C)A 1993, s. 211. See Chap. 15.

B. Invalidity Pension

4–25   Invalidity pension is a payment for people who are incapable of work in the long term due to sickness or disability.[41]

(1) Qualification conditions

4–26   In order to be entitled to invalidity pension one must:

(a) be permanently incapable of work; and

(b) satisfy the contribution conditions.[42]

4–27   The definition of "incapacity for work" has already been discussed in relation to disability benefit (see para. 4–15). A person will be regarded as being permanently incapable of work if, immediately before the date of claim of invalidity pension:

(a) he or she has been continuously incapable of work for a period of one year and it is shown to the satisfaction of a deciding officer or an appeals officer that the person is likely to continue to be incapable of work for at least a further year; or

(b) the person is incapable of work and evidence is adduced to establish to the satisfaction of a deciding officer or an appeals officer that the incapacity for work is of such a nature that the likelihood is that the person will be incapable of work for life.

4–28   However, s/ he will not be so regarded where it is subsequently shown to the satisfaction of a deciding officer or an appeals officer that he or she is no longer likely to continue to be incapable of work for at least a further year or for life, as the case may be.[43]

4–29   In practice, most claimants of invalidity pension will have been in receipt of disability benefit for considerably more than one year before qualifying for pension. Generally speaking, where a medical referee examining somebody for disability benefit considers that he or she is likely to qualify for invalidity pension, the medical referee will recommend to the Department that the person be transferred to invalidity pension. The Department will then inform the person of this option. It is, of course, open to a person to submit a claim for invalidity pension in any other case.

---

[41] The provisions in relation to invalidity pension are set out in SW(C)A 1993, ss. 95–99 and in SW(CPP)R 1994, arts 52–54.

[42] SW(C)A 1993, s. 95.

[43] SW(CPP)R 1994, art. 52.

(2) Contribution conditions

4–30 In order to qualify for invalidity pension, one must have:

(a) at least 260 paid contributions since entry into insurance; and

(b) at least 48 paid or credited contributions in the last complete contribution year (*i.e.* tax year) before the "relevant date".[44]

4–31 "Relevant date" means any day subsequent to the completion of one year of continuous incapacity for work where the insured person has entered into a continuous period of incapacity for work and he or she is subsequently proved to be permanently incapable of work, or any date subsequent to the commencement of a period of incapacity for work where evidence is produced to the satisfaction of a deciding officer or an appeals officer to establish that the incapacity for work is of such a nature that the likelihood is that the person will be incapable of work for life.[45]

(3) Payments

4–32 Invalidity pension is payable at a flat rate, with increases for qualified adults and qualified children as appropriate.[46] "Secondary benefits" are generally payable with invalidity pension. Any person who satisfies the above contribution conditions may receive invalidity pension indefinitely, as it is payable beyond pension age where a person does not qualify for an old age pension at a higher rate.

(4) Disqualifications

4–33 A person will be disqualified for receiving invalidity pension if and so long as he or she fails, without good cause, to observe the following Rules of Behaviour.[47] These provide that a person:

(1) must attend for medical or other examination at such time or place as may be required by an officer of the Minister, provided that not less than seven days' notice in writing has been given;

(2) must obey any instructions, relating to the person's behaviour or any other matter concerning the incapacity, of a doctor attending on the person or of a medical referee;

---

[44] SW(C)A 1993, s. 96.
[45] *ibid.*, s.96 and SW(CPP)R 1994, art. 53.
[46] SW(C)A 1993, ss. 98 and 99.
[47] *ibid.*, s. 95(3) and SW(CPP)R 1994, art. 54 and Sched. F.

(3) must not refuse unreasonably to see an officer of the Department and to answer any reasonable enquiries by any such officer related to the claim;

(4) must not engage in work whether on the person's own account or on behalf of any other person.

4–34 The person may, with the prior written permission of an officer of the Minister, be exempted from the operation of Rule 4 for any period during which:

(a) having become permanently incapable of following his or her usual occupation he or she is undergoing a course of training with a view to taking up some other occupation; or

(b) he or she is engaged in work in the nature of rehabilitation or occupational therapy; or

(c) he or she is engaged in light work for which no remuneration is or would ordinarily be payable.[48]

Persons who take up these options can still retain their invalidity pension.

4–35 A person is also disqualified if he or she is undergoing penal servitude, imprisonment or detention in legal custody (subject to certain exceptions).[49]

C. Disability Allowance

4–36 Disability allowance (DA) is a means-tested payment for people who are substantially handicapped in undertaking employment in the long term due to sickness or disability.[50] This payment replaces the disabled persons maintenance allowance administered by the regional health boards under the auspices of the Department of Health. Responsibility for this payment transferred from the Department of Health to the Department of Social Welfare on October 2, 1996.

(1) Qualification conditions

4–37 In order to be entitled to disability allowance a person must:

(1) be between the ages of 16 and pension age (currently 66);

---

[48] SW(CPP)R 1994, art. 54 (2).
[49] SW(C)A 1993, s. 211 and see Chap. 15.
[50] The provisions in relation to disability allowance are set out in SW(C)A 1993, ss. 191A–D (as inserted by SWA 1996, s.13) and in SW(CPP)R 1994, Chap. 6A (as inserted by S.I. No. 297 of 1996).

(2) be substantially handicapped, by reason of a specified disability, in undertaking employment of a kind which, if the person were not suffering from that disability, would be suited to his or her age, experience and qualifications; and

(3) satisfy the means test.[51]

4–38 For the purposes of section 191B, a person is regarded as being substantially handicapped in undertaking suitable employment by reason of a specified disability where he or she suffers from an injury, disease, congenital deformity or physical or mental illness or defect which has continued or, in the opinion of a deciding officer or an appeals officer, may reasonably expect to continue for a period of at least one year. However, he or she shall not be so regarded where it is subsequently shown to the satisfaction of a deciding officer or an appeals officer that he or she is no longer likely to continue to be substantially handicapped for a period of at least one year.[52]

(2) Means test

4–39 The means test,[53] which is broadly similar to that applying to unemployment assistance includes means from:

• most property owned by the person and/or by his or her spouse (but excluding property personally used or enjoyed by the person);

• all income which the person and/or spouse may reasonably expect to receive in the coming year (with certain exceptions);

• the value of any advantage accruing to the person or spouse from the use of property (other than a domestic dwelling or farm building, owned and occupied, furniture and personal effects) which is personally used or enjoyed by the person or spouse and the value of any advantage from the leasing of a farm of land;

• any property which the person or spouse have deprived themselves of either directly or indirectly in order to qualify for assistance.

It should be noted that the assessment of "benefit and privilege" does not apply to disability allowance.

4–40 The detailed provisions of the means tests are set out below. Part I of the Third Schedule provides that in the calculation for the purposes of disability allowance, the following are deemed to constitute the means of a person.

---

[51] SW(C)A 1993, s. 191B.
[52] SW(CPP)R 1994, art. 86A as inserted by S.I. No. 297 of 1996.
[53] See SW(C)A 1993, Pt I of Third Sched.

(a) Rule 1(1)

4–41   Other than in such circumstances and subject to such conditions and for such periods as may be prescribed, the weekly value of any property belonging to the person (not being property personally used or enjoyed by the person or a farm of land leased by him or her) which is invested or is otherwise put to profitable use by the person or which, though capable of investment or profitable use is not invested or put to profitable use by the person, is taken into account. The weekly value of the property is calculated as follows:

(i)   the first €12,697 of the capital value of the property shall be excluded; and

(ii) the weekly value of so much of the capital value of the property as exceeds €12,697 but does not exceed €25,394.76 shall be assessed at €1.27 per each €1,269.74; and

(iii) the weekly value of so much of the capital value of the property as exceeds €25,394.76 but does not exceed €38,092.14 shall be assessed at €2.54 per each €1,269.74; and

(iv) the weekly value of so much of the capital value of the property as exceeds €38,092.14 shall be assessed at €5.08 per each €1,269.74.

4–42   Thus, Rule 1(1) provides for a system of notional assessment of means from capital. It does not matter whether the actual income from capital is greater or lesser than the notional assessment, as the latter is deemed to constitute the weekly means of a person from such capital. In practice, it would be administratively impossible to operate a system of assessment of actual income, as this would vary constantly with, for example, varying interest rates on deposit accounts or variation in returns from shares, leading to frequent fluctuations in the level of pension payable. In addition, the notional system is designed to favour those with relatively small amounts of capital, as can be seen from the exclusion of the first €12,697 from assessment.

4–43   For the purposes of Rules 1(2) and 1(5), the income of a person is, in the absence of other means of ascertaining it, taken to be the income actually received during the year immediately *preceding* the date of calculation.

(b) Rule 1(2)

4–44   All income which the person or his or her spouse may reasonably expect to receive during the succeeding year in cash, whether as contributions to the expenses of the household or otherwise, is taken into account. The following are excluded:

1(2)(a): such amount as may be prescribed of all moneys earned by his or her spouse from insurable employment[54];

1(2)(b): any moneys received by way of benefit, pension, assistance, allowance, supplement or continued child payment under Part II, III, IV, V or VA, or by way of a payment corresponding to child benefit under Part IV from another Member State of the E.U.;

1(2)(c): any income arising from a bonus under a scheme administered by the Minister for the Gaeltacht for the making of special grants to parents or guardians resident in the Gaeltacht or Breac-Gaeltacht of children attending primary schools;

1(2)(d): in the case of a qualified applicant under a scheme administered by the Minister for the Gaeltacht and known as Scéim na bhFoghlaimeoirí Gaeilge, any income received under that scheme in respect of a person who is temporarily resident with the qualified applicant, together with any other income received in respect of such temporary resident;

1(2)(e): an amount of an allowance, dependant's allowance, disability pension or wound pension under the Army Pensions Acts 1923 to 1980, or a combination of such allowances and such pensions so far as such amount does not exceed €101.60 per year;

1(2)(f): any moneys received from a charitable organisation, being a body whose activities are carried on otherwise than for profit (but excluding any public or local authority) and one of whose functions is to assist persons in need by making grants of money to them;

1(2)(g): such amount, as may be prescribed, of income from employment by a health board or by a person approved by a health board, as a home help;

1(2)(h): any moneys received by way of training allowance from an organisation while undergoing a course of rehabilitation training provided by the organisation (being an organisation approved of by the Minister for Health for the purposes of the provision of such training);

[1(2)(hh) applies to unemployment assistance only];

1(2)(i): any moneys, except so far as they exceed €132.08 per year, received by such person or by the spouse of such person in respect of work as an outworker under a scheme that is, in the opinion of the Minister, charitable in character and purpose;

1(2)(j): where his or her spouse is engaged on a seasonal basis in the occupation of fishing, one-half of so much of the income derived therefrom as does not exceed €152.40 per year and one-third of so

---

[54] See SW(CPP)R 1994, art. 90A(2) as inserted by S.I. No. 83 of 2000.

much of such income as exceeds €152.40 per year but does not exceed €381 per year[55];

[1(2)(jj) does not apply to DA];

1(2)(k): payments by a health board in respect of a child who is boarded out;

1(2)(kk): payments in respect of not more than two persons boarded out under section 10 of the Health (Nursing Homes) Act 1990 (insofar as the aggregate amount received in respect of each person does not exceed the maximum amount of the old age (non-contributory) pension)[56];

[1(2)(l) and (ll) do not apply to DA];

1(2)(m): in such circumstances as may be prescribed, any moneys received by way of a maintenance grant under the Higher Education Grants scheme, the Maintenance Grants Scheme for Students attending Post-Leaving Certificate Courses, the Vocational Education Committees Scholarship Scheme, or the Third-Level Maintenance Scheme for Trainees[57];

1(2)(n): any moneys received by way of a mobility allowance payable under section 61 of the Health Act 1970;

[1(2)(o) and (p) do not apply to DA];

1(2)(q): payments by a health board in respect of the provision of accommodation for a child under section 5 of the Child Care Act 1991;

[1(2)(r) does not apply to DA];

1(2)(s): any sums received by way of assistance in the maintenance at home of handicapped children under section 61 of the Health Act 1970 and known as domiciliary care allowance, and such amount as may be prescribed of earnings from employment or self-employment of a rehabilitative nature (currently €120)[58];

1(2)(t): any moneys received by his or her spouse in respect of participation in the Vocational Opportunities Scheme;

1(2)(u): any moneys received by his or her spouse in respect of participation in the Back to Work Allowances, Back to Education Allowance or Part-Time Job Incentive Schemes;

1(2)(v): any moneys received by his or her spouse in respect of participation in a FÁS course;

---

[55] Amended by SWA 1999.
[56] Inserted by SWA 2001.
[57] Substituted by SWA 2001.
[58] SW(CPP)R 1994, art. 90A(1) as amended by S.I. No. 120 of 2002.

1(2)(w) such other income received by a person or his or her spouse as may be prescribed.[59]

4-45 Thus, Rule 1(2) covers income received by a person but subject to the extensive list of exclusions set out above. It should be noted that these exclude income from employment and from some forms of self-employment which are dealt with separately by Rules 1(7) and (8), discussed below.

<u>(c) Rule 1(3)</u>

4-46 The means of a person are deemed to include the yearly value ascertained in the prescribed manner of any advantage accruing to him or to his spouse from:

(a) the use of property (other than a domestic dwelling or farm building owned and occupied, furniture and personal effects) which is personally used or enjoyed by him or by his spouse; and

(b) the leasing by him or by his spouse of a farm of land.[60]

<u>(d) Rule 1(4)[61]</u>

4-47 All income and the yearly value ascertained in the prescribed manner of all property of which he or his spouse have directly or indirectly deprived themselves in order to qualify for the receipt of disability allowance are included. However, where such income or the yearly value of the property so ascertained has reduced since the date of calculation, the calculation may be revised, subject to such conditions and in such circumstances as may be prescribed, provided that any such Regulations shall not cause the income or yearly value of the property taken to be part of the means to be increased.

<u>(e) Rule 1(7)[62]</u>

4-48 In the case of a person engaged in employment under a contract of service, the value, ascertained in the prescribed manner of any moneys derived from the said employment and the value so calculated shall be deemed to constitute the weekly means of that person from such employment.

---

[59] Amended by SWA 1997, s. 26 and SWA 2001, s. 24. SW(CPP)R 1994, art. 90A(3) (as inserted by S.I. No. 297 of 1996) prescribes income from an award relating to Hepatitis C from the Compensation Tribunal or a court, and compensating arising from thalidomide.
[60] Amended by SWA 1997, s. 37.
[61] Amended by SWA 1996, s. 15 and SWA 2000, s. 17.
[62] Inserted by SWA 1996, s. 22. Rules 1(5), (6) and (6A) do not apply to DA.

(f) Rule 1(8)[63]

4–49   In the case of a fisherman, means include the gross income derived from any form of self-employment, less: (a) any expenses necessarily incurred in carrying on any form of self-employment, and (b) where the fisherman has a qualified child who normally resides with him or her, an amount of €254 per annum in respect of the first two qualified children and €381 per annum in respect of each qualified child, calculated at 70 per cent.

(g) Rule 2A[64]

4–50   Notwithstanding the provisions of other Rules, for the purposes of disability allowance, the gross proceeds derived from the sale of the principal residence of the claimant or beneficiary or, in the case of a married couple who are living together, the spouse of the claimant or beneficiary shall not, subject:

(a) to such limit,

(b) to such conditions,

(c) in such circumstances, and

(d) for such periods,

as shall be prescribed, be taken into account in calculating the means of the claimant or pensioner.

4–51   In this Rule "gross proceeds derived from the sale of the principal residence" means:

(a) the agreed sale price of the residence, or

(b) where the claimant or beneficiary purchases alternative accommodation, the difference between the agreed sale price of the former residence and the agreed purchase price of the replacement residence.

4–52   Paragraphs (1) and (2) do not apply to any sums arising from the investment or profitable use of the gross proceeds derived from the sale of the principal residence. Thus, where a person sells his or her principal residence, the gross proceeds of the sale up to a maximum figure (currently €190,460.71) are exempted from the means test where the residence has been sold on or after April 1, 2001 so as to enable the person to:

---

[63] Inserted by SWA 1999, s. 22 and amended by SWA 2000, s. 19. While not specifically excluding DA, this rule is unlikely to be of relevance to DA claimants.
[64] Inserted by SWA 2001, s. 13.

- purchase or rent alternative accommodation, which he or she occupies as his or her only or main residence; or
- move into a private nursing home which has been registered under section 4 of the Health (Nursing Home) Acts 1990.[65]

4-53 From April 5, 2002, this provision was extended to any of the categories of people outlined above who:

- move in with a recipient of carer's allowance or benefit, where the recipient is that pensioner's carer; or
- move to sheltered or special housing in the voluntary co-operative, statutory or private sectors that is funded under the Capital Assistance Scheme operated by the Department of the Environment and Local Government.[66]

(h) Rule 3

4-54 In the application of these rules, "spouse" means each person of a married couple who are living together or a man and woman who are not married to each other but are cohabiting as husband and wife.[67]

(3) Payments

4-55 Disability allowance is payable at a flat rate with increases for qualified adults and qualified children as appropriate.[68] "Secondary benefits" are generally payable with disabilty allowance. Any person who satisfies the above contribution conditions may receive disability allowance up to pension age.

(4) Disqualifications

4-56 A person may be disqualified for receiving disability allowance if he or she fails, without good cause, to attend for or to submit himself or herself to such medical or other examinations as may be required or to observe Rules of Behaviour.[69] The Rules of Behaviour provide that a person:

(1) must attend for medical or other examination at such time or place as may required by the Department, provided that the person has been given not less than seven days' notice in writing;

(2) must obey any doctor's instructions relating to the disability; and

---

[65] As amended by S.I. No. 132 of 2001.
[66] As amended by S.I. No. 120 of 2002.
[67] Substituted by SWA 1995, s. 16.
[68] SW(C)A 1993, s. 191C.
[69] See SW(C)A 1993, s. 191D and SW(CPP)R 1994, art. 86B and Sched. O.

(iii) must not unreasonably refuse to see an officer of the Department and answer any reasonable enquiries by such officer relating to the claim.

4–57   A person is not entitled to receive disability allowance for any period during which he or she is resident in an institution except:

- where a person has an existing entitlement to disability allowance and goes into institutional care after August 1, 1999, in which case entitlement to disability allowance will continue as long as he or she satisfies the qualifying conditions for award of disability allowance; or

- where he or she entered the hospital or institution before August 1, 1999, and he or she was resident there on a temporary basis to receive medical or other treatment for a period not exceeding 13 weeks, *i.e.* DA is payable for up to 13 weeks in these circumstances.[70]

4–58   "Institution" means a hospital, convalescent home or home for people suffering from physical or mental disability or ancillary accommodation, a nursing home for the care and maintenance of dependent elderly people, and any other similar establishment providing residence, maintenance or care where the cost of a person's maintenance therein is being met in whole or in part by or on behalf of a health board.[71] The definition does not include, however, community-based houses or hostels, sometimes called "Low Support Hostels", funded or approved by health boards. DA is payable to persons who are resident there provided that the health board is not funding their maintenance.

4–59   These provisions originally meant that people with disabilities in residential accommodation or institutional care were not entitled to receive disability allowance. In recent years they have been substantially modified as set out above. However, there is a group of people who entered institutional care prior to August 1999 who still are not entitled to DA. In some cases, such persons may be paid some form of "pocket money" by the institution.

4–60   A person is also not entitled to disability allowance if he or she is absent from the State or undergoing penal servitude, imprisonment or detention in legal custody (subject to certain exceptions).[72]

D. Blind Person

4–61   Blind pension (BP) is a means-tested payment payable to blind persons.

---

[70] SW(C)A 1993, ss. 191B(3), (3A) (as inserted by SWA 1999, s. 20 and amended by SWA 2000, s. 21) and (3B) as amended by SWA 1999, s. 20.

[71] *ibid.*, s. 191A.

[72] *ibid.*, s. 211. See Chap. 15.

It is basically, the old age (non-contributory) pension payable below pension age.[73]

(1) Qualification conditions

4–62 In order to qualify for BP, a person must be "blind", must have attained the age of 18 years and must satisfy the mean test. Section 141 provides that in order to qualify for BP a person must be "so blind that he either cannot perform any work for which eyesight is essential or cannot continue his ordinary occupation".

(2) Means test

4–63 The means test for BP is broadly the same as that for the old age (non-contributory) pension (see Chapter 3). However, in the case of a blind person, Rule 1(4) excludes:

(i) earnings (including wages and profit from any form of self-employment) other than employment of a rehabilitative nature as a blind person except and in so far as the annual amount of such earnings is calculated to exceed an amount made up as follows:

€396.24, plus €264.16 if his or her spouse is living with or is wholly or mainly maintained by him or, being a single person, widow or widower, is maintaining wholly or mainly a person over the age of 16 years having the care of one or more than one qualified child who normally resides or reside with him or her, plus €132.08 for each qualified child normally residing with him or her of whom account has not already been taken in accordance with this paragraph in calculating the means of another person;

(ii) such amount as may be prescribed (currently €120) of his or her earnings from employment of a rehabilitative nature[74]; or

(iii) any income arising from a grant or allowance in pursuance of a scheme for promoting the welfare of the blind prepared under section 2 of the Blind Persons Act 1920 (*i.e.* a blind welfare allowance payable by the health boards).[75]

---

[73] See the discussion in *Harvey v. Minister for Social Welfare* [1989] I.R. 213, in which the Supreme Court rejected an argument that the blind pension was not an old age (non-contributory) pension and upheld Blayney J.'s decision that it was merely the old age pension payable at an earlier age to a person who suffers from blindness.

[74] SW(CPP)R 1994, art. 89B as amended by S.I. No. 120 of 2002.

[75] Rule 1(4)(h) as substituted by SWA 1997, s. 26.

4–64 In addition, in the case of blind pension, Rule 1(4) excludes any moneys received by way of a maintenance grant under the Higher Education Grants scheme, the Maintenance Grants Scheme for Students attending Post-Leaving Certificate Courses, the Vocational Education Committees Scholarship Scheme, or the Third-Level Maintenance Scheme for Trainees.[76]

4–65 It should be noted that a number of the provisions of the OAP means test do not apply in the case of a blind person.[77]

(3) Payments

4–66 BP is payable at a flat rate, with increases for qualified children as appropriate.[78] It is payable over pension age. The normal "qualified adult" rules do not apply to BP. Increases are payable where the claimant is living with, or is wholly or mainly maintaining, his or her spouse and the spouse is not in receipt of a payment.[79] However, where the spouse is aged over 66, he or she will normally qualify for an OAP in his or her own right. Additional payments are made where the person is aged over 80 or living alone. "Secondary benefits" are generally payable with BP.

(4) Disqualifications

4–67 A person is generally disqualified for payment of BP where he or she is receiving a contributory pension.[80] A person is also disqualified while undergoing penal servitude, imprisonment or detention in legal custody.[81] An increase for a qualified adult or qualified child can still be paid. BP is not normally payable outside the State.[82]

---

[76] Rule 1(4)(n) as substituted by SWA 2001, s. 13.
[77] *e.g.* Rule 1(4)(i) and (k).
[78] SW(C)A 1993, s. 136.
[79] *ibid.*, s. 137. Spouse includes a party to a marriage that has been validly dissolved or a man and woman who are not married to each other but are cohabiting as husband and wife: see s. 132.
[80] *ibid.*, s. 139, subject to s. 135.
[81] *ibid.*, s. 211; see Chap. 15.
[82] *ibid.*, s. 211; see Chap. 15.

CHAPTER 5

Occupational Injuries Benefits and Deductability of Benefits from Awards of Damages for Personal Injury

5–01 This chapter looks at the occupational injuries code. It also looks at the issue of the deductibility of social welfare benefits from awards of damages. Although the scope of this issue extends beyond occupational injuries and includes, for example, deductibility of disability benefit entitlements from motor accident awards, it is of particular relevance to occupational injuries and it seems appropriate to address it in this chapter.

1. Background

5–02 The workmen's compensation legislation was introduced in 1897 by Joseph Chamberlain to reform the existing procedures whereby workers injured in the course of their employment had to seek compensation under tort law from their employer.[1] The courts had construed the employer's responsibilities in a very narrow manner and, in contrast, the workmen's compensation legislation provided that compensation at a set amount was automatically payable by the employer where an injury arose "out of and in the course of employment".[2] Only a narrow range of hazardous industries was originally covered but this was extended to agriculture in 1900 and subsequently to most manual and lower-paid employments by the Liberal Government in 1906. Compensation was to be paid directly by the employer and there was no obligation on the employer to insure against liability, although many did. Compensation was payable during incapacity for work as a proportion of previous earnings or, in the case of a fatal accident, as a lump sum to a person's dependants. The State was only involved to a limited extent in supervising the scheme and in providing the main forum for the adjudication of disputes through the courts.

[1] J. Bartrip, *Workmen's Compensation in Twentieth Century Britain: Law, History and Social Policy* (Ashgate, London, 1987).
[2] *Report of the Commission on Workmen's Compensation* (Stationery Office, Dublin, 1963), Chap. II.

5–03 The workmen's compensation legislation was consolidated by the Fianna Fáil Government in 1934, following the report of a Departmental Committee in 1927, but there were relatively few changes to the scheme itself. Consideration was given to including the reform of workmen's compensation amongst the issues to be addressed in the 1949 White Paper and subsequent legislation, but these plans were shelved. However, dissatisfaction with this scheme led to the establishment of a Commission in 1955 to review this whole area of the law. The Majority Report of the Commission in 1962 recommended retention of a modified workmen's compensation scheme, but the Minority Report recommended that workmen's compensation be replaced by a system of social insurance for occupational injuries. Following on this latter recommendation, the occupational injuries code was established in 1966. This was a system of insurance financed by employers and administered by the Department from which benefits were paid to employees suffering from occupational injuries or diseases. A feature which distinguished the occupational injuries code from other social insurance schemes was that claimants of occupational injuries benefits (OIB) did not have to satisfy any contribution conditions, reflecting the fact that because the code partly replaced the employer's liability in law, the system was financed entirely by employers though a separate Occupational Injuries Fund and no contributions were levied on employees. However, these distinctive features were considerably modified over the years. The separate OIB fund was abolished in 1990 and occupational injury benefits are now funded from the general Social Insurance Fund. Occupational injury benefits were originally paid at a higher rate than general social welfare benefits. However, this was gradually eroded over time and the differential was largely abolished in 1992.

2. Current Situation

A. Scope of the Occupational Injuries Code

5–04 The scope of the occupational injuries code is determined by two factors – first, the claimant must be working in insurable (occupational injuries) employment (see Chapter 14) and, secondly, the illness must be due to an occupational accident or prescribed disease or injury. In general terms, the vast majority of employees irrespective of age are covered for occupational injuries. However, self-employed persons are *not* covered for OIB.

(1) Occupational accidents and prescribed diseases and injuries

5–05 The occupational injuries code applies in respect of personal injuries caused by accidents arising out of and in the course of employment (occupational accidents) and in respect of prescribed diseases and prescribed personal injury not so caused but which are due to the nature of the employment (occupational diseases). The accident or disease must have occurred or developed on or after May 1, 1967.

(a) Occupational accidents

5–06 The meaning of the term "accident" is not self-evident and considerable case law has been built up around the meaning of this word.[3] An accident has been held to include deliberate acts by a third party, and the fact that the event was foreseeable has been held not to prevent it being considered to be an accident.[4] The main use of the term has been to distinguish an event (which can be an accident) from a process (which cannot).[5] Thus, an injury sustained as a result of an ongoing series of incidents, none of which could be regarded as an accident, will not be regarded as having been caused by an occupational accident. (Such an injury might, however, constitute a prescribed disease, depending on the circumstances.)

The House of Lords has recently reviewed the law in relation to the distinction between an accident and a process.[6] A fireman claimed industrial injuries benefit (the U.K. equivalent of injury benefit) on the basis that he had attended many fatal accidents which had resulted in his suffering from post-traumatic stress disorder. The House of Lords held that it was necessary to identify an accident which had caused injury to the claimant; the fact that a claimant had suffered stress or developed a physical or psychological illness as a result of a stressful occupation would not of itself qualify the claimant for an award of benefit. Even so, it was possible to find that persons in stressful occupations might have suffered an accident or a series of accidents (although the distinction between an accident and a process might be difficult to discern). "Accident" required to be given its ordinary meaning and regard should be had to such factors as expectation and forseeability, whether an incident was exceptional, and to the nature of the claimant's occupation.

---

[3] Ogus, Barendt and Wikely, *The Law of Social Security* (4th ed., Butterworths, London, 1995), pp. 302–5; Clark, *Annotated Guide to Social Welfare Law* (Sweet & Maxwell, London, 1995), pp. 127–130. There are very few Irish cases interpreting the occupational injuries code. In contrast, there are numerous workmen's compensation cases on issues such as the term "accident" – many of which are referred to by Clark – but one would have to question how relevant many of them are today given the significant changes in work practices.

[4] *Trim Joint District School v. Kelly* [1914] A.C. 667.

[5] *Chief Adjudication Officer v. Faulds* [2000] 2 All E.R. 961.

[6] *ibid.* See *Kelly v. Cement Ltd* [1940] I.R. 86 and the discussion in the Northern Ireland case of *R. (Curry) v. National Insurance Commissioners* [1974] N.I. 102. In *Mullen v. Secretary of State for Work and Pensions* [2002] S.C. 251 the Court of Sessions found, on the facts of that case, that repeated back injuries were accidents rather than a process.

5–07   An occupational accident is one which arises "out of and in the course of employment".[7] This phrase – which has given rise to even more debate than the meaning of the word "accident" – is generally accepted to mean that: (a) the accident must have been caused or linked to some risk relating to the claimant's employment; and (b) it must have occurred during the course of employment.[8] The meaning of this phrase has been modified by section 51 of SW(C)A 1993, which sets out certain rules for determining when an accident may be regarded as having arisen out of and in the course of employment. There is a presumption that an accident which occurred *in the course of* employment arose *out of* that employment.[9] This presumption is rebuttable, however, so that in appropriate cases, an employer may be able to show that even though the claimant suffered an injury while at work, the accident was not attributable to the employment.

5–08   In addition, where an accident:

(a) arises in the course of employment;

(b) is caused by another person's misconduct, negligence or misbehaviour or by steps taken in consequence of any such misconduct, negligence or misbehaviour or by the behaviour or presence of an animal or is caused by or consists in the insured person being struck by any object or by lightning; and

(c) the insured person did not directly or indirectly contribute cause or contribute to the happening of the accident by his conduct outside the employment or by any act not incidental to the employment,

such accident *shall be* treated as having arisen out of the insured person's employment.[10]

5–09   Disobeying instructions does not necessarily debar an employee from claiming occupational injuries benefits. The fact that, at the time of the accident, the employee was acting in contravention of any statutory or other regulations pertaining to the employment or of any orders given by the employer or was acting without instructions from the employer shall not affect a claim for benefit provided that: (a) the accident would have been deemed to be an occupational accident had the act not been done in contravention of regulations or without instructions from the employer, as the case may be; and (b) the act is done for the purposes of and in connection with the employer's trade or business.[11]

---

[7] Ogus, Barendt and Wikely, above, n.3, pp. 306–323; Clark, above, n.3, pp. 130–135.
[8] *Chief Adjudication Officer v. Rhodes* [1999] 2 All E.R. 859.
[9] Social Welfare (Consolidation) Act 1993 (SW(C)A 1993), s. 51(1).
[10] *ibid.*, s. 51(2).
[11] *ibid.*, s. 51(3).

5–10 Accidents occurring while commuting to and from work (to or from the normal place of residence) are deemed to be occupational accidents provided they occur in the course of an unbroken journey to or from work to carry out or having carried out the duties of employment.[12] Accidents happening to an insured person at the place of employment and while that person is taking steps, in an actual or supposed emergency, to rescue persons or property are also deemed to have arisen out of and in the course of employment.[13]

5–11 The position of apprentices injured while on training is governed by section 51(6), which creates a rebuttable presumption that accidents occurring to an apprentice while attending a technical school or other place of training or instruction are occupational accidents if attendance was with the employer's consent or under his or her direction or if attendance was required by the contract of apprenticeship.

5–12 Finally, where a claim for occupational injuries benefit is made (or a declaration is sought that an accident or disease is an occupational accident or disease), the Minister may direct that the relevant employment shall be treated as having been insurable (occupational injuries) employment notwithstanding that, by reason of a breach of a statutory provision passed for the protection of employed persons, the contract of employment was void or the employee was not lawfully employed.[14]

5–13 Except where regulations otherwise provide, occupational injuries benefits are not payable in respect of an accident happening while the insured person is outside of the State.[15] This exclusion is subject to the E.U. Regulations on social security for migrant workers (Regulation 1408/71[16] as amended). These provide that where a person is working for an employer in another E.U. country, he or she is generally covered by the social security laws of that country. However, if a person is posted by an Irish employer to work in another E.U. country and remains subject to Irish social welfare law, cover for occupational injuries benefit continues under Irish legislation. In addition, the E.U. Regulation provides that where a person subject to Irish legislation has left the territory of a Member State to proceed, in the course of his or her

---

[12] See SW(C)A 1993, s. 51(4) and the Social Welfare (Amendment of Miscellaneous Social Insurance Provisions) Regulations 1986 (S.I. No. 81 of 1986), art. 11. See an appeals officer's decision on the meaning of "unbroken" in *Social Welfare Appeals Office Report 1997*, p. 20.
[13] SW(C)A 1993, s. 51(5).
[14] *ibid.*, s. 52(1).
[15] *ibid.*, s. 52(3).
[16] [1971] O.J. L149/2.

employment, to another Member State and sustains an accident before arriving there, his or her entitlement to benefit shall be established as if the accident had occurred in Ireland.[17]

(b) Prescribed diseases and personal injuries not caused by accidents

5–14 Section 66(1) provides that the occupational injuries code shall apply in respect of prescribed diseases and prescribed personal injuries that are not caused by an accident but that are due to the nature of the employment. Subsection (2) obliges the Minister to prescribe a disease or injury for the purpose of this section in relation to insured persons if: (a) it ought to be treated as a risk of their occupations and not as a risk common to all persons; and (b) it is such that, in the absence of special circumstances, the attribution of particular cases to the nature of the employment can be established or presumed with reasonable certainty. The relevant Regulations list over 50 medical conditions which are prescribed as occupational diseases or injuries in respect of specified occupational activities.[18] In relation to the vast majority of these conditions, the Regulations provide for a rebuttable presumption that the condition is due to the nature of the employment. The Regulations also provide for the determination of the time at which a person is to be treated as having developed a prescribed disease or injury and regulate the circumstances in which any such disease or injury is to be treated as having recrudesced or as having been contracted or received afresh.

B. Occupational Injuries Benefit

5–15 There are currently four different occupational injury payments. The main payments are the disablement benefit (not to be confused with the general disability benefit), which provides compensation for a "loss of faculty", and injury benefit, which is a short-term income maintenance payment (broadly the equivalent of disability benefit).

---

[17] [1971] O.J. L149/2, Annex VI (A) point G.3.

[18] Social Welfare (Occupational Injuries) (Prescribed Diseases) Regulations 1983 (S.I. No. 392 of 1983), as amended by S.I. No.102 of 1985. The E.U. has drawn up recommendations on occupational diseases: Recommendation to the Member States of July 23, 1962 concerning the adoption of a European schedule of occupational diseases [1962] O.J. B80/2188 and Commission Recommendation 66/462 of July 20, 1966 on the conditions for granting compensation to persons suffering from occupational diseases [1966] O.J. P147/2696. These are not legally binding but the ECJ has held that national courts are required to take them into account in interpreting national provisions: Case 322/88, *Grimaldi v. Fonds des maladies professionnelles* [1989] E.C.R. 4407.

(1) Disablement benefit

(a) Conditions of entitlement

5–16 A person who suffers from an occupational injury or disease is entitled to disablement benefit where he or she suffers as a result of the accident from a loss of physical or mental faculty assessed at not less than 1 per cent.[19] It is not necessary to prove incapacity to work in order to be entitled to disablement benefit. Assessment of loss of faculty is made by a deciding officer in accordance with the general principles set out in section 54(3). Thus, the disabilities to be taken into account are all disabilities to which one may be expected to be subject during the period taken into account as compared with a person of the same age and sex whose physical and mental condition is normal. Such disabilities are treated as having been incurred as a result of the relevant loss of faculty except where they were the result of a congenital defect or an injury or disease received or contracted before the relevant accident or disease, or an injury or disease received or contracted after, and not directly attributable to, such accident. The assessment is made without reference to the particular circumstances of the claimant other than age, sex and physical and mental condition, and is made by reference to disabilities that are prescribed by Regulation as amounting to 100 per cent disablement.

5–17 Section 54(4) provides that Regulations may direct that a prescribed loss of faculty shall be treated as resulting in a prescribed degree of disablement.[20] Section 54(5) provides for the making of a provisional assessment of disablement where there is a possibility of change in the condition of the claimant.

5–18 Finally, disablement benefit is not payable for the first three days after the accident occurred or the disease was contracted. Moreover, if a person is incapable of work as a result of the accident or disease, he or she cannot claim disablement benefit while remaining so incapable during the period of

---

[19] SW(C)A 1993, s. 54(1). See Ogus, Barendt and Wikely, above, n.3, pp. 328–338; Clark, above, n.3, pp. 142–144.

[20] Art. 5 of the Social Welfare (Occupational Injuries) Regulations 1967 (S.I. No.77 of 1967) (SW(OI)R 1967), read in conjunction with the First Schedule thereto, sets out the prescribed degrees of disablement for 55 different types of injury (seven of which are assessed at 100% disablement), while the Social Welfare (Occupational Injuries) Regulations 1983 (S.I. No. 391 of 1983) specifies the rules to be followed in assessing degrees of disablement in respect of occupational deafness. SW(OI)R 1967, art. 5(3) does provide, however, that the prescribed degree of disablement may be adjusted to such figure as is reasonable in the circumstances where the claimant may be expected to be subject to greater disabilities as a result of the injury than would normally be incurred as a result of such an injury, or where the part of the body by which the injury was sustained would not, apart from that injury, have been normal at the date of the assessment.

156 days (excluding Sundays) beginning with the day of the relevant accident or commencement of illness.[21]

(b) Rates of benefit

5–19   Where disablement is assessed at less than 20 per cent, benefit is normally payable as a gratuity fixed in accordance with a prescribed scale.[22] However, where such disablement is assessed at not less than 10 per cent, and where the period of assessment is for life or a period exceeding seven years, a person may opt, before the gratuity is paid, for the substitution of a weekly pension for the gratuity. (The minimum threshold of 10 per cent disablement does not apply in respect of disablement commencing before May 1, 1990.) Again, the rate of pension is fixed in accordance with a prescribed scale. Where disablement is assessed as amounting to 20 per cent or more, disablement benefit is payable as a weekly pension which varies in accordance with the degree of disablement from a prescribed minimum where the claimant has suffered 20 per cent disablement to a prescribed maximum where the claimant has suffered 100 per cent disablement.[23]

5–20   Unemployability supplement is payable as an increase to disablement benefit where a person is incapable of work and likely to remain permanently so incapable.[24] A person in receipt of such a supplement also qualifies for further increases in respect of qualified adult and children.[25]

5–21   Where disablement is assessed as amounting to 50 per cent and where, as a result of the relevant loss of faculty, a person requires constant attendance, the disablement pension is supplemented by a constant attendance allowance, except where the person is receiving medical treatment as an in-patient in a hospital or similar institution.[26]

5–22   Where a person suffers two or more successive accidents covered by the code, he or she is not entitled (apart from increases in respect of a qualified adult or child) to receive an aggregate of injury benefit and disablement

---

[21] SW(C)A 1993, s. 54(2).

[22] *ibid.*, s. 54(7). This scale is updated annually by Regulation.

[23] See SW(C)A 1993, Pt III of Second Sched. as amended annually. S.I. No.114 of 1990, art. 3 provides for special provision for the payment of disablement pension to sufferers of pneumoconiosis and byssinosis whose disablement is assessed at less than 20% but more than 10%.

[24] SW(C)A 1993, s. 56.

[25] *ibid.*, s. 55(4). The Social Welfare Act 1994 (SWA 1994), s. 20(9) provides for the repeal of SW(C)A 1993, s. 55, but this provision has not come into force at the time of writing.

[26] SW(C)A 1993, s. 57 as inserted by SWA 1996, s. 39 and amended by SWA 2001, s. 19.

pension, or two or more disablement pensions, in excess of the appropriate maximum rate of disablement pension.[27]

(c) Disqualification

5–23 A person is disqualified for receiving disablement benefit for such period not exceeding nine weeks if he or she fails without good cause:

(1) to attend for, or to submit himself or herself to, medical examination;

(2) to submit himself or herself to such medical treatment as is considered appropriate in his or her case by the registered medical practitioner in charge of the case or by a medical referee (provided that he or she shall not be disqualified for receiving disablement benefit for refusing to undergo a surgical operation not being one of a minor character).[28]

5–24 A person is disqualified for receiving unemployability supplement for a period not exceeding nine weeks if he or she fails without good cause to observe any of the rules of behaviour specified in the Third Schedule to the 1967 Regulations.[29] These are as follows:

(1) he or she shall obey the instructions of the doctor in attendance and answer any reasonable enquiries by the Minister or his or her officers relating to the claim;

(2) he or she shall refrain from behaviour likely to retard his or her recovery;

(3) if the person absents himself or herself from the place of residence, he or she shall leave word as to where he or she may be found;

(4) he or she shall not refuse unreasonably to see the Minister's sickness visitor;

(5) he or she shall do no work unless it is work in respect of which the earnings do not, on the average, exceed a prescribed amount per week. By virtue of article 18(5), the Minister may exempt a person from the operation of this rule for such period as he or she may think fit where the work is part-time and by way of rehabilitation or occupational therapy or where the person has become incapable of following his or her usual occupation and is undergoing a course of training with a view to fitting himself or herself to take up some other occupation.

5–25 A person is disqualified for receipt of, *inter alia,* disablement pension

---

[27] SW(C)A 1993, s. 58. See also SW(OI)R 1967, arts 10 and 11.
[28] See SW(C)A 1993, s. 70 and SW(OI)R 1967, art. 18(1), as amended by S.I. No. 81 of 1986.
[29] See SW(OI)R 1967, art. 18(2) as amended.

while he or she is undergoing penal servitude, imprisonment or detention in legal custody.[30] The disqualification is relaxed where: (a) the claimant is detained (other than as a criminal lunatic) in an institution for the treatment of mental or infectious diseases; or (b) the detention is in respect of the claimant having been charged with a criminal offence, the charge is subsequently withdrawn or the claimant is acquitted and immediately before the detention he or she was entitled to the said benefit or would have been but for the "waiting days" rule; or (c) imprisonment is undergone as an alternative to payment of a fine.[31]

5–26 Finally, article 18(3) provides for the suspension of proceedings on a claim for or payment of disablement benefit for such period as may be determined under the Act in any case to which either article 18(1) or article 18(2) applies. The Act does not appear to impose any limitation on the duration of such suspension.

(2) Injury benefit[32]

(a) Conditions of eligibility

5–27 If a person is incapable of work as a result of an occupational accident or disease occurring after May 1, 1967, he or she is entitled to injury benefit from the fourth day of such period of incapacity.[33] A claim cannot be made in respect of any day of paid holiday leave.[34] Injury benefit can only be claimed for a maximum of 156 days (excluding Sundays) beginning with the date of the accident. A person under the age of 16 is not entitled to injury benefit except in so far as may be provided by Regulations.[35] Injury benefit is not payable in respect of pneumoconiosis, byssinosis, occupational asthma, vibration-induced white finger, or occupational deafness.[36] In such cases, apparently, the person must claim disablement benefit.

(b) Rates of benefit

5–28 The personal rate of injury benefit is currently equivalent to the personal

---

[30] SW(C)A 1993, s. 211.

[31] See *ibid.*, s. 211 and SW(OI)R 1967, arts 12 and 13.

[32] Note that Social Welfare Act 1994 (SWA 1994), s. 20 anticipates the eventual integration of injury benefit into the disability benefit scheme. This has not come into effect at the time of writing.

[33] SW(C)A 1993, s. 53(1).

[34] *ibid.*, s. 53(2)

[35] *ibid.*, s. 53(3). S.I. No. 82 of 1992 provides for the payment of injury benefit to such persons.

[36] S.I. No. 392 of 1983, art. 20 as amended by S.I. No. 102 of 1985. See SW(C)A 1993, s. 66(5).

rate of disability benefit. Section 55 provides for increases of benefit in respect of qualified adults and/or children. Where a person suffers two or more successive accidents covered by the code, he or she shall not be entitled (apart from increases in respect of a qualified adult or child) to receive, *inter alia*, an aggregate of injury benefit and disablement pension in excess of the appropriate maximum rate of disablement pension.[37]

(c) Disqualifications

5–29   The grounds of disqualification for injury benefit are essentially the same as for unemployability supplement payable with disablement benefit except that a person may additionally be disqualified for receipt of injury benefit if he or she engages in work other than: (a) light work for which no remuneration is, or would ordinarily be, payable; (b) work undertaken primarily as a definite part of treatment while a patient in a hospital, sanatorium or other similar institution, provided earnings do not exceed a prescribed amount per week; or (c) work under a scheme that is, in the opinion of the Minister, charitable in character and purpose and where the earnings do not exceed a prescribed amount per week.

(3) Death benefit

5–30   Death benefit is payable where an insured person in insurable (occupational injuries) employment dies, after May 1, 1967, as a result of an accident arising out of and in the course of employment, or where immediately before death he or she was entitled to disablement pension assessed at 50 per cent or more, in the following circumstances[38]:

(i)   The widow(er) of the deceased is entitled to death benefit.[39] A widow(er) is disqualified for benefit if he or she remarries or if and so long as he or she and any person cohabit as husband and wife.[40] However he or she will not lose entitlement to death benefit merely because he or she is divorced from the former spouse.[41] Increases in the rate of death benefit are payable (a) where the claimant has qualified children and (b) where he or she has reached pensionable age and is living alone.

(ii) A parent of the deceased is entitled to death benefit if, at the date of the deceased's death, such parent was being wholly or mainly maintained by

---

[37] SW(C)A 1993, s. 58.

[38] *ibid.*, ss. 59 and 60 as substituted by SWA 1997, s. 14 and amended by SWA 2001, s. 15.

[39] *ibid.*, s. 60(1).

[40] *ibid.*, s. 60(3) and (4).

[41] *ibid.*, s. 60(10) as inserted by SWA (No. 2) 1995, s. 2.

the child or would have been so maintained but for the accident.[42] Different rates of pension are payable, depending on the marital status of the deceased and the circumstances of the parents.[43] The maximum rate is payable only where the deceased was a widower, widow or single person and (where the parent is the father), the parent is permanently incapable of self-support by reason of some physical or mental infirmity, or (where the parent is the mother) the parent is a widow or a wife whose husband does not qualify for the maximum pension. In any other situation, a reduced pension only is payable. Mothers are disqualified upon marriage, re-marriage or cohabitation, as the case may be. There are no comparable disqualifications for fathers. It is questionable whether the varying treatments of men and women in this context are legally valid having regard to Directive 79/7,[44] although this issue is almost irrelevant in practice given that the numbers involved are tiny.

(iii) Death benefit is payable to an orphan of the deceased who was wholly or mainly maintained by the deceased at the date of his death.[45]

(iv) Finally, a lump sum payment (currently €635) is payable to the person paying funeral expenses.[46]

(4) Medical Care Allowance

(a) Conditions of eligibility

5–31   The cost of medical care which, in the opinion of the Minister, is reasonably and necessarily incurred by the insured person as a result of an occupational injury or disease and which is not otherwise provided for under the Health Acts, the Mental Treatment Acts or the treatment benefit scheme is payable out of the Social Insurance Fund.[47] For the purpose of this scheme, medical care comprises general practitioner and specialist care; nursing care at home (except where a constant attendance allowance is payable) and institutional nursing care; pharmaceutical and other medical or surgical supplies; dental and optical treatment and appliances; care provided by professionals allied to the medical profession, such as physiotherapists and chiropodists; and travelling expenses to and from the place where medical care is provided. As the decision on a claim for medical care allowance is entrusted to the Minister, as opposed to a deciding officer, it would appear

---

[42] SW(C)A 1993, s. 61(1).
[43] *ibid.*, s. 61(3).
[44] [1979] O.J. L6/24.
[45] SW(C)A 1993, s. 62.
[46] *ibid.*, s. 63(1).
[47] *ibid.*, s. 65(1).

that there is no statutory right of appeal against such decision to an appeals officer.

(b) Amount of allowance

5–32 The amount of allowance payable is the cost of the medical care reasonably and necessarily incurred less the cost or value of such treatment provided for under the Health Acts, the Mental Treatment Acts or the treatment benefit scheme, regardless of whether the claimant actually avails himself of the services or benefits provided pursuant to such legislation. The appropriate cost for the care provided is determined by the Minister. The Minister may decide to pay the allowance to such persons as he or she thinks fit and, in particular, where the cost of medical care is due to a health board, to the health board.

(5) Miscellaneous

(a) Appeals

5–33 In general, if a person is dissatisfied with a decision in relation to an occupational injury benefit, including an interim decision in relation to a provisional assessment of the degree of disablement for the purposes of disablement benefit, he or she can appeal to the Social Welfare Appeals Office (see Chapter 18) (although see above in relation to medical care allowance).

(b) Notice of accidents

5–34 By virtue of section 67, Regulations may provide for requiring an insured person to give notice of any accident in respect of which injury benefit or medical care allowance may be claimed to his employer within a prescribed time. (Where the insured person dies as a result of the accident within this prescribed time, the obligation to notify may pass to another prescribed person.) Section 68 provides that Regulations may require employers to report such accidents to a prescribed person within a prescribed time, to furnish to such person any information required for the determination of claims for injury benefit, and to take such other steps as may be prescribed to facilitate the giving of notices of accidents in respect of which injury benefit may be claimed, the making of claims for such benefit and the determination of such claims.[48]

---

[48] The relevant regulations for both of these sections are the Social Welfare (Claims and Payments) Regulations 1967 (S.I. No. 85 of 1967), arts 11 and 12 as amended by S.I. No. 81 of 1986.

(c) Rehabilitation

5–35 By virtue of section 73, the Minister may make such contributions towards the cost of rehabilitation services for persons entitled to disablement benefit as he or she may, with the consent of the Minister for Finance, determine.

(d) Medical research

5–36 Section 74 empowers the Minister to promote research into the causes, incidence and methods of prevention of occupational accidents and diseases and to finance such research from the Social Insurance Fund.

3. The Deductability of Benefits from Personal Injury Awards

5–37 This section looks at the deduction of social welfare payments from damages for personal injuries and fatal accidents. The position in relation to the deductibility of social welfare from awards of damages is unfortunately complicated and there is a lack of clarity as to the policy issues involved.[49] The English courts, over four decades ago, described this as an area in which "logic is conspicuous by its absence" and it can not be said that logic has blossomed in the interim.

A. Statutory Non-Deductibility in Personal Injury Claims

(1) Civil Liability (Amendment) Act 1964

5–38 Section 2 of the Civil Liability (Amendment) Act 1964 provides that:

> "In assessing damages in an action to recover damages in respect of a wrongful act (including a crime) resulting in personal injury not causing death, account shall not be taken of:
> (a) any sum payable in respect of the injury under any contract of insurance,
> (b) any pension, gratuity or other like benefit payable under statute or otherwise in consequence of the injury."

The general rule, therefore, in personal injury claims is one of non-deductibility

---

[49] See generally J. White, *Irish Law of Damages* (Butterworths, Dublin, 1989); R. Clark, "Damages and the Social Welfare 'Overlap'" (1984) 19 Ir. Jur. 40; Law Reform Commission, *Consultation Paper On Section 2 Of The Civil Liability (Amendment) Act, 1964: The Deductibility Of Collateral Benefits From Awards Of Damages* (LRC, Dublin, 1999); McMahon and Binchy, *Law of Torts* (Butterworths, Dublin, 2000), para. 44–112—44–142; R. Lewis, *Deducting Benefits from Damages for Personal Injury* (Oxford University Press, 2000).

of collateral benefits. Insofar as they are not specifically brought into account (as discussed below) social welfare payments payable in consequence of the injury are *not* to be deducted.

(2) Position at common law

5–39   While section 2 provides a comprehensive code for the treatment of social welfare benefits (insofar as it applies), it is necessary to examine the common law position in order to establish the full scope of section 2. Unfortunately, the Irish case law is sparse and uninformative, while foreign authorities must be approached with some caution given the different legal background involved.

5–40   Some social welfare payments are not, in any case, payable in consequence of the injury, nor are they intended to compensate for the loss suffered. For example, retirement pensions or old age (contributory) pensions become payable automatically upon reaching the ages of 65 and 66 years respectively. Entitlement to these pensions is therefore entirely separate from any losses arising from an injury. In general, these payments should not be taken into account in assessing damages. It has been held, in a number of jurisdictions, that old age and retirement pensions are not deductible from damages for loss of earnings.[50]

5–41   Social welfare payments that are intended to compensate for loss of earnings have, in general, be held to be deductible at common law. So, for example, several jurisdictions have held that unemployment benefits should be deducted from damages for loss of earnings.[51] The same approach has been adopted with occupational injuries type payments.[52] However, insofar as these benefits are payable "in consequence of the injury", they are excluded by section 2 (although see below in relation to the statutory inclusion of specific social welfare payments). U.K. authority would suggest that social welfare payments that are intended to meet the costs of care (insofar as these exist in Ireland) are also deductible at common law.[53]

---

[50] *Hewson v. Downs* [1970] 1 Q.B. 73; *Redding v. Lee* (1983) C.L.R. 117.

[51] *Hill v. Cunningham* [1968] N.I. 58; *Nabi v. British Leyland (U.K.) Ltd* [1980] 1 All E.R. 667; *Redding v. Lee* (1983) C.L.R. 117. Compare *Jack Cewe Ltd v. Jorgenson* (1980) 111 D.L.R. (3rd) 577, in which the Supreme Court of Canada held that unemployment benefits were not deductible as they were granted independent of the cause of action, and *Fitzpatrick v. Moore* [1962] N.I. 152 (subsequently overruled in *Hill*).

[52] *Manser v. Spry* (1994) 181 C.L.R. 428; *Salmi v. Greyfriar Developments Ltd*, [1985] 17 D.L.R. (4th) 186 (although the later case refers to a wrongful dismissal rather than a personal injury claim).

[53] *Hodgson v. Trapp* [1989] A.C. 807. However, it should be noted that such Irish payments

5–42 The U.K. courts have also held, in a number of cases, that means-tested payments may be assessed against a claim for loss of earnings. It would appear that the correct basis for these decisions is to avoid overcompensation of the plaintiff, so deductibility will normally only arise in relation to the period to the date of trial (or, strictly speaking, to judgment), as subsequent entitlement to a means-tested payment may well be affected by the award of damages.[54]

5–43 Social welfare payments which fall outside the scope of section 2, *i.e.* which do not arise in consequence of an injury, may, therefore, be relevant to an award of damages. This issue was considered in the decision of Costello P. in *Ryan v. Compensation Tribunal*.[55] The Tribunal had based its award for future loss of earnings on the appellant's previous earnings from a community employment scheme less the amount of two social welfare payments which were payable to her, namely what the Judge referred to as single parent's allowance (presumably lone parent's allowance) and deserted wife's allowance. The appellant challenged the Tribunal's award for loss of future earnings on the basis that two social welfare payments fell within section 2 and ought not to have been deducted. Costello P. held that those payments were not payable in consequence of an accident but rather because the plaintiff was treated as a single parent and deserted wife within the meaning of the social welfare legislation. Consequently, the Tribunal did not err in deducting the payments from the plaintiff's gross income in order to award damages on the basis of loss of net income.

It appears to have been assumed that the payments in question would be deductible if they were not excluded by section 2. However, it is not clear that this assumption was correct and that the payments in question, which were not specifically intended to compensate for loss of earnings and which did not necessarily do so, should have been taken into account in assessing damages.[56] It would appear that the award of damages in this case could, in strict law, have led to a reduction in (or the extinguishment of) entitlement to the means-tested payments in question, which would have led to under-compensation of the plaintiff. While the law has subsequently been amended to exclude compensation under the Hepatitis C compensation scheme from assessment as means,[57] this would suggest that public policy is for non-

---

as exist are not on all fours with the U.K. benefits considered in that case, and again the position would be affected by s. 2.

[54] *Lincoln v. Hayman* [1982] 1 W.L.R. 488. In *Gaskill v. Preston* [1981] All E.R. 427 it was held that family credit (broadly equivalent to the Irish family income supplement) was deductible, in principle, from both past and future damages for loss of earnings; but as possible future payment of family credit was unascertainable, no deduction for the future was made in practice.

[55] [1997] 1 I.L.R.M. 194 at 205 *et seq.*

[56] The facts of the case are unfortunately obscure.

[57] S.I. No. 374 of 1996.

deductibility of social welfare payments in such cases. These arguments do not appear to have been considered by the Court, and it submitted that this aspect of the decision should be considered to have been arrived at *per incuriam*. It is submitted that the correct approach should be that social welfare payments that are not payable in consequence of the injury (and that are not, therefore, excluded by section 2) are only deductible insofar as this is necessary to avoid overcompensation of the plaintiff and that this will normally arise, in the case of means-tested payments, only up to the date of trial.

(3) Scope of section 2

5–44 It is clear that social welfare "benefits", *i.e.* social insurance and occupational injuries payments, are generally excluded by section 2. There is some debate as to whether social assistance (means-tested) payments are covered by the principle of non-deductibility set out in section 2, which refers to "benefit". On the one hand, it can be argued that the word "benefit" is used in the section in its ordinary and natural sense, *i.e.* to mean advantage. Thus "benefit payable under statute" is broad enough to encompass all social welfare payments, and social assistance payments are therefore included in the scope of the section.[58] The Supreme Court in *Murphy v. Cronin* took a broad view of the term "benefit" and did not confine it to social welfare benefits as defined in the Social Welfare Acts.[59] It is submitted that this is the correct approach.[60]

5–45 Even if they are not included in the term "benefits", it can be argued that social assistance payments are not relevant to the deductibility of collateral benefits due to the use of a means test in order to determine entitlement.[61] Clark argues that social assistance payments are not covered by section 2, but that "[p]roblems of dual compensation in social assistance cases are more apparent than real, because the statutory disregard provisions have no applicability in cases where a means test is involved."[62] Once the plaintiff receives damages, it may be that he or she will no longer satisfy the means test, in which case assistance payments would cease. If, subsequent to the receipt of damages, the injured party still satisfies a means test, this is

---

[58] White, above, n. 49, para. 4.10.15.

[59] [1966] I.R. 699. This case involved the Civil Liabilities Act 1961, s. 50 but the language used is the same as section 2. However, the specific point discussed here was not at issue in this case and the statement was *obiter*.

[60] In most available Irish cases it appears to be assumed that section 2 applies to both benefit and assistance payments. See for example *Ryan v. Compensation Tribunal* [1997] 1 I.L.R.M. 194 and *Kiely v. Carrig* (Trinity and Michaelmas, 1996) D.P.I.J. 209.

[61] Law Reform Commission, above, n. 49, para. 7.61.

[62] Clark, above, n. 49, p. 57. White, above, n. 49, also argues that social assistance payments are not deductible at common law (para. 4.10.16), but it is submitted that this is incorrect.

presumably due to circumstances obtaining prior to the accident (as the damages award will theoretically have placed the injured party in the same position, insofar as that is possible, as before the accident). In these circumstances it can be argued that the assistance payments are not related to the accident. As outlined above, however, this line of argument is correct only in relation to future damages, and the U.K. courts have held means-tested payments to be deductible in certain circumstances. Decisions such as *Ryan* show that social assistance payments may, in practice, be taken into account and it would appear that the key issue concerning the scope of section 2 is not whether the payment is means tested but whether the payment is payable in consequence of the injury.

5–46 In *Kiely v. Carrig*,[63] the issue arose as to whether unemployment assistance should be taken into account in assessing damages in respect of loss of earnings to date. The plaintiff, who was a self-employed person, became unemployed shortly before his accident. He was not entitled to an insurance benefit and so unemployment assistance was paid. Barr J. held that had the accident not happened, the plaintiff would probably have found employment. It followed, therefore, that unemployment assistance was a benefit "payable in consequence of the injury" within the meaning of section 2 and accordingly was not to be deducted. This case indicates that the Court would have deducted unemployment assistance from the loss of earnings to date but for section 2. It is submitted that this decision is a correct statement of the law.

B. Statutory Inclusion of Certain Benefits

5–47 However, the general exclusion of social welfare benefits has been modified in relation to a number of social welfare payments. First, section 75 of the Social Welfare (Consolidation) Act 1993 provides that:

> "Notwithstanding section 2 of the Civil Liability (Amendment) Act, 1964, and section 236 of this Act, in an action for damages for personal injuries (including any such action arising out of a contract) there shall in assessing those damages be taken into account, against any loss of earnings or profits which has accrued or probably will accrue to the injured person from the injuries, the value of any rights which have accrued or will probably accrue to him therefrom in respect of injury benefit (disregarding any right in respect of injury benefit payable by virtue of section 210, after the death of the injured person) or disablement benefit (disregarding any increase thereof under section 57 in respect of constant attendance) for the 5 years beginning with the time when the cause of action accrued."[64]

---

[63] (Trinity and Michaelmas, 1996) D.P.I.J. 209.
[64] SW(C)A 1993 s. 75(4)–(6) provides for the exclusion of certain compensation under the Garda Síochána (Compensation) Acts.

5–48   Secondly, section 237(1) of the 1993 Act provides that:

"Notwithstanding section 2 of the Civil Liability Act, 1964, and section 236, in assessing damages in any action in respect of liability for personal injuries not causing death relating to the use of a mechanically propelled vehicle (within the meaning of section 3 of the Road Traffic Act, 1961), there shall be taken into account the value of any rights arising from such injuries which have accrued, or are likely to accrue, to the injured person in respect of disability benefit (including any amount payable therewith by way of pay-related benefit) or invalidity pension under Part II for the period of 5 years beginning with the time when the cause of action accrued."

5–49   The Law Reform Commission points out that

"Section 75 originated as section 39 of the Social Welfare (Occupational Injuries) Act, 1966 and was influenced by the analogous English provision which provided for the deduction of half of the value of certain social security benefits paid or likely to be paid up to five years from the date of the accrual of the cause of action. The justification put forward for the Irish provision was that the occupational injuries scheme was entirely financed by the employer, and therefore not to take the payments into account would essentially result in a double charge on employers; furthermore, the worker is obliged to give credit for the payments as he has not purchased the benefits by direct contributions. Of note in the Minister for Social Welfare's explanation is the statement that, 'if the workers have to pay a contribution, naturally the amount of the benefit that should be taken into account in the reduction of common law damages would be less'."[64]

Section 237 arose from a concern to reduce the cost of motor insurance by reducing the size of compensation awards.[66]

(1) Interpretation of statutory provisions

5–50   Section 75(2) provides that the reference in section 75(1) to assessing the damages for personal injuries must, in cases where the damages otherwise recoverable are subject to reduction under the law relating to contributory negligence or are limited by or under any Act or by contract, be taken as referring to the total damages which would have been recoverable apart from the deduction or limitation. In other words, deductibility is applied to the total damages which would be payable before these are reduced by reason of contributory negligence (or otherwise). This provision favours the defendant, who has his or her notional damages reduced by the amount of the relevant social welfare payment rather than the lesser actual damages. Section 237(2)

---

[65] Law Reform Commission, above, n. 49, para. 7.56.
[66] *ibid.* para. 7.45.

applies the same rule of deductibility from total damages as applied by section 75(2) (see above).

5–51 The phrase "there shall ... be taken into account" means that the benefits in question must be deducted and leaves no discretion to the court.[67] The use of the phrase "rights which have accrued" in both sections raises the question as to whether deductibility applies only to benefits which the person has received or whether it applies where the person would have an entitlement but fails to claim the benefit. The position at Irish law would appear to be that a claim is a necessary prerequisite to entitlement and, therefore, it is only where the benefits have been claimed that deductibility applies.[68] This appears to be how the provisions are interpreted in practice.

5–52 In the case of section 75, it is relevant that in some cases disablement benefit may be payable as a gratuity (a lump sum) in respect of a period of years. It is submitted that the wording of section 75, which refers to "the value of any rights which have accrued or will probably accrue to him therefrom in respect of ... disablement benefit ... for the 5 years beginning with the time when the cause of action accrued", means that only that proportion of the gratuity which relates to the five years is to be taken into account.[69]

5–53 The U.K. courts have held that the benefit to be taken into account under the equivalent of section 75 is not restricted to the period during which loss was suffered, *i.e.* entitlement to benefit may be taken into account for up to the full five years even though the damages may be claimed in respect of s shorter period.[70] It is submitted that this is a correct interpretation of the law.

5–54 White has pointed out that while section 75 confines deductibility to loss of earnings, section 237 is not so limited by the wording of the section. He argues, nonetheless, that the basic principle governing deductibility requires that benefits should only be set off against damages for loss of earnings or profits and that section 237 should be interpreted in this light.[71] While this

---

[67] *Kelly v. Farrans* [1954] N.I. 41: *Flowers v. George Wimpey & Co Ltd* [1956] 1 Q.B. 73; *Hultquist v. Universal Pattern and Precision Engineering* [1960] 2 Q.B. 467.

[68] See *Eley v. Bedford* [1972] 1 Q.B. 155.

[69] *Perez v. CAV* [1959] 1 W.L.R. 724.

[70] *Stott v. Wimpey* [1953] 2 Q.B. 92; *Flowers v. George Wimpey & Co Ltd* [1956] 1 Q.B. 73. In *Flowers* Devlin J. held that this approach applied whether or not the benefit had been paid in error and that it was not for the Court to enquire whether the benefit had been paid by mistake. In the absence of fraud or other compelling reason for the Court to investigate the circumstances of payment of benefit, this approach seems right both in principle and in practical terms.

[71] Above, n. 49, para. 4.10.22.

approach would appear to be correct in principle, it is not clear that the plain language of the section requires such an interpretation.[72] However, if deductibility against general damages were to be allowed, recent decisions of the U.K. courts have indicated that where a person is in receipt of a social welfare payment prior to injury and where no claim for loss of earnings arises, a claim for the loss of social welfare benefits (which are deductible from general damages under U.K. law) may lie.[73]

(2) The five-year rule

5–55   Thus, certain social welfare payments are an exception to the general rule of non-deductibility from awards of damages, for a period of five years from the date of the cause of action. As the Law Reform Commission points out, there are considerable practical difficulties with the deduction of social welfare payments due to a variety of factors, such as inflation, social welfare increases, changes in eligibility for payments due to changes in the nature of the injury, statutory regulations and changes in social welfare policy. There have been conflicting Irish decisions as to the application of this provision.

5–56   In *O'Loughlin v. Teeling* MacKenzie J. effectively refused to apply that provision to future benefits. He said that the jury, in making the award for future loss of earnings, was making a finding about the plaintiff's future prospects of work and was considering him to be capable of employment within a short period of time. If the Department of Social Welfare were confronted with that evidence, it could cut off the plaintiff's disability benefit. Therefore, the Judge could not say with any probability that the plaintiff would still be in receipt of the benefit in the near future and so he would not deduct possible future benefits from the award.[74]

5–57   A subsequent case, *O'Sullivan v. Iarnrod Éireann*, reflects an alternative interpretation of the statutory provision.[75] The plaintiff had argued that there was no evidence as to what might happen to disablement benefit into the future and therefore the most that should be taken into account under section 75 were the benefits that had accrued prior to the date of the action. However, Morris J. held that the onus was on the plaintiff to show that the Department intended to alter the status quo. He found that there was no indication of any such intention on the part of the Department to do so and

---

[72] See *Hassall v. Secretary of State for Social Security* [1995] 3 All E.R. 909 for a strict interpretation of a similar point, although the statutory language is entirely different.
[73] *ibid.*; *Donnelly v. McCoy* [1995] N.I. 220.
[74] [1988] I.L.R.M. 617 at 619.
[75] Unreported, High Court, Morris J., March 14, 1994.

therefore deducted an amount for future as well as past benefits. It is submitted that the latter view is an accurate interpretation of Irish law as it stands at present.

5–58 Finally, the treatment of foreign social security benefits has been considered in a number of cases. In *Van Keep v. Surface Dressing Contractors*,[76] Budd J. considered how a Dutch social insurance payment was to be treated. He held that the payment, which arose from payment of contributions under a statutory occupational insurance scheme, was an insurance scheme and that payments were excluded under section 2(a) or, if he was wrong on this point (which he probably was as the scheme in question was a statutory one), that they were "other benefits" under section 2(b), which appears to be the correct basis for the decision.

5–59 In *McKenna v. Best Travel*,[77] Lavan J. considered whether two types of Israeli social welfare payments were to be deducted from damages. One type of payment related to reimbursement of medical and dental fees, while the second was a monthly disability payment. Lavan J. held that a flexible approach should be taken as to the treatment of such benefits "capable of responding to the individual issues presented in each case" and on that basis he determined both payments to be non-deductible.[78]

C. Fatal Injuries

5–60 In relation to fatal injuries, section 50 of the Civil Liability Act 1961 provides that in assessing damages for fatal injuries

"... account shall not taken of –
(a) any sum payable on the death of the deceased under any contract of insurance,
(b) any pension, gratuity or other like benefit payable under statute or otherwise in consequence of the death of the deceased."

5–61 The wording of this section is the same as that of section 2 discussed above and broadly the same issues arise. In *State (Hayes) v. Criminal Injuries Compensation Tribunal*,[79] Finlay P. said that section 50 clearly excluded the deduction of "any social welfare benefit payable to a dependant" from an award of damages.[80]

---

[76] Unreported, High Court, June 11, 1993.
[77] [1998] 3 I.R. 57.
[78] Following the quoted statement of Walsh J. in *Grehan v. Medical Incorporated* [1986] I.L.R.M. 627 at 638.
[79] [1982] I.L.R.M. 210.
[80] [1982] I.L.R.M. 210 at 212, albeit that the statement was *obiter*.

5–62 Section 75(3) of the Social Welfare (Consolidation) Act 1993 provides that, notwithstanding section 50 of the 1961 Act, in assessing damages in respect of a person's death under Part IV of that Act, account may be taken of any death benefit (by way of a grant under sections 63 in respect of funeral expenses) resulting from the person's death.

5–63 Section 236 of the S(C)WA provides that in assessing damages in any action under the Fatal Injuries Act 1956 or Part IV of the Civil Liability Act 1961, the following shall not be taken into account: child benefit, widow(er)'s (contributory) pension, orphan's (contributory) allowance, one parent family payment in the case of a widow(er), and widow's and orphan's (non-contributory) pension.[81] White has argued that this section is otiose as these payments would not be deductible in any case having regard to section 50.[82]

D. Law Reform

5–64 This area of law has recently been reviewed in a consultation report by the Law Reform Commission. The Commission provisionally recommended that the public interest in reducing or eliminating double compensation required that a broad principle of deduction of all collateral benefits should be established in Irish law. While recognising that there were situations which would justify an exemption to that rule, the Commission did not believe that social welfare benefits should be so excluded. The Commission noted that social insurance payments are funded on a pay-as-you-go basis rather than being fully funded. The Commission believed that the absence of an actuarial link, in conjunction with the obligatory nature of PRSI payments, and the fact that social insurance is funded by society as a whole, removed this type of pension from the scope of the exception justified in the public interest.

5–65 The Commission accepted that such an approach "may appear to shift the windfall gain from the plaintiff (who under a rule of non-deductibility may be doubly compensated) to the defendant who is financially liable to pay less where collateral benefits are deducted".[83] To meet this objection, some legal systems have allowed the provider of the collateral benefit to recoup the value of the benefit from the defendant. However, while the Commission recognised the moral and intellectual attractiveness of reimbursement of the collateral benefit provider, it provisionally (and somewhat unconvincingly)

---

[81] As amended by SWA 1996, ss. 19 and 27 and by SWA 1997, s.20.
[82] Above, n. 49, para 9.4.09.
[83] It is in fact obvious that this would be the effect of such a move – subject of course to the fact that the gain would in many cases go to the defendant's insurers rather than the defendant.

recommended that such an option was not viable in Ireland, as it felt the mechanisms currently available in Irish law to retransfer the loss from the benefit provider to the tortfeasor were insufficient to base a general policy of reimbursement.[84]

---

[84] It should be noted that such a system of reimbursement works effectively in the U.K. See Lewis, above, n. 49.

Table: Deductibility and social welfare payments

	Benefit	Authority
1. Benefits deductible against damages for personal injuries in respect of any loss of earnings or profits for five years in the case of occupational injuries	Injury benefit, disablement benefit	SW(C)A 1993, s.75
2. Benefits deductible against damages for personal injuries for five years in the case of road traffic accidents	Disability benefit, invalidity pension	SW(C)A 1993, s.237
3. Benefits fully deductible	Social welfare payments not payable in consequence of the injury and having a compensatory effect	*Ryan v. Compensation Tribunal* [1997] 1 I.L.R.M. 194
	[including means-tested payments giving rise to over-compensation (insofar as not specifically excluded by CL(Am)A 1964 s. 2)]	*Lincoln v. Hayman* [1982] 1 W.L.R. 488
4. Benefits not deductible	All social welfare benefits payable in consequence of the injury (other than those listed at 1 and 2 above)	CL(Am)A, 1964 s. 2
	Old age and retirement pensions	*Hewson v. Downs* [1970] 1 Q.B. 73; *Redding v. Lee* (1983) C.L.R. 117
	Other social welfare payments not related to cause of action and not having a compensatory effect (Including, means-tested payments not giving rise to overcompensation)[83]	*Redding v. Lee* (1983) C.L.R. 117

---

[85] There is no Irish authority for this point, and in fact *Ryan v. Compensation Tribunal* would appear to be authority for the deductibility of such payments. It is suggested above that this case should be considered to have been incorrectly decided on this point.

CHAPTER 6

Employment and Unemployment Payments

6–01 This chapter looks at support for employed and unemployed persons under the social welfare system.

1. Background

6–02 "Unemployment" and "the unemployed" were terms invented in the late nineteenth century.[1] While problems of lack of work and underemployment had existed prior to then, they had not been conceptualised in the way which unemployment came to be understood. The solution adopted by the Liberal Government in the United Kingdom to unemployment in the early twentieth century involved both decasualisation of the unemployed, putting unemployed persons in contact with employers seeking workers, and the payment of financial support during periods of unemployment.[2] Labour exchanges were to play a key role both in requiring men to register as unemployed and in matching them to available work. A Labour Exchange Act was adopted in 1909 to provide for such a system on a nationwide basis. This was also intended as a structure through which a system of unemployment insurance could be operated.

6–03 Unemployment insurance proposals were published in 1911 in conjunction with the national insurance proposals. In contrast to national insurance, the unemployment insurance legislation provided for a national system of insurance administered though the employment exchanges and branch employment offices. Only seven major trades were to be covered initially. Benefit was payable at a rate of 7 shillings per week for up to 15 weeks in any period of 12 months – distinguishing neither on grounds of sex nor region. In order to qualify, unemployed workers had to have been employed in an insured trade for at least 26 weeks and be capable of and unable to obtain suitable employment. In addition, workers who had lost employment

---

[1] C. Topalov, *Naissance du chomeur* (Albin Michel, Paris, 1994); W. Walters, "The discovery of 'unemployment': new forms for the government of poverty" (1994) 23 *Economy and Society* at 265–290.

[2] J. Harris, *Unemployment and Politics: A Study of English Social Policy, 1886–1914* (Clarendon, 1972).

through misconduct or who had voluntarily given up their job without just cause were disqualified. Trade unions were encouraged to administer unemployment benefits for their members and to pay larger unemployment benefits than those payable under the legislation. However, this had only a limited impact in Ireland.

6–04 The scope of unemployment insurance was expanded during the First World War.[3] After the war, a non-contributory "out-of-work donation" was introduced for demobilised soldiers and subsequently extended to civilian workers. This was payable at (relatively high) subsistence rates and, unlike the unemployment insurance scheme, included payments for dependants. The unemployment insurance scheme itself was effectively remade in 1920. Unemployment insurance was extended to all manual workers and to non-manual workers earning less than £250 per annum. Most civil and public servants, who were in permanent employment and therefore not subject to the risk of unemployment, remained outside the scheme. However, the extended unemployment insurance scheme came into effect at a time when unemployment was rising sharply, which led, in Fraser's words, to "the grafting-on to the insurance scheme of a series of devices which sought to preserve the fiction of insurance but in reality were a system of thinly disguised outdoor relief".[4] In 1921, additional payments for dependants were included in the unemployment insurance scheme. Few changes were made in the first decade of independence.

6–05 In 1933, following the report of an inter-departmental committee, the Fianna Fáil Government legislated for a means-tested unemployment assistance scheme (UA) and this was brought into effect in 1934.[5] The qualification conditions for UA were modelled on the existing unemployment insurance scheme but, unlike insurance claimants, assistance claimants were required to show that they were "genuinely seeking work". This new scheme led to a massive increase in the level of recorded unemployment as unemployed and underemployed people claimed UA. It is clear that, at least from this time on (if not before), the main emphasis of the administration was on providing payment to unemployed persons rather than attempting to find them work. During the later 1930s the numbers unemployed fell due to a combination of growth in employment, creation of public works, and restrictions of those entitled to UA. This trend continued during the war years, with heavy emigration to the United Kingdom accounting for low levels of unemployment in Ireland.

---

[3] B. Gilbert, *British Social Policy 1914–1939* (Batsford, London, 1970), Chap 2.
[4] D. Fraser, *Evolution of the British Welfare State* (Macmillan, London), p. 184.
[5] M. Cousins, *The Birth of Social Welfare* (Four Courts, Dublin, 2002).

6–06   The 1949 White Paper on Social Security and the subsequent 1952 legislation saw the unification of the various social insurance schemes and the establishment of broadly similar qualification conditions for unemployment and disability benefit. Benefit was to be payable for a period of up to six months once a person had at least six months' paid contributions and the "waiting period" during which benefit was not paid was reduced from six days to three. Unemployment benefit (UB) was extended to most private-sector employments. In comparative terms, Ireland, in line with other English-speaking countries, tended to have relatively high levels of unemployment insurance coverage – reaching close to full coverage by the 1960s. There were few changes to the unemployment payments in the decades after the establishment of a unified social welfare scheme. Despite the changes in the workforce with a decline in agricultural employment, recorded unemployment remained relatively low in the 1950s, 1960s and early 1970s – with high emigration accounting for this in the 1950s and economic and employment growth paying a key role in later years. As non-agricultural employment expanded, the numbers on UB rose relative to those on UA. The extension of the duration of UB to 12 months (1967) and subsequently to 15 months (1976) also affected this balance.

6–07   A number of improvements were made in the unemployment schemes from a gender perspective in the 1970s and 1980s (see Chapter 9). The overall level of unemployment benefit payments had tended to be internationally average – remaining at about 40 per cent of average net industrial earnings in the period from the 1930s to the 1970s.[6] In 1974, a pay-related benefit scheme was introduced for all short-term benefits. This provided an earnings-related supplement to the existing flat-rate unemployment benefit payment being funded entirely by employers' and employees' contributions. This led to a significant increase in the replacement rate to about 70 per cent by 1985.

6–08   Following the establishment of a Department of Labour in 1966, the administration of employment exchanges was transferred to this new department. However, in line with the recommendations of a review of the placement service carried out by the Institute of Public Administration (1968), a National Manpower Service was established in 1971 under the Department of Labour. In line with thinking at the time, this was to separate the placement service from the unemployment benefit system. Accordingly, the employment exchanges – now solely responsible for paying benefits – were transferred back to the Department of Social Welfare. The "manpower service" approach wanted to separate placement and benefit functions almost entirely, seeing

---

[6]   E. Carroll, *Emergence and Structuring of Social Insurance Institutions* (Swedish Institute for Social Research, Stockholm, 1999).

the placement service as being a mainstream service for the generality of employers and employees. The image of this service was not to be tarnished by any association with the unemployed. Indeed, not only was compulsory registration of unemployed people not recommended, people were not even to be encouraged to contact the placement service when they signed on.[7] This approach – originally adopted in response to the clear failure of the employment exchanges to function effectively as placement services and with close to full employment – was almost as, if not more, unsuccessful than the approach which it replaced.[8]

6–09 In fact, the average annual number on the Live Register remained at about 100,000 up to 1980. However, it increased dramatically thereafter, reaching 230,000 by 1985.[9] Unemployment assistance increased very significantly over this period. By the time of the Commission on Social Welfare, over 25 per cent of the working age population was in receipt of social welfare, with unemployment payments being by far the largest component. The Commission reported that much of the recent growth in social welfare expenditure and beneficiaries was accounted for by the increase in unemployment. In tandem with the overall increase in unemployment, there was a significant increase in the duration of unemployment, with the proportion of those unemployed for over 12 months doubling between 1975 and 1985 (from 20.6 per cent to 41.2 per cent). The Commission, however, had few proposals to remedy this situation. It focused on palliative responses, suggesting that the requirement that persons be "available for work" should not be strictly enforced in a period of prolonged recession, and recommending a relaxation of signing arrangements and allowing unemployed people to engage in educational courses.

6–10 The Commission also reviewed the link between the Departments of Social Welfare and Labour and their respective functions. As outlined above, the placement and payments services had been separated in the 1970s, just before the significant rise in unemployment. But it was not until 1982 that, following a Government direction, the main focus of the National Manpower Service (NMS) was directed at the unemployed. However, no structured co-ordination between the two services was put in place. The Commission on Social Welfare recommended "the closest co-operation" between the two services, but did not consider that there was any case for an amalgamation of

---

[7] NESC, *Manpower Policy in Ireland* (NESC, Dublin, 1985), p. 208–209.
[8] The review by the NESC in 1985 (*ibid.*, p. 214) found that "the degree of [market] penetration achieved by the national employment service is not very substantial and has not increased over the years, notwithstanding the re-organisation of the service and the allocation of additional resources of a fairly considerable scale."
[9] *Report of the Commission on Social Welfare* (Stationery Office, Dublin, 1986), p. 331.

functions. The NMS was amalgamated with the public training agency ANCO and the Youth Employment Service to form FÁS in 1987; but this only led to a further diminution in the emphasis on placement, with resources increasingly going towards "social" and "community" employment schemes, which rose significantly over the period to 2000.

6–11   In the 1980s, the Fine Gael-led coalition had begun a reduction in the level of pay-related benefit and introduced a "genuinely seeking work" requirement for unemployment benefit. The Coalition also introduced the first "in-work benefit", *i.e.* family income supplement (FIS). This was a payment to low-income families in employment modelled on the similar U.K. benefit. It was intended to ensure that persons were always better off in work than on unemployment payments. The return of Fianna Fáil to office in 1987 saw a number of further measures to reduce expenditure, including an increase in the contributions required for unemployment benefit from 26 to 39, the gradual abolition of pay-related benefit, and the introduction of a "Jobsearch" programme. However, the average numbers on the Live Register remained extremely high peaking at an average of 294,000 in 1993.

6–12   The economic boom of the 1990s saw a dramatic change in this situation and the unemployment payments scheme has been transformed in recent years – albeit without any real change in the underlying legislation. The massive increase in the number of people at work of about 400,000 between 1997 and 2002 meant that there was now a significant demand for workers with unemployment falling to below 4 per cent. The numbers on the Live Register fell from an average of 254,000 in 1997 to a low of 135,000 in May 2001 before rising again – one hopes temporarily – in the light of both Foot and Mouth Disease initially and, subsequently, the world economic downturn.

6–13   Over the 1990s a range of measures were introduced to encourage unemployed people to return to education (Back to Education Allowance) and to return to employment. The Back to Work scheme (BTW), started in 1993, provided an incentive to people to return to employment or self-employment and to retain a proportion of their unemployment payment. In many cases, this allowed people to regularise their existing irregular employment situation. Unlike community employment schemes which provided publicly subsidised social employment, BTW concentrated on getting people into the labour market. Evaluations of this scheme found that it was quite successful in returning people to employment and that the displacement and dead-weight was quite low.[10] A subsequent review found that the level of

---

[10] Work Research Centre, *Developing Active Welfare Policy* (Department of Social,

dead-weight was rising in the light of the improved economic situation and arising from this review the period of unemployment required to avail of BTW was increased from 12 months to 15 months.[11]

6–14 The main change in the administration of unemployment payments arose from the introduction of the Employment Action Plan (EAP), involving structured co-operation between FÁS and the Department in 1998 (this had been prefigured by a pilot Youth Progression programme in 1996). Under the EAP, people under 25 who were signing on for six months were referred by the Department to FÁS for interview. Persons attending FÁS were interviewed and, where possible, offered training or work opportunities. Those refusing to attend have their entitlements reviewed and increasing numbers of claimants were disqualified for not being available for or genuinely seeking work. But the striking thing was the number of claimants who simply signed off when requested to go to FÁS. The EAP was subsequently extended to people aged up to 25 passing 18 months' unemployment and to all adults between 25 and 55 passing 12 and subsequently nine months' unemployment. In addition, whereas the general EAP adopted a preventative approach to the flow of unemployed people at a particular point, a process of "full engagement" was carried out with the stock of all unemployed people (over six months) in a number of local areas. While the EAP itself engaged with a relatively small proportion of the 250,000–300,000 or so people who sign on in any one year, the whole process of activation and structured co-ordination with FÁS was also to be seen in a range of other activities carried out by the Department.

2. Current Situation

6–15 There are two main unemployment payments: contributory un-employment benefit and means-tested unemployment assistance. There is also a pre-retirement allowance (PRETA), which is payable to people aged over 55 who have been in receipt of long-term unemployment assistance. Such persons are not required to be available for work. Farm assist is a means-tested payment payable to low-income farmers. In addition, there are administrative Back to Work and Back to Education schemes for persons on social welfare payments who wish to take up work or education. Finally, there is the family income supplement scheme for families in low-income employment.

Community and Family Affairs, Dublin, 1997); Work Research Centre, *Self Employment and the Long Term Unemployed* (Department of Social, Community and Family Affairs, Dublin, 1997).

[11] Indecon, *An Evaluation of the BTWAS and AAE Schemes* (Stationery Office, Dublin, 2000).

A. Unemployment Benefit[12]

6–16   A person is entitled to unemployment benefit (UB) for any "day of unemployment" which forms part of a "period of interruption of employment" provided he or she is under pensionable age, *i.e.* 66 on the day for which the benefit is claimed, proves unemployment in the prescribed manner, satisfies the contribution conditions, and has sustained a substantial loss of employment in any period of six consecutive days (except in the case of a person engaged in casual employment).[13]

(1) Qualification conditions

(a) Period of interruption of employment

6–17   The rule in relation to entitlement to unemployment benefit is that benefit is payable in respect of any "day of unemployment" which is part of a "period of interruption of employment". Period of interruption of employ-ment is defined as any three "days of interruption of employment" (*i.e.* a day of unemployment or of incapacity for work),[14] whether consecutive or not, within a period of six consecutive days. Any two such periods not separated by a period of more than 13 weeks are to be treated as one period of interrup-tion of unemployment. Periods spent on various work experience and train-ing schemes, not exceeding one year in duration, do not break a period of interruption of employment.[15] The result of these rules is that entitlement to unemployment benefit is established on a daily basis. However, in order to establish initial entitlement, one must be out of work due to unemployment or incapacity for any three days in a period of six consecutive days. Benefit is not payable for the first three days in any period of interruption of employ-ment.[16]

(b) "Day of unemployment"

6–18   A day is not treated as a day of unemployment[17] unless: the person is

---

[12] The details of the payment are set out in the Social Welfare (Consolidation) Act 1993 (SW(C)A 1993), ss. 42–47 and the Social Welfare (Consolidation Payments Provisions) Regulations 1994 (SW(CPP)R 1994), arts 8–8B as amended.

[13] See SW(C)A 1993, s. 42(1) and (4). And see generally Clarke's extensive discussion of the relevant sections: R. Clarke, *Annotated Guide to Social Welfare Law* (Sweet & Maxwell, London, 1995).

[14] SW(C)A 1993, s. 42(4)(b).

[15] *ibid.*, s. 42(5).

[16] *ibid.*, s. 42(3).

[17] On the concept of unemployment, see *Louth v. Minister for Social Welfare* [1993] 1 I.R. 339; *Director-General for Social Services v. Thomson* (1981) 38 A.L.R. 624; *McAuliffe*

capable of work; he or she is available for work (or is deemed to be or exempted from being so available); and he or she is genuinely seeking, but is unable to obtain, employment suitable for him or her having regard to age, physique, education, normal occupation, place of residence and family circumstances.[18] Sunday (or such other day of the week as may be prescribed) is not treated as a day of unemployment or incapacity for work and is disregarded in computing any period of consecutive days.[19] A day is not treated as a day of unemployment if the person does any paid or remunerative work on that day unless that work could have been done by the person in addition to his or her usual employment and outside the ordinary working hours of that employment and either the remuneration or profit from the occupation does not exceed €12.70 per day or at least 117 contributions have been paid by the person in either of the last three years or the last three complete contribution years.[20]

(c) "Available for employment"

6–19   A person must be "available for employment" (or be deemed to be or exempted from being available).[21] A person is regarded as being available for employment if he or she can show to the satisfaction of the Minister that he or she is willing and able, at once, to take up an offer of suitable full-time employment.[22] It is accepted that, in practice, a person may require a day or two to make necessary arrangements. The relevant Regulations provide that a person will not be regarded as being available for employment if he or she imposes unreasonable restrictions on: (a) the nature of the employment; (b) the hours of work; (c) the rate of remuneration; (d) the duration of the employment; (e) the location of the employment; or (f) other conditions of employment that he or she is prepared to accept.[23] In determining what constitutes suitable full-time employment, regard must be had to: (a) the skills, qualifications and experience of the person concerned; (b) the period for which the person has been unemployed; and (c) the availability of employment vacancies within travelling distance from his or her residence. The requirement that the person be available to take up "full-time" work may have a disproportionate impact on women, as more women than men wish to available of part-time work – often due to family responsibilities. If this requirement

---

v. Secretary, Department of Social Security (1990) 23 A.L.D. 284, upheld at (1992) 28 A.L.D. 609.

[18] SW(C)A 1993, s. 42(4)(a).

[19] *ibid.*, s. 42(4)(d).

[20] SW(CPP)R 1994, art. 26.

[21] SW(C)A 1993, s. 42(4). In relation to exemptions see SW(CPP)R 1994, art. 73 as amended by S.I. No. 54 of 1998 and S.I. No. 408 of 2001.

[22] See SW(CPP)R 1994, art. 8A as amended by S.I. No. 137 of 1998 and D/SFA Unemployment Benefit Guidelines for Deciding Claims.

[23] *ibid.*

was to be challenged under E.U. law, it would require to be objectively justified, *i.e.* to be shown that it was a necessary part of the overall unemployment payment system which aims to compensate people who are unable to find full-time work and not to act as a subsidy to those who only wish to work part-time.[24]

6–20 Departmental guidelines provide that a person who moves to a location where his or her prospects of getting suitable employment have been significantly reduced will not be considered to be available for work. In deciding whether a move to a location imposes unreasonable restrictions on availability for work, regard should be had to the reasons for the move. For example, the guidelines state that people who relocate to be near family or relatives or under a resettlement programme would be regarded as indigenous residents.[25]

In the short term, a person could be regarded as available where he or she is seeking to be re-employed in his or her usual employment. However, over a longer period, a person would be required to be available for any suitable employment having regard to his or her skills, qualifications, experience and health status. A person who is not legally able to work (*e.g.* a non-E.U. national without a work permit) could not be considered available for employment.

(d) Genuinely seeking work

6–21 A person must be genuinely seeking work which is suitable for him or her, having regard to his or her age, physique, education, normal occupation, place of residence and family circumstances.[26] The relevant Regulations provide that a person is regarded as genuinely seeking employment if he or she can show that he or she has, in the relevant period, taken reasonable steps which offer him or her the best prospects of obtaining employment.[27] These "steps" include:

> "(*a*) applications for employment made to persons—
>   (i)   who have advertised the availability of employment, or
>   (ii) who appear to be in a position to offer employment,
>
> (*b*) seeking information on the availability of employment from—
>   (i)   employers,

---

[24] See *CJSA/1434/2000*, in which a Social Security Commissioner upheld similar U.K. legislation, albeit that U.K. rules excluded those with caring responsibilities from the requirement.

[25] This approach is broadly supported in Canadian jurisprudence: *Canada (A.G.) v. Whiffen* (1994) 165 N.R. 145.

[26] SW(C)A 1993, s. 42 (4).

[27] See SW(CPP)R 1994, art. 8B as amended S.I. No. 137 of 1998 and D/SFA Unemployment Benefit Guidelines for Deciding Claims.

(ii) advertisements,

(iii) persons who have placed advertisements which indicate that employment is available, or

(iv) employment agencies,

(c) availing of reasonable opportunities for training which is suitable in his or her circumstances,

(d) acting on advice given by an officer of the Minister, FÁS or other placement service concerning the availability of employment, and

(e) taking steps towards establishing themselves in self-employment."[28]

6–22 The taking of one step on a single occasion is not considered to be sufficient to prove that a person is genuinely seeking work, unless taking it is all that is reasonable for the person concerned to do. In deciding whether a person has taken the steps which are reasonable in his or her case, regard must be had to his or her circumstances, including in particular: (a) his or her skills, qualifications and experience; (b) the steps which he or she has taken previously to seek employment; (c) the availability and location of vacancies for employment; (d) the duration of his or her period of unemployment; and (e) his or her family circumstances.

(2) Contribution conditions

6–23 The contribution conditions require a person to have: (a) at least 39 reckonable contributions paid in the period between entry into insurance and the day for which the benefit is claimed; and (b) 39 contributions paid or credited in the last complete contribution year before the beginning of the benefit year for which the benefit is claimed; and (c) reckonable weekly earnings in excess of a fixed amount (€88.88 in 2002) in the relevant contribution year.[29] Reduced rates of UB are payable where the average reckonable weekly earnings are less than that amount. As an alternative to the second contribution requirement, a person must have at least 26 reckonable contributions paid in each of the last two complete contribution years before the beginning of the benefit year in which the claim is made.[30] This is to facilitate atypical workers (such as job sharers) in qualifying for benefit.

(3) Payments

6–24 Unemployment benefit is payable at a flat rate, with increases for qualified adults and qualified children as appropriate.[31] Non-statutory

---

[28] SW(CPP)R 1994, art. 8B.
[29] SW(C)A 1993, s. 43.
[30] SWA 2001, s. 20.
[31] SW(C)A 1993, ss. 44 and 45.

"secondary benefits" are not generally payable with unemployment benefit. Benefit is payable for up to 390 days (*i.e.* 15 months) or for 156 days (six months) in the case of a person under 18 years of age.[32] Once this benefit period has been exhausted, a person must have 13 weeks of insurable employment before requalifying for UB.

(4) Disqualifications

6–25 A range of disqualifications for benefit is set out in the legislation. A person is disqualified if he or she is absent from the State (subject to exceptions, including those under E.U. law).[33] However, a person is not disqualified for the first two weeks of a period of holidays or while representing Ireland in an amateur capacity at an international sporting event.[34] A person is also disqualified if he or she is undergoing penal servitude, imprisonment or detention in legal custody.[35] Persons on a FÁS community employment scheme are also disqualified for UB.[36]

6–26 A person may be disqualified for UB for up to nine weeks if he or she:

(1) has lost his or her employment though his or her own misconduct or has voluntarily left employment without just cause[37];

(2) has refused an offer of suitable employment[38];

(3) has without good cause refused or failed to avail himself or herself of any reasonable opportunity of receiving training provided or approved by FÁS as suitable in his or her case;

(4) has failed or neglected to avail himself or herself of any reasonable opportunity of obtaining suitable employment.[39]

---

[32] SW(C)A 1993, s. 46.

[33] *ibid.*, s. 211. See Chaps 15 and 17.

[34] Social Welfare (Absence from the State) Regulations 1988 (S.I. No. No. 154 of 1988).

[35] SW(C)A 1993, s. 211.

[36] *ibid.*, s. 47(3).

[37] On misconduct, see *Canada (A.G.) v. Tucker* [1986] 2 F.C. 329; *Canada (A.G.) v. Brissette* [1994] 1 F.C. 684; *Smith v. Canada (A.G.)* [1998] 1 F.C. 529; *Foley v. Department of Family and Community Services* [2002] A.A.I.A. 626. On voluntary leaving, see *Crewe v. Social Security Commissioner* [1982] 2 All E.R. 745; *Tanguay v. C.E.I.C.* (1985) 68 N.R. 154.

[38] Employment is not deemed to be suitable if it is in a situation vacant as a result of a trade dispute, employment in the district where the person was last employed at a rate of pay lower or on conditions less favourable than he or she would be used to or employment in another district at a rate of pay lower or conditions less favourable that those generally observed; see SW(C)A 1993, s. 47(6).

[39] SW(C)A 1993, s. 47(4)(a)–(d). See generally Clarke, above, n.13 and Ogus and Barendt, *The Law of Social Security* (3rd ed., Butterworths, London, 1988), pp. 97–110.

6–27 Disqualification for up to nine weeks will also apply to a person, under 55 years of age, who is made redundant and receives a redundancy payment of €19,046.07 or more.

6–28 A person who has lost employment by reason of a stoppage of work which was due to a trade dispute at the factory, workshop, farm or other premises or place at which he or she is employed is disqualified for benefit so long as the stoppage of work continues, except in a case where he or she has, during the stoppage of work, become bona fide employed elsewhere in the occupation which she usually follows or has become regularly engaged in some other occupation.[40] This disqualification does not apply to a person who is not participating in or directly interested in the trade dispute which caused the stoppage of work. The purpose of this disqualification is to attempt to ensure "neutrality" in relation to trade disputes, *i.e.* that the State was not seen to subvent strikers. However, the perceived harshness of this approach led to the establishment in 1982 of a Social Welfare Tribunal to consider further cases of this kind. Where a person has been found by a deciding officer or an appeals officer to be subject to the trade dispute disqualification, the person may apply to the Tribunal for an adjudication that he or she is entitled to benefit (notwithstanding the disqualification). The Tribunal has regard, *inter alia*, to the reasonableness or otherwise of employers and employees in relation to the trade dispute.[41]

B. Unemployment Assistance[42]

6–29 A person is entitled to unemployment assistance (UA) for any "day of unemployment" which forms a part of a "period of interruption of employment", provided he or she is aged over 18 and under pensionable age, *i.e.* 66 on the day for which the assistance is claimed, proves unemployment in the prescribed manner, and qualifies under the means test.[43] Where a person is entitled to UA and UB, he or she may opt for either payment – whichever is more beneficial.[44] This allows, for example, community employment workers reverting to an unemployment payment to claim long-term UA (and the associated secondary benefits), which might be more advantageous than claiming UB. However, a person cannot claim both payments in respect of the same day.

---

[40] SW(C)A 1993, s. 47. On the "trade dispute" disqualification, see Clarke, above, n.13 and Kerr and Whyte, *Irish Trade Union Law* (Butterworths, 1985).

[41] *ibid.*, ss. 274–276 as amended by SWA 1996, s. 33. See Clarke, above, n.13 for an extensive note.

[42] The main provisions are in SW(C)A 1993, ss. 119–126 and SW(CPP)R 1994, arts 8–8B and 68–74 as amended.

[43] SW(C)A 1993, s. 120.

[44] *ibid.*, s. 125 as amended by SWA 2000, s. 27.

(1) Qualification conditions

6–30   As in the case of unemployment benefit, in order to qualify for UA, a person must be available for employment (or be deemed to be or exempted from being so available) and be genuinely seeking employment.[45] The rules in relation to "day of unemployment" availability for work, genuinely seeking work, disqualifications and so on are, in general, very similar if not identical to those which apply in relation to unemployment benefit, and will not be discussed again here in detail.

6–31   As in the case of UB, one is not entitled to UA for the first three days of unemployment. In addition, UA is not payable for less than a day. A person is not regarded as unemployed in respect of any day on which he or she is working under a contract of employment (written or otherwise) or is in receipt of wages.

6–32   Any period of continuous employment under a community employment scheme or various other training and employment schemes of up to 52 weeks, or receipt or entitlement to PRETA between any two continuous periods of employment, is disregarded in treating them as one continuous period of employment.[46]

(2) Means test

6–33   The means test includes means from:

- most property owned by the person and/or by his or her spouse (but excluding property personally used or enjoyed by the person);
- all income which the person and/or spouse may reasonably expect to receive in the coming year (which certain exceptions);
- the value of any advantage accruing to the person or spouse from the use of property (other than a domestic dwelling or farm building, owned and occupied, furniture and personal effects) which is personally used or enjoyed by the person or spouse and the value of any advantage from the leasing of a farm of land;
- any property which the person or spouse have deprived themselves of either directly or indirectly in order to qualify for assistance;
- the value of any "benefit and privilege" enjoyed by the person or spouse including the estimated value to the household of all income earned by the spouse from employment or self-employment.

---

[45] SW(C)A 1993, s. 120(3A) as inserted by SWA 1996, s. 22.
[46] *ibid.*, s. 120(5) as amended by SWA 2002, s. 6.

6–34 The detailed provisions of the means test are set out below. Part I of the Third Schedule provides that in the calculation of the means of a person for the purposes of unemployment assistance (and pre-retirement allowance), the following are deemed to constitute the means of a person under the rules.

(a) Rule 1(1)

6–35 Other than in such circumstances and subject to such conditions and for such periods as may be prescribed, the weekly value of any property belonging to the person (not being property personally used or enjoyed by the person or a farm of land leased by him or her) which is invested or is otherwise put to profitable use by the person or which, though capable of investment or profitable use is not invested or put to profitable use by the person is taken into account. The weekly value of the property is calculated as follows:

(i) the first €12,697 of the capital value of the property shall be excluded; and

(ii) the weekly value of so much of the capital value of the property as exceeds €12,697 but does not exceed €25,394.76 shall be assessed at €1.27 per each €1,269.74; and

(iii) the weekly value of so much of the capital value of the property as exceeds €25,394.76 but does not exceed €38,092.14 shall be assessed at €2.54 per each €1,269.74; and

(iv) the weekly value of so much of the capital value of the property as exceeds €38,092.14 shall be assessed at €5.08 per each €1,269.74.

6–36 Thus, Rule 1(1) provides for a system of notional assessment of means from capital. It does not matter whether the actual income from capital is greater or lesser than the notional assessment, as the latter is deemed to constitute the weekly means of a person from such capital. In practice, it would be administratively impossible to operate a system of assessment of actual income, as this would vary constantly with, for example, varying interest rates on deposit accounts or variation in returns from shares leading to frequent fluctuations in the level of pension payable. In addition, the notional system is designed to favour those with relatively small amounts of capital as can be seen from the exclusion of the first €12,697 from assessment.

(b) Rule 1(2)

6–37 All income which the person or his or her spouse may reasonably expect to receive during the succeeding year in cash, whether as contributions to the expenses of the household or otherwise, is taken into account, but excluding:

1(2)(a): such amount as may be prescribed of all moneys earned by his spouse from insurable employment;

1(2)(b): any moneys received by way of benefit, pension, assistance, allowance, supplement or continued child payment under Part II, III, IV, V or VA, or by way of a payment corresponding to child benefit under Part IV from another Member State of the E.U.;

1(2)(c): any income arising from a bonus under a scheme administered by the Minister for the Gaeltacht for the making of special grants to parents or guardians resident in the Gaeltacht or Breac-Gaeltacht of children attending primary schools;

1(2)(d): in the case of a qualified applicant under a scheme administered by the Minister for the Gaeltacht and known as Scéim na bhFogh-laimeoirí Gaeilge, any income received under that scheme in respect of a person who is temporarily resident with the qualified applicant, together with any other income received in respect of such temporary resident;

1(2)(e): an amount of an allowance, dependant's allowance, disability pension or wound pension under the Army Pensions Acts 1923 to 1980, or a combination of such allowances and such pensions so far as such amount does not exceed €101.60 per year;

1(2)(f): any moneys received from a charitable organisation, being a body whose activities are carried on otherwise than for profit (but excluding any public or local authority) and one of whose functions is to assist persons in need by making grants of money to them;

1(2)(g): such amount as may be prescribed of income from employment by a health board or by a person approved by a health board, as a home help;

1(2)(h): any moneys received by way of training allowance from an organisation while undergoing a course of rehabilitation training provided by the organisation (being an organisation approved of by the Minister for Health for the purposes of the provision of such training);

1(2)(hh): any moneys, subject to such limit as may be prescribed, received by way of repayment of expenses necessarily incurred in relation to travel and meals while undergoing a course of education, training or development approved by the Minister[47];

1(2)(i): any moneys, except so far as they exceed €132.08 per year, received by such person or by the spouse of such person in respect of work as an outworker under a scheme that is, in the opinion of the Minister, charitable in character and purpose;

---

[47] Inserted by SWA 2001, s. 13.

1(2)(j): where his or her spouse is engaged on a seasonal basis in the occupation of fishing, one-half of so much of the income derived therefrom as does not exceed €152.40 per year and one-third of so much of such income as exceeds €152.40 per year but does not exceed €381 per year[48];

1(2)(jj): other than in the case of disability allowance, and subject to Rule 1(8) (below), any income derived by a fisherman from any form of self-employment[49];

1(2)(k): payments by a health board in respect of a child who is boarded out,

1(2)(kk): payments in respect of not more than two persons boarded out under section 10 of the Health (Nursing Homes) Act 1990 (insofar as the aggregate amount received in respect of each person does not exceed the maximum amount of the old age (non-contributory) pension)[50];

1(2)(1): other than in the case of disability allowance and subject to Rule 1(7) (below), all moneys earned by him or her of current personal employment under a contract of service;

1(2)(11): other than in the case of disability allowance, any expenses necessarily incurred in carrying on any form of self-employment;

1(2)(m): in such circumstances as may be prescribed, any moneys received by way of a maintenance grant under the Higher Education Grants scheme, the Maintenance Grants Scheme for Students attending Post-Leaving Certificate Courses, the Vocational Education Committees Scholarship Scheme, or the Third-Level Maintenance Scheme for Trainees[51];

1(2)(n): any moneys received by way of a mobility allowance payable under section 61 of the Health Act 1970;

1(2)(o): other than in the case of disability allowance, such income as may be prescribed, arising from such activities as may be prescribed[52];

1(2)(p): other than in the case of disability allowance and subject to Rules 1(6) and (6A), any moneys earned by the person or by his or her spouse from insurable employment of a seasonal nature[53];

1(2)(q): payments by a health board in respect of the provision of accommodation for a child under section 5 of the Child Care Act 1991;

1(2)(r): other than in the case of disability allowance, an amount of €2,539

---

[48] Amended by SWA 1999, s. 22.
[49] Inserted by SWA 1999, s. 22.
[50] Inserted by SWA 2001, s. 13.
[51] Substituted by SWA 2001, s. 13.
[52] SW(CPP)R 1994, art. 88 prescribes income from seaweed harvesting up to €1,270.
[53] Inserted by SWA 1998, s. 10.

together with one-half of any amount in excess of €2,539 under the Rural Environment Protection Scheme (REPS) and the Special Areas of Conservation Scheme;

[1(2)(s): relates to DA];

1(2)(t): any moneys received by his or her spouse in respect of participation in the Vocational Opportunities Scheme;

1(2)(u): any moneys received by his or her spouse in respect of participation in the Back to Work Allowances, Back to Education Allowance or Part-Time Job Incentive Schemes;

1(2)(v): any moneys received by his or her spouse in respect of participation in a FÁS course;

1(2)(w): such other income received by a person or his or her spouse as may be prescribed.[54]

6–38 Thus, Rule 1(2) covers income received by a person but subject to the extensive list of exclusions set out above. It should be noted that these exclude income from employment and from some forms of self-employment which are dealt with separately by Rules 1(6), (6A), (7) and (8), discussed below.

6–39 For the purposes of Rule 1(2), the income of a person is, in the absence of other means of ascertaining it, taken to be the income actually received during the year immediately *preceding* the date of calculation.[55]

(c) Rule 1(3)

6–40 The means of a person are deemed to include yearly value ascertained in the prescribed manner of any advantage accruing to him or to his spouse from:

(a) the use of property (other than a domestic dwelling or farm building owned and occupied, furniture and personal effects) which is personally used or enjoyed by him or by his spouse; and

(b) the leasing by him or by his spouse of a farm of land.[56]

---

[54] Amended by SWA 1997, s. 26 and SWA 2001, s. 24. SW(CPP)R 1994, art. 90B prescribes income from an award relating to Hepatitis C from the Compensation Tribunal or a court, and compensation arising from thalidomide.

[55] See SW(C)A 1993, Rule 2 of Pt I of Third Sched.

[56] Amended by SWA 1996, s. 37. See SW(CPP)R 1994, art. 87 as substituted by S.I. No. 313 of 2000.

(d) Rule 1(4)[57]

6–41 All income and the yearly value ascertained in the prescribed manner of all property of which he or his spouse have directly or indirectly deprived themselves in order to qualify for the receipt of disability allowance, unemployment assistance or pre-retirement allowance are included. However, where such income or the yearly value of the property so ascertained has reduced since the date of calculation, the calculation may be revised, subject to such conditions and in such circumstances as may be prescribed, provided that any such Regulations shall not cause the income or yearly value of the property taken to be part of the means to be increased.

(e) Rule 1(5)[58]

6–42 The yearly value of any benefit or privilege enjoyed by a person or by his or her spouse is included, including the estimated value to the household in the succeeding year deriving from all income earned by his spouse from insurable employment and insurable self-employment. "Benefit and privilege" is calculated in accordance with departmental guideslines.[59]

6–43 For the purposes of Rule 1(5), the income of a person is, in the absence of other means of ascertaining it, taken to be the income actually received during the year immediately *preceding* the date of calculation.[60]

(f) Rule 1(6)[61]

6–44 In the case of a person who makes a claim for unemployment assistance during a period in which he is engaged in insurable employment of a seasonal nature, the value, ascertained in the prescribed manner, of any moneys derived from the said employment is included. The value so calculated is deemed to constitute the weekly means of that person from such employment.

---

[57] Amended by SWA 1996 and SWA 1997.

[58] Amended by SWA 1996, s.15 and SW(CPP)R 1994, art. 89F as inserted by S.I. No. 324 of 1999.

[59] Department of Social and Family Affairs, Unemployment Assistance – Benefit and Privilege Guidelines. See *R. v. Supplementary Benefits Commission, ex parte Singer* [1973] 1 W.L.R. 713, which held that the essential feature of income was an element of recurrence and that *ad hoc* receipts could not be income as a benefit and privilege. Gibson J. in *R. (Rooney) v. Local Government Board* [1920] 2 I.R. 347 took the view that a casual and temporary benefit did not come within the definition of "the yearly value of any benefit and privilege".

[60] SW(C)A 1993, Rule 2 of Pt I of Third Sched.

[61] Inserted by SWA (No. 2) 1995, s.11 and amended by SWA 1996, s.11 and SW(CPP)R 1994, art. 89E as inserted by S.I. No. 324 of 1999.

6–45   Under this rule, earnings from employment of a seasonal nature are assessed as means.

(g) Rule 1(6A)[62]

6–46   The value of all moneys derived by his or her spouse from insurable employment of a seasonal nature, ascertained in the prescribed manner, during the period in which his or her spouse is engaged in such employment is included. The value so calculated is deemed to constitute the weekly means of that person from such employment.

6–47   Under this rule, earnings *by a spouse* from employment of a seasonal nature are assessed as means.

(h) Rule 1(7)[63]

6–48   In the case of a person engaged in employment under a contract of service, the value, ascertained in the prescribed manner of any moneys derived from the said employment is included. The value so calculated is deemed to constitute the weekly means of that person from such employment.

6–49   Under this rule, earnings from employment under a contract of service are assessed as means.

(i) Rule 1(8)[64]

6–50   In the case of a fisherman, means include the gross income derived from any form of self-employment, less: (a) any expenses necessarily incurred in carrying on any form of self-employment, and (b) where the fisherman has a qualified child who normally resides with him or her, an amount of €254 per annum in respect of the first two qualified children and €381 per annum in respect of each qualified child, calculated at 70 per cent.

6–51   "Fisherman" is defined as a person engaged in seafishing as a self-employed person (a) on a fishing boat entered in the Register of Fishing Boats, or (b) on a fishing boat and in a place in respect of which a fishing licence (under section 3 of the Fisheries (Consolidation) Act 1959) for fishing for salmon at sea has been issued.[65]

---

[62] Inserted by SWA 1998, s.10 and SW(CPP)R 1994, art. 89G as inserted by S.I. No. 324 of 1999.

[63] Inserted by SWA 1996, s.22 and SW(CPP)R 1994, art. 89D as inserted by S.I. No. 324 of 1999.

[64] Inserted by SWA 1999, s. 22 and amended by SWA 2000, s. 14.

[65] Rule 3 as inserted by SWA 1999, s. 22.

6–52 Under this rule, earnings from self-employment as a fisherman are assessed as means at a rate of 70 per cent, subject to a disregard in respect of qualified children. This treatment of means is similar to that applicable in the case of farm assist.

(j) Rule 3

6–53 In the application of these Rules, "spouse" means each person of a married couple who are living together or a man and woman who are not married to each other but are cohabiting as husband and wife.[66]

(3) Payments

6–54 Unemployment assistance is payable at a flat rate, with increases for qualified adults and qualified children as appropriate.[67] Where both of a couple are entitled to UA, the amount payable is limited to that which would be payable were the couple treated as a claimant and qualified adult (*i.e.* about 1.7 times the individual rate).[68] While higher rates of payment have in the past been payable to persons who were "long-term" unemployed, the standard rates are currently the same for all UA claimants. Limited "secondary benefits" (*e.g.* Christmas bonus) are payable with long-term unemployment assistance (*i.e.* persons who have been unemployed for 15 months or more). Assistance is payable indefinitely to pension age.

(4) Disqualifications

6–55 A person is disqualified for UA while he or she is an inmate of an institution maintained wholly or partly out of public moneys or by a local authority, or where he or she is employed on a community employment scheme.[69] The general disqualifications which apply to UB in relation to imprisonment, absence from the State, trade disputes, leaving or losing employment, refusing work or training, etc., also apply to UA.[70] There is also a specific disqualification for residence outside the State.

6–56 A person is not entitled to receive UA while attending a course of study, other than in limited prescribed circumstances.[71] "Course of study"

---

[66] Substituted by SWA 1995, s. 16.
[67] SW(C)A 1993, ss. 121–124.
[68] *ibid.*, s. 122.
[69] SW(C)A 1993, s. 125(1).
[70] See above, paras 6–25—6–28. See above, SW(C)A 1993, ss. 125(3)–(6) and 211.
[71] There are a number of decisions in other jurisdictions in relation to similar (but not identical) provisions. See, in particular, *Secretary, Department of Social Security v.*

means a full-time day course of study, instruction or training at any institution of education.[72] A person is regarded as attending a course of study for three months immediately following the completion of second-level education or the completion of the Leaving Certificate (whichever is later), for the duration of the academic year (including term vacations), or for the period immediately following the completion of one academic year (other than the final academic year). This disqualification does not apply to mature students nor to students on "second chance" education.[73] The main purpose of this disqualification, introduced in 1993, is to ensure that students do not qualify for UA during the term holidays – particularly the summer holidays.[74] An administrative Student Summer Job Scheme was introduced to ensure that disadvantaged students had access to some income over the summer months.

C. Pre-Retirement Allowance

6–57 Pre-retirement allowance (PRETA) is a payment, analogous to unemployment assistance, which is payable to older, long-term unemployed persons and limited other groups of long-term claimants. Such persons are not required to be available for or genuinely seeking work. In fact, such persons are required to be "retired".

(1) Qualification conditions

6–58 Pre-retirement allowance is payable in respect of any period of retirement to a person:

(a) who has attained the age specified by regulations (currently 55)[75] but has not attained pensionable age (*i.e.* 66);

(b) who satisfies a means test; and

Jordan [1998] 604 F.C.A.; *Chief Adjudication Officer v. Weber* [1997] 4 All E.R. 274; *Flemming v. Secretary of State for Work and Pensions* [2002] E.W.C.A. Civ. 641.

[72] SW(C)A 1993, s. 126. "Institute of education" means a school, university or college of an university, an institution of higher education designated under the Higher Education Authority Act 1971, any institution to which the National Council for Education Awards Act 1979 applies, any institution established under the Regional Technical Colleges Act 1992, any institution incorporated under the Dublin Institute of Technology Act 1992, any other institution to which the Local Authorities (Higher Education Grants) Acts 1968 to 1992 apply, and any other institution as may be prescribed.

[73] SW(CPP)R 1994, art. 74

[74] Prior to the provision, a full-time student would not, in general, have been entitled to UA, as he or she would not have been available for employment. See *Landry v. Canada (A.G.)* (1992) 152 N.R. 164; but see also the more flexible approach taken by the Australian Federal Court in *Director-General of Social Services v. Thomson* (1981) 38 A.L.R. 624.

[75] See SW(CPP)R 1994, art. 75 as substituted by S.I. No. 426 of 1996.

(c) (i) who has been in receipt of unemployment benefit or unemployment assistance for not less than 390 days for any continuous period of unemployment in the immediately preceding period as construed in accordance with section 120(3);

(ii) being a separated (including divorced) spouse, has not been engaged in remunerative employment or self-employment at any time in a preceding prescribed period; or

(iii) immediately before the week in respect of which PRETA is claimed was in receipt of one-parent family payment but has ceased to be entitled to such payment by virtue of no longer being regarded as a qualified parent within the meaning of section 157(1), or carer's allowance but has ceased to be entitled to such allowance because he or she is no longer regarded as a carer within the meaning of section 163(1).[76]

6–59 Thus, while the primary client group for PRETA is those who have been long-term unemployed, persons over 55 who cease to be lone parents or carer's and, thereby, cease to qualify for the relevant payments may also transfer to PRETA.

6–60 Any period during which a person does not engage in insurable employment or insurable self-employment shall be regarded as a period of retirement.[77] Section 120(6) provides that the requirement of continuous receipt of UA or UB (set out in section 127(1)(c)) does not apply in the case of a person in respect of a continuous period of retirement, *i.e.* any two periods of retirement not separated by more than 52 weeks.[78]

(2) Means test

6–61 The means test for PRETA is very similar to that applicable to UA outlined above.

6–62 Where the spouse of a claimant for pre-retirement allowance is not the claimant's qualified adult, the means of the claimant shall be taken to be one-half the assessed means.

(3) Payments

6–63 PRETA is payable at a flat rate, with increases for qualified adults and

---

[76] SW(C)A 1993, s. 127 as substituted by SWA 1998, s. 18.
[77] SW(CPP)R 1994, art. 76.
[78] As inserted by SWA 2002, s. 6.

qualified children as appropriate.[79] Where both of a couple are entitled to PRETA, the amount payable is limited to that which would be payable were the couple treated as a claimant and qualified adult (*i.e.* about 1.7 of the individual rate).[80] Limited "secondary benefits" (*e.g.* Christmas bonus) are payable with PRETA). PRETA is payable indefinitely to pension age.

(4) Disqualifications

6–64   The general disqualifications in relation to imprisonment and absence from the State also apply to PRETA.[81] In addition, the specific disqualification for residence outside the State which is applicable to UA under section 211(6) also applies to PRETA. Finally, in the case of person who qualifies for PRETA having been a separated spouse under section 127(1)(c)(ii), PRETA is no longer payable where the person remarries or cohabits as husband and wife.[82]

D. Farm Assist

6–65   Farm Assist (FA) is a means-tested scheme for low-income farmers.[83] Unlike the previous smallholders assistance, which was unemployment assistance payable to farmers, who were not included on the Live Register, farm assist provides a partial disregard for earned income and thus provides a greater incentive for small farmers to generate income from farming.

(1) Qualification conditions

6–66   To qualify for farm assist, a person must be aged between 18 and 66 years, be engaged in farming, and satisfy a means test.[84]

6–67   "Farmer" is defined as a person engaged in farming while "farming" is defined as farming farmland in the State, including commonage, which is:

(a) owned and used for the purposes of husbandry; or

(b) leased and used for the purposes of husbandry; or

(c) does not form part of a larger holding and is used for the purposes of husbandry,

by the claimant.[85]

---

[79] SW(C)A 1993, s. 128.

[80] *ibid.*, s. 122.

[81] *ibid.*, s. 211.

[82] *ibid.*, s. 127(2)(b). On cohabitation see Chap.11.

[83] The main provisions are at SW(C)A 1993, ss. 191L–Q (as inserted by SWA 1999, s.15) and S.I. No. 324 of 1999.

[84] SW(C)A 1993, s. 191M as inserted by SWA 1999, s. 15.

[85] *ibid.*, s. 191L(1).

6–68 "Husbandry" means the working of the land with the object of extracting the traditional produce of the land.[86] This includes the cultivation of crops or trees (forestry) and the keeping of livestock and poultry.

6–69 Departmental guidelines state that tenure in the land should be verified by reference to relevant source documentation, *e.g.* Land Registry Office, lease agreement, etc. Ownership may include joint ownership. Where the land is neither owned nor leased, farm assist may be payable only where the land used does not form part of a larger holding. This includes cases where the claimant is farming a holding in respect of which he or she has an intestacy share which has not been officially registered. It also includes situations where two or more siblings with an intestacy share in a farm jointly manage the same holding.

6–70 Where two or more persons farm what may originally have been a single unit, but is now claimed to be made up of separate units, the guidelines state that deciding officers must satisfy themselves that what was the original farm is now managed as two separate entities/businesses, *e.g.* that the claimant has his or her own herd number.

6–71 It is not sufficient for a person simply to own a farm of land. As outlined above, the legislation prescribes that the claimant himself or herself must be engaged in farming. Therefore, a person who owns a farm of land, but leases, lets or rents out the entire holding does not satisfy this condition and cannot, therefore, qualify for FA. If, however, the claimant is personally engaged in farming part of the holding and leases, and lets or rents a portion of the farm to another person, he or she may qualify for a payment.

6–72 There is no minimum acreage requirement. However, the guidelines also state that deciding officers must satisfy themselves that the land would reasonably be considered to be a farm which is used by the claimant for the purposes of husbandry. For example, where a claimant resides in a dwelling on a large site, *e.g.* one or two acres, and he or she has a large vegetable garden, it may be reasonable to conclude that while the claimant may be engaged in husbandry, the land does not constitute a farm of land and the person is not engaged in farming Conversely, the claimant may be engaged in intensive farming on a small acreage, *e.g.* pig or mushroom farming, which would satisfy the condition.

---

[86] SW(C)A 1993, s. 191L(1).

(2) Means test

6–73 The means test for farm assist is set out in Part IV of the Third Schedule.[87] In calculating the means of a farmer, account must be taken of the following rules.

(a) Rule 1(1)[88]

6–74 The means are deemed to include the gross yearly income which the farmer or his or her spouse may be reasonably expected to receive from farming or from any other form of self-employment less:

(a) any expenses necessarily incurred in carrying on farming or other form of self-employment; and

(b) in the case of a farmer who has a qualified child who normally resides with him, an amount of €254 per annum in respect of each of the first two qualified children, and €381 per annum in respect of each subsequent qualified child

calculated at the rate of 70 per cent.

(b) Rule 1(2)

6–75 Other than in such circumstances and subject to such conditions and for such periods as may be prescribed, the weekly value of any property belonging to the person (not being property personally used or enjoyed by the person or a farm of land leased by him or her) which is invested or is otherwise put to profitable use by the person or which, though capable of investment or profitable use, is not invested or put to profitable use by the person is taken into account. The weekly value of the property is calculated as follows:

(i) the first €12,697 of the capital value of the property shall be excluded; and

(ii) the weekly value of so much of the capital value of the property as exceeds €12,697 but does not exceed €25,394.76 shall be assessed at €1.27 per each €1,269.74; and

(iii) the weekly value of so much of the capital value of the property as exceeds €25,394.76 but does not exceed €38,092.14 shall be assessed at €2.54 per each €1,269.74; and

(iv) the weekly value of so much of the capital value of the property as exceeds €38,092.14 shall be assessed at €5.08 per each €1,269.74.

---

[87] As inserted by SWA 1999, s. 16.
[88] Substituted by SWA 2000, s. 18.

6–76 Thus, Rule 1(1) provides for a system of notional assessment of means from capital. It does not matter whether the actual income from capital is greater or lesser than the notional assessment, as the latter is deemed to constitute the weekly means of a person from such capital. In practice, it would be administratively impossible to operate a system of assessment of actual income, as this would vary constantly with, for example, varying interest rates on deposit accounts or variation in returns from shares leading to frequent fluctuations in the level of pension payable. In addition, the notional system is designed to favour those with relatively small amounts of capital, as can be seen from the exclusion of the first €12,697 from assessment.

<u>(c) Rule 1(3)</u>

6–77 All other income which the person or his or her spouse may reasonably expect to receive during the succeeding year in cash, whether as contributions to the expenses of the household or otherwise, is taken into account, but excluding:

1(3)(a): any moneys received by way of benefit, pension, assistance, allowance, supplement or continued child payment under Part II, III, IV, V or VA, or by way of a payment corresponding to child benefit under Part IV from another Member State of the E.U.;

1(3)(b): any income arising from a bonus under a scheme administered by the Minister for the Gaeltacht for the making of special grants to parents or guardians resident in the Gaeltacht or Breac-Gaeltacht of children attending primary schools;

1(3)(c): in the case of a qualified applicant under a scheme administered by the Minister for the Gaeltacht and known as Scéim na bhFogh-laimeoirí Gaeilge, any income received under that scheme in respect of a person who is temporarily resident with the qualified applicant, together with any other income received in respect of such temporary resident;

1(3)(d): an amount of an allowance, dependant's allowance, disability pension or wound pension under the Army Pensions Acts 1923 to 1980, or a combination of such allowances and such pensions so far as such amount does not exceed €101.60 per year;

1(3)(e): any moneys received from a charitable organisation, being a body whose activities are carried on otherwise than for profit (but excluding any public or local authority) and one of whose functions is to assist persons in need by making grants of money to them;

1(3)(f): such amount as may be prescribed of income from employment by a health board or by a person approved by a health board, as a home help;

1(3)(g):   any moneys received by way of training allowance from an organisation while undergoing a course of rehabilitation training provided by the organisation (being an organisation approved of by the Minister for Health for the purposes of the provision of such training);

1(3)(h):   any moneys, except so far as they exceed €132.08 per year, received by such person or by the spouse of such person in respect of work as an outworker under a scheme that is, in the opinion of the Minister, charitable in character and purpose;

1(3)(j):   payments by a health board in respect of a child who is boarded out[89];

1(3)(jj): payments in respect of not more than two persons boarded out under section 10 of the Health (Nursing Homes) Act 1990 (insofar as the aggregate amount received in respect of each person does not exceed the maximum amount of the old age (non-contributory) pension)[90];

1(3)(k):   all moneys earned by the farmer or his or her spouse in respect of current personal employment under a contract of service;

1(3)(l):   in such circumstances as may be prescribed, any moneys received by way of a maintenance grant under the Higher Education Grants scheme, the Maintenance Grants Scheme for Students attending Post-Leaving Certificate Courses, the Vocational Education Committees Scholarship Scheme, or the Third-Level Maintenance Scheme for Trainees[91];

1(3)(m):   any moneys received by way of a mobility allowance payable under section 61 of the Health Act 1970;

1(3)(n):   an amount of €1,270 per annum from the harvesting of seaweed;

1(3)(o):   subject to Rule 1(5), any moneys earned by the person or by his or her spouse from insurable employment of a seasonal nature;

1(3)(p):   payments by a health board in respect of the provision of accommodation for a child under section 5 of the Child Care Act 1991;

1(3)(q):   an amount of €2,540 together with one-half of any amount in excess of €2,540 (plus any expenses necessarily incurred in participating in these schemes) under the Rural Environment Protection Scheme (REPS) and the Special Areas of Conservation Scheme;

1(3)(r):   any moneys received by his or her spouse in respect of participation in the Vocational Opportunities Scheme;

---

[89] Rule 1(3)(i) deleted by SWA 2000, s. 18.
[90] Inserted by SWA 2001, s. 13.
[91] Substituted by SWA 2001, s. 13.

1(3)(s): any moneys received by his or her spouse in respect of participation in the Back to Work Allowances, Back to Education Allowance or Part-Time Job Incentive Schemes;

1(3)(t): any moneys received by his or her spouse in respect of participation in a FÁS course;

1(3)(u): such other income received by a person or his or her spouse as may be prescribed.[92]

6–78 Thus, Rule 1(3) covers income received by a person but subject to the extensive list of exclusions set out above. The income is taken to be the income actually received during the year immediately preceding the date of calculation – in the absence of other means of ascertaining it.[93] However, in exceptional circumstances income will be assessed on a current basis where it is possible to do so. For example, where a farmer had stock destroyed as a result of Foot and Mouth disease and therefore would have no income from this aspect of farming, this would be taken into account in assessing current entitlement to farm assist.

(d) Rule 1(4)[94]

6–79 All income and the yearly value ascertained in the prescribed manner of all property of which he or his spouse have directly or indirectly deprived themselves in order to qualify for the receipt of disability allowance, unemployment assistance or pre-retirement allowance are included. However, where such income or the yearly value of the property so ascertained has reduced since the date of calculation, the calculation may be revised, subject to such conditions and in such circumstances as may be prescribed, provided that any such Regulations shall not cause the income or yearly value of the property taken to be part of the means to be increased.

(e) Rule 1(5)[95]

6–80 In the case of a farmer or his or her spouse engaged in current personal or seasonal employment, the value, ascertained in the prescribed manner, of any moneys derived from this employment is taken into account.

---

[92] SW(CPP)R 1994, art.90B (as inserted by S.I. No. 324 of 1999) prescribes income from an award relating to Hepatitis C from the Compensation Tribunal or a court, and compensation arising from thalidomide.

[93] SW(C)A 1993, Rule 2 of Pt IV of Third Sched.

[94] Amended by SWA 2000, s. 17.

[95] Amended by SWA 1996 and SW(CPP)R 1994, arts 89D–H as inserted by S.I. No. 324 of 1999.

(f) Rule 3

6–81 In the application of these Rules, "spouse" means each person of a married couple who are living together or a man and woman who are not married to each other but are cohabiting as husband and wife.[96]

(g) Rule 4

6–82 Rule 4 provides that the Minister may vary the provisions of Rule 1 by regulation. However, this Rule must be read in the light of the judicial interpretation of the separation of powers.

6–83 Where the spouse of a claimant for farm assist is not the claimant's qualified adult, the means of the claimant shall be taken to be one-half of the assessed means.[97]

(3) Payments

6–84 Farm assist is payable at a flat rate, with increases for qualified adults and qualified children as appropriate.[98] Where both of a couple are entitled to FA, the amount payable is limited to that which would be payable were the couple treated as a claimant and qualified adult (*i.e.* about 1.7 times the individual rate).[99] Limited "secondary benefits" (*e.g.* Christmas bonus) are payable with FA. FA is payable indefinitely to pension age.

(4) Disqualifications

6–85 A person is disqualified for farm assist while he or she is employed under community employment, or participating in Back to Work or the Part-Time Job Incentive.[100] In addition, a farmer is not entitled to farm assist while attending a course of study (other than in prescribed circumstances).[101]

6–86 The general disqualifications in relation to imprisonment and absence from the State also apply to FA.[102] In addition, the specific disqualification for residence outside the State which is applicable to UA under section 211(6) also applies to FA.[103]

---

[96] Substituted by SWA 1995.
[97] SW(C)A 1993, s. 191M(2).
[98] *ibid.*, ss. 191N and 191O.
[99] *ibid.*, s. 191P.
[100] *ibid.*, s. 191Q(1).
[101] *ibid.*, s. 191Q(2)–(4). This disqualification is the same as that applicable to UA, see above, para. 6–56.
[102] SW(C)A 1993, s. 211.
[103] As amended by SWA 1999, s. 17.

E. Family Income Supplement

6–87 Family income supplement (FIS) is a payment to low-income families in employment.[104] The purpose is to ensure that families in employment are better off than they would be if they were not employed and in receipt of a social welfare payment.

(1) Qualification conditions

6–88 In order to qualify for FIS a person must be a member of a *"family"*, must be engaged in *remunerative full-time employment* as an employee (self-employment is *not* eligible) and must satisfy a means test. "Family" is defined in section 197 as: (a) a person who is engaged in remunerative[105] full-time employment as an employee; (b) where such person is living with or mainly maintaining his or her spouse, that spouse; and (c) a child or children.[106] "Child" means a qualified child as defined in section 2(3) who normally resides with that family and "spouse" includes a party to a marriage that has been validly dissolved, or a man and woman who are not married to each other but are cohabiting as husband and wife.[107] Where family income supplement is payable in respect of a particular family for any period, no person who was included in that family at the beginning of such period is to be regarded as a member of any other family during that period.[108]

6–89 Regulations provide that a person is to be regarded as being engaged in remunerative full-time employment as an employee where he or she is engaged in remunerative employment (other than employment under a scheme administered by FÁS and known as community employment) which is expected to continue for a period of a minimum of three months and the number of hours worked per fortnight is not less than 38, or where the aggregate number of hours worked by him and his spouse is not less than 38 per fortnight.[109]

6–90 In *Healy v. Minister for Social Welfare*[110] the plaintiff claimed that the

---

[104] The main provisions are in SW(C)A 1993, ss. 197–203 and SW(CPP)R 1994, arts 94–98 as amended.

[105] In *RI/93(FC)* a Northern Ireland Social Security Commissioner held that a student nurse in receipt of a bursary was not in *remunerative* work.

[106] As amended by SWA (No. 2) 1995, s. 9.

[107] As substituted by SWA (No. 2) 1995, s. 9.

[108] SW(C)A 1993, s. 200(2).

[109] SW(CPP)R 1994, art. 97 as amended by S.I. No. 189 of 1996. In *R. v. Ebbw Vale and Methyr Tydfil Supplementary Benefits, ex parte Lewis* [1982] 1 W.L.R. 420, the Court of Appeal held that a person who was absent from work through illness was not engaged in remunerative work for the purposes of the U.K. family income supplement scheme.

[110] [1999] 1 I.L.R.M. 72

disqualification of persons employed in community employment by regulation was *ultra vires* the Minister. However, Carroll J. held that the general definition of remunerative full-time employment by regulation was a valid exercise of the ministerial power to promulgate delegated legislation in that it filled in the detail and gave effect to principles and policies contained in the statute itself. She did not find it necessary, on the facts of that case, to decide whether the specific exclusion of community employment was *ultra vires* the Minister.

(2) Payments

6–91 The rate of FIS is calculated as a percentage of the difference between the "weekly family income" and a set scale which varies in accordance with the size of the family. This scale is normally adjusted on an annual basis in line with general increases in social welfare rates. Section 199 provides that the weekly rate of family income supplement is to be 60 per cent of the amount by which the weekly family income is less than the amount appropriate in the particular case under section 198. Once a person qualifies for FIS it is payable at a minimum rate (currently €13 per week).

6–92 Family income supplement is payable for a period of 52 weeks beginning on the date on which it is receivable and, except where Regulations otherwise provide, the weekly rate of family income supplement payable is not affected by any change of circumstances during that period.[111] However, in practice, FIS rates are increased in line with the general increases in social welfare rates, although this is not specifically provided for by the legislation.

6–93 Family income supplement is payable to the member of the family (other than a child) who is engaged in remunerative full-time employment as an employee or, where there are two members of the family so engaged, to the member whose weekly income as calculated for the purposes of family income supplement forms the greater part of the weekly family income.[112]

(3) Means test

6–94 "Weekly family income" is defined as the amount of *net* income received in a week by a family (*i.e.* less tax, PRSI and levies), less any income of a child of that family.[113] Regulations provide that weekly family income is to be calculated or estimated:

---

[111] SW(C)A 1993, s. 200. S.I. No. 189 of 1996 provides for an increase for additional children.
[112] *ibid.*, s. 201.
[113] *ibid.*, s. 197.

(a) insofar as it comprises earnings from employment as an employee, by reference to the weekly average of the amount of such earnings received in the two months immediately prior to the date on which the claim for family income supplement has been made where such earnings are received at monthly intervals, or in the four weeks immediately prior to such date where such earnings are received at weekly or fortnightly intervals;

(b) insofar as it comprises income from any form of self-employment, by reference to the weekly amount of such income calculated or estimated by dividing the income in the 12 months preceding the date of claim by 52;

(c) insofar as it consists of income from any other source, by reference to the normal weekly amount of such income.[114]

6–95 Where in any case a deciding officer or appeals officer considers that the periods mentioned above would not be appropriate to determine the amount of weekly family income, he or she may have regard to such other period which appears to him or her to be appropriate for that purpose.

6–96 In calculating or estimating weekly family income the following items are disregarded:

(a) any sums received by way of death benefit by way of orphan's pension, orphan's (contributory) allowance, carer's benefit, orphan's (non-contributory) pension, carer's allowance, supplementary welfare allowance, child benefit or family income supplement;

(b) any sums received by way of allowance for domiciliary care of handicapped children under the Health Act 1970;

(c) any sums received by way of an allowance under regulations made under section 23 of the Housing (Private Rented Dwellings) Act 1982;

(d) any sums from the investment or profitable use of property (not being property personally used or enjoyed by the person concerned);

(e) payments by a health board in respect of a child who is boarded out;

(f) in the case of a qualified applicant under a scheme administered by the Minister for the Gaeltacht and known as Scéim na bhFoghlaimeoirí Gaeilge, any income received under that scheme in respect of a person who is temporarily resident with the qualified applicant, together with any other income received in respect of such temporary resident;

---

[114] SW(CPP)R 1994, art. 95.

(g) any moneys received from a charitable organisation being a body whose activities are carried on otherwise than for profit (but excluding any public or local authority) and one of whose functions is to assist persons in need by making grants of money to them; and

(h) any income arising from employment of a casual nature by a health board as a home help.[115]

(4) Disqualifications

6–97   The general disqualifications in relation to absence from the State and imprisonment apply in the case of FIS.[116]

---

[115] SW(CPP)R 1994, art. 96
[116] SW(C)A 1993, s. 211.

CHAPTER 7

Supplementary Welfare Allowance

1. Background

7–01 The Supplementary Welfare Allowance (SWA) scheme is the direct descendant of the first social welfare scheme: the Poor Law. The Elizabethan Poor Laws did not apply in the Kingdom of Ireland and only limited measures to deal with the poor, primarily applying to the main towns and cities, were adopted prior to 1800.[1] However, after the Union and faced by a rapidly growing population, a number of public commissions were appointed to consider the relief of the poor and related issues in the first decades of the nineteenth century. Reflecting the position in England and Wales, where public debate eventually led to the establishment of the "New Poor Law" in 1834,[2] legislation was adopted by the U.K. Parliament in 1838. This divided the country into 130 Poor Law Unions, which were to be responsible for the relief of poverty in their own areas. Each Union was governed, subject to the overall supervision of the U.K. Poor Law Commissioners, by a board of guardians, partly appointed *ex officio* and partly elected.

7–02 Unlike the position in the United Kingdom, where outdoor relief was allowed in certain circumstances, relief was to be provided only in workhouses which were to be established in each Union. However, the Irish Poor Law had hardly even been established when it was hit by a disaster of a scale with which it had never been designed to deal. One enduring legacy of that period was that, in 1847, the restriction of relief to those in workhouses was abandoned and the law was amended to allow outdoor relief in certain circumstances.

7–03 After the Famine, the overall position of the Irish population improved

---

[1] On the position in Ireland, see D. Dickson, "In Search of the Old Irish Poor Law" in R. Mitchison and P. Roebuck eds., *Economy and Society in Scotland and Ireland 1500-1939* (John Donald, Edinburgh, 1988); F. Powell, *The Politics of Irish Social Policy* (Edwin Mellen, Lewiston, 1992), Chap. 1.

[2] *The Poor Law Report of 1834* (S.G. and E.O.A. Checkland eds, Penguin, Harmondsworth, 1974); K. Williams, *From Pauperism to Poverty* (Routledge and Kegan Paul, London, 1981); G. Himmelfarb, *The Idea of Poverty* (Faber and Faber, London, 1984); A. Brundage, *The Making of the New Poor Law 1832–39* (Hutchinson, London, 1978).

significantly – largely from the fall in the population – and the numbers relying on the Poor Law fell up to the 1870s. From the 1870s on there was an intensified struggle between Irish tenants and their landlords. In the 1880s, arising both from economic conditions and from the increasing political agitation, the cost of outdoor relief increased significantly in nationalist-dominated Connacht and Munster, and the Local Government Board dissolved several boards of guardians.[3] In the late 1880s and early 1890s, Poor Law relief was tightened up and a programme of largely successful relief works was initiated instead, with the Congested Districts Board being established in 1891 with a long-term, developmental role. The 1898 reform of local government led to substantial changes in the structure of the boards of guardians, with the *ex officio* membership being abolished, and membership of the boards became the same as that of the newly established local authorities, with separate boards of guardians being retained in urban areas – elected on the same franchise as the new urban district councils.

7–04 By the turn of the century, the need for reform of the Poor Law system was becoming apparent. In Ireland, the Lord Lieutenant established a Viceregal Commission and this reported in 1906. The Commission's report was, to some extent, overshadowed by the appointment of a Royal Commission to investigate the Poor Laws. The Royal Commission published majority and minority reports in 1909. In brief, the majority favoured a reform of the existing Poor Law, the establishment of voluntary aid committees and a national system of labour exchanges, whereas the minority favoured breaking up the Poor Law into discrete services to support children, the sick, the mentally defective, the aged and infirm and so on.[4] No action had been taken to implement the reports of these Commissions when war broke out in 1914.

7–05 The outbreak of the Troubles in 1916 and the renewed conflict from 1919 significantly affected the Poor Law in Ireland. One of the key objectives of Sinn Féin was to establish a *de facto* state and one of the main areas in which it succeeded in doing so was in relation to the takeover of local government, including the Poor Law. Three issues came together, namely, Sinn Féin's desire to create a real state, the long recognised need for Poor Law reform, and the need for economy in local government caused by the withdrawal in 1920 of British financial support to local authorities. The Dáil ministry, in a relatively short period of time, carried through the most

---

[3] M. Daly, *The Buffer State: The Historical Roots of the Department of the Environment* (Institute of Public Administration, Dublin, 1997), p. 21.
[4] For a more detailed discussion see A.W. Vincent, "The Poor Law Reports of 1909 and the Social Theory of the Charity Organisation Society" in D. Gladstone ed., *Before Beveridge: Welfare before the Welfare State* (Institute of Economic Affairs, London, 1999).

fundamental reform of the Poor Law system, significantly reducing the number of workhouses, switching the emphasis from indoor to outdoor relief, and replacing the system of local Unions and boards of guardians with a county-based system.

7–06 The Cumman na nGeadheal Government introduced legislation to give formal legal effect to these reforms in the Local Government (Temporary Provisions) Act 1923. However, a very significant reform of the administration of relief was implemented by way of ministerial regulation in 1923. In place of the wide range of approaches set out in the original County Schemes, all the existing schemes were amended in June 1923 to bring them into a uniform order. This provided that County Boards of Health were to be established. Each area was to have a County Home for the Aged and Infirm and a County Hospital for medical, surgical and maternity cases. No person was to be relieved in an institution unless this could be done at less cost than in any other lawful way. Any new schemes subsequently approved also followed this standard approach so that by 1925 all counties except Dublin were now following a broadly uniform approach, at least in theory. A further standardisation of the administration of outdoor relief (or what became known as home assistance) was introduced in 1923 and 1924, whereby each Board of Health was to appoint a superintendent assistance officer and assistance officers whose duty it was to receive and investigate applications for assistance, which the superintendent then submitted to the Board of Health for its decision.

7–07 Fianna Fáil introduced an extensive Bill on reform of the home assistance legislation in 1939. The legislation was to consolidate the existing position rather than to bring forward new provisions. The legislation, which also applied to Dublin, largely codified the existing position, although the public assistance bodies now became the local county council rather than a committee of the council. This change formed part of the overall reform of local government.[5] The legislation did mark the last step in the change from direct "democratic" control of assistance payments to its replacement with bureaucratic decision-making. Decisions in relation to entitlement under the Poor Law were made by the (at least partially) elected board of guardians following investigation by relieving officers.[6] The County Board of Health (Assistance) Order 1924 provided that the superintendent assistance officers

---

[5] LXXVI *Dáil Debates* Cols 519–520 (June 6, 1939). See generally Daly, above, n.3.

[6] That this function was not simply nominal or one which could be delegated had been shown in the High Court case of *R. (O'Mahony) v. Ellis* [1898] 2 I.R. 57, in which the Fermoy guardians were surcharged by the Poor Law auditor because of their practice of only approving the first weekly payment of relief and of then simply retrospectively sanctioning payments already made by the relieving officer. The High Court held that the guardians must grant authority in each case *before* payments were made.

were to "receive, examine and investigate" all applications, which were then to be submitted to the public assistance authority for decision. However, this decision now became the function of the county manager.[7] Thus, in a period of just over 40 years, the administration of poor relief underwent a fundamental shift from being purely a matter for the elected guardians to a position, following the coming into effect of the County Management Act 1940, whereby elected members of the Boards of Assistance were excluded from the decision-making process on individual claims for home assistance.

7–08   Reform of public assistance did not form part of the 1949 White Paper and there were, in fact, few significant changes in the operation of the system in the period to the 1970s. The inadequacies of the system were highlighted in a study by Séamus Ó Cinnéide in the late 1960s and the old Poor Law system was finally abolished in 1975 and replaced by the supplementary welfare allowance – modelled on supplementary benefit in the United Kingdom.[8] The scheme was to be operated by the regional health boards on behalf of the Department rather than by the Department itself. This was intended as residual income support scheme for those who did not qualify for one of the main social welfare payments and it also included additional payments in relation to rent, emergencies and once-off needs. The economic downturn of the 1980s created considerable pressures on the scheme in the 1980s, although this has abated somewhat in more recent years. It should be noted that the Social Welfare Act 2000 allows the Minister to transfer the administration of certain supplementary welfare allowance payments from the health boards to the Department.[9] This provision has not been brought into effect at the time of writing. A major review of the objectives and operation of the scheme is ongoing at the time of writing.

2. Current Situation

A. Qualification Conditions

7–09   Section 171 of the Social Welfare (Consolidation) Act 1993 provides that subject to the Act, every person in the State whose means are insufficient to meet his or her needs and the needs of any qualified adult or child dependant shall be entitled to supplementary welfare allowance. Thus, subject to specific groups who are disqualified for SWA (see below), the only qualification condition to be satisfied is need. The needs of a person are be taken to be the

---

[7] County Management Act 1940 and Public Assistance (General Regulations) Order 1942.

[8] S. Ó Cinnéide, *A Law for the Poor* (Institute of Public Administration, Dublin, 1968).

[9] Social Welfare Act 2000 (SWA 2000), s. 41.

rate of SWA appropriate to that person (and his or her dependants).[10] Therefore, if the person has an income less than the current SWA rate, he or she will be entitled to payment.

7–10 Section 176 provides that a health board *may*, subject to Regulations, determine that a person shall not be entitled to supplementary welfare allowance unless: (a) he or she is registered for employment in such manner as the Minister may prescribe;[11] and (b) he or she makes application for any statutory or other benefits or assistance to which he or she may be entitled, including such benefits or assistance from countries other than the State.[12] It should be noted that this provision allows but does not require a board to oblige a person either to register for employment or make application for benefits. Clearly, a board should consider the specific circumstances in coming to a decision as to whether to exercise its discretion in each individual case. In addition, regulations provide that section 176(a) shall not apply to a person who satisfies the board that s/he is incapable of work due to some specific disease or bodily or mental disablement.[13]

B. Means Test

7–11 The means test is set out in Part III of the Third Schedule to SW(C)A 1993. The detailed provisions are set out below. It should be noted that the SWA means test is the strictest of those applying in the area of social welfare and that fewer disregards and concessions apply than in relation to the other two main means tests. In calculating the amount of supplementary welfare allowance payable to any person where (a) a husband and wife, or (b) a man and woman who are not married to each other but are cohabiting as husband and wife, are members of the same household, their needs and means are aggregated and are regarded as the needs and means of the claimant. In the case of a person with a child dependant, his or her needs are taken to include the needs of that child dependant. Where the needs of any person are taken into account in determining the entitlement of any other person to supplementary welfare allowance, only such other person is entitled to an allowance.[14]

---

[10] Social Welfare (Consolidation) Act 1993 (SW(C)A 1993), s. 177. The main provisions concerning SWA are set out in SW(C)A 1993, ss. 170–191 and in the Social Welfare (Consolidated Supplementary Welfare Allowance) Regulations 1995 (S.I. No. 382 of 1995) as amended (SW(CSWA)R 1995).

[11] SW(CSWA)R 1995, art. 8(2) prescribes that a person shall be required to prove unemployment in accordance with Regulations made under s. 120(1)(b), *i.e.* as in the case of unemployment assistance.

[12] The use of the word "entitled" implies that this provision does not extend to requiring persons to seek charitable support.

[13] SW(CSWA) 1995, art. 8.

[14] SW(C)A 1993, s. 177(2).

7–12 The means test provides that in calculating the weekly means of a person for supplementary welfare allowance, account shall be taken of the following rules.

(1) Rule 1(1)

7–13 All income in cash is taken into account, including the net cash value of any non-cash earnings derived from personal exertions and the actual or estimated amount of any household income, whether as contributions to the expenses of the household or otherwise. The following are excluded:

1(1)(a): any sums received by way of child benefit under Part IV;

1(1)(b): payments by a health board in respect of a child who is boarded out;

1(1)(bb): payments in respect of not more than two persons boarded out under section 10 of the Health (Nursing Homes) Act 1990 (insofar as the aggregate amount received in respect of each person does not exceed the maximum amount of the old age (non-contributory) pension)[15];

1(1)(c): in the case of a qualified applicant under a scheme administered by the Minister for the Gaeltacht and known as Scéim na bhFogh-laimeoirí Gaeilge, any income received under that scheme in respect of a person who is temporarily resident with the qualified applicant, together with any other income received in respect of such temporary resident;

1(1)(d): any sums received by way of allowance for domiciliary care of handicapped children under section 61 of the Health Act 1970;

1(1)(e): any sums arising from the investment or profitable use of property (not being property personally used or enjoyed by such person or a farm of land leased by him or her);

1(1)(f): any moneys received from a charitable organisation, being a body whose activities are carried on otherwise than for profit (but excluding any public or local authority) and one of whose functions is to assist persons in need by making grants of money to them;

1(1)(g): such amount, as may be prescribed, of income from employment by a health board or by a person approved by a health board, as a home help;

1(1)(h): any moneys received by way of a training allowance from an organisation while undergoing a course of rehabilitative training provided by an organisation approved by the Minister for Health and Children for the provision of such training;

---

[15] Inserted by SWA 2001, s.13.

1(1)(i): any moneys received by way of a mobility allowance payable under section 61 of the Health Act 1970, to the person;

1(1)(j): such income, as may be prescribed, arising from such activities as may be prescribed;

1(1)(k): any income arising from a grant or allowance under section 2 of the Blind Persons Act 1920 (*i.e.* blind welfare allowance);

1(1)(l): payments by a health board in respect of the provision of accommodation for a child under section 5 of the Child Care Act 1991;

1(1)(m): such amount, as may be prescribed, of earnings from employment of a rehabilitative nature (currently €120)[16];

1(1)(n): in such circumstances as may be prescribed, any moneys received by way of a maintenance grant under the Higher Education Grants scheme, the Maintenance Grants Scheme for Students attending Post-Leaving Certificate Courses, the Vocational Education Committees Scholarship Scheme, or the Third-Level Maintenance Scheme for Trainees[17];

1(1)(o): such other income received by a person or his or her spouse as may be prescribed[18];

1(1)(p): prescribed amount of rent supplement (see below, para. 7–30);

1(1)(q): any moneys received by his or her spouse in respect of participation in the Vocational Training Opportunities Scheme;

1(1)(r): any moneys received by his or her spouse in respect of participation in the Back to Work, Back to Education, or Part-time Job Initiative schemes;

1(1)(s): any moneys received by his or her spouse in respect of participation in a course approved by FÁS.

(2) Rule 1(2)[19]

7–14 The value of any property belonging to the person (not being property personally used or enjoyed by him or a farm of land leased by him or her) which is invested or is otherwise put to profitable use or which, though capable

---

[16] SW(CSWA)R 1995, art. 33 as inserted by S.I. No. 190 of 1996 and amended by S.I. No. 119 of 2002.

[17] Substituted by SWA 2001, s.13.

[18] Substituted by SWA 1997, s.26. Under this provision, compensation relating to Hepatitis C awarded by the Compensation Tribunal or a court and compensation relating to thalidomide are excluded from assessment as means. SW(CSWA)R 1995, art.34 as inserted by S.I. No. 334 of 1997.

[19] Amended by SWA 1996, s.37.

of investment or profitable use, is not invested or put to profitable use is taken into account. The yearly value of the first €507.90 of the property is taken to be 5 per cent of the capital value and the yearly value of so much of the capital value of the property as exceeds the sum of €507.90 is taken to be 10 per cent of the capital value. The weekly value of the property is calculated as one fifty-second part of the yearly value so calculated.

7–15 Regulations may modify these provisions in relation to the calculation of the yearly value of property.[20]

7–16 Thus, the more favourable disregards for capital which apply to most social welfare payments do not apply to SWA.

(3) Rule 1(3)[21]

7–17 The means of a person are deemed to include the value of any advantage accruing to the person from:

(a): the use or enjoyment of property (other than a domestic dwelling or a farm building owned and occupied, or furniture and personal effects) which is personally used or enjoyed by him or her; and

(b): the leasing by him or her of a farm of land.

(4) Rule 1(4)

7–18 The value of any benefit or privilege enjoyed by the person is taken into account.

(5) Rule 1(5)

7–19 All income and the value of all property of which the person has directly or indirectly deprived himself in order to qualify himself for the receipt of supplementary welfare allowance is taken into account.

7–20 Rule 2 provides that the Minister may vary the provisions of Rule 1 by Regulations. However, the provision must be interpreted in line with judicial decisions on the separation of powers.

---

[20] Rule 1(2A) as inserted by SWA 1996, s.37.
[21] Amended by SWA 1996. s.37.

C. Payments

(1) Weekly payments

7–21 SWA is payable at a flat rate, with increases for qualified adults and child dependants as appropriate.[22] The general definitions of qualified adult and qualified child do not apply to SWA. For the purposes of the SWA scheme, "qualified adult" is defined as: (a) the spouse of the beneficiary who is being wholly or mainly maintained by him or her; or (b) a person over the age of 16 years being wholly or mainly maintained by the beneficiary and having the care of one or more than one qualified child who normally resides with the beneficiary where the beneficiary is:

(i) a single person,

(ii) a widow,

(iii) a widower, or

(iv) a married person who is not living with and is neither wholly nor mainly maintaining, nor being wholly or mainly maintained by, such married person's spouse.[23]

7–22 "Child dependant" is defined as any child, not being a qualified child, who is dependent on that beneficiary for support and who is under the age of 18 years or is of or over the age of 18 and is regarded as attending a course of study within the meaning of section 126(3)(a), *i.e.* for the period of three months immediately following the completion or the leaving by that person of second-level education or the completion of the Leaving Certificate (whichever is the later).[24]

7–23 Section 177(2)(c) provides that where the needs of any person are take into account in determining the entitlement of any other person to SWA, only such other person shall be entitled to an allowance. As sections 177(2)(a) provides that where a husband and wife, or a man and woman who are not married to each other but are cohabiting as husband and wife, are members of the same household, their needs are aggregated, this means that – unlike other social welfare payments – only one SWA payment may be paid to a couple.

7–24 As SWA is often paid as an "interim" payment while a claim for a main social welfare payment is pending, where any SWA is paid to or in respect of a person who becomes entitled to a social welfare payment, the

---

[22] SW(C)A 1993, s. 178.

[23] *ibid.*, s. 170.

[24] *ibid.*, 170 as substituted by SWA 1994, s.23.

SWA is treated as having been paid "on account" and is deducted from any arrears of social welfare due to the person.[25]

(2) Weekly or monthly supplements

7–25 Section 179 provides that in the case of a person whose means are insufficient to meet his or her needs, Regulations may provide for a weekly or monthly payment to supplement that person's income.[26] The Regulations may prescribe the class(es) or persons to whom supplement may be paid and the conditions and circumstances in which a supplement may be paid. Supplements can be paid in relation to rent, mortgage, and diet costs and in "exceptional circumstances".

(3) Rent supplement

7–26 A person may be entitled to a supplement towards the amount of rent payable by him or her in respect of his or her residence. "Rent" is defined as any periodical payment in the nature of rent made in return for a special possession of a dwelling or for the use, occupation or enjoyment of a dwelling, but does not include so much of any rent or payment as: (a) relates to the provision of goods or services; (b) is paid or made to defray the cost of maintenance of, or repairs to, a dwelling for which in the absence of agreement to the contrary the tenant would be liable; or (c) relates to any right or benefit other than the bare right to use, occupy and enjoy the dwelling as a residence. "Residence" means a residential premises, other than an institution, that is used as the sole or main residence of the claimant where "residential premises" means a building or part of a building, used or suitable for use, as a dwelling and any land which the occupier of a building or part of a building used as a dwelling has for his own occupation and enjoyment with the said building or part thereof as its garden.[27]

7–27 Such entitlement is subject to a range of conditions in relation to the housing needs of the person.[28] In particular it is necessary that:

(a) he or she is a bona fide tenant;

(b) he or she has made application, on being so required by the health board,

---

[25] SW(C)A 1993, s. 184. The same approach applies in relation to persons who become entitled to payments from other E.U. countries; s. 184A as inserted by SWA 1995, s. 21.

[26] As amended by SW(C)A 1993, para. 3 of the Sixth Sched. with effect from January 1, 1996 replacing the previous s. 179, which arguably provided a direct statutory entitlement to a supplement where a person's means were insufficient to met his needs: see *State (McLoughlin) v. Eastern Health Board* [1986] I.R. 416.

[27] SW(CSWA)R 1995, art.3.

[28] *ibid.*, art.9.

to a housing authority to be assessed for a housing need under section 9 of the Housing Act 1988;

(c) his or her name has not been excluded from an assessment made by a housing authority pursuant to section 9 of the Housing Act 1988 by reason of failure to accept an offer of accommodation or if his or her name has been so excluded, the health board is satisfied that there was valid reason for the failure to accept such offer;

(d) he or she has not vacated accommodation provided by a housing authority or if he or she has vacated such accommodation, the health board is satisfied that he or she had good cause for so doing;

(e) he or she is not in receipt of, or entitled to, an allowance in accordance with regulations made under section 23 of the Housing (Private Rented Dwellings) Act 1982;

(f) the person beneficially entitled to the rent payable under the tenancy is not:
   (i) a housing authority,
   (ii) a health board,
   (iii) a body which provides services on behalf of, or similar or ancillary to, a health board using residential care staff and which receives a subvention from the Minister for Health in respect of the claimant, or
   (iv) a voluntary housing body which receives a subsidy under the scheme, known as the "rental subsidy scheme", administered by housing authorities under section 7 of the Housing (Miscellaneous Provisions) Act 1992;

(g) the health board is satisfied that:
   (i) the claimant is in need of accommodation and is unable to provide for it from his or her own resources,
   (ii) the residence is reasonably suited to the residential and other needs of the claimant, and
   (iii) the rent payable by the claimant is just and proper having regard to the nature, character and location of the residence and for this purpose the health board shall at such time and in respect of such class or classes of persons as the Minister may direct, determine the appropriate maximum amount of rent in respect of which a supplement is payable having regard to the family circumstances and the location of the residence of such persons, and

(h) where the person beneficially entitled to the rent payable under the tenancy is an approved body in receipt of assistance under the scheme of capital assistance for the provision of housing accommodation operated under section 6 of the Housing (Miscellaneous Provisions) Act 1992 and section 15 of the Housing Act 1988, the health board receives confirmation from the relevant housing authority that the rent has been fixed in accordance with the terms of the scheme.

7–28 The amount of a supplement payable – in the case of a person who has not reached 65 years of age – is the difference between the person's weekly needs (*i.e.* the appropriate rate of SWA to which he or she would be entitled), less a certain minimum rent payment (currently €7.62) and his or her weekly means, less the weekly amount of rent payable. In the case of a person aged 65 or over the amount of the supplement is €10 plus the difference between the person's weekly needs less €7.62 and his or her weekly means, less the weekly amount of rent payable. However, the amount is not to exceed such amount as the health board considers reasonable to meet the residential needs of the claimant. Where a person, other than a qualified adult or a child dependant, resides with the claimant other than as a sub-tenant, the health board is required to reduce the amount of the supplement payable, by such amount which in the opinion of the health board is reasonably attributable to that other person.[29]

7–29 Where the tenancy is with an approved body which is in receipt of assistance under the scheme of capital assistance, the maximum supplement payable is currently set at €40 for a couple or €37 in other cases. This is to take account of the fact that the capital costs of the building have been assisted by the State and that, therefore, the body should be in a position to charge a reduced rent.[30]

7–30 In order to provide an incentive for persons in receipt of rent supplement to take up employment, the means test for SWA was modified in the Social Welfare Act 2000 to provide that €50 per week was to be disregarded from the amount of income derived from net earnings from employment.[31]

7–31 Rent supplement payable can continue to be payable for the period in which the beneficiary resides continuously in the same residence. Any period of absence from the residence by virtue of temporary residence in an institution for any period which does not exceed 13 weeks is to be disregarded.[32]

---

[29] SW(CSWA)R 1995, art.12 as substituted by S.I. No. 101 of 2001 and amended by S.I. No. 653 of 2001.
[30] *ibid.*, art.13 as amended by S.I. No. 101 of 2001.
[31] Rule 1(1)(p) as inserted by SWA 2000, and SW(CSWA)R 1995, art.9(3) as inserted by S.I. No. 653 of 2000.
[32] SW(CSWA)R 1995, art.11.

(4) Mortgage interest supplement

7–32 A person may be entitled to a supplement towards the amount of mortgage *interest* payable by him or her in respect of his or her residence, provided that: (a) the loan agreement was entered into at a time when, in the opinion of the health board, the claimant was in a position to meet the repayments thereunder; and (b) the residence in respect of which the loan is payable is not offered for sale.[33] It should be noted that supplement is payable only on the amount of mortgage *interest* and not on capital repayments. "Mortgage interest" means such proportion of a loan as is for the time being attributable to interest, other than interest payable by virtue of a delay or default in making a repayment under the loan agreement, entered into by the claimant for the purpose of defraying money employed in the purchase, repair or improvement of a residence or in paying off another loan used for such purpose.[34] It is a condition of entitlement to a mortgage supplement that the health board is satisfied that: (a) the amount of the mortgage interest payable by the claimant does not exceed such amount as the health board considers reasonable to meet his or her residential and other needs; and (b) it is reasonable to award a supplement having regard to the amount of any arrears outstanding on the loan. However, a health board may award a supplement where the amount of mortgage interest payable by the claimant exceeds such "reasonable" amount for not more than 12 months from the date on which the claim is made.

7–33 The level of, and duration of, mortgage supplement is calculated in the same general manner as applies to rent supplement, as set out above.

(5) Diet supplement

7–34 A claimant is entitled to a supplement towards the cost of a specified diet which he or she or a qualified adult or child dependant has been prescribed by virtue of a specified medical condition.[35] The following diets are specified[36]:

(a) in the case of a person who is of or over the age of 18 years:
    (i) diabetic diet,
    (ii) low-fat, low-cholesterol diet,
    (iii) reducing (calorie-restricted) diet,
    (iv) high-fibre diet,
    (v) low-fat diet,

---

[33] SW(CSWA)R 1995, art.10. The defintion of "loan" in art.3 has been amended by S.I. No. 190 of 1996.
[34] *ibid.*, art.3.
[35] *ibid.*, art.15.
[36] *ibid.*, as amended by S.I. No. 190 of 1996.

    (vi) high-protein, high-calorie diet,
   (vii) gluten-free diet,
 (viii) low-protein, high-calorie diet,
   (ix) liquidised (altered consistencies) diet,
    (x) low-lactose, milk-free diet,
   (xi) high-protein, low-salt diet, and
  (xii) modified-protein high-calorie diet, and

(b) in the case of a person who is under the age of 18 years:
    (i) reducing (calorie-restricted) diet,
   (ii) high-fibre diet,
  (iii) low-fat diet,
  (iv) diabetic diet,
   (v) high-protein, high-calorie diet,
  (vi) gluten-free diet,
 (vii) low-protein, high-calorie diet,
(viii) low-lactose, milk-free diet,
  (ix) high-protein, low-salt diet.

7–35 It is a condition of any claimant's entitlement to a diet supplement that: (a) it is certified by a hospital consultant or registrar that the person or dependant has been prescribed a specified diet by virtue of a specified medical condition, or, in relation to the diets at (i), (ii) and (vii) that this has been specified by a registered medical practitioner; and (b) the nature and duration of the diet which has been prescribed is verified by the registered medical practitioner or by a qualified dietician.[37] A diet supplement is not payable for any period during which the person is in an institution.

7–36 For the purposes of diet supplement, a "child dependant" means any child, not being an adult dependant who is dependent on that claimant for support and who is: (a) under the age of 18 years; or (b) of or over the age of 18 years and under the age of 22 years and is receiving full-time education within the meaning of section 2(3).

7–37 The amount of supplement paid in respect of an adult or child dependant between the ages of 18 and 22, is either €34.28 or €44.44, and the amount of supplement in respect of a child under 18 years will be either €6.35 or €10.16 depending on the type of diet, less a proportion of the applicant's weekly income. The amount of any benefit or assistance paid in respect of a child dependant is not assessed as income when calculating a diet supplement in respect of an adult.

---

[37] SW(CSWA)R 1995, art.15(3) as amended by S.I. 190 of 1996, which also inserts a definition of "registered medical practitioner". "Qualified dietician", etc., is defined in SW(CSWA)R 1995.

(6) Exceptional circumstances

7–38 Finally, a health board may award a supplement in any case where it appears to the board that the circumstances of the case so warrant.[38] In particular, a board may award a supplement where: (a) a claimant is living alone or only with a qualified adult or child dependants and has, due to ill-health or infirmity or that of any of the persons living with him or her, exceptional needs by reason of having to maintain a high standard of heating in the residence; or (b) a claimant has exceptional needs other than those already specified in the 1995 Regulations.

(a) Exceptional needs payments

7–39 Section 181 provides that a health board may, in any case where it considers it reasonable, having regard to all the circumstances of the case, so to do, determine that supplementary welfare allowance shall be paid to a person by way of a single payment to meet an exceptional need. This discretionary provision allows health boards to make once-off payments to meet exceptional needs. The concept of "exceptional needs" is not defined in the legislation. Departmental guidelines state that payments would be for such items as: (a) special clothing in the case of a person who has a serious illness; (b) bedding or cooking utensils for someone setting up a home for the first time; or (c) costs in relation to funerals or visiting relatives in hospital or prison.

(b) Emergency payments

7–40 Section 182 provides that the general disqualification of students, full-time workers and persons affected by trade disputes set out in sections 172, 173 or 174 (see below) do not prevent the payment of supplementary welfare allowance in an urgent case. In addition, in determining whether an allowance is payable in an urgent case and the amount or nature of the allowance, the health board is allowed to disregard the conditions for the grant of SWA set out in section 176 and the normal means test where this appears to it to be inappropriate in the circumstances of the case. Thus, SWA payments may be made in an urgent case effectively to any person. This might apply, for example, were there flooding or a domestic fire and people who would not normally qualify for SWA required once-off assistance in cash or kind. However, where SWA is paid to a person who is engaged in remunerative full-time work, a

---

[38] SW(CSWA)R 1995, art.31. In *McDougall v. Secretary of State for Social Services* [1981] S.L.T. 259, the House of Lords held that a high cost of living in a particular area could never by itself amount to exceptional circumstances. In *Vaughan v. United Kingdom* (December 12, 1987), the European Commission of Human Rights held that a failure to provide a payment under the supplementary benefits scheme to meet the applicant's travel costs to see his children was not in breach of Art. 8 of the European Convention on Human Rights.

health board may, if it is satisfied that in all the circumstances of the case it would be equitable so to do, determine that the whole or part of the allowance is to be recoverable from that person.[39]

(c) Benefits in kind

7–41   Section 180 provides that whenever it appears to a health board that by reason of exceptional circumstances the needs of a person can best be met by the provision of "goods or services" instead of the payment to which the person would otherwise be entitled, the health board may determine that such goods or services be provided for him or her under arrangements made by the board. In making a determination under this section to meet sudden and urgent need, the health board may dispense with inquiry into means or other circumstances and with compliance with any regulations.

(d) Burials

7–42   A health board may provide for the burial of: (a) a person who died within the functional area of the health board and in respect of whose burial suitable arrangements are not otherwise being made; and (b) a person who has been drowned and cast ashore within its functional area or who has otherwise perished and been found dead within that area and whose body has not been claimed for burial.[40]

7–43   In addition, a health board may, in any case in which it thinks proper, bring into and bury in its functional area the body of a person eligible for supplementary welfare allowance who has died outside such functional area. A health board may defray all expenses necessarily incurred in the burial under this section of a person or in the bringing of the body of a person into its functional area for burial.

7–44   Where a health board incurs expenses in relation to the body of a deceased person, it may obtain repayment of such expenses from the estate of the deceased person or from any person who was liable to maintain the deceased person immediately before his death. These provisions are in addition to the payment of once-off payments in respect of funeral expenses under section 181.

D. Disqualifications

7–45   Three groups of people are specifically excluded from entitlement to

---

[39] SW(C)A 1993, s. 182(2).
[40] *ibid.*, s. 185.

SWA (other than in exceptional circumstances), namely, students, persons in remunerative full-time work, and persons involved in a trade dispute.

7–46 Section 172 provides that a person shall not be entitled to receive supplementary welfare allowance while attending a course of study (within the meaning of section 126) other than in such circumstances and subject to such conditions as may be prescribed.[41] "Course of study" means a full-time day course of study, instruction or training at any institution of education.[42] A person is regarded as attending a course of study for three months immediately following the completion of second-level education or the completion of the Leaving Certificate (whichever is later), for the duration of the academic year (including term vacations), or for the period immediately following the completion of one academic year (other than the final academic year). This disqualification does not apply to mature students or to students on a Vocational Training Opportunities Scheme, the Back to Education scheme, or such other course of education as approved by the Minister.[43] This disqualification is without prejudice to the entitlement of any person to receive supplementary welfare allowance in respect of a qualified adult or child dependant.[44] Notwithstanding subsection (1), supplementary welfare allowance may, where there are *exceptional circumstances*, be granted to a person who would be entitled to receive supplementary welfare allowance but for that subsection.[45]

7–47 Section 173 provides that a person shall not, other than in such circumstances and subject to such conditions as may be prescribed, be entitled to supplementary welfare allowance in relation to any period during which he or she is engaged in remunerative full-time work.[46] The SWA Regulations state that a person will be regarded as being involved in full-time work where he or she is so engaged for not less than 30 hours in a week.[47] However,

---

[41] As amended by SWA 1994, s.24.

[42] SW(C)A 1993, s. 126. "Institute of education" means a school, university or college of a university, an institution of higher education designated under the Higher Education Authority Act 1971, any institution to which the National Council for Education Awards Act 1979 applies, any institution established under the Regional Technical Colleges Act 1992, any institution incorporated under the Dublin Institute of Technology Act 1992, any other institution to which the Local Authorities (Higher Education Grants) Acts 1968 to 1992 apply, and any other institution as may be prescribed.

[43] SW(CSWA)R 1995, art.7

[44] SW(C)A 1993, s. 172(2).

[45] *ibid.*, s. 173(3).

[46] As amended by SWA 1994, s.25. The U.K. courts have consistently held that in the case of self-employment, "remunerative" means "paid" rather than "profitable": *Perrot v. Supplementary Benefits Commission* [1980] All E.R. 110; *Smith v. Chief Adjudication Officer*, reported in R(IS) 21/91; *Chief Adjudication Officer v. Ellis*, reported in R(IS) 22/95. This approach does not appear to be followed in practice in this jurisdiction.

[47] SW(CSWA)R 1995, art.6(3)

subsection (2) provides that the Minister may by Regulations provide for the postponement of the operation of subsection (1) in respect of any class of persons becoming engaged in remunerative full-time work until such period after the commencement of the engagement as may be specified in the Regulations. This power has been exercised to allow persons who take up employment to continue to be eligible for SWA for a 30-day period after taking up employment or the date of which he or she receives remuneration, whichever is earlier (to allow for possible delays in being paid by an employer).[48] In addition, persons engaged in remunerative full-time work while participating in the Back to Work scheme or in community employment are also not disqualified for SWA. Section 173 (3) provides that subsection (1) does not apply in the case of any person engaged in remunerative full-time work where the earning power of such person is, by reason of any physical or mental disability, substantially reduced in comparison with the earning power of other persons engaged in similar work.

7–48 Finally, section 174 provides that in any case where, by reason of a stoppage of work due to a trade dispute at his or her place of employment, a person is without employment for any period during which the stoppage continues, and such person has not, during that stoppage, become bona fide employed elsewhere in the occupation which he or she usually follows, or has not become regularly engaged in some other occupation, his or her needs for that period shall be disregarded for the purpose of ascertaining his or her entitlement to supplementary welfare allowance, except in so far as such needs include the need to provide for his or her adult or child dependants. This exclusion is similar to that which applies in relation to unemployment assistance.[49] This disqualification does not apply to any person who is not participating in or directly interested in the trade dispute which caused the stoppage of work.[50]

7–49 "Place of employment" means the factory, workshop, farm or other premises or place at which the person was employed, but, where separate branches of work which are commonly carried on as separate businesses in separate premises or at separate places are in any case carried on in separate departments on the same premises or at the same place, each of those departments shall, for the purposes of this section, be deemed to be a separate factory or workshop or farm or separate premises or a separate place, as the case may be.

---

[48] SW(CSWA)R 1995, art.6
[49] See the discussion at paras 6–28 and 6–55.
[50] SW(C)A 1993, s. 174(2).

7–50 In addition, the general disqualifications in relation to residence, temporarily or permanently, outside the State or the undergoing of penal servitude, imprisonment or detention in legal custody apply to SWA.[51]

---

[51] See SW(CSWA)R 1995, Sched. B.

CHAPTER 8

Social Welfare and Family Structures

8–01 This chapter provides an overview of the manner in which social welfare payments relate to family structures and the extent to which the Irish Constitution and the European Convention on Human Rights influence the treatment of different types of family. It looks in detail at the manner in which increases are payable in respect of qualified adults. Social welfare support for particular "family" contingencies – such as lone parenthood and caring – is outlined in subsequent chapters.

1. Background

8–02 The treatment of families and households under the social welfare code is a matter of ongoing importance in all countries. This is particularly the case in Ireland, where there have been very significant changes in the composition of households and an increase in the number of married women and women with children in the paid labour force. The role of the Constitution is also of particular importance in an Irish context.

A. Constitutional Provisions

8–03 Article 41 of the Constitution, entitled "The Family", provides in relevant part that:

"1.1° The State recognises the Family as the natural primary and fundamental unit group of Society, and as a moral institution possessing inalienable and imprescriptible rights, antecedent and superior to all positive law.

2° The State, therefore, guarantees to protect the Family in its constitution and authority, as the necessary basis of social order and as indispensable to the welfare of the Nation and the State.

2. 1° In particular, the State recognises that by her life within the home, woman gives to the State a support without which the common good cannot be achieved.

2° The State shall, therefore, endeavour to ensure that mothers shall not be obliged by economic necessity to engage in labour to the neglect of their duties in the home.

3. 1° The State pledges itself to guard with special care the institution of

Marriage, on which the Family is founded, and to protect it against attack ..."

8–04 While the provisions of Article 41.2 in relation to women's "life within the home" have not received any detailed judicial consideration, the general recognition of the family based on marriage has received extensive judicial consideration, including a number of cases specifically in relation to social welfare.[1] In *Hyland v. Minister for Social Welfare*,[2] the Supreme Court held that a provision of the Social Welfare Acts which treated an unmarried couple more favourably than a married couple was a breach of the positive obligation cast upon the State by Article 41.3.1°. However, in *Mhic Mathúna v. Ireland*,[3] the Supreme Court held that the provision of specific social welfare benefits for unmarried mothers was not in beach of the Constitution and that there were abundant grounds for distinguishing between the needs and requirements of single parents and those of married parents living and rearing a family together.

8–05 The *Hyland* case arose from a reform of the social welfare code resulting from the implementation of the E.U. Directive on equal treatment in social welfare (discussed in Chapter 9). Prior to the enactment of the Social Welfare (No. 2) Act 1985, married women were generally not allowed to claim unemployment assistance unless their husbands were incapable of self-support. The E.U. Directive required the removal of this discriminatory provision. However, the 1985 Act imposed a limitation on the amount of social welfare which an unemployed married couple might receive. This limitation did not apply to an unmarried couple. The applicant argued that this limitation on the entitlements of a married couple constituted a failure by the State to carry out its obligations under Article 41.3.1°. Unsurprisingly, given the clear evidence that an unmarried couple in the same situation would have been financially better off, the Supreme Court agreed and held that the limitation was in breach of the Constitution.[4]

8–06 However, the courts were less willing to find unconstitutionality where a claim involved a much more complex comparison between the tax and welfare benefits provided by the State to a married couple and the benefits

---

[1] See generally G. Hogan and G. Whyte, *The Irish Constitution* (Butterworths, Dublin, 2002).

[2] [1989] I.R. 624. See also the similar approach in *H. v. Eastern Health Board* [1988] I.R. 747, a case involving a similar provision in relation to disabled person's maintenance allowance.

[3] [1995] 1 I.R. 484.

[4] In the event the Oireachtas chose to impose a similar limitation on unmarried couples rather than to remove the limitation on married couples.

provided to an unmarried parent. In *Mhic Mathúna*, the applicants contended that the overall state policy in relation to supports for a married couple with children *vis-à-vis* an unmarried parent constituted invidious discrimination against them (as a married couple with children) and was in breach of the constitutional provisions. In particular, they challenged the abolition of general tax allowances in respect of children. However, Finlay C.J., speaking for the Supreme Court, held that there were abundant grounds for distinguishing between the needs and requirements of single parents and those of married parents living apart and rearing a family together. Once just a justification existed, the Court was satisfied that it could not interfere by seeking to assess what the extent of the disparity should be.[5]

8–07 The Court did state that it was clearly conceivable that under certain circumstances statutory provisions, particularly those removing in its entirety financial support for the family, could constitute a beach of the constitutional duty of the State under Article 41. However, no such "total removal of support" arose in this case. Rather, it was contended that the level of support had become insufficient. However, Finlay C.J. pointed out that social welfare provisions were not the only means of financial support for children provided by the State and that state contributions to free education, medical services and other matters would also have to be considered in deciding whether the level of support was a proper discharge of the constitutional duty. In addition, the Chief Justice stated that there was also the "vital question" as to whether the level of support was appropriate "bearing in mind the other constitutional duties of the State and the other demands properly to be made upon the resources of the State".[6] These matters were peculiarly "within the field of national policy to be decided by a combination of the executive and the legislature that cannot be adjudicated upon by the courts".[7]

8–08 Thus, the lesson from the case law would appear to be that the courts would find a breach of the Constitution where a married couple is treated less favourably than an unmarried couple in the same circumstances. However, the courts would be much slower to attempt to interfere where there are clear grounds for distinguishing between the circumstances of a married couple and a comparator such as a single parent. Finally, while Finlay C.J. suggested that there could be circumstances in which the courts would hold that a total removal of state financial support for the family was in breach of the Constitution, the numerous *caveats* which followed that statement indicate that it would only be exceptionally, if at all, that the courts would make such a finding.

---

[5] [1995] 1 I.R. 484 at 499.
[6] *ibid.*
[7] *ibid.*

B. European Convention on Human Rights

8–09 The European Convention on Human Rights also includes provisions relevant to the family. In particular, Article 8 of the Convention provides that:

"1. Everyone has the right to respect for his private and family life ...

2. There shall be no interference by a public authority with the exercise of this right except such as is in accordance with the law and is necessary in a democratic society in the interests of ... the economic well-being of the country ..."

8–10 Article 8 has been considered in a number of social security cases. In *Petrovic v. Austria*[8] the applicant argued that an Austrian law which entitled mothers to a parental leave allowance but gave no such entitlement to fathers was in breach of Article 14 (non-discrimination) taken with Article 8. The applicant argued that financial assistance enabling parents to stop working in order to look after their children affected family life and therefore came within the scope of Article 8, whereas Austria argued that it was not within the scope of Article 8 as that Article did not contain any general obligation to provide financial support to parents in these circumstances and that it was a matter of welfare policy which was not to be included within the concept of family life. The Court agreed that Article 8 in itself did not impose any positive obligation on states to provide a parental leave allowance.[9] However, the Court held that the allowance was intended to promote family life and necessarily affected the way in which the latter was organised as, in conjunction with parental leave, it enabled one of the parents to stay at home to look after the children.

8–11 The Court held that Article 14 came into play whenever "the subject-matter of the disadvantage ... constitutes one of the modalities of the exercise of a right guaranteed" or where the measures complained of were "linked to the exercise of a right guaranteed". It ruled that by granting parental leave allowance states were able to demonstrate their respect for family life within the meaning of Article 8 of the Convention; the allowance therefore came within the scope of that provision. Accordingly, it fell to be decided whether the different treatment of men and women was in breach of Article 14.[10] Under

---

[8] (1988) 33 E.H.R.R. 14.

[9] In general, it has been held that the right of respect for family life does not impose an obligation on states to provide financial assistance to ensure that individuals can enjoy family life to the fullest: *Vaughan v. United Kingdom*, December 12, 1997.

[10] The Court has consistently held that Article 14 complements the other substantive provisions of the Convention and has no independent existence since it has effect solely in relation to "the enjoyment of the rights and freedoms" safeguarded by those provisions. Although the application of Article 14 does not presuppose a breach of those provisions – and to this extent it is autonomous – there can be no room for its application unless the facts at issue fall within the ambit of one or more of the latter.

the Court's case law, a difference in treatment was discriminatory for the purposes of Article 14 if it "has no objective and reasonable justification", that is if it did not pursue a "legitimate aim" or if there was not a "reasonable relationship of proportionality between the means employed and the aim sought to be realised".[11]

8–12   The applicant argued that the different treatment of mothers and fathers with regard to parental leave allowance was not justified at all. The allowance was not intended to protect mothers as it was not paid until eight weeks after the birth and until the right to receive maternity benefit had been exhausted, but to assist parents – whether mothers or fathers – who wished to take leave to look after their very young children.

8–13   Austria submitted that the fact that there was no common European standard in the matter meant that the decision to pay a parental leave allowance only to mothers fell within the margin of appreciation left to states in respect of welfare policy. Furthermore, the provisions in question reflected the outlook of society at the time, according to which the mothers had the primary role in looking after young children.

8–14   The Court noted that at the time parental leave allowances were paid only to mothers, not to fathers, once a period of eight weeks had elapsed after the birth and the right to a maternity allowance had been exhausted. Maternity leave and the associated allowances were primarily intended to enable the mother to recover from the fatigue of childbirth and to breastfeed her baby if she so wished. Parental leave and the parental leave allowance, on the other hand, related to the period thereafter and were intended to enable the beneficiary to stay at home to look after the infant personally. While aware of the differences which may exist between mother and father in their relationship with the child, the Court started from the premise that so far as taking care of the child during this period was concerned, both parents were "similarly placed". The Court stated that the advancement of the equality of the sexes was a major goal in the Member States of the Council of Europe and very weighty reasons would be needed for such a difference in treatment to be regarded as compatible with the Convention.[12] However, the Court noted that states enjoyed a certain margin of appreciation in assessing whether and to what extent differences in otherwise similar situations justified a different treatment in law. The scope of the margin of appreciation would vary according to the circumstances, the subject matter and its background; in this respect,

---

[11] *Petrovic*, above, n.8, at para. 30.
[12] Citing *Schuler-Zgraggen v. Switzerland*, June 24, 1993, Series A no. 263, pp. 21–22, and *Van Raalte v. The Netherlands* (1997) 24 E.H.R.R. 503.

one of the relevant factors might be the existence or non-existence of common ground between the laws of the states.

8–15 At the material time, that is at the end of the 1980s, there was no common standard in this field, as the majority of the Contracting States did not provide for parental leave allowances to be paid to fathers. The Court took the view that the idea of the state giving financial assistance to the mother or the father so that the parent concerned could stay at home to look after the children was relatively recent and that welfare measures of this sort were primarily intended to protect mothers and to enable them to look after very young children. Only gradually, as society has moved towards a more equal sharing between men and women of responsibilities for the bringing up of their children, had states introduced measures extending to fathers, such as entitlement to parental leave. The Court therefore found it difficult to criticise the Austrian legislature for having introduced in a gradual manner, reflecting the evolution of society in that sphere, legislation which was, all things considered, very progressive in Europe. The Court noted that there still remained a very great disparity between the legal systems of the Contracting States in this field. While measures to give fathers an entitlement to parental leave had been taken by a large number of states, the same was not true of the parental leave allowance, which only a very few states granted to fathers. The Court ruled, therefore, that Austria's refusal to grant the applicant a parental leave allowance had not exceeded the margin of appreciation allowed to them and, consequently, the difference in treatment complained of was not discriminatory within the meaning of Article 14.

8–16 In recent cases before the European Court of Human Rights it has been argued that the failure to provide a pension to a widower and to the surviving member of an unmarried couple living together as man and wife (where a pension was paid to a widow) was in breach of Article 8.[13] However, in both cases, the Court decided the cases on the basis of Article 14 and did not give detailed consideration to the Article 8 argument. Article 8 may have implications for the operation of the liable relatives provisions considered in Chapter 11.

2. Legislation and Practice

8–17 The concepts of "family" and "household" are not specifically defined in relation to social welfare payments.[14] However, both are of fundamental

---

[13] *Shackell v. United Kingdom*, April 27, 2000; *Willis v. United Kingdom* (2002) 35 E.H.R.R. 21.
[14] There is a specific definition of family in relation to the family income supplement: see Social Welfare (Consolidation) Act 1993 (SW(C)A 1993), s. 197.

importance to the operation of the social welfare code. In practice, varying concepts of both family and household are utilised in different parts of the social welfare system. In some cases, entitlement to a payment is entirely unrelated to whether or not the claimant is living alone or as part of any particular family or household type. In other cases, the circumstances of a spouse or partner and any children may be taken into account. In other cases again, the circumstances of broader family members (*e.g.* parents or step-parents) may be relevant.

8–18 In the following sections we look at three key issues in relation to family structures: first, the extent to which the basic payment varies in accordance with a person's membership of a family[15]; secondly, the extent to which benefits are increased to meet the needs of other family members; and, finally, the extent to which a person's payment may be reduced because he or she is a member of a family or household.[16]

A. Payment to Individuals/Family Members

8–19 The earliest social welfare payment, the Poor Law, was intended to provide a minimum means of support to persons unable to support themselves through work. Support was provided on a family basis but no specific rates were set for families of different sizes. This payment was means-tested and, with a view to enforcing the subsidiary nature of the support and to keeping the cost to a minimum, members of the immediate and extended family were liable to repay to the boards of guardians any support paid to a claimant. Under the Poor Relief (Ireland) Act 1838 husbands were liable to support their wives and children up to the age of 15; fathers, widows and unmarried parents were liable to support their children; and children were liable to support their parents.

8–20 Social insurance payments, introduced in 1911, were, in contrast, paid without a means test and regardless of the income of other members of the family. This was based on the assumption that the occurrence of one of the contingencies insured against (unemployment and illness) was, for the class of insured persons, a very good indicator of lack of income. However, this assumption was not applied in the same way to all persons. Reflecting the fact that women generally received a lower level of earnings, lower rates of

---

[15] As will be seen, no such variation now exists.

[16] The policy issues in relation to the social welfare treatment of families and households have been addressed in a number of recent reports including, the Household Review Group (1991) , the Commission on the Family (1997), and the Working Group on the Treatment of Married, Cohabiting and One-Parent Families under the Tax and Social Welfare Codes (1999).

sickness benefits were payable to women – although the same rate was payable to men and women in relation to unemployment and disablement benefit. Unmarried persons aged under 21 were assumed to have lower needs and thus received reduced rates of sickness benefit unless such a person proved that members of his or her family were wholly dependent on him or her.[17] Married women received reduced entitlement to benefits on marriage unless they continued to be employed in insurable employment. Over time, however, these distinctions have been removed so that there is now one flat rate of payment to all persons regardless of age or sex (see Chapter 9).[18]

B. Payment for Dependants

8–21 Two different approaches were taken in the early social welfare schemes to ensure that the breadwinner's social welfare income was sufficient to support not only himself but also any dependants.[19] The first was the payment of an earnings-related benefit. Here the claimant was paid a large proportion of his previous wage on the assumption that this would be sufficient to support him and any dependants. This system applied under the workmen's compensation scheme and continued in Ireland up to the 1960s. This approach has been followed in many continental countries. However, the Beveridge report opted for flat-rate benefits, with the payment of adult dependency increases. This approach, initiated as an emergency measure in 1918 and gradually extended to most social welfare schemes, was followed in the Irish White Paper in 1949. However, while a married woman was assumed to be dependent on her husband, an increase was only payable in respect of a married man if it could be shown that he was unable to support himself because of physical or mental infirmity and, consequently, was dependent on his wife.

8–22 These different rules in relation to dependency for men and women could not be continued in the light of the E.U. Directive on equal treatment and, as a result, a factual test of dependency was introduced in 1986 (see below). In 1997, adult dependants were renamed as qualified adults, but without any underlying change in the legislation.

---

[17] Unemployed persons aged 17 were paid at half the standard rate, which was payable from the age of 18.

[18] There are still variations between the amount of welfare paid to different categories of claimant and claimants over pension age receive higher rates of payment.

[19] The structure of social welfare support in relation to children is discussed in Chap. 13. The focus here is on adult dependants.

C. Payments to "Assumed Dependants"

8–23   The other side of this coin is the extent to which the social welfare payment of a claimant is reduced because of the fact that he or she is a member of a family or household. As we have seen above, there is no longer any variation in the basic rate of payment on the basis of such membership. However, in a number of circumstances, that basic rate may be reduced in the case of means-tested payment.

8–24   The social insurance system generally (albeit implicitly) adopts the concept of the immediate family as the relevant unit. The only persons taken into account are the husband and wife (or cohabitees) and any children. Social insurance payments are payable on an individual basis and are not reduced because of membership of an immediate or extended family (although, as we have seen, they may be increased where the immediate family includes "dependants").

8–25   In relation to social assistance, or means-tested payments, however, a varied approach is taken. A person's entitlement to, or level of, payment is affected by a number of different family circumstances, in particular:

(1) Marriage – In the case of a married person, the income of the spouse will normally be taken into account as means.

(2) Cohabitation – In the case of lone parents payments (*e.g.* one-parent family payment (OFP)), cohabitation with another person as man and wife acts as a total bar to payment (see Chapter 11). In relation to unemployment assistance (UA), cohabitation results in the cohabitee's income, if any, being taken into account in the same way as if the couple were married.

(3) Couple limitation – In the case of UA, a limitation applies to payment to a couple (whether married or cohabiting) whereby if both qualify for unemployment assistance (or a range of other payments), they will not receive two full rates but instead will be limited to the amount which would have been payable if one person claimed for the other as a qualified adult (about 1.7 times the personal rate).

(4) Benefit and privilege – In the case of supplementary welfare allowance (SWA) and UA, the concept of the extended family or household has been retained by way of the "benefit and privilege" rule. This forms part of the means test and provides that the value of any "benefit and privilege" enjoyed by the person is to be taken into account. This is not statutorily defined. However, departmental guidelines state that, in the case of UA, where a person is living with a parent or step-parent in the family home, an assessment will be made of the benefit and privilege derived from the parents' income. This will not be assessed where the person is living with

other relatives or with non-relatives. In addition, the "benefit and privilege" rule is not applied where a married child is living with his or her parents. Thus, in this case, the concept of an extended family is applicable. The "benefit and privilege" rule does not apply to most other means-tested payments such as disability allowance and OFP.

8–26 Thus, in the case of most means-tested payments, the person's personal rate of payment may be reduced because of membership of an immediate or extended family. However, the precise manner in which this is done varies from payment to payment and the detailed treatment is outlined in the chapters which deal with each payment. We go on, in this chapter, to look at the rules in relation to payment of an increase in respect of a qualified adult.

3. Current Situation

A. Increase for a Qualified Adult

8–27 In the case of most weekly social welfare payments, an increase is payable where the claimant has a qualified adult. This entitlement is provided for in the sections of the Acts dealing with the individual payment.[20] Old age (non-contributory) pension and blind pension have different rules which are outlined in Chapter 3. A somewhat different approach also applies in relation to SWA (see Chapter 7). An increase in respect of a qualified adult (IQA) is not payable with carer's allowance or benefit or with maternity benefit. IQAs are not payable with the lone parents and widow(er)'s payments.

8–28 Section 2(2) of SW(C)A 1993, as amended, defines "qualified adult", subject to sections 114 (bereavement grant), 170 (SWA), and 245A (tapered IQAs), as meaning, in relation to any person:

(a) a spouse who is wholly or mainly maintained by that person but does not include:

(i) a spouse in employment (other than subsidiary employment or employment of inconsiderable extent as specified in paragraph 4 or 5 of Part II of the First Schedule); or

(ii) a spouse who is self-employed; or

(iii) a spouse who is entitled to, or is in receipt of, any benefit, pension, assistance or allowance (other than supplementary welfare allowance) under Parts II or III of the Act[21]; or

---

[20] For example, entitlement to an IQA in the case of disability benefit is set out in SW(C)A 1993, s. 34.

[21] Amended by the Social Welfare Act 1995 (SWA 1995), s. 15 and SWA 1996, s. 15.

(iv) a spouse who, by virtue of the provisions of section 47(1) or 125(3) relating to trade disputes, is or would be disqualified for receiving unemployment benefit or assistance in his or her own right, with the exception of a spouse who qualifies as a qualified adult by virtue of Regulations made under paragraph (c); or

(v) a spouse who is entitled to or is in receipt of an allowance the rate of which is related to the rates of unemployment assistance or benefit payable in respect of a non-craft full-time course approved by FÁS under the Industrial Training Act 1967; or

(vi) a spouse who is entitled to or in receipt of an allowance in respect of participation in the Vocational Training Opportunities Scheme; or

(vii) a spouse who is entitled to or in receipt of an allowance in respect of participation in the Back to Education Allowance, Back to Work Allowance, or Part-time Job Incentive[22];

or

(b) a person over the age of 16 years who is wholly or mainly maintained by that person and having the care of one or more than one qualified child who normally resides with that person where that person is: (i) a single person, (ii) a widow, (iii) a widower, or (iv) a married person who is not living with and is neither wholly or mainly maintaining, nor being wholly or mainly maintained by, such married person's spouse; or

(c) such person as the Minister may by Regulations specify to be a qualified adult for the purposes of the Act.

8–29 For the purposes of determining entitlement to an IQA, references to "spouse" are construed as including: (a) a party to a marriage that has been validly dissolved; or (b) a man and a woman who are not married to each other but are cohabiting as husband and wife.[23]

8–30 Section 2(2)(a) would have meant that any person who was in employment (other than subsidiary employment or employment of inconsiderable extent) or self-employment or in receipt of most social welfare payments was not classified as a qualified adult, even if he or she was "wholly or mainly maintained" by the claimant. However, in exercise of the power provided under section 2(2)(c), Regulations provide a spouse who is wholly or mainly maintained by a person is, subject to sections 170 and 245A, to be a qualified adult in relation to that person, where the spouse is:

---

[22] Amended by SWA 2001, s. 24.
[23] SW(C)A 1993, s. 3(13) as substituted by SWA(No. 2) 1995, s. 10.

"(a) in employment or self-employment, or

(b) entitled to or in receipt of disablement benefit, death benefit, orphan's (contributory) allowance, orphan's (non-contributory) pension and to no other benefit or assistance (other than supplementary welfare allowance)."[24]

8–31 A person (who is a member of a married couple living together or who is one of a man and woman not married to each other but cohabiting as husband and wife) is considered to be wholly or mainly maintaining his or her spouse where that spouse's weekly income does not exceed €88.88.[25] A person who is one of a married couple not living together is considered to be wholly or mainly maintaining his or her spouse where that spouse is not cohabiting with another person as husband and wife, where that spouse's weekly income does not exceed €88.88, and where the person is contributing towards the maintenance of his or her spouse by a weekly amount which is equal to or in excess of the amount of the IQA payable with unemployment assistance. Thus, this provision brings within the definition of qualified adult a person who is in employment or self-employment but whose income does not exceed €88.88 per week and who is wholly or mainly maintained by the claimant (as defined above). It also brings in persons who are in receipt of the limited number of social welfare payments with specific purposes outlined in Article 6(b).

8–32 A person who is: (i) a single person; (ii) a widow; (iii) a widower; or (iv) a married person who is not living with and is neither wholly or mainly maintaining, nor being wholly or mainly maintained by, his or her spouse, is considered to be wholly or mainly maintaining another person where that other person, being over the age of 16 years and having the care of one or more than one qualified child of the first-mentioned person, resides with the first-mentioned person and his or her weekly income does not exceed €88.88. This provision provides a definition of "wholly or mainly maintaining" for the purposes of section 2(2)(b).

8–33 Weekly income is calculated as follows:

(a) insofar as it comprises earnings from employment as an employee, by reference to the weekly average of the gross amount of all such earnings received in the previous two months where earnings are received monthly, or in the previous six weeks where earnings are received weekly or fortnightly;

---

[24] Social Welfare (Consolidated Payments Provisions) Regulations 1994 (SW(CPP)R 1994), art. 6 as amended by S.I. No. 95 of 1996.
[25] SW(CPP)R 1994, art. 6A, as inserted by S.I. No. 95 of 1996.

(b) insofar as it comprises income from any form of self-employment, by reference to the weekly amount of such income calculated by dividing the income in the last complete income tax year by 52;

(c) insofar as it consists of income from property (other than property referred to in paragraph (d)) which is invested or otherwise put to profitable use or is capable of being but is not invested or put to profitable use, by reference to one 52nd part of the yearly value of the property, calculated as follows:
  (i) the first €12,697.38 of the capital value of the property shall be excluded;
  (ii) the weekly value of so much of the capital value of the property as exceeds €12,697.38 but does not exceed €25,394.76 shall be assessed at €1.27 per each €1,269.74; and
  (iii) the weekly value of so much of the capital value of the property as exceeds €25,394.76 but does not exceed €38,092.14 shall be assessed at €2.54 per each €1,269.74; and
  (iv) the weekly value of so much of the capital value of the property as exceeds €38,092.14 shall be assessed at €5.08 per each €1,269.74, and

(d) insofar as it consists of income from any other source (including rent or any other periodical payment receivable for the possession and use of property in all lands, tenements and hereditaments), by reference to the normal weekly amount of such income.[26]

8–34 In calculating this weekly income, any sums received by way of disablement benefit, death benefit, child benefit, orphan's (contributory) allowance or orphan's (non-contributory) pension, or sums received by way of domiciliary care allowance, are disregarded. A deciding officer or appeals officer who considers that the periods mentioned above would not be appropriate in any case to determine the amount of weekly income may have regard to such other period which appears to be appropriate for that purpose.

8–35 Thus, the definition of "qualified adult" covers three different groups of person: (i) spouses (including cohabitees) who are wholly or mainly dependent on the claimant (subject to the list of exclusions set out above, including those in employment, self-employment or in receipt of social welfare and certain other allowances); (ii) a person over 16 who is caring for the claimant's child(ren); and (iii) spouses specified by Regulations to be qualified

---

[26] SW(CPP)R 1994, art. 6B as inserted by S.I. No. 95 of 1996 and amended by S.I. No. 81 of 2000.

adults, *i.e.* persons wholly or mainly maintained by the claimant who are in employment or self-employment but are earning less than €88.88 per week.

8–36 In the case of section 2(2)(b), a lower age limit of 16 is provided. However, no specific age limit is set in relation to subsections (a) and (c). Departmental guidelines suggest that while social welfare legislation does not specify the age a person has to be in order to be considered a qualified adult, it is reasonable for deciding officers to refuse to award an IQA for a person under the age of 18 on the basis that he or she is not an adult (except where he or she is legally married or in section 2(2)(b) cases). This is on the basis, *inter alia*, of the fact that legal definitions of adult include "a person who attains full age" and of the age of majority as "age 18 years or, if married before that age, age on marriage". It might, however, be desirable to underpin this approach in legislation, given the fact that, in some cases, persons under the age of 18 are considered to be "adults" for the purposes of an IQA.

8–37 Where a claimant or beneficiary of disability benefit, unemployment benefit, injury benefit, unemployability supplement, invalidity pension, old age (contributory) or retirement pension, unemployment assistance, farm assist, pre-retirement allowance or disability allowance, would be entitled to an increase in respect of his or her spouse but for the fact that the spouse's weekly income exceeds the prescribed limit, and where the spouse's weekly income is less than a maximum amount (currently €196.81 per week), a tapered rate of increase is payable depending on the precise level of income. This is in order to ensure that persons whose income is somewhat over the basic €88.88 per week limit do not lose the entire IQA.[27]

8–38 The rate of the IQA varies from scheme to scheme and is currently set at about 66–70 per cent of the main rate. However, in the case of qualified adults over pension age of pensioners, the IQA is significantly higher and the objective has been set of increasing this to the full old age (non-contributory) rate over time.

8–39 An IQA is not normally payable in respect of a person who is absent from the State or undergoing imprisonment or detention in legal custody, but this rule is subject to certain exceptions (see Chapter 15).[28]

---

[27] SW(C)A 1993, s. 245A (as inserted by SWA 1995, s.15 and amended by SWA 2000, s. 20) and SW(CPP)R 1994, art. 6C as inserted by S.I. No. 492 of 1997 and amended by S.I. No. 81 of 2000.

[28] SW(C)A 1993, s. 211.

CHAPTER 9

The Implementation of the E.U. Equality Directive

9–01 This chapter looks at the implementation of the E.U. Directive on equal treatment for men and women in social security (Directive 79/7) in the Irish social welfare code.[1]

1. Background

9–02 Social welfare benefits have traditionally been granted on the basis of the claimant's status within a family or household rather than on a purely individual basis (Chapter 8). There has been a tendency over time to move away from taking into account the circumstances of the extended family (although this can still be found in many social assistance schemes) towards a greater emphasis on the immediate family (spouse or partner) or on the individual. At the present time, there is a tension in social welfare policy worldwide between the move towards individualisation (*i.e.* granting benefits without taking account of the family circumstances) and a contrary tendency towards emphasis on intra-family solidarity. The tendency towards individualisation is encouraged by the increase in the number of married women participating in the paid labour force, by the emphasis on equal treatment for men and women in social security in E.U. policy and by the increasing number of people living in non-traditional family units (*e.g.* the increase in the number of people living alone, in the number of lone parents and in the level of marital breakdown). The reliance on family solidarity has largely arisen from concerns about the costs of social welfare and the desire to limit costs by transferring responsibility for support of individuals from the State to the family. This involves a move from a broader community or national solidarity to a narrower concept of solidarity and an increased emphasis on

---

[1] [1979] O.J. L6/24. Art. 14 of the European Convention on Human Rights prohibits discrimination on a range of grounds, including sex. However, Art. 14 has effect solely in relation to the enjoyment of the rights and freedoms safeguarded by the other provisions of the Convention, for example, rights in relation to family life, possessions and a fair hearing. The relevant case law is, accordingly, discussed as it arises in relation to specific issues. See, in particular, Chaps 2, 8 and 18.

subsidiarity (in one of its many guises). The issue of individualisation can involve intergenerational as well as gender aspects, but in this chapter we concentrate on the latter.

A. Women in the Social Welfare Code (1911–79)

9–03 The Irish social welfare system, as we saw in Chapter 8, has traditionally seen married women as part of the immediate family and dependent on their husbands. The National Insurance Act 1911 reinforced this construction. Indeed, under this Act, reflecting the lower rates of pay received by women generally, all women paid lower rates of contributions and received lower rates of benefit. As we saw in Chapter 1, this construction of women as dependants was reinforced by the Cumann na nGaedheal Government in 1929, which provided that women's membership of the national insurance scheme terminated on marriage, with women receiving a once-off marriage benefit. This change had been recommended by the (all-male) Committee of Inquiry into Health Insurance and Medical Services (1925) and was not opposed by Fianna Fáil or Labour. The result of this was that married women were not generally entitled to national insurance benefits (including sickness benefit and maternity benefit payable on their own insurance) and women who continued working after marriage were treated as new entrants to insurance. The Social Welfare Act 1952 abolished some aspects of direct discrimination in relation to single women, who, in future, received the same level of benefit, although paying a lower contribution rate. However, differential treatment for married women proved more enduring. The 1952 Act provided that a married woman was disqualified for unemployment, disability and treatment benefit, maternity allowance and maternity grant (on her own insurance) after marriage unless she worked in insurable employment for at least six months after marriage. In return for the termination of her insurance in this way, she received a lump sum marriage grant of between £3 and £10. If she did re-enter insurance and qualify for unemployment or disability benefit, she received a lower rate of benefit as she was deemed to be dependent on her husband (unless her husband was incapable of self-support), although she paid the full contribution rate for a woman. The husband, however, when entitled to a social welfare payment, was automatically entitled to an increase in respect of his wife, who was deemed to be dependent on him, even if she was in fact in receipt of benefit herself or in employment (although in 1961 only 5 per cent of women over the age of 15 years were active in the paid labour force).

9–04 The above remained the position at the time of the report of the Commission on the Status of Women (1972). The Commission pointed out that "it is becoming increasingly common for women to continue in employment after marriage and it seems to us to be unfair and discriminatory that they should be debarred from benefit for a period of time solely due to the fact of their marriage".[2] The Commission recommended that women should retain their rights to benefit and that the marriage grant should be abolished: this change was implemented in 1973. In relation to the lower rates of benefit, the Commission was "in sympathy with the ultimate objective that a woman, should not, because she is married, suffer any reduction relative to other persons in the rate of social welfare benefit payable to her"[3]; however, it felt unable to make any short-term detailed recommendations. Instead, the Commission but recommended that the Department of Social Welfare should have as an objective the abolition of the lower rate for married women and its replacement by the single person's rate. In relation to the amount of (then flat-rate) contribution, the Commission felt that the differentiation between men and women was reasonable in view of the fact that women received lower rates of pay. The Commission felt that the best way to resolve this issue was to introduce a pay-related contribution scheme. As we have seen, such a scheme was introduced in the period 1973–79. Among the other areas of discrimination, one of the most important was the treatment of women claimants of unemployment assistance. In order to qualify for assistance, a widow or a single woman was required to have at least one dependant or to have been insured for at least one year in the four years preceding the claim. A married woman was completely debarred from claiming unemployment assistance unless her husband was incapable of self-support or, if neither was a dependant of the other, she had one or more child dependants. The Commission on the Status of Women explained that the limitations on single women arose from the fact that when the scheme was introduced in 1933 it was feared that "large numbers of single women, especially in rural areas, not really in the labour market"[4] would claim assistance with consequent costs to the scheme and without any real possibility that such women would find work. The Commission recommended the abolition of this limitation and this was implemented in 1978. The exclusion of most married women was motivated by the view that such women did not form part of the labour force. Surprisingly, the Commission made no recommendation on the position of married women and the Government took no action until the constitutionality of part of this limitation was legally challenged in 1981. That case had questioned the constitutionality of the rule requiring married women to have child dependants in order to claim assistance and was settled after the rule had been abolished in the Social Welfare Act 1982. However, no alteration was made in the general rule whereby most women were deemed to be dependent on their husbands until the implementation of the equality Directive (see below).

---

[2] Report of the Commission on the Status of Women (Stationery Office, Dublin, 1972), para. 339.

[3] *ibid.*, para. 343.

[4] *ibid.*

9–05 Amongst the other recommendations of the Commission were that children's allowance should normally be paid to the mother rather than to the father (implemented in 1974), and that payments for unmarried mothers and prisoners' wives should be introduced (implemented in 1973 and 1974). The Commission also considered the extent to which changes in the social welfare system were necessitated by the proposed introduction of equal pay in order to comply with E.U. law. In order to ensure that certain families – those in which the mother was unable, due to the age or number of her children, to take up employment and benefit from equal pay, and those in which the mother would have to pay for childcare if she did enter employment – did not have their relative standards of living affected by the introduction of equal pay, the Commission recommended that an allowance be paid to families with at least one child under the age of five or, where there were two or more children, where the youngest was under the age of seven. This was to be in addition to any other social welfare entitlements. Thus, the allowance was intended to compensate for the woman's inability to enter employment and to assist with the cost of childcare. This proposal, however, was never implemented.

9–06 Hence, we can see the notion of equal treatment in social welfare is one which predates the E.U. Directive on equality and significant developments had taken place in Ireland prior to the implementation of that Directive. One can also see that the development of equality has not been a progressive movement from inequality in 1911 to a greater degree of equality in the 1970s. Indeed, the relative position of women clearly worsened after Independence in the 1920s and 1930s, with the exclusion of married women from national insurance in 1929 and the exclusion of most women from entitlement to unemployment assistance in 1933. These developments reflect the economic difficulties of the time, the conservative views of the Cumann na nGaedhcal Government, the equally conservative views of Fianna Fáil in relation to the role of women, and the ideology of the Catholic Church. Indeed, similar developments can be seen in relation to many other employment-related issues, including the marriage bar for married women in the civil service and the teaching profession and the restrictions on women's work imposed by the Conditions of Employment Act 1936. This tendency can also be seen in relation to a range of "social" issues, including divorce and contraception. The position improved somewhat after the 1952 reforms, with single woman becoming entitled to equal rates of benefit and the introduction of a maternity allowance. However, few further improvements occurred until the 1970s, when significant changes were made, including the ending of the exclusion of married women from entitlement to many social insurance benefits on marriage, the introduction of equal pay-related contributions, the establishment of a number of payments for lone mothers and the payment of children's allowance to mothers. However, there remained significant instances of direct discrimination against married women, in addition to the fact that the whole social welfare code was based on discriminatory assumptions about the roles of men and women. While the changes which were achieved in this period predated the adoption of the Directive on equal treatment in social security, they must be seen in the context of Ireland's obligations under E.U. law, which led to the abolition of the ban on married women's employment in the public service (1973) and the legislation on equal pay (1974) and equality in access to employment (1977), which had consequences for the structure of the social welfare system.

B. E.U. Equality Law and the Directive on Social Security

9–07 Article 119 of the Treaty of Rome provides that men and women are to receive equal pay for equal work.[5] The inclusion of this Article in the Treaty was motivated by economic as well as social reasons in that Member States, in particular France, wished to ensure that no Member State could improve its economic competitiveness by relying on cheap female labour. In 1976, the European Court of Justice held that this provision had direct legal effect in the national legal systems (*i.e.* it created enforceable rights which could be relied on by an individual before the national courts).[6] While the Court held that social welfare payments did not fall within the meaning of "pay" within the terms of Article 119,[7] it was clear that the employment and social welfare systems were so closely bound up that it would be impossible to achieve equality in employment without also introducing legislation in the area of social welfare. In 1975 the E.U. Council of Ministers adopted a Directive in relation to equal pay and in 1976 it adopted a second equality Directive on equal treatment in relation to access to employment, vocational training and working conditions. The latter was originally intended to apply to social security as well, but due to the difficulties involved it was decided to adopt a third Directive specifically in relation to statutory social security schemes. A proposal was published by the Commission in 1977 and was adopted with relatively minor amendments (at least so far as the Irish system was concerned) on December 19, 1978. An unusually long implementation period of six years was allowed and the Directive did not come into force in Ireland until December 23, 1984. As can be seen from its ancestry in the second Directive, the purpose of the social security Directive was largely to achieve equality in work-related areas. It applies only to work-related social welfare schemes and to members of the working population (the legal detail of the Directive is discussed below).

---

[5] S. Prechal and N. Burrows, *Gender Discrimination Law of the European Community* (Dartmouth, Aldershot, 1990); M. Bolger and C. Kimber, *Sex Discrimination Law* (Round Hall, Dublin 2000).

[6] Case 43/75 *Defrenne v. SABENA* [1976] E.C.R. 455.

[7] Case 80/70 *Defrenne v. SABENA* [1971] E.C.R. 445.

9–08 The Directive does not apply to all social welfare schemes or to all social welfare claimants. Family and survivors benefits are excluded from the scope of the Directive and the effect of subsequent decisions of the European Court of Justice has been that general means-tested payments (such as supplementary welfare allowance) are also excluded. Only persons at work and persons who are looking for work or whose work has been interrupted by one of the risks referred to in the Directive (sickness, invalidity, old age, occupational accidents and diseases and unemployment) are covered by the Directive. The Directive rules out all discrimination, direct and indirect, on grounds of sex in relation to all aspects of social welfare within its scope, including the calculations of contributions and of benefits.[8] However, the Directive itself, with its close links to the paid labour force, is based on differentiated assumptions as to the role of men and women. Thus, people who give up employment in order to care for children (the vast majority of whom are women) are not covered by the Directive. The Council of Ministers adopted a fourth Directive on equal treatment in occupational pension schemes and a further Directive on equal treatment in self-employment in 1986.[9] The latter has only very limited relevance in the area of social welfare.

9–09 The E.U. Commission published a further proposed Directive to "complete" the implementation of the principle of equal treatment in social security in 1985.[10] This proposal has not been adopted by the Council of Ministers to date and there appears to be little prospect of its adoption. This proposal would have had the effect of implementing the principle of equality in relation to areas excluded from the scope of the third Directive, including family and survivors benefits. However, the proposal did not go so far as to require individualisation of benefits, nor did it require that protection be provided in areas of particular relevance to women, such as lone parents payments. Thus, while the proposal, if adopted, might have achieved full formal equality between men and women in most areas of the social welfare code, it would not necessarily have ensured improved provision for women who remained excluded from or marginal to the paid labour force, nor would it necessarily have made it easier for such women to gain access to improved social protection. To a large extent, the E.U. Directives only provide for equality for women in so far as women participate in the paid labour force in the same way as men. However, more recently the Council of Ministers has adopted E.U. Commission proposals for specific Directives in relation to issues such as maternity, atypical work and parental leave.

---

[8] Indirect discrimination arises where a provision that is formally neutral as between sexes has a disproportionate impact to the disadvantage of one sex and where the provision cannot be objectively justified on grounds unrelated to sex.

[9] See Prechal and Burrows, above, n.5.

[10] COM (87) 494 final.

C. The Implementation of the Equal Treatment Directive in Ireland (1979–94)[11]

9–10 As we saw in the first part of this chapter, while the Government had taken several steps to remove discrimination against women in the 1970s, at the time of the adoption of the Directive in 1979 there remained several important areas where direct and indirect discrimination still continued. The main areas of direct discrimination were:

(1) married women in receipt of various benefits (such as unemployment and disability benefit) received lower rates of pay than married men and single persons;

2) married women received unemployment benefit for only 12 months as opposed to the normal 15 months (this had been increased from six months in 1979);

(3) married women were generally not allowed to claim unemployment assistance unless their husbands were incapable of self-support;

(4) married women were deemed to be dependent on their husbands (again, unless the husband was incapable of self-support), with the result that the husband generally received dependent increases for his wife and children while the wife generally did not receive such increases.

The first two areas did not raise any great conceptual problems and indeed were ultimately resolved simply by raising the level and period of payment for married women to those applying to other claimants. However, as we will discuss in more detail below, the issues around dependency and access to unemployment assistance raised much more important issues of principle. The main area of possible indirect discrimination related to the exclusion from social insurance of part-time workers (generally speaking, at that time people working less than 18 hours per week), the vast majority of whom were women.[12]

9–11 Despite the six-year implementation period, successive governments took little action to remove the existing areas of discrimination. It was not until late 1984 that a Bill was published to make the necessary changes to the social welfare scheme in relation to the directly discriminatory aspects. This was eventually passed by the Oireachtas in 1985 but was not brought into effect until May and November 1986.[13] The delay in implementation led to

---

[11] For a detailed legal analysis of the case law involved, see G. Whyte, *Social Inclusion and the Legal System* (Institute of Public Administration, Dublin, 2002), pp. 141–151.

[12] See Whyte, *Sex Equality, Community Rights and Irish Social Welfare Law* (Irish Centre for European Law, Dublin, 1988) for other areas of discrimination.

[13] Social Welfare (No. 2) Act 1985. In the first of the *Cotter* and *McDermott* cases, the

increased costs for the Government and, despite the time taken to introduce the new structures, to transitional provisions which continued to discriminate against married women until their abolition in 1992. The Social Welfare (No. 2) Act 1985 provided that the rates of social welfare payable to married women were to increase to the same level as those payable to other adults, and unemployment benefit was to be payable for the normal 15 months. Thus, in this area, the reformed social welfare system treated married women as individuals for the first time, with no assumption that their personal needs were less because of an assumed dependency of their husbands. The Irish legislation did not, for example, follow the Belgian approach of introducing separate (higher) rates for "heads of household" (predominantly men) and lower rates for "single persons" and "cohabitees" (a person living with another person with an occupational or welfare income), both made up predominantly of women. While these groups are formally neutral as to the sex of the claimant, they reinforce existing gender constructions – although the Court of Justice held that the Belgian legislation was not in breach of the Directive.[14]

9–12 The other areas of direct discrimination created more difficult conceptual problems. In relation to the notion of dependency, the Department was faced with the option of extending to married women the existing system, whereby a married man received a dependency increase for his wife and children even if she was not, in fact, dependent on him. This would have led to a massive increase in the number of payments as, while the majority of married women were, in fact, still dependent on their husbands, this was not true of the majority of married men. Such an approach would have led to "dependency" increases being paid to households which already had adequate incomes in many cases. A second approach would have been to abolish dependency increases altogether. However, this would have led to severe cuts in payments to many poor households, which could only have been overcome by a major increase in the level of payment made to all claimants or the introduction of a system of individualised payments. Faced with these alternatives, the decision was made to retain the existing concept of dependency but to require factual proof of dependency in all cases. In practice this meant that dependency increases were payable only where the spouse was in receipt of earned income of less than £50 per week and was not in receipt of a welfare payment in her or his own right. Where a spouse was not dependent, any child dependency increases due were paid at half the full rate. This was implemented in November 1986 but also led to income losses in many low-income households as the husbands of wives in receipt of relatively low

---

ECJ held that the Directive had direct effect from December 1984 and that women were entitled to rely on its provisions in the absence of any implementing legislation: Case 286/85 *McDermott v. Minister for Social Welfare* [1987] E.C.R. 1453.

[14] Case 229/89 *Commission v. Belgium* [1991] E.C.R. I–2205.

incomes (but over £50 per week) lost the dependency increases. Transitional payments were introduced to compensate such families. However, as these were paid to married men and not to married women, they continued to discriminate contrary to the terms of the equality Directive.[15] Thus, in this area the social welfare system arguably retained the notion of women's dependency, replacing the concept of notional dependency with a more factual approach. While one might argue that this is only a reflection of the factual situation, research has shown that the structure of dependency in the social welfare system made it difficult for women to take up anything other than low-paid employment and, in reflecting women's existing dependency, thereby also reinforced it. Efforts have been made to overcome this issue by introducing tapered increases for qualified adults where that person is in work over a certain weekly income.

9–13 Difficulties also arose in relation to the entitlement of married women to unemployment assistance. A simple removal of the exclusion would have led to an increased number of women claiming assistance (with little opportunity of obtaining employment), leading to an increase in the level of recorded unemployment and extra costs for the system. It is interesting to note that these are almost precisely the same reasons why women were granted only restricted access to unemployment assistance in the 1930s. As a result, while married women were allowed to claim assistance, a cap was placed on the amount of social welfare payable to a family, so that families where the wife claimed assistance would be no better off than families where the wife remained as an adult dependant (see Chapter 8). As there was no financial benefit in claiming (and, in some cases, financial disadvantages), not surprisingly many married women chose not to exercise their new-found right to claim assistance. Although these provisions obviously had the effect of continuing the existing exclusion of married women from the labour force, it would seem from decisions of the Court of Justice that such measures are not in breach of the Directive.[16] However, in this area the implementing strategy chosen clearly reinforced the notion of women's dependency rather than creating an individual right to benefits. As we have seen in Chapter 8, a successful constitutional challenge to these provisions in the *Hyland* case led to the extension of the cap on payments to cohabiting as well as to married couples.[17]

9–14 The delay in implementing the Directive was condemned in several

---

[15] As the ECJ held in the second of the *Cotter* and *McDermott* cases: Case C–377/89 *Cotter v. Minister for Social Welfare* [1991] E.C.R. I–1155.

[16] Case 229/89 *Commission v. Belgium* [1991] I–2205

[17] *Hyland v. Minister for Social Welfare* [1989] I.R. 624.

cases brought before the Court of Justice.[18] Ultimately, after a campaign involving a range of Irish groups including the Free Legal Advice Centres (FLAC), and faced with a threat of legal action by the European Commission, the Government agreed to pay arrears of about £60 million to Irish women who were entitled to equal treatment in the period from 1984 to the dates of implementation of the Directive in 1986. Subsequently, in 1995, following further ECJ decisions and a High Court decision,[19] the Rainbow Government accepted that it was liable for further payments in respect of, for example, transitional payments made from 1986 to 1992. A further £250 million was paid to up to 77,500 women in final settlement of these claims.

9–15 The delay in implementing the Directive has been attributed to the particular structure of the Irish social welfare system and the fact that the implementation period in Ireland coincided with "a period of particular economic difficulties and political instability".[20] Nor, indeed, were such difficulties confined to Ireland, with the Netherlands also failing to implement the Directive in time. However, Cook and McCashin[21] have pointed out that, in the period in question, social welfare expenditure grew rapidly and not simply because of rising numbers of claimants, as real levels of payment also increased. They argue that a more strategic approach at administrative and political levels would have allowed the phasing in of what was bound to be a problematic structural change. The failure to take this opportunity is attributed to institutional failings in the policy-making process. While this is no doubt correct, it perhaps underestimates the institutional paralysis created by the political and administrative systems' inability to cope with the economic reverses of the 1970s and 1980s after a long period of economic growth.

2. Current Situation

9–16 As we have seen, Council Directive 79/7 of December 19, 1978 on the progressive implementation of the principle of equal treatment for men

---

[18] Including the first and second of the *Cotter* and *McDermott* cases [1987] E.C.R. 1453 and [1990] E.C.R. I–1155; Case 208/90 *Emmott v. Minister for Social Welfare* [1991] E.C.R. I–4269. See Whyte, above, n.11.

[19] *Tate v. Minister for Social Welfare* [1995] 1 I.R. 418.

[20] G. Mangan, "Social Protection and the Single Market" in S. Ó Cinnéide (ed.), *Social Europe: EC Social Policy and Ireland* (Institute of European Affairs, Dublin, 1993) and see Comptroller and Auditor General, *Report 1992* (Stationery Office, Dublin, 1993).

[21] A. McCashin and G. Cook, "Male Breadwinner: A Case Study of Gender and Social Security in the Republic of Ireland" in A. Byrne and M. Leonard (eds), *Women and Irish Society – A Sociological Reader* (Beyond the Pale Publications, Belfast, 1997), pp. 167–180.

and women in matters of social security was adopted in 1979 and came into effect in December 1984.[22] The objective of the Directive is to implement the principle of equal treatment in statutory social security schemes offering protection against the risks of sickness, invalidity, old age, accidents at work, occupational diseases and unemployment and in social assistance.

A. Personal Scope

9–17 The Directive applies to the working population (including self-employed persons); to workers and self-employed persons whose activity is interrupted by illness, accident or involuntary unemployment; to persons seeking employment; and to retired or invalided workers and self-employed persons.[23] The European Court of Justice has held that persons in employment which is regarded as minor (because it consists of fewer than 15 hours work a week and attracts remuneration of up to one-seventh of the average monthly salary) form part of the working population within the meaning of Article 2 and therefore fall within its personal scope.[24] The Court held that the fact that a person's earnings from employment do not cover all his or her needs could not prevent him or her from being a worker or a member of the working population under E.U. law.

9–18 However, the Court has imposed one important restriction on the personal scope of the Directive in ruling that it is confined to workers or to persons whose activity (or search for work) was interrupted by one of the contingencies covered by the Directive (see below). The effect of this decision has been to narrow the personal scope of the Directive significantly by excluding persons (mainly women) whose activity was interrupted due to taking on family responsibilities (*i.e.* due to marriage, childbirth or childcare).[25] Thus, in the *Achterberg* case,[26] a woman seeking to claim that Dutch pension rules discriminated against her on grounds of sex was held not to be entitled to bring a claim, as she fell without the personal scope of the Directive. In *Drake*, the Court held that a woman who had given up work in order to care for her disabled mother was within the personal scope of the Directive as she had given up work due to the invalidity of her mother – a risk listed in Article 3.[27] However, the Court subsequently ruled in *Züchner* that a woman who was providing nursing care to her husband in the home was not within the

---

[22] [1979] O.J. L6/24.
[23] Art. 2.
[24] Case C–317/93 *Nolte v. Landesversicherungsanstalt* [1995] E.C.R. I–4625.
[25] Case 31/90 *Johnson v. Chief Adjudication Officer* [1991] E.C.R. 3723.
[26] Joined Cases 48, 106 & 107/88 *Achterberg-te Riele v. Sociale Verzekeringsbank* [1989] E.C.R. 1963.
[27] Case 150/85 *Drake v. Chief Adjudication Officer* [1986] E.C.R. 1995.

scope of the Directive as she had not given up employment to do so nor had she interrupted efforts to find work.[28] The Court held that the term "activity" in Article 2 could be construed only as referring at the very least to an economic activity, *i.e.* an activity undertaken for remuneration in the broad sense, and so providing unpaid nursing care did not make the applicant a "worker" for the purposes of the Directive.

B. Material Scope

9–19 The Directive applies to statutory schemes which provide protection against the classic social security risks, *i.e.* sickness, invalidity, old age, accidents at work and occupational diseases, to unemployment, and to social assistance, in so far as it is intended to supplement or replace such schemes.[29] The Directive does not, however, apply to provisions concerning survivors' benefits or to family benefits except in the case of family benefits granted by way of increases of benefits due in respect of the risks referred to in Article 3(1).[30] The Court of Justice has, in general, given a reasonably broad definition to the material scope of the Directive. It has, for example, held that a carer's payment fell within the scope of the Directive as being directly and effectively linked to the protection provided against one of the risks specified in the Directive (*i.e.* invalidity).[31] The Court has held that a statutory right to free medicines is within the scope of the Directive as being linked to the contingency of sickness[32] and that a statutory winter fuel payment payable only to older people was within the scope of the Directive.[33] Conversely, the Court held that a scheme to provide concessionary fares to certain groups including older people did not fall within the scope of the Directive, as while protection against the risk of old age was *a* purpose it was not *the* purpose, as other groups could also qualify.[34] The Court has also held that the U.K. housing benefit falls outside the scope of the Directive.[35]

9–20 The Court has ruled one important type of payment outside the scope of the Directive, *i.e.* general mean-tested payments which have the objective

---

[28] Case C–77/95 *Züchner v. Handelskrankenkasse Bremen* [1996] E.C.R. I–5689.

[29] Art 3 (1).

[30] Art. 3(2). See Joined cases C–245 & 312/94 *Hoever v. Land Nordrhein-Westfalen* [1996] E.C.R. I–4895.

[31] Case 150/85 *Drake v. Chief Adjudication Officer* [1986] E.C.R. 1995.

[32] Case C–137/94 *R. v. Secretary of State for Health, ex parte Richardson* [1995] E.C.R. I–3407.

[33] Case C–382/98, *R. v. Secretary of State for Social Security, ex parte Taylor* [1999] E.C.R. I–8955.

[34] Case C–228/94 *Atkins v. Wreknin District Council* [1996] E.C.R. I–3633.

[35] Case 243/90 *R. v. Secretary of State for Social Security, ex parte Smithson* [1992] E.C.R. I–467.

of keeping people out of poverty.[36] This is not so significant in Ireland, where most means-tested payments are linked to specific contingencies, but would, however, mean that a general payment such as supplementary welfare allowance is almost certainly outside the Directive. It is of considerably more significance in the United Kingdom whether the general mean-tested income support payment is outside the scope of the Directive.

C. Principle of Equal Treatment

9–21 The principle of equal treatment means that there should be no discrimination whatsoever on grounds of sex, either directly or indirectly, by reference in particular to marital or family status, specifically as concerns:

- the scope of the schemes and the conditions of access thereto;
- the obligation to contribute and the calculation of contributions;
- the calculation of benefits, including increases due in respect of a spouse and for dependants and the conditions governing the duration and retention of entitlement to benefits.[37]

9–22 Direct discrimination, *i.e.* where a person of one gender is treated less well than a person of the other gender, is generally self-evident. The early cases dealt with by the Court of Justice frequently dealt with cases of clear direct discrimination where the Member State argued that the Directive did not have direct effect or with cases where direct discrimination was carried over in transitional measures. The issue of indirect discrimination is considerably more complicated. It has been considered in a number of cases before the Court, which has now established a reasonably clear interpretation of the concept – albeit one under which almost all claims of indirect discrimination fail.

9–23 Indirect discrimination arises where a provision that is formally neutral as between the sexes has a disproportionate impact to the disadvantage of one sex and where the provision cannot be objectively justified on grounds unrelated to sex. Exclusion of part-time employment from compulsory social insurance – something which was the case in Ireland up to 1991 – is a good example of the issues involved in indirect discrimination cases. The exclusion is formally gender neutral, *i.e.* it does not specifically apply to women. However, in almost all E.U. countries the vast majority of part-time workers are women and, therefore, an exclusion of part-time workers disproportionately affects one gender. The issue to be decided is whether this is allowed under

---

[36] Joined Cases C–63–64/91 *Jackson v. Chief Adjudication Officer* [1992] E.C.R. I–4737.
[37] Art. 4(1).

E.U. law. The Court has consistently held that the Directive precludes the application of a national measure which, although formulated in neutral terms, works to the disadvantage of far more women than men, *unless* that measure is based on objective factors unrelated to any discrimination on grounds of sex. Such objective justification is provided where the measures chosen reflect a legitimate social policy aim of the Member State whose legislation is at issue, are appropriate to achieve that aim and are necessary in order to do so.[38] In practice, the Court has allowed a "reasonable margin of discretion" to Member States in producing such justification.

9–24 In the *Nolte* case – a case involving the exclusion of persons working less than 15 hours from German social insurance – it was accepted that the exclusion of such workers disproportionately affected women.[39] However, the German Government – supported by the United Kingdom and Ireland – argued that the exclusion of part-time workers corresponded to a structural principle of the German social security scheme. It was stressed that in contributory social security schemes equivalence must be maintained between the contributions paid by employees and employers and the benefits paid. It was argued that the structure of the scheme could not be maintained in its present form if the provisions excluding part-time workers had to be abolished. The German Government further argued that it was responding to the social demand for part-time employment by fostering the supply of such employment and that the only way of doing so was to exclude part-time employment from social insurance. The Court, in response, noted that, in the current state of E.U. law, social policy was a matter for the Member States and, consequently, it was for the Member States to choose the measures capable of achieving the aim of their social and employment policy. In exercising that competence, the Court held that Member States have a broad margin of discretion. In a somewhat tautologous construction, the Court noted that the social and employment policy relied on by Germany was objectively unrelated to any discrimination on grounds of sex and that, in exercising its competence, the national legislature was reasonably entitled to consider that the legislation in question was necessary in order to achieve that aim. Accordingly, the Court held that the legislation could not be described as indirect discrimination. As can be seen, the Court has applied quite a weak check to the exercise of

---

[38] Case C–343/92 *De Weerd v. Bestuur van de Bedrijfsvereniging voor de Gezondheid* [1994] E.C.R. I–571; Case C–317/93 *Nolte v. Landesversicherungsanstalt* [1995] E.C.R. I–4625. And see Case C–280/94 *Posthuma-van Damme v. Bestuur van de Bedrijfsvereniging voor Detailhandel, Ambachten en Huisvrouwen* [1996] E.C.R. I–179; Case C–8/94 *Laperre v. Bestuurscommissie beroepszaken in de provincie Zuid-Holland* [1996] E.C.R. I–273 for other decisions in which the Court allowed a wide margin of discretion to Member States.

[39] Case C–317/93 *Nolte v. Landesversicherungsanstalt* [1995] E.C.R. I–4625.

Member States' discretion in relation to indirect discrimination in social security. The Court has held that to justify disproportionate treatment it must be shown that the measures reflect a legitimate social policy aim of the Member State, are appropriate to achieve that aim and are necessary in order to do so. In *Nolte*, the Court accepted that the social policy aim, claimed by the German Government of encouraging part-time employment was legitimate. However, it does not seem to have given any consideration as to whether the exclusion of part-time workers was appropriate to achieve that aim, unless its unsupported statement that the policy was "objectively unrelated" to discrimination on grounds of sex is supposed to do so. The Court simply accepted that the national legislature was "reasonably entitled to consider" that it was necessary. Given this approach, it is unsurprising that there have been no recent indirect discrimination cases before the Court.

9–25   Article 4(2) provides that the principle of equal treatment is without prejudice to the provisions relating to the protection of women on the grounds of maternity.[40]

D. Implementation

9–26   Article 5 requires that Member States take the measures necessary to ensure that any laws, regulations and administrative provisions contrary to the principle of equal treatment are abolished. Article 6 requires Member States to introduce into their national legal system such measures as are necessary to enable all persons who consider themselves wronged by failure to apply the principle of equal treatment to pursue their claims by judicial process, possibly after recourse to other competent authorities. Unlike the earlier E.U. Directives on equal pay and equal treatment, no specific institutions were established in Irish law in relation to claims under Directive 79/7, which are heard initially by the social welfare adjudication and appeals systems (see Chapter 18) and subsequently in the courts.

9–27   The Court of Justice has held that Article 5 does not require that an individual should be able to obtain interest on arrears of social security benefit where the delay in the payment of the benefit is the result of discrimination prohibited by the Directive[41] – although the conditions laid down by national

---

[40] See Prechal and Burrows, above, n.5, pp. 177–178.

[41] Case C–66/95 *R. v. Secretary of State for Social Security, ex parte Sutton* [1997] E.C.R. I–2163. The ECJ again imposed lower standards in this area than it has done in relation to employment cases and it refused to follow its case law on the issue in Case C–271/91 *Marshall v. Southampton and South West Hampshire Area Health Authority* [1993] E.C.R. I–4367. The Irish courts had previously held that compensation should be increased by an appropriate amount in line with the consumer price index to compensate for late payment: *Tate v. Minster for Social Welfare* [1995] 1 I.R. 418 at 434.

law relating to compensation must not be less favourable than those relating to similar domestic claims and must not be framed so as to make it virtually impossible or excessively difficult to obtain reparation.[42] As compensation is payable in respect of payments delayed for a period exceeding 12 months "due solely or mainly to circumstances within the control of the Department" under Irish law (see Chapter 15), this general principle would require the same approach to be taken in relation to claims under E.U. law (in so far as it is relevant), despite the decision in *Sutton*.[43]

9–28 In *Emmott*, the Court of Justice considered the issue of time-limits for bringing claims in relation to the equal treatment Directive.[44] It ruled that so long as a Directive had not been properly transposed into national law, individuals were unable to ascertain the full extent of their rights. Only the proper transposition of the Directive brought that state of uncertainty to an end and it was only then that the legal certainty, which must exist if individuals are to be required to assert their rights, is created. The Court held that it followed that E.U. law precluded a Member State from relying on national procedural rules relating to time-limits for bringing proceedings so long as that Member State has not properly transposed the Directive into its domestic legal system.

9–29 In *Steenhorst-Neerings*, the Court subsequently considered the status of a national rule restricting the retroactive effect of a claim for benefits.[45] It was suggested to the Court that, following *Emmott*, the time-limits for proceedings brought by individuals seeking to avail themselves of their rights were applicable only when a Member State has properly transposed the Directive. The Court, however, distinguished *Emmott* on the basis that, unlike the rule of domestic law fixing time-limits for bringing actions (as in *Emmott*), a rule restricting the retroactive effect of a claim for benefits did not affect the right of individuals to rely on Directive 79/7 in proceedings before the national courts against a defaulting Member State. It merely limited the retroactive effect of claims made for the purpose of obtaining the relevant benefits. The Court took the view that the aim of the rule restricting the retroactive effect of claims for benefits was quite different from that of a rule imposing mandatory

---

[42] Joined Cases C–6 &9/90, *Francovich v. Italy* [1991] E.C.R. I–5357.
[43] Social Welfare (Consolidation) Act 1993, s. 206A as inserted by Social Welfare Act 1998, s. 11.
[44] Case C–208/90 *Emmott v. Minister for Social Welfare* [1991] E.C.R. I–4269.
[45] Case C–338/91 *Steenhorst-Neerings v. Bestuur van de Bedrijfsvereniging voor Detailhandel, Ambachten en Huisvrouwen* [1993] E.C.R. I–5475. See also Case C–410/92, *Johnson v. Chief Adjudication Officer* [1994] E.C.R I–5483; N. Hyland, "A case note on *Johnson v. Chief Adjudication Officer*" (1995) 13 I.L.T 62–65. On the position under the European Convention on Human Rights, see *Walden v. Liechtenstein*, March 16, 2000.

time-limits for bringing proceedings. The Court held, therefore, that E.U. law did not preclude the application of a national rule which limits the period prior to the bringing of the claim in respect of which arrears of benefit are payable, provided that those conditions were no less favourable than those relating to similar domestic actions and that they were not framed so as to render virtually impossible the exercise of rights conferred by E.U. law.

9–30 While the distinction between *Emmott* (which concerns the right to bring a case) and *Steenhorst-Neerings* (which concerns the right to arrears of benefit) can certainly be made in principle, in practice the distinction is often much less clear. This is exemplified by the *Tate* case, in which Carroll J. had to decide whether claims in relation to social welfare payments under the equal treatment Directive were barred by the Statute of Limitations.[46] The High Court held that a breach of obligation by the State to observe Community law was a tort within the meaning of section 111(2) of the Statute of Limitations 1957. It was argued that the decision in *Emmott* precluded the State from pleading the statute. Carroll J. held that while the Statute of Limitations did provide that no tort action shall be brought after the expiration of six years from the cause of action (and was thus a rule imposing time-limits for bringing a case), the reality was that where there was a continuing breach it, in effect, limited the period in respect of which arrears of benefit could be claimed.[47] She took the view that, in the light of the subsequent cases, *Emmott* did not have the wide general application which it appeared to have on first reading and that it did not prevent the State pleading the statute in respect of payments which fell due more than six years before the action brought.

E. Exclusions

9–31 Article 7 provides that the Member States may exclude from the scope of the Directive:

- the determination of pensionable age for the purposes of granting old-age and retirement pensions and the possible consequences thereof for other benefits;
- advantages in respect of old-age pension schemes granted to persons who have brought up children; the acquisition of benefit entitlements following periods of interruption of employment due to the bringing-up of children;
- the granting of old-age or invalidity benefit entitlement by virtue of the derived entitlements of a wife;

---

[46] *Tate v. Minister for Social Welfare* [1995] 1 I.R. 418. See M. Cousins, "Equal Treatment in Social Security: The Final Round?" [1995] 4 I.J.E.L.
[47] [1995] 1 I.R. 418 at 446.

- the granting of increases of long-term invalidity, old-age, accidents at work and occupational disease benefits for a dependent wife;

- the consequences of the exercise, before the adoption of the Directive, of a right of option not to acquire rights or incur obligations under a statutory scheme.

9–32 The Member States are required periodically to examine whether it is justified to maintain the exclusions in the light of social developments. This is an area in which much of the case law currently coming before the Court of Justice is concentrated. This applies in particular in relation to article 7(1) concerning different pension ages and the consequences thereof for other benefits. However, this has no relevance to Ireland, where we have always had equal statutory pension ages for men and women.

F. Directive 76/207[48]

9–33 It should be noted that the European Court of Justice has held in general that social security matters do not come within the scope of the equal treatment Directive 76/207. However, it has held that a social security scheme can fall within its scope in so far as its subject matter concerns access to employment. In particular, it held that the U.K. family credit payment was within the scope of that Directive, which implies that the very similar Irish family income supplement is also within its scope.[49]

---

[48] [1976] O.J. L39/40.
[49] Case C–116/94 *Meyers v. Adjudication Officer* [1995] E.C.R. I–2131.

CHAPTER 10

Social Welfare Support for Informal Caring

1. Background

10–01 Social welfare provision for informal carers in Ireland dates from 1968, when increases in pensions for the elderly (then over 70 years of age) were introduced for claimants who were so incapacitated as to require full-time care and attention where a "prescribed female relative" lived with the claimant to provide such care.[1] The only female relatives initially prescribed by regulation were a daughter and stepdaughter. The increase was only payable where the prescribed relative had left insurable employment in order to provide full-time care and attention, and where she had paid 156 weeks' employment contributions within the five years before leaving employment. The payment was paid to the pensioner. The weekly rate represented 69 per cent of the then non-contributory old age pension and 62 per cent of the higher contributory pension. The payment, which became known as the prescribed relative's allowance (PRA), was thus very restrictive. First, it was only paid to persons aged over 70 in receipt of a pension, thus ruling out younger persons who required care and persons over 70 who were not entitled to a social welfare pension. Secondly, the categories of prescribed female relative were extremely restrictive and initially applied only to the claimant's daughters (or step-daughters) who had been regularly employed and who had given up work to care for him or her. The restrictions meant that few persons qualified for PRA and, in the following year, the contribution rule was abolished and the definition of prescribed relative was extended to include a wider range of female relatives.[2] The then Minister for Local Government explained that by this extension of the scheme "an inducement is being given to people to keep their aged relatives at home rather than have them go into institutions".[3] In 1972, the scheme was extended to the corresponding male relatives and in following years it was extended to a wider range of relatives.

---

[1] In addition, under the occupational injuries scheme introduced in 1967, a constant attendance allowance is payable to a person who, as a result of an occupational accident or disease, is suffering from at least 50% disablement and who, as a result, requires "constant attendance" (see Chap. 5).

[2] 240 *Dáil Debates* Col. 411.

[3] 241 *Dáil Debates* Col. 1146.

10–02 Separately, in 1973, a scheme of allowances for domiciliary care of severely handicapped children was introduced by the Department of Health. The scheme was aimed at severely mentally or physically handicapped children who were living at home and who required constant care. It was "designed to alleviate, in some measure, the additional burdens created by the retention of such children in the home".

10–03 The prescribed relatives scheme was subsequently extended to persons in receipt of an invalidity pension below retirement age in 1982. PRA remained quite restrictive in that the prescribed relative could not be engaged in employment outside the home of the person for whom full-time care and attention was being provided. In addition, if the prescribed relative was in receipt of a social welfare payment, no PRA was payable. Finally, the prescribed relative could not be a married person who was being wholly or mainly maintained by his or her spouse. This effectively disqualified most married women from qualifying as a prescribed relative – a group which made up a large percentage of actual carers. The rationale given for this exclusion was that the scheme was intended to compensate for a situation which does not normally arise and therefore situations in which a wife cared for her husband (or for other relatives in the matrimonial home) were excluded.[4] From 1986, this rule was arguably in breach of the E.U. Directive on equal treatment for men and women.[5]

10–04 The limited and unsatisfactory nature of PRA led to several proposals for the introduction of a less restrictive payment for carers. The Commission on Social Welfare (1986) recommended that prescribed relatives should have entitlement in their own right to a means-tested payment as part of a comprehensive social assistance scheme. This recommendation was supported by the National Council for the Elderly, which also recommended that this payment should be extended to cover carers who were married and other persons not already covered by the existing scheme.[6] As a first step in this direction, the Social Welfare Act 1989 provided that PRA was to be paid directly to the carer. As might be expected, given the very restrictive eligibility conditions, the numbers in receipt of PRA were always quite low. In the 1970s over 3,000 persons received the allowance but this subsequently declined to only 1,850 in December 1989 just before the introduction of the carer's allowance. The vast majority of the persons in receipt of care were elderly, although precise figures are not available.

---

[4] 248 *Dáil Debates* Col 1699.

[5] See Case 150/85 *Drake v. Chief Adjudication Officer* [1986] E.C.R. 1995 and Whyte, "Social Welfare Law 1985/1986 – The Year in Review" 5 *J.I.S.L.L.* (1986) 135–150 at 149.

[6] National Council for the Aged, *Caring for the Elderly* (Dublin, 1988).

10–05 The Social Welfare Act 1990 introduced a means-tested carer's allowance to replace PRA. This is payable to a person who resides with and provides full-time care and attention to a person in receipt of a range of social welfare payments who is so incapacitated as to require full-time care and attention. The qualifying persons were initially confined to those in receipt of an Irish pension who were over the age of 66 or those under that age in receipt of a long-term invalidity or blind payment. The Social Welfare Act 1991 extended this to apply to corresponding social insurance payments from other E.U. countries or countries with which Ireland has a reciprocal agreement.

10–06 The Minister for Social Welfare, Michael Woods T.D., introducing the new legislation, said that despite changes in society, such as the greater mobility of young people and the increased participation by married women in the paid labour force, the family continued to be the strongest and most reliable source of care for elderly incapacitated people.[7] The aims of the legislation, as expressed by the Minister, were to give "official recognition to the role of carer" and to provide "a secure and independent source of income" while ensuring that resources were directed at those who need them most.[8] Accordingly, the allowance was subject to a strict means test and the disregard for income was minimal (although an increased disregard for spousal income was introduced in 1994). In addition, the means of the claimant were to include such amount as the person cared for "could reasonably be expected to contribute", although this provision has never been implemented in practice. The carer was originally required not to "be engaged in employment or self-employment outside his [or her] home", although this was subsequently modified. A person who is in receipt of another social welfare payment or in respect of whom a qualified adult increase is being paid is not entitled to carer's allowance. However, all married persons are now eligible to claim the allowance. It had been estimated by the Department of Social Welfare that over 8,000 persons would be entitled to carer's allowance; but by December 1993 only 4,328 were in receipt of the payment.[9]

10–07 In recent years the carer's allowance has been broadened out significantly – following a major review of the payment – with the numbers in receipt of the allowance increasing from 7,000 in 1995 to over 20,000 by 2002.[10] This was achieved through a relaxation of the means test (particularly in relation to the carer's spouse's income); relaxation of the qualification conditions (*e.g.* extending the residency rule and allowing people to work for

---

[7] 397 *Dáil Debates* Col. 755.
[8] *ibid.* Cols 755, 757 and 1042.
[9] *ibid.* Col. 756.
[10] *Review of Carer's Allowance* (Department of Social, Community and Family Affairs, Dublin, 1998).

up to 10 hours per week outside the home); and extending eligibility to carers of all ages, including children. In addition, a new carer's leave and benefit was introduced, whereby persons in employment are entitled to take up to 15 months off work to care for a person while retaining the entitlement to return to work at the end of that period and being paid a social-insurance-based carer's benefit while on leave.

10–08 The majority of recipients are women (79 per cent in 2000), which figure broadly corresponds to general estimates of the sexual division of caring responsibilities. However, the carer's allowance is heavily concentrated on carers in the 40–64 age group (70 per cent). Only 11 per cent of payments go to people of 65 years and over, compared to an estimated 25 per cent of carers of the elderly in this age bracket. This suggests that elderly carers are themselves likely to be in receipt of an old age pension (or persons in respect of whom a qualified adult increase is in payment) and are therefore ineligible for carer's allowance. There are about 500 people in receipt of carer's benefit. Like the allowance, it is expected that this will slowly but significantly increase in coming years. The vast majority (96 per cent) are women. Unfortunately, no indication is given of the age of the persons requiring care and attention; but it seems likely that the carer's allowance is largely concentrated on the elderly who require care.

2. Current Situation

10–09 The two main payments in respect of carers are the carer's allowance and carer's benefit. The details of the domiciliary care allowance scheme operated by the health board are set out below (see para. 10–41).

A. Carer's Allowance

(1) Qualification conditions

10–10 The carer's allowance is a means-tested payment to persons providing full-time care and attention for a "relevant person" who is disabled.[11] In order to be entitled to a carer's allowance one must be a carer, *i.e.* a person must be residing with and providing full-time care and attention to a relevant person.[12] In limited circumstances, a person not residing with the caree but providing full-time care and attention can qualify for the allowance. In addition, the carer:

---

[11] Social Welfare (Consolidation) Act 1993 (SW(C)A 1993), ss. 163–169 and Pt II of Third Sched. and Social Welfare (Consolidated Payments Provisions) Regulations 1994 (SW(CPP)R 1994) (S.I. No. 417 of 1994), arts 84–86 as amended.

[12] SW(C)A 1993, s. 163.

(1) must not be engaged in employment or self-employment outside the home for more than 10 hours per week;

(2) must be at least 18 years old; and

(3) must not be residing in an institution.[13]

10–11 The following additional conditions apply to a non-resident carer:

(1) there must be a direct system of communication (such as a telephone or alarm system) between the carer's residence and that of the caree;

(2) the caree must not already be receiving full-time care and attention within his or her own residence from another person.[14]

10–12 "Institution" means: (a) a hospital, convalescent home or home for persons suffering from physical or mental disability or accommodation ancillary thereto and any other similar establishment providing residence, maintenance or care for the persons therein; or (b) a private dwelling where a person is boarded out under an arrangement with a health board.[15]

10–13 "Relevant person" means a person (other than a person in receipt of a constant attendance allowance under the occupational injuries scheme) who has such a disability that he or she requires full-time care and attention and who has attained the age of 16, or who is under 16 and is a person in respect of whom an allowance is paid for domiciliary care of disabled children under section 61 of the Health Act 1970.[16]

10–14 A relevant person is regarded as requiring full-time care and attention where:

(a) he or she has such a disability that he or she requires from another person:
   (i) continual supervision and frequent assistance throughout the day in connection with normal bodily functions, or
   (ii) continual supervision in order to avoid danger to him or herself; and

(b) he or she is likely to require full-time care and attention for at least 12 months; and

(c) the nature and extent of his or her disability has been certified by a doctor.[17]

---

[13] SW(C)A 1993, s. 164 and SW(CPP)R 1994, art. 85.

[14] SW(CPP)R 1994, art. 85B as substituted by S.I. No. 340 of 2000.

[15] *ibid.*, art. 84.

[16] SW(C)A 1993, s. 163 as amended by SWA 1999, s. 10 and SWA 2000, s. 28.

[17] *ibid.*, s. 163(3) as amended by SWA 1999, s. 13 and SWA 2000, s. 28. A person may be required to attend for or submit to such medical or other examination as may be required and may be disqualified for failing to do so without good cause; s. 168B as inserted by SWA 2000, s. 11.

10–15 The terms "requires ... continual supervision and frequent assistance throughout the day in connection with normal bodily functions" and "continual supervision in order to avoid danger to him or herself" are based on U.K. legislation in relation to attendance allowance and, subsequently, disability living allowance. There has been extensive judicial consideration of the meaning of these terms by the U.K. courts.[18] However, the precise language used is not the same as the Irish wording, the legislative context is not the same, nor are the U.K. decisions self-evidently correct.[19] So it could not be said that the Irish courts would (or indeed should) necessarily the U.K. interpretation in this regard.

10–16 A carer will continue to be regarded as providing full-time care and attention to a relevant person where he or she would qualify for payment of an allowance but for the fact that either he or she or the relevant person is undergoing medical or other treatment of a temporary nature in an institution for a period of not longer than 13 weeks.[20]

(2) Means test

10–17 The means test (which is broadly similar to the OAP means test) includes means from:

- property owned by the person and/or by his or her spouse (but excluding property personally used or enjoyed by the person);

- all income which the person and/or spouse may reasonably expect to receive in the coming year (which certain exceptions);

- the value of any advantage accruing to the person or spouse from the use of property (other than a domestic dwelling or farm building, owned and occupied, furniture and personal effects) which is personally used or enjoyed by the person or spouse and the value of any advantage from the leasing of a farm of land;

- any property which the person or spouse have deprived themselves of either directly or indirectly in order to qualify for assistance.

---

[18] *R. v. National Insurance Commissioner ex parte Secretary of State for Social Services* [1981] 1 W.L.R. 1017; *In re Woodling* [1984] 1 W.L.R. 384; *R. v. Secretary of State for Social Services ex parte Connolly* [1986] 1 All E.R. 998; *Mallinson v. Secretary of State for Social Security* [1994] 1 W.L.R. 630; *Cockburn v. Chief Adjudication Officer* and *Secretary of State for Social Services v. Fairey* [1997] 3 All E.R. 844; *Stewart v. A.G. for Scotland*, reported in R(DLA) 2/00. See D. Pollard, "Attention in connection with bodily functions" (1998) 5 *J.S.S.L.* 175.

[19] The U.K. legislation relates to qualification by a person with a disability for a "cost of disability" payment, whereas the Irish legislation refers to the qualifying conditions of the caree in relation to the entitlement of a carer.

[20] SW(CPP)R 1994, art. 86 as amended by S.I. No. 333 of 1997.

10–18 The detailed means test provides that in calculating the means of a person for the purposes of the carer's allowance, account shall be taken of the following rules.

(a) Rule 1(1)[21]

10–19 Other than in such circumstances and subject to such conditions and for such periods as may be prescribed, the weekly value of any property belonging to the person (not being property personally used or enjoyed by the person or a farm of land leased by him or her) which is invested or is otherwise put to profitable use by the person or which, though capable of investment or profitable use, is not invested or put to profitable use by the person is taken into account. The weekly value of the property is calculated as follows:

(i)   the first €12,697 of the capital value of the property shall be excluded; and

(ii) the weekly value of so much of the capital value of the property as exceeds €12,697 but does not exceed €25,394.76 shall be assessed at €1.27 per each €1,269.74; and

(iii) the weekly value of so much of the capital value of the property as exceeds €25,394.76 but does not exceed €38,092.14 shall be assessed at €2.54 per each €1,269.74; and

(iv) the weekly value of so much of the capital value of the property as exceeds €38,092.14 shall be assessed at €5.08 per each €1,269.74;

but no account shall be taken under any other provision of these Rules of any appropriation of the property for the purpose of current expenditure.

10–20 Thus, Rule 1(1) provides for a system of notional assessment of means from capital. It does not matter whether the actual income from capital is greater or lesser than the notional assessment, as the latter is deemed to constitute the weekly means of a person from such capital. In practice, it would be administratively impossible to operate a system of assessment of actual income, as this would vary constantly with, for example, varying interest rates on deposit accounts or variation in returns from shares leading to frequent fluctuations in the level of pension payable. In addition, the notional system is designed to favour those with relatively small amounts of capital, as can be seen from the exclusion of the first €12,697 from assessment.

---

[21] SW(C)A 1993, Pt II of Third Sched. as substituted by SWA 2000, s. 17. See SW(CPP)R 1994, art. 87A as substituted by S.I. No. 324 of 1999.

(b) Rule 1(4)[22]

10–21 All income in cash which the person may reasonably expect to receive during the year succeeding the date of calculation is taken into account, but excluding:

1(4)(a): any sums arising from the investment or profitable use of property (not being property personally used or enjoyed by the person or a farm of land leased by him or her)[23];

1(4)(b): any sums received by way of benefit, pension, assistance, allowance, supplement or continued payment under Part II, III, IV, V or VA, or by way of a payment corresponding to child benefit under Part IV from another Member State of the E.U.;

1(4)(c): any income arising from a bonus under a scheme administered by the Minister for Education for the making of special grants to parents or guardians resident in the Gaeltacht or Breac-Gaeltacht of children attending primary schools;

1(4)(d): in the case of a qualified applicant under a scheme administered by the Minister for the Gaeltacht and known as Scéim na bhFogh-laimeoirí Gaeilge, any income received under that scheme in respect of a person who is temporarily resident with the qualified applicant, together with any other income received in respect of such temporary resident;

1(4)(e): any moneys from a charitable organisation, being a body whose activities are carried on otherwise than for profit (but excluding any public or local authority) and one of whose functions is to assist persons in need by making grants of money to them;

1(4)(f) any income arising by way of:
   (i) infectious diseases maintenance allowance to or in respect of the person or the person's dependants;
   (ii) payments by a health board in respect of a child who is boarded out;
   (iii) payments in respect of not more than two persons boarded out under section 10 of the Health (Nursing Homes) Act 1990 (insofar as the aggregate amount received in respect of each person does not exceed the maximum amount of the old age (non-contributory) pension)[24]; or
   (iv) a mobility allowance payable under section 61 of the Health Act 1970, to the person;

---

[22] Substituted by SWA 1997, s. 26. Rule 1(2) was dropped in SWA 1997 and Rules 1(2A) and 3 refer to transitional measures.

[23] Thus, actual income from capital which is subject to assessment under Rule 1(1) is excluded from the scope of Rule 1(4).

[24] Inserted by SWA 2001, s. 13.

1(4)(g): subject to Rule 5 (this should, in fact, read Rule 6), an amount of an allowance, dependant's allowance, disability pension or wound pension under the Army Pensions Acts 1923 to 1980 (including, for the purposes of this subparagraph, a British war pension) or of a combination of such allowances and such pensions except so far as such amount exceeds €101.60 per year;

[1(4)(h) relates to blind pension];

1(4)(i): in the case of a person who is not a blind person or a lone parent (within the meaning of section 157), and who has a qualified child who normally resides with him or her, all his or her earnings except and in so far as the annual amount of such earnings is calculated to exceed €132.08 for each such child of whom account has not already been taken in accordance with this paragraph in calculating the means of another person;

[1(4)(j) relates to OFP];

1(4)(k): in the case of a person who is not a blind person, any moneys, except so far as they exceed €66.04 per year, received by the person in respect of employment as an outworker under a scheme that is, in the opinion of the Minister, charitable in character and purpose;

1(4)(l): such amount as may be prescribed of income from employment by a health board or by a person approved by a health board as a home help;

1(4)(m): any moneys received by way of a training allowance from an organisation while undergoing a course of rehabilitative training provided by an organisation approved by the Minister for Health and Children for the provision of such training;

[1(4)(mm) relates to OFP];

[1(4)(n) relates to BP or OFP];

1(4)(o): such income as may be prescribed, arising from such activities as may be prescribed;

1(4)(p): payments by a health board in respect of the provision of accommodation for a child under section 5 of the Child Care Act, 1991;

1(4)(q): an amount of €2,540 together with one-half of any amount in excess of €2,540 under the Rural Environment Protection Scheme (REPS) and the Special Areas of Conservation Scheme;

1(4)(r): in the case of a person who has attained pensionable age, any moneys received under the Early Retirement Scheme from Farming operated under E.U. Council Regulation 2079/92;

[1(4)(s) relates to OFP];

1(4)(t): any moneys in respect of rent from a person who resides with the claimant or beneficiary and but for the residence of such person the claimant or beneficiary would reside alone[25];

1(4)(u): any moneys received by his or her spouse in respect of participation in the Vocational Opportunities Scheme;

1(4)(v): any moneys received by his or her spouse in respect of participation in the Back to Work Allowances, Back to Education Allowance or Part-Time Job Incentive Schemes;

1(4)(w): any moneys received by his or her spouse in respect of participation in a FÁS course;

1(4)(x): such other income received by a person or his or her spouse as may be prescribed.[26]

10–22 Income assessed under Rule 1(4) is, in the absence of other means for ascertaining it, taken to be that actually received during the year immediately preceding the date of calculation. However, where such income is attributable to a period prior to the year immediately preceding the date of calculation but is received in a subsequent year, it is regarded as having been received in the year to which it is attributable.

10–23 Thus, Rule 1(4) provides for the assessment of all income in cash but subject to a lengthy list of exceptions. Many of these are now of a largely historical nature and affect relatively few people. Even the more recent exclusions tend to affect relatively few people. Although there are a number of clauses which allow general exclusion of income by regulation,[27] the practice has been to legislative for specific exclusions as these arise.

(c) Rule 1(5)

10–24 The means of a person are deemed to include the yearly value of any advantage accruing to the person from:

(a) the use or enjoyment of property (other than a domestic dwelling or a farm building, owned and occupied, furniture and personal effects) which is personally used or enjoyed by the person; and

(b) a farm of land leased by the person[28];

---

[25] Substituted by SWA 1998, s. 10.

[26] SW(CPP)R 1994, art. 90B (as inserted by S.I. No. 324 of 1999) prescribes income from an award relating to Hepatitis C from the Compensation Tribunal or a court, and compensation fro thalidomide.

[27] Rule 1(4)(o) and (x).

[28] Amended by SWA 1996, s. 37.

but for the purposes of this Rule a cottage provided under the Labourers Acts 1883 to 1965, and vested in the person or the spouse of that person pursuant to those Acts or pursuant to the Housing Acts 1966 to 1984, shall not be treated as property which is personally used or enjoyed by that person or the spouse of that person so long as payment of the purchase annuity has not been completed.

<u>(d) Rule 3</u>

10–25 If it appears that any person has, whether before or after the commencement of the Act, directly or indirectly deprived himself or herself of any income or property in order to qualify himself or herself for the receipt of the pension or allowance in question, or for the receipt thereof at a higher rate than that to which he or she would otherwise be entitled, that income or the yearly value of that property shall for the purposes of these Rules be taken to be part of the means of that person.

10–26 However, Rule 3(2)(a) provides that this does not apply to any assignment:

(i) which is an assignment to a child or children of the assignor; and

(ii) which is an assignment of property consisting of a farm of land (together with or without the stock and chattels thereon) the rateable value of which (including the buildings thereon) does not exceed £30 and of which the assignor is the owner and the occupier or the occupier only.

10–27 But Rule 3(2)(b) goes on to provide that subparagraph (a) does not apply to an assignment by a person who, at any time within the three years ending when the relevant claim for a pension or application for an increase of a pension is made, was the owner and/or occupier of any agricultural lands *exceeding* £30 in rateable value. "Assignment" includes any form of conveyance, transfer or other transaction by which a person parts with the ownership or possession of property.

10–28 A transfer will generally be accepted by the Department where the farm or business is transferred due to advanced age and / or failing health of the claimant or where the transfer is considered to be part of a genuine family settlement.

10–29 Where the income or the value of the property taken to be part of the person's means has reduced since the date of calculation, the calculation may be revised, subject to such conditions and in such circumstances as may be prescribed; but Regulations shall not cause the income or the yearly value of the property taken to be part of his or her means to be increased.

(e) Rule 4

10–30 The following provisions apply when calculating the means of a person who is one of a couple living together:

(a) the means of the person shall be taken to be one-half of the total means of the couple;

(b) the person shall be deemed to be entitled to one-half of all property to which the person or the other member of the couple is entitled or to which the person and the other member of the couple are jointly entitled;

(c) for the purposes of this Rule, the means of each member of the couple shall first be determined in accordance with these Rules (each being regarded as an applicant for a pension or a pension at a higher rate or carer's allowance, as the case may be) and the total means shall be the sum of the means of each member as so determined;

(d) where one member of the couple dies, nothing which was reckoned for the purposes of pension, or would (if such deceased member had been entitled to receive any pension) have been so reckoned, as means of the deceased member shall be so reckoned as means of the surviving member for the purpose of reducing the pension of the surviving member if any payment in respect of that pension was made before the death of the deceased member or becomes payable in respect of a period previous or part of which was previous to that death.

10–31 "Couple" means a married couple who are living together or a man and woman who are not married to each other but are cohabiting as husband and wife. In calculating the means of a person who is one of a married couple living apart from his spouse, any sum paid by him to his spouse under a separation order shall be deducted in calculating his means.

10–32 Rule 4(1A) provides that in the case of carer's allowance, in calculating the weekly means of the other member of the couple the following are excluded:

(a) an amount, not exceeding the maximum rate of the old age (contributory) pension, of a social security payment payable under the legislation of another state; and

(b) an amount, not exceeding half the amount of the increase in respect of a qualified child payable with OACP of a social security payment payable under the legislation of another state in respect of each qualified child for which an increase is granted under section 165(1).

Rule 4(1B) provides for a significant disregard for spousal earnings in the case of carer's allowance. Under this Rule, in calculating the weekly means of the couple (other than means derived from a social security payment payable under the legislation of another state), a prescribed amount (currently €382 per week in the case of a married/co-habiting person or €191 per week in the case of a single person) is disregarded.[29]

(f) Rule 5

10–33 Where:

(a) an old age (non-contributory) pension, blind pension, widow(er)'s (non-contributory) pension, orphan's (non-contributory) pension, one parent family payment or carer's allowance is in course of payment to or in respect of a person or the spouse of the person or both of them; and

(b) a pension or pensions (in this Rule referred to as "the other pension"), not being a pension or pensions mentioned in paragraph (a), is in course of payment to or in respect of the person or the spouse of the person or both of them;

in calculating the means of the person or of the spouse or of both of them for the purposes of old age (non-contributory) pension, blind pension, widow(er)'s (non-contributory) pension, orphan's (non-contributory) pension, one parent family payment or carer's allowance (as the case may require), any portion of the amount of an increase in the other pension or the aggregate increase, where more than one increase in the other pension has occurred, which, if it were reckoned as means, would result in a reduction in the amount of the pension or combined pensions (as the case may be) which would be greater than the amount by which the other pension has been increased, shall not be reckoned as means.[30]

(g) Rule 6

10–34 The amount of any allowance, special allowance, dependant's allowance, disability pension or wound pension under the Army Pensions Acts 1923 to 1980, or pension under the Military Service (Pensions) Acts 1924 to 1964, arising out of service in the period commencing on April 23, 1916, and ending on September 30, 1923, or pension under the Connaught Rangers (Pensions) Acts 1936 to 1964, is disregarded in the calculation of means.

---

[29] SW(CPP)R 1994, art. 89(2) as amended by S.I. No. 120 of 2002.
[30] Amended by SWA 1995, s. 23, SWA 1996, s. 19 and SWA 1997, s. 20.

(3) Payments

10–35 CA is payable at a flat rate, with increases for qualified children as appropriate (no increases for qualified adults apply).[31] "Secondary benefits" are generally payable with CA. The rate of the allowance is currently somewhat higher than the standard social assistance rate for people aged under 65/66, while the rate for those over 66 is set at the same level as the old age pension. Where a person is caring for more than one person, a 50 per cent increase in the payment is made. An annual respite care grant is payable to the carer.[32]

(4) Disqualifications

10–36 A person is not entitled to carer's allowance if he or she is absent from the State or if he or she is undergoing penal servitude, imprisonment or detention in legal custody (subject to certain exceptions).[33]

B. Carer's Benefit

(1) Qualification conditions

10–37 Carer's Benefit (CB) is a payment made to insured people who leave the workforce to provide full-time care and attention to persons who require full-time care and attention.[34] While entitlement to carer's leave and benefit are intended to operate in a complementary manner, entitlement to leave – which is set out in the Carer's Leave Act 2001 – is separate from entitlement to benefit, *i.e.* unlike maternity benefit, entitlement to carer's benefit is not dependent on entitlement to carer's leave. In order to be entitled to a carer's benefit one must be at least 16 years old and a carer, *i.e.* a person must be residing with and providing full-time care and attention to a relevant person.[35] In addition, the carer:

(1) must have been engaged in remunerative full-time employment as an employed contributor for the three-month period prior to the first day in respect of which the claim is made[36];

---

[31] SW(C)A 1993, s. 165.

[32] *ibid.*, s. 168A as substituted by SWA 2001, s. 14 and SWA 2002, s. 3.

[33] *ibid.*, s. 211.

[34] See SW(C)A 1993, ss. 82A–J (inserted by SWA 2002, s. 10) as amended. The main regulations relating to Carer's Benefit are contained in SW(CPP)R 1994, arts 35A–G (inserted by S.I. No.340 of 2000).

[35] SW(C)A 1993, s. 82A. Again, as in the case of carer's allowance, in limited circumstances persons not residing with the caree but providing full-time care may qualify for benefit. See above para. 10–11. The definition of relevant person is identical to that set out above in relation to the carer's allowance.

[36] That is, employment for an aggregate of not less than 34 hours in each period of a

(2) must not engage in employment or self-employment of more than 10 hours per week[37]; and

(3) must satisfy the contribution conditions.

(2) Contribution conditions

10–38 The contribution conditions are that the person must have at least 156 paid contributions and must have 39 paid or credited contributions in the last contribution year before the benefit year in which the claim is made, or in the 12 months immediately prior to the first day for which the benefit is claimed, or 26 weeks in each of the last two contribution years before the beginning of the benefit year (the latter condition is to allow job-sharers to benefit).[38]

(3) Payments

10–39 CB is payable at a flat rate, with increases for qualified children as appropriate (no increases for qualified adults apply).[39] "Secondary benefits" are not generally payable with CB, as it is considered to be a short-term payment. Where a person is caring for more than one person, a 50 per cent increase in the payment is made. The rate of benefit is currently set at an intermediate rate above that payable in respect of all other social insurance payments to those of working age and about 10 per cent above the rate of carer's allowance. Benefit is payable for up to 65 weeks, whether consecutive or not. An annual respite care grant is payable to the carer.

(4) Disqualifications

10–40 A person is not entitled to carer's benefit if he or she is absent from the State or if he or she is undergoing penal servitude, imprisonment or detention in legal custody (subject to certain exceptions).[40] A person who, having been in receipt of benefit for a period of less than six weeks, ceases to be entitled to such benefit is disqualified for receipt of benefit in respect of the same person for six weeks from the last day which he or she was entitled to benefit.[41]

---

fortnight within the three-month period prior to the claim. SW(C)A, s. 82B(5) as amended by SWA 2002, s. 15. But see s. 82B(6).

[37] SW(C)A 1993, s. 82(B)(b) and SW(CPP)R 1994, art. 35E.

[38] *ibid.*, s. 82C.

[39] *ibid.*, s. 82D.

[40] *ibid.*, s. 211.

[41] *ibid.*, s. 82I.

C. Domiciliary Care Allowance

10–41   The domiciliary care allowance scheme is operated under section 61 of the Health Act 1970, which enables arrangements to assist in the maintenance at home of sick or infirm persons or a person who would otherwise require maintenance otherwise than at home. No statutory instrument was made in relation to the scheme and it is operated on the basis of a circular. The scheme applies to children up to the age of 16 years who "require from another person constant care or supervision, *i.e.* continual or continuous care or supervision substantially greater than that which would normally be required by a child of the same age and sex". The scheme is intended to apply to long-term disabilities only, *i.e.* which are likely to continue for at least one year, and is not intended to apply to disabilities which only intermittently or infrequently give rise to a need for "constant care". The care may be provided by the parent(s) or by another person or persons. The allowance is normally to be paid to the mother of the child but may be paid to the father or to the person who is caring for the child. Only the means of the child are taken into account in determining eligibility. In this context, means includes payments of compensation for injuries or disabilities. The payment is currently payable at €179.80 per month. It appears that the design of the scheme was influenced by the U.K. attendance allowance[42]; but the Irish payment is significantly different in that, first, it is confined to children and, secondly, unlike attendance allowance, the purpose of the payment is explicitly to compensate for the "additional burden" of caring for a child.

---

[42] See Ogus and Barendt, *The Law of Social Security* (2nd ed., Butterworths, London, 1982), pp. 171–177.

CHAPTER 11

Lone Parent Payments

11–01 This chapter looks at support for lone parents under the social welfare code and, in particular, at the one-parent family payment (OFP), which is currently the main social welfare support for lone parents.

1. Background

11–02 The financial needs of "lone parents" or "one-parent families" had not been provided for in any comprehensive way under the social welfare system until recently.[1] Originally, lone parents would have been dependent on the general Poor Law (subsequently home assistance). However, "lone parents" in the nineteenth century would have been predominantly widows rather than separated or unmarried parents. The vast majority of such parents were – and are – women. Official views tended to be much more favourable towards widows than towards unmarried mothers. The 1834 Poor Law Commission, referring to the position in Britain, had noted that widows alone had "established a right to public support" independent of any claim to be unable to find employment. In contrast, the Viceregal Commission on the Poor Laws, which reported in 1906, recommended that the different classes be segregated into different institutions appropriate to their needs. Mothers of illegitimate children were "on the occasion of their first lapse" to be sent to a special institution but "more depraved cases" were to be separated from their children and boarded in religious houses or the labour houses to which vagrants were also to be committed.

11–03 Independence did not bring any dramatic change in the attitude to widows and unmarried mothers. In the case of the Poor Law, attitudes towards women – and, in particular, different categories of mothers – were strikingly displayed in the report of the Commission on the Relief of the Poor (1927). The Commission divided unmarried mothers into two categories: those who were "amenable to reform" and "less hopeful cases". The first group, referred

---

[1] As the Report of the Commission on Social Welfare (Stationery Office, Dublin, 1986, p. 354) pointed out, such terms are "a convenient but misleading shorthand for a complex variety of family situations".

to as "first offenders," required moral upbuilding. However, the "women who had fallen more than once" should be housed in separate institutions. The Commission was concerned that there was no power to detain unmarried mothers in institutions "even where it is clearly necessary" for their own protection, and recommended that there should be power to retain a person, although this was to be in no sense penal but for the benefit of the woman and her child. In contrast, the Commission took a much more positive view of widows and deserted mothers, recommending a mother's pension and commenting favourably on the United Kingdom widow's contributory pension as having "many attractive features". The recommendation for separate institutional accommodation for unmarried mothers was implemented, at least in part, but the majority of unmarried mothers remained in general poor law institutions. The Government, in response to a Dáil 1928 motion calling for a contributory widow's pension, promised to establish an inquiry; but no action had been taken when the Government went out of office in 1932.

11–04 Subsequently, payments were introduced to cover specific groups (which included but were not exclusively lone parents) based on their status. Thus, the Fianna Fáil Government introduced a widow's pension in 1935. Originally this was intended to be a mainly contributory pension (with limited means-tested pensions for specific groups of widows who would not qualify for a contribution-based payment). However, because of the large number of widows not qualifying, it was effectively remade in 1936 as a dual contributory and non-contributory pension.[2]

11–05 Payments for lone parents received relatively little attention in subsequent decades and did not feature strongly in the 1949 White Paper, although a number of changes were made to the widow's pensions in the late 1940s and early 1950s. It was not until the 1970s that further major contingency payments were introduced, with deserted wife's allowance in 1970, deserted wife's benefit and unmarried mother's allowance in 1973, and prisoner's wife's allowance in 1974. These payments were to be paid on a long-term basis and without any requirement that a woman should seek employment at any stage. Many lone parents – in particular separated persons and unmarried fathers – were excluded from the scope of these payments and had to rely on the lowest social welfare payments. The Commission on Social Welfare recommended an overall restructuring of social assistance in terms of the income needs of claimants rather than on a categorical basis and envisaged that this would entitle all one-parent families to a payment.

11–06 The Social Welfare Act 1989 introduced a deserted husband's

---

[2] M. Cousins, *The Birth of Social Welfare* (Four Courts Press, Dublin, 2002), Chap. 3.

allowance and a widower's (non-contributory) pension; but rather than introducing a further categorical payment this was, in effect, a step towards a major unification of payments. This took place in the Social Welfare Act 1990, which provided for a lone parent's allowance, which was brought into effect in November 1990. This was a means-tested payment and was payable to a lone parent of either sex who had at least one qualified child residing with him or her. Thus, the categorical basis, which had existed up to 1990, was ended and, as a result, lone parents in receipt of existing payments were automatically transferred to the lone parent's allowance. Two social insurance (or contributory) payments which applied only to women – the widow's (contributory) pension and the deserted wife's benefit – were retained and thus there continued to be discrimination against widowers and deserted husbands.

11–07 The Irish courts have twice held that discrimination against deserted husbands in this way is not unconstitutional.[3] The E.U. Directive on equal treatment in matters of social security (see Chapter 9) provides that the Directive does not apply to survivor's benefits or to family benefits, and thus is not relevant in relation to these areas. The E.U. Commission proposed a Directive on completing the implementation of the principle of equal treatment in social security (COM (87) 494 final) in 1987, which would have provided for the extension of the principle of equal treatment to both survivors and family benefits. This proposed Directive would have required the abolition of all discrimination between men and women as regards these payments. Although the proposal was never agreed by the Council of Ministers of the E.U., it is likely that it had some effect on the decisions by the Irish Government to prospectively eliminate equal treatment in relation to these areas.

11–08 The Social Welfare Act 1994 transformed the existing widow's (contributory) pension into a survivor's pension (subsequently renamed widow's and widower's pension) for both sexes (see Chapter 3). Subsequently, in 1996, Minister Proinsias de Rossa introduced a one-parent family payment to subsume the lone parent's allowance, and deserted wife's benefit was abolished for new claimants. It had originally been stated that this payment would not to be means-tested[4] (hence, perhaps, the unusual title of "payment" rather than allowance). In fact, OFP is broadly similar to lone parent's allowance but with a comparatively generous disregard for income from employment.

---

[3] *Dennehy v. Minister for Social Welfare*, unreported, High Court, July 26, 1984; *Lowth v. Minister for Social Welfare* [1998] 4 I.R. 321. See below para. 11–43 for further discussion.
[4] Department of Social Welfare Press Release, February 19, 1995.

2. Current Situation

11–09 In addition to the one-parent family payment, a number of lone parents continue to claim deserted wife's benefit and allowance. However, these payments have been discontinued as regard new claims. In addition, several thousands of lone parents qualify for the widow's (contributory) pension (see Chapter 3).

A. One-Parent Family Payment[5]

(1) Qualification conditions

11–10 In order to qualify for one-parent family payment (OFP), a person must be a "qualified parent", *i.e.* a widow/er, separated spouse, an unmarried person, or a person whose spouse has been committed in custody to a prison or place of detention for a period of not less than six months, who has at least one qualified child normally residing with him or her.[6] A widow/er who has remarried is not regarded as a widow/er for these purposes.

(a) Separated spouse

11–11 A person is to be regarded as being a separated spouse if :

(a) she and her spouse have lived apart from one another for a continuous period of at least three months immediately preceding the date of her claim for one-parent family payment and continue to so live apart; and

(b) she makes and continues to make appropriate efforts, in the particular circumstances, to obtain maintenance from a liable relative.[7]

11–12 The term "lived apart" is one which features in family law both in this jurisdiction (in section 5 of the Family Law (Divorce) Act 1996) and in the United Kingdom, and it has received extensive judicial consideration. There would appear to be no reason why the interpretation applied would not also be relevant in the context of social welfare law. In *McA. v. McA.*[8] the High Court discussed the meaning of the term "lived apart". Following the

---

[5] The main provisions are set out in Social Welfare (Consoidation) Act 1993 (SW(C)A 1993), ss. 157–162 (as inserted by Social Welfare Act 1996 (SWA 1996), s. 17) and in Social Welfare (Consolidation Payments Provisions) Regulations 1994 (S.I. No. 417 of 1994) (SW(CPP)R 1994), arts 79–83B (as inserted by S.I. No. 426 of 1996) as amended.

[6] SW(C)A 1993, s. 157 as inserted by SWA 1996, s. 17.

[7] SW(CPP)R 1994, art. 80 as amended by S.I. No. 139 of 1999.

[8] [2000] 1 I.R. 457. This case has been followed by an Appeals Officer in a recent decision: see Social Welfare Appeals Office, *Annual Report 2001* (Stationery Office, Dublin, 2002), p. 23.

English decision in *Santos v. Santos*,[9] McCracken J. held that the phrase "lived apart" must be construed as meaning something more than mere physical separation. He stated:

"Marriage is not primarily concerned with where the spouses live or whether they live under the same roof, and indeed there can be a number of circumstances in which the matrimonial relationship continues even though the parties are not living under the same roof as, for example, where one party is in hospital or an institution of some kind, or is obliged to spend a great deal of time away from home in the course of his or her employment. Such separations do not necessarily constitute the persons as living apart from one another. Clearly there must be something more than mere physical separation and the mental or intellectual attitude of the parties is also of considerable relevance. I do not think one can look solely either at where the parties physically reside, or at their mental or intellectual attitude to the marriage. Both of these elements must be considered, and in conjunction with each other."[10]

Accordingly, McCracken J. had "no doubt that, just as parties who are physically separated may in fact maintain their full matrimonial relationship, equally parties who live under the same roof may be living apart from one another".

(b) Unmarried person

11–13 A person is to be regarded as being an unmarried person if, not being a married person, he or she is the parent of a qualified child and he or she makes reasonable efforts to obtain maintenance from a liable relative. The term "parent" is deemed to include the adoptive parent, in the case of a child who has been adopted under the Adoption Acts 1952 to 1991 (or under such other form of adoption as the Minister considers appropriate in the circumstances).[11]

(c) Prisoner's spouse

11–14 A person is to be regarded as being a prisoner's spouse if he or she is the spouse of a person who: (a) is in a prison or place of detention; and (b) has for a period of not less than six months immediately preceding the date of claim been in custody by order of a court or a responsible authority, or is

---

[9] [1972] 2 All E.R. 246.

[10] [2000] 1 I.R. 457. See also the approach of the Australian courts in *Staunton-Smith v. Secretary, Department of Social Security* (1991) 14 A.A.R. 325.

[11] SW(CPP)R 1994, art. 81 as amended by S.I. No. 426 of 1996. While a separated spouse is required to make *appropriate* efforts to obtain maintenance, an unmarried person is required to make *reasonable* efforts. It appears that nothing turns on this difference in language.

committed in custody by a court or a responsible authority for a period of not less than six months.[12]

(d) Normal residence of qualified child

11–15 A qualified child is regarded as normally residing with a qualified parent where: (a) the child is resident with that parent; and (b) that parent has the main care and charge of the child.[13] A qualified child who is resident in an institution is regarded as normally residing with the qualified parent where that parent contributes towards the cost of the child's maintenance in the institution and is the person with whom the child would be regarded as normally residing if the child were not resident in an institution. "Institution" means:

(a) a hospital, convalescent home or home for persons suffering from physical or mental disability or accommodation ancillary thereto;

(b) any other similar establishment providing residence, maintenance or care for the persons therein; or

(c) any prison, place of detention or other establishment to which articles 23 and 24 of the Social Welfare (Social Assistance) Regulations 1993 apply.

(e) Efforts to obtain maintenance

11–16 Thus, separated spouses are required to make appropriate efforts to obtain maintenance as a precondition and as an ongoing condition of their claim. The Departmental guidelines provide that the efforts condition is regarded as being satisfied:

- if the separated couple is involved in a structured mediation process which addresses the spouse's liability to maintain the claimant and dependent children;

- if the spouse is working in this country or abroad and the claimant approaches the District Court Clerk and requests that a maintenance summons be served on him or her;

- if the claimant takes the spouse to court for maintenance;

- if the claimant cannot trace the spouse and has made an effort to do so, for example by reporting them as missing to the Gardaí, etc.;

- if the spouse is in receipt of social welfare payment only, the claimant is not required to take any action;

- if the current income of the spouse is too low to reasonably expect that any maintenance payment can be made; or

---

[12] SW(CPP)R 1994, art. 82 as amended by S.I. No. 426 of 1996.
[13] *ibid.*, art. 83 as amended by S.I. No. 426 of 1996.

- if evidence is available to prove allegations that the spouse is violent and that there is a consequent risk to the claimant in the event of further contact.

11–17   An unmarried person is obliged to make reasonable efforts to obtain maintenance from a liable relative. However, the efforts condition is not treated as a *precondition* to the award of the claim for new unmarried applicants, although unmarried claimants are required to make such efforts subsequent to any award. This requirement is applicable to new claims on or after May 1, 1997.

(2) Means test

11–18   OFP is a mean-tested payment and the means test is set out in Part II of the Third Schedule to SW(C)A 1993. This is broadly similar to the means test applying to the old age (non-contributory) pension (see Chapter 3). However, income assessed under Rule 1(4) includes, in the case of OFP, the net cash value of such non-cash benefits as may be prescribed, and such income received by a qualified child or qualified children as may be prescribed. In addition, in the case of OFP, in order to encourage the employment of lone parents, claimants of OFP are allowed to earn gross weekly earnings (including wages and profit from any form of self-employment) of up to €146.53 per week before their OFP is affected and up to €293.07 before the payment is withdrawn entirely.[14] Where a person's weekly earnings exceed the lower amount, an amount of €146.53 and half the weekly earnings in excess of that amount is disregarded (subject to the upper threshold at which entitlement ceases). Persons exceeding this limit can retain a portion of OFP for a transitional period of up to 12 months.[15] In addition, persons in receipt of OFP are allowed to retain a certain amount of maintenance paid by the spouse or absent parent.[16]

11–19   The means test includes means from:
- most property owned by the person and/or by his or her spouse (but excluding property personally used or enjoyed by the person);
- all income which the person and/or spouse may reasonably expect to receive in the coming year (with certain exceptions);
- the value of any advantage accruing to the person or spouse from the use of property (other than a domestic dwelling or farm building, owned and

---

[14] See SW(C)A 1993, s. 158(3) (as amended by SWA 1999, s. 31) and Pt II of Third Sched. as amended by SWA 1999.

[15] SW(C)A 1993, s. 158(4) as amended by SWA 2001, s. 21 and SW(CPP)R 1994, art. 83A as amended by S.I. No. 103 of 2001.

[16] Rule 1(4)(s) below.

occupied, furniture and personal effects) which is personally used or enjoyed by the person or spouse and the value of any advantage from the leasing of a farm of land;

- any property which the person or spouse have deprived themselves of either directly or indirectly in order to qualify for assistance.

11–20 The detailed means test provides that in calculating the means of a person for the purposes of the old age (non-contributory) pension, account shall be taken of the following rules.

(a) Rule 1(1)[17]

11–21 Other than in such circumstances and subject to such conditions and for such periods as may be prescribed, the weekly value of any property belonging to the person (not being property personally used or enjoyed by the person or a farm of land leased by him or her) which is invested or is otherwise put to profitable use by the person or which, though capable of investment or profitable use is not invested or put to profitable use by the person is taken into account.The weekly value of the property is calculated as follows:

(i) the first €12,697 of the capital value of the property shall be excluded; and

(ii) the weekly value of so much of the capital value of the property as exceeds €12,697 but does not exceed €25,394.76 shall be assessed at €1.27 per each €1,269.74; and

(iii) the weekly value of so much of the capital value of the property as exceeds €25,394.76 but does not exceed €38,092.41 shall be assessed at €2.54 per each €1,269.74; and

(iv) the weekly value of so much of the capital value of the property as exceeds €38,092.41 shall be assessed at €5.08 per each €1,269.74;

but no account shall be taken under any other provision of these Rules of any appropriation of the property for the purpose of current expenditure.

11–22 Thus, Rule 1(1) provides for a system of notional assessment of means from capital. It does not matter whether the actual income from capital is greater or lesser than the notional assessment, as the latter is deemed to constitute the weekly means of a person from such capital. In practice, it would be administratively impossible to operate a system of assessment of actual income, as this would vary constantly with, for example, varying interest rates on deposit accounts or variation in returns from shares leading to frequent

---

[17] See SW(C)A 1993, Pt II of the Third Sched. as substituted by SWA 2000, s. 17.

fluctuations in the level of pension payable. In addition, the notional system is designed to favour those with relatively small amounts of capital, as can be seen from the exclusion of the first €12,697 from assessment.

(b) Rule 1(4)[18]

11–23 All income in cash (including the net cash value of prescribed non-cash benefits)[19] which the person may reasonably expect to receive during the year succeeding the date of calculation is taken into account, but excluding:

1(4)(a):   any sums arising from the investment or profitable use of property (not being property personally used or enjoyed by the person or a farm of land leased by him or her)[20];

1(4)(b):   any sums received by way of benefit, pension, assistance, allowance, supplement or continued payment under Part II, III, IV, V or VA, or by way of a payment corresponding to child benefit under Part IV from another Member State of the E.U.;

1(4)(c):   any income arising from a bonus under a scheme administered by the Minister for Education for the making of special grants to parents or guardians resident in the Gaeltacht or Breac-Gaeltacht of children attending primary schools;

1(4)(d):   in the case of a qualified applicant under a scheme administered by the Minister for the Gaeltacht and known as Scéim na bhFogh-laimeoirí Gaeilge, any income received under that scheme in respect of a person who is temporarily resident with the qualified applicant, together with any other income received in respect of such temporary resident;

1(4)(e):   any moneys from a charitable organisation, being a body whose activities are carried on otherwise than for profit (but excluding any public or local authority) and one of whose functions is to assist persons in need by making grants of money to them:

1(4)(f):   any income arising by way of:
     (i) infectious diseases maintenance allowance to or in respect of the person or the person's dependants;
     (ii) payments by a health board in respect of a child who is boarded out;

---

[18] Substituted by SWA 1997, s. 26. Rule 1(2) was dropped in SWA 1997 and Rules 1(2A) and 3 refer to transitional measures.

[19] SW(CPP)R 1994, art. 89 (as substituted by S.I. No. 461 of 2002) prescribes the value of housing costs paid by a liable relative and the value of "direct provision" provided by the Department of Justice, Equality and Law Reform to certain asylum seekers.

[20] Thus, actual income from capital which is subject to assessment under Rule 1(1) is excluded from the scope of Rule 1(4).

(iii) payments in respect of not more than two persons boarded out under section 10 of the Health (Nursing Homes) Act, 1990 (insofar as the aggregate amount received in respect of each person does not exceed the maximum amount of the old age (non-contributory) pension)[21]; or

(iv) a mobility allowance payable under section 61 of the Health Act 1970 to the person;

1(4)(g): subject to Rule 5 (this should, in fact, read Rule 6), an amount of an allowance, dependant's allowance, disability pension or wound pension under the Army Pensions Acts 1923 to 1980 (including, for the purposes of this subparagraph, a British war pension) or of a combination of such allowances and such pensions except so far as such amount exceeds €101.60 per year;

[1(4)(h) relates to blind pension];

[1(4)(i) does not apply to OFP];

1(4)(j): in the case of a qualified parent within the meaning of section 157 and subject to Rule 1(7), any moneys received by way of earnings (inlcuding wages and profit from any form of self-employment)[22];

1(4)(k): in the case of a person who is not a blind person, any moneys, except so far as they exceed €66.04 per year, received by the person in respect of employment as an outworker under a scheme that is, in the opinion of the Minister, charitable in character and purpose;

1(4)(l): such amount as may be prescribed, of income from employment by a health board or by a person approved by a health board as a home help;

1(4)(m): any moneys received by way of a training allowance from an organisation while undergoing a course of rehabilitative training provided by an organisation approved by the Minster for Health and Children for the provision of such training;

1(4)(mm): in the case of OFP, any moneys, subject to such limit as may be prescribed, received by way of repayment of expenses necessarily incurred in relation to travel and meals while undergoing a course of education, training or development approved by the Minister[23];

1(4)(n): in the case of OFP, any moneys received by way of a maintenance grant under the Higher Education Grants scheme, the Maintenance Grants Scheme for Students attending Post-Leaving Certificate

---

[21] Inserted by SWA 2001, s. 13.
[22] Amended by SWA 1999, s. 31.
[23] Inserted by SWA 2001, s. 13.

Courses, the Vocational Education Committees Scholarship Scheme, or the Third-Level Maintenance Scheme for Trainees[24];

1(4)(o): such income as may be prescribed, arising from such activities as may be prescribed;

1(4)(p): payments by a health board in respect of the provision of accommodation for a child under section 5 of the Child Care Act 1991;

1(4)(q): an amount of €2,540 together with one-half of any amount in excess of €2,540 under the Rural Environment Protection Scheme (REPS) and the Special Areas of Conservation Scheme;

1(4)(r): in the case of a person who has attained pensionable age, any moneys received under the Early Retirement Scheme from Farming operated under E.U. Council Regulation 2079/92;

1(4)(s): for the purposes of OFP, moneys received by way of maintenance payments (incluing payments made to or in respect of a qualified child) in so far as they do not exceed the annual housing costs actually incurred by the qualified parent (subject to such maximum as may be prescribed) together with one-half of any amount of maintenance in excess of the amount disregarded in respect of housing costs[25];

1(4)(x): such other income received by a person as may be prescribed.[26]

11–24 Income assessed under Rule 1(4) is, in the absence of other means for ascertaining it, taken to be that actually received during the year immediately preceding the date of calculation. However, where such income is attributable to a period prior to the year immediately preceding the date of calculation but is received in a subsequent year, it is regarded as having been received in the year to which it is attributable.

11–25 Thus, Rule 1(4) provides for the assessment of all income in cash but subject to a lengthy list of exceptions. Many of these are now of a largely historical nature and affect relatively few people. Even the more recent exclusions tend to affect relatively few people. Although there are a number of clauses which allow general exclusion of income by regulation,[27] the practice has been to legislative for specific exclusions as these arise.

---

[24] Substituted by SWA 2001, s. 13.

[25] *ibid.*, s. 21. This is discussed below, see para. 11–39. See SW(CPP)R 1994, art. 89C as inserted by S.I. No. 426 of 1996.

[26] SW(CPP)R 1994, art. 90B (as inserted by S.I. No. 324 of 1999) prescribes income from an award relating to Hepatitis C from the Compensation Tribunal or a court, and compensation arising from thalidomide.

[27] Rule 1(4)(o) and (x).

(c) Rule 1(5)

11–26 The means of a person are deemed to include the yearly value of any advantage accruing to the person from:

(a) the use or enjoyment of property (other than a domestic dwelling or a farm building, owned and occupied, furniture and personal effects) which is personally used or enjoyed by the person; and

(b) a farm of land leased by the person[28];

but for the purposes of this Rule, a cottage provided under the Labourers Acts 1883 to 1965, and vested in the person or the spouse of that person pursuant to those Acts or pursuant to the Housing Acts 1966 to 1984, shall not be treated as property which is personally used or enjoyed by that person or the spouse of that person so long as payment of the purchase annuity has not been completed.

(d) Rule 1(7)[29]

11–27 In the case of a qualified parent who has earnings (including wages and profits from any form of self-employment), the gross weekly earnings are deemed to constitute the weekly means of that parent from earnings. In order to provide an incentive to take up employment, an amount of €146.53 per week together with half the gross weekly earnings in excess of that amount are disregarded in calculating the assessable "gross weekly earnings".

(e) Rule 2

11–28 Notwithstanding the provisions of other Rules, for the purposes of OFP where the claimant has reached pension age (66), the gross proceeds derived from the sale of the principal residence of the claimant or beneficiary or, in the case of a married couple who are living together, the spouse of the claimant or beneficiary where such spouse has attained pensionable age, shall not, subject:

(a) to such limit;

(b) to such conditions;

(c) in such circumstances; and

(d) for such periods,

---

[28] Amended by SWA 1996.

[29] Inserted by SWA 1999, s. 31. SW(C)A 1992, s. 158(3)–(5) (as amended by SWA 1999, s. 31) provides that OFP is not payable to a person whose gross weekly earnings exceed €293.07 per week subject to transitional provisions.

as shall be prescribed, be taken into account in calculating the means of the claimant or pensioner.

11–29 In this rule "gross proceeds derived from the sale of the principal residence" means:

(a) the agreed sale price of the residence; or

(b) where the claimant or beneficiary purchases alternative accommodation, the difference between the agreed sale price of the former residence and the agreed purchase price of the replacement residence.

11–30 The exemptions do not apply to any sums arising from the investment or profitable use of the gross proceeds derived from the sale of the principal residence.

11–31 Thus, where a person sells his or her principal residence, the gross proceeds of the sale up to a maximum figure (currently €190,460.71) are exempted from the means test where the residence has been sold so as to enable the person to:

• purchase or rent alternative accommodation, which he or she occupies as hihe or sher only or main residence; or

• move into a private nursing home which has been registered under section 4 of the Health (Nursing Home) Acts 1990.[30]

11–32 From April 5, 2002, this provision was extended to any of the categories of people outlined above who:

• move in with a recipient of carer's allowance or benefit, where the recipient is that pensioner's carer or

• move to sheltered or special housing in the voluntary co-operative, statutory or private sectors that is funded under the Capital Assistance Scheme operated by the Department of the Environment and Local Government.[31]

(f) Rule 3

11–33 If it appears that any person has, whether before or after the commencement of the Act, directly or indirectly deprived himself or herself of any income or property in order to qualify himself or herself for the receipt of the pension or allowance in question, or for the receipt thereof at a higher rate than that to which he or she would otherwise be entitled, that income or

---

[30] SW(CPP)R 1994, art. 90 as amended by S.I. No. 132 of 2001 and S.I. No. 120 of 2002.
[31] S.I. No. 120 of 2002.

the yearly value of that property shall for the purposes of these Rules be taken to be part of the means of that person.

11–34　However, Rule 3(2)(a) provides that this does not apply to any assignment:

(i)　which is an assignment to a child or children of the assignor; and

(ii)　which is an assignment of property consisting of a farm of land (together with or without the stock and chattels thereon) the rateable value of which (including the buildings thereon) does not exceed £30 and of which the assignor is the owner and the occupier or the occupier only.

11–35　But Rule 3(2)(b) goes on to provide that subparagraph (a) does not apply to an assignment by a person who, at any time within the three years ending when the relevant claim for a pension (or allowance) or application for an increase of a pension is made, was the owner and/or occupier of any agricultural lands *exceeding* £30 in rateable value. "Assignment" includes any form of conveyance, transfer or other transaction by which a person parts with the ownership or possession of property.

11–36　A transfer will generally be accepted by the Department where the farm or business is transferred due to advanced age and/or failing health of the claimant or where the transfer is considered to be part of a genuine family settlement.

11–37　Where the income or the value of the property taken to be part of the person's means has reduced since the date of calculation, the calculation may be revised, subject to such conditions and in such circumstances as may be prescribed, but Regulations shall not cause the income or the yearly value of the property taken to be part of his or her means to be increased.

(g) Rule 5[32]

11–38　Where:

(a)　an old age (non-contributory) pension, blind pension, widow(er)'s (non-contributory) pension, orphan's (non-contributory) pension, one-parent family payment or carer's allowance is in course of payment to or in respect of a person or the spouse of the person or both of them; and

(b)　a pension or pensions (in this Rule referred to as "the other pension"), not being a pension or pensions mentioned in paragraph (*a*), is in course

---

[32] Rule 4 relates to the means of couples and is not relevant to OFP.

of payment to or in respect of the person or the spouse of the person or both of them;

in calculating the means of the person or of the spouse or of both of them for the purposes of old age (non-contributory) pension, blind pension, widow(er)'s (non-contributory) pension, orphan's (non-contributory) pension, one-parent family payment or carer's allowance (as the case may require) any portion of the amount of an increase in the other pension or the aggregate increase, where more than one increase in the other pension has occurred, which, if it were reckoned as means, would result in a reduction in the amount of the pension or combined pensions (as the case may be) which would be greater than the amount by which the other pension has been increased, shall not be reckoned as means.[33]

11–39 As set out above (see para. 11–16), a person is obliged to seek maintenance from the other spouse or parent. Both personal and child maintenance payable by the other spouse or parent are assessed as means. However, housing costs of up to €95.23 a week can be offset against maintenance payments with half the balance of maintenance being assessed as means in establishing entitlement to one-parent family payment.[34] "Housing costs" means rent or repayment of a loan entered into solely for the purpose of defraying money employed in the purchase, repair or essential improvement of the residence in which the qualified parent is residing, while "maintenance payments" mean any payments received under or pursuant to such maintenace arrangments as may be prescribed.[35]

11–40 Where a recipient of one-parent family payment is receiving maintenance payments by way of a court order (*i.e.* a maintenance order or an order of the court made on foot of a separation agreement),[36] he or she is liable to transfer any payments received to the Minister.[37] In practice, this may be applied where the maintenance payments have not been assessed in deciding his or her rate of payment. Failure to comply with a request to transfer maintenance payments may result in reduction of the one-parent family payment by the amount which the person is liable to transfer.[38]

---

[33] Amended by SWA 1995, s. 23, SWA 1996, s. 19 and SWA 1997, s. 20.

[34] Rule 1(4)(s) as amended by SWA 2001, s. 21. SW(CPP)R 1994, art. 89C as inserted by S.I. No. 426 of 1996.

[35] *ibid.* SW(CPP)R 1994, art. 89C(2) prescribes all forms of formal and informal arrangements, whether by court order or otherwise.

[36] SW(C)A 1993, s. 284(1) as amended by SWA 1997,s. 29.

[37] *ibid.*, s. 298.

[38] *ibid.*, s. 298 (3).

(3) Payments

11–41 OFP is payable at a flat rate, with increases for qualified children as appropriate.[39] Certain "secondary benefits" are payable with OFP.

(4) Disqualifications

11–42 A person is not entitled to OFP if he or she is absent from the State or if he or she is undergoing penal servitude, imprisonment or detention in legal custody (subject to certain exceptions).[40] The marriage or remarriage of a parent terminates entitlement to OFP.[41] A person is also disqualified for OFP if and so long as he or she and another person are "cohabiting as man and wife".[42]

3. Legal Issues

A. Discrimination between Men and Women

11–43 As outlined above, both lone parents' and widow/ers' payments are now made on a sex-neutral basis. However, there remains "historical" discrimination between the sexes in that a number of single-sex schemes still exist, although these are no longer open to new claims. The largest of these schemes is the deserted wife's benefit where there were still about 12,000 claims in payment in 2002. The E.U. Directive on equal treatment does not apply, as the deserted wife's benefit, does not fall within the material scope of the Directive.[43] In a number of cases, discrimination against men was challenged before the Irish courts on constitutional grounds. Most recently, in *Lowth v. Minister for Social Welfare*,[44] a deserted husband argued that the failure to provide a deserted husband's payment was in breach of Articles 40.1, 40.3 and 41 of the Constitution. However, the Supreme Court held against the plaintiff on the basis that Article 40.1 did not require that all citizens be treated identically without recognition of differences in relevant circumstances. Persons could be classified and treated differently once this classification was for a legitimate legislative purpose. In the particular circumstances, the Court was satisfied that there were ample grounds for the Oireachtas to

---

[39] SW(C)A 1993, ss. 159.
[40] *ibid.*, s. 211. See Chap. 15.
[41] *ibid.*, s. 158(2).
[42] *ibid.*, s. 160.
[43] Art. 3 of Directive 79/7 and see *Lowth v. Minister for Social Welfare* [1998] 4 I.R. 321 at 329–330.
[44] [1998] 4 I.R. 321.

conclude that deserted wives were in general likely to have greater needs than deserted husbands so as to justify the legislation.

B. The Cohabitation Disqualification

11–44 The cohabitation disqualification applies to the various payments which can be loosely described as lone parent's or survivor's payments.[45] Where a person is cohabiting, he or she is thereby disqualified from receiving any of these payments. Cohabitation, in this context, is thus an absolute bar to payment and not merely a factor which is taken into account in deciding the level of payment to be made. The concept of cohabitation is defined in the Social Welfare Acts as involving "living with another person as man and wife". There has been no attempt to provide a more detailed statutory definition and when the issue came before the High Court, Gannon J. stated that he considered "it unwise for the Court to supply a definition when the legislature has refrained from doing so".[46]

11–45 The Department guideslines state that no single criterion can necessarily support a decision that a couple are living together as husband and wife and that a number of factors of the relationship should be considered in deciding if cohabitation exists.[47] In particular, officers of the Department are instructed to have regard to five criteria. The first two relate to the "living together" aspect, while the remaining three focus on the relationship of husband and wife. In order to be considered to be "living together", the persons must be co-resident, although temporary or part-time absence from the residence is not considered to be inconsistent with co-residence. Secondly, the Department seeks to establish whether there is a sharing of financial and household responsibilities. The three remaining criteria relate to the stability of the relationship, the social nature of the relationship (*e.g.* do the couple act socially or represent themselves to others as husband and wife) and the sexual relationship of the couple. Proof of sexual relations is stated not to be an essential element of cohabitation, but admittance of such a relationship is stated to be "strong evidence" of cohabitation. It is not necessary that all of the five elements be established; but some elements must be established.

---

[45] See SW(C)A 1993, s. 160 (OFP); s. 101(3) (widow/er's (contributory) pension; s. 110(3) (DWB); s. 146 (widow's (non-contributory) pension; s. 154 (DWA); s. 156 (PWA).

[46] *Foley v. Moulton* [1989] I.L.R.M. 169. On the position in the U.K. see *Crake v. SBC* and *Butterworth v. SBC* [1982] 1 All E.R. 498; *Robson v. Secretary of State for Social Services* (1982) 3 F.L.R. 232; *Re J.* [1995] 1 F.L.R. 660. See generally Ogus, Barendt and Wikely, *The Law of Social Security* (4th ed., Butterworths, London, 1995), pp. 389–393.

[47] See "Guidelines for Officers in relation to Cohabitation" in D/SCFA, *Review of the One-Parent Family Payment* (Stationery Office, Dublin, 2000), App. VI.

11–46 Thus, it is not necessary that there be any financial support of the claimant by the "cohabitee" in order that cohabitation should exist. The Department's interpretation of the law on this point has been upheld by the High Court in a case in which the Court rejected the argument that the cohabitation rule should be interpreted in a purposive manner so as only to apply where actual financial support was being provided.[48] In that case, Gannon J. approved the comments of the English courts in *Thomas v. Thomas*,[49] in which it was stated:

> "'Cohabitation' means living together as husband and wife and ... consists in the husband acting as a husband towards the wife and the wife acting as a wife towards the husband ..."

11–47 Gannon J. refused to follow a number of Canadian cases in which it had been held that the concept of "living together as husband and wife" should be construed in the light of the purposes of the legislation so as to refer to the economic relationship of the couple and not to their sexual or social relationship.[50]

C. Support from the Spouse/Parent

(1) The obligation to seek maintenance

11–48 Under the deserted wife's scheme, there was, until November 1990, a requirement that in order to qualify for a payment, the claimant must have made "reasonable efforts" to trace and obtain maintenance from his or her spouse. In practice, this requirement was interpreted in a strict manner. Claimants were often required to make an application to court for maintenance even in circumstances where it was clear that there was little possibility of obtaining support from the spouse. If a court order was made but was not paid, the claimant would then be expected to go back to court – possibly on several occasions – in an attempt to have the order enforced. It was, in practice, extremely difficult in many cases for claimants to bring their cases to court. If and when they did get to court, the awards made were very low. Ward[51] reported that in 80 per cent of orders in the District Court, the total order was less than

---

[48] *Foley v. Moulton* [1989] I.L.R.M. 169. See G. Whyte, "Social Welfare Law – The Cohabitation Rule" (1989) 11 D.U.L.J. 187.

[49] [1848] 2 K.B. 294.

[50] *Re Proc and Minister for Community and Social Services* (1975) 53 D.L.R. (3d) 512; *Re Stoikiewicz and Filas* (1979) 92 D.L.R. (3d) 128. A similar approach has been adopted by the New Zealand courts (see *Ruka v. Department of Social Welfare* [1997] 1 N.Z.L.R. 154) but rejected in Australia: *Lambe v. Director-General of Social Services* (1981) 38 A.L.R. 405; *Lynam v. Director-General of Social Services* (1983-84) 52 A.L.R. 128.

[51] P. Ward, *Financial Consequences of Marital Breakdown* (Combat Poverty Agency, Dublin, 1989).

£60 per week with over half the awards being for £40 or less. He also showed that 60 per cent of all current orders were below the then level of supplementary welfare allowance and that no less than 81 per cent of such orders were less than the rate of deserted wife's benefit. Ward showed that even where a maintenance order was made, such orders were not paid regularly in 87 per cent of all cases.

11–49   The reform of the lone parents payment in 1990 changed the requirement of having to make "reasonable efforts" to one requiring the claimant to "make and continue to make appropriate efforts" to obtain maintenance.[52] However, this small change in wording masks a more fundamental change in approach. From 1990 on, the practice of the Department has been to interpret this provision in a much more flexible way than the previous rules and it is only in situations where the Department feels that the claimant should reasonably be able to obtain maintenance that the Department will insist on the institution of court proceedings. In other circumstances, the Department may grant the payment to the claimant and then pursue the spouse under the liable relative provisions set out below.

(2) The liability to maintain

11–50   The Social Welfare Acts of 1989 and 1990 introduced the provisions concerning the liability of family members to maintain persons and to repay payments to the Department.[53] A person is now liable to maintain his or her spouse (including a divorced spouse)[54] and children aged under 18, and children aged over 18 and under 21 who are receiving full-time education or instruction by day at any university, college, school or other educational establishment.[55] The provisions apply to OFP and supplementary welfare allowance but we will focus here on OFP.

11–51   The Department can require any liable relative to repay some or all of the amount of a payment made to a claimant. The maximum amount to be deducted cannot exceed the total social welfare payment being paid to the

---

[52] As we have seen, reference to reasonable efforts crept back in in 1996 in relation to unmarried spouses, but this does not appear to imply a reversion to a tougher test.

[53] While such liable relative provisions have existed for many years in relation to the Poor Law, home assistance and supplementary welfare allowance, these provisions were not applied to any great extent in recent years.

[54] SW(C)A 1993, s. 284(1) as amended by SWA 1999, s. 29. By implication, a decree of nullity would terminate liability in respect of the "spouse" (although not of any children).

[55] See *ibid.*, ss. 284–299, as amended and the Social Welfare (Liable Relative) Regulations 1999 (S.I. No. 138 of 1999) (SW(LR)R 1999) and the Social Welfare (Liable Relative) (Amendment) Regulations 2000 (S.I. No. 314 of 2000).

claimant. If the liable relative does not contribute, the Department can apply to the District Court for an order directing the person to make the repayments.[56]

11–52 The detailed provisions in relation to the determination of the contribution are set out in Regulations prescribed under section 286(1A).[57] When a claim for one-parent family payment is being investigated, the claimant is asked for the identity of the liable relative, who may not be interviewed at claim stage, but is informed of his or her potential liability by letter. After a claim is awarded and if it is deemed that the liable relative may be in a position to contribute, then he or she is contacted by the Department at that stage, and may be interviewed. The liable relative and his or her employer are obliged to provide information to the Department in relation to the amount of a contribution.[58] Failure to provide requested information constitutes an offence.[59]

11–53 The financial and family situation of each liable relative is assessed in detail. The amount which the liable relative is liable to contribute is: (a) the weekly value of any property belonging to the liable relative (not being property personally used or enjoyed by him or her) which is (or which is capable of being) invested or otherwise put to profitable use calculated as set out above in Rule 1(1); and (b) the other gross income actually received or likely to be received in the contribution year in which the calculation of liability is begin completed (or a different year if the deciding officer or appeals officer feels the former is not appropriate), less income tax and PRSI, any maintenance payments being paid by the liable relative in respect of the spouse and/or children where such payments have been taken into account in deciding the amount of OFP payable, and an allowance in respect of rent or repayment of a loan for the purposes of defraying money employed in the purchase, repair or essential improvement of the residence in which the liable relative is residing up to €4,953 per annum. If, however, the liable relative has remarried or is cohabiting as husband and wife with a person who is in employment or self-employment, then only half of the capital value of property is assessed up to €2,476.50.[60]

11–54 The following deductions are also allowed:
- a personal allowance set at the equivalent of the maximum personal weekly rate of one-parent family payment plus €19.00;
- the current amount of the increase in respect of a qualified child payable

[56] SW(C)A 1999, s. 286 as amended by SWA 1996, s.19 and SWA 1999, s. 29.
[57] Inserted by SWA 1999, s. 29.
[58] SW(C)A 1993, s. 212(2) and S.I. No. 138 of 1999, art. 7.
[59] *ibid.*, s. 212(6) as amended by SWA 1999, s. 26.
[60] SW(LR)R 1999, art. 5 as amended by S.I. No. 314 of 2000.

with OFP in respect of each qualified child residing full-time with the liable relative for whom he or she has the main care and charge.[61]

11–55 The weekly contribution due by the liable relative will be the lower of the following: the amount calculated in accordance with article 4, the weekly rate of OFP in payment to the spouse or parent as the case may be, or in the case of a qualified child of an unmarried person, an amount not exceeding the maximum amount set in section 23 of the Family Law (Maintenance of Spouses and Children) Act 1976 as amended in respect of each qualified child.[62] An explanation of the assessment and allowances is furnished to each liable relative, with a copy of the decision on the amount he or she is liable to contribute and the liable relative can appeal to the Social Welfare Appeals Office within 21 days if he or she is not satisfied with the deciding officer's decision.

11–56 The Minister is empowered to take an action in the District Court to seek enforced payment of contributions due, by way of instalment orders or attachment of earnings order.[63] The latter order is directed to the person who has the liable relative in his or her employment to make specified deductions from his or her earnings and to pay the amounts deducted to the District Court clerk for transmission to the Department. Such actions would normally only be considered where the liable relative had failed to comply with the determination on contributions due although it appears that no such action has in fact gone to court to date. The Minister may apply to the District Court for an order directing the arrest and imprisonment of the person for non-compliance with an order.

11–57 Maintenance payments made under a court order offset in whole or in part contributions due by a liable relative as do any maintenance payments transferred to the Department in accordance with section 298.[64]

11–58 There are several issues in regard to the practical operation of this legislation. First, the Supreme Court held, in relation to the enforcement of earlier liable relative provisions, that the question as to the claimant's initial entitlement to the payment (and any consequent liability to maintain) may be reopened in the District Court.[65] Section 286(4) of the Act was amended in

---

[61] SW(LR)R 1999, art. 4 as amended by S.I. No. 314 of 2000.
[62] *ibid.*, art. 4 as amended by S.I. No. 314 of 2000.
[63] SW(C)A 1993, ss. 286–296.
[64] *ibid.*, s. 297 and SW(LR)R 1999, art. 6.
[65] *Board of Public Assistance for the South Cork Public Assistance District v. O'Regan* [1949] I.R. 415. In that case, the Supreme Court considered a case stated in relation to an application to the District Court to enforce recovery of payments made to the

1998 to remove the power of the District Court to "fix the amount of the contribution to be made" but this does not address the issue as to whether a contribution is due at all or not.

11–59 Secondly, it is unclear if the liable relative will be allowed to rely on defences such as the fact that the circumstances of the case (including the conduct of the claimant) would make it repugnant to justice to order the liable relative to contribute. In the area of family law, such a defence would mean that the relative would not be liable for maintenance, but it is not clear if the same rules will apply in the social welfare area. In *National Assistance Board v. Wilkinson*,[66] the Divisional Court, considering similar U.K. legislation, held that a husband was not liable to contribute if his wife had been guilty of adultery or desertion. However, the Court of Appeal in *National Assistance Board v. Parkes*[67] held that the correct basis for this decision was the phrase in the U.K. legislation which required the court to "have regard to all the circumstances".[68] The Irish legislation contains no such phrase and the old Irish case of *McEvoy v. Guardians of the Kilkenny Union*,[69] which interprets the Irish Poor Law provisions from which our current legislation is derived, is authority for the proposition that liability to maintain is absolute and that the behaviour of the spouse is irrelevant.

11–60 Finally, there is an issue as to whether an agreement between the parties to transfer property might affect liability to maintain. One spouse may agree to transfer property to the other on the basis that no maintenance or only a low maintenance payment is to be made. It is well established that one party cannot contract out of his or her right to maintenance.[70] Nonetheless, should a subsequent application for maintenance be made, the courts may take into account all the relevant facts including any property transfer.[71] The U.K. authorities are unanimous that an agreement between the parties will not relieve a spouse from liability to maintain although, under the U.K. legislation, it could be taken into account in deciding the appropriate

---

respondent's wife. A majority of the Court held that the wife was not eligible to receive public assistance and that, therefore, the public assistance authority was not entitled to recover from the husband. However, O'Byrne J. did say that he was not to be taken as dealing with a case where the granting of assistance depended upon a disputed question of fact (as opposed to law).

[66] [1952] 2 All E.R. 255.

[67] [1955] 2 All E.R. 1.

[68] See Casey, "The Supplementary Benefits Act: Lawyer's Law Aspects" (1968) 19 N.I.L.Q. 1.

[69] (1896) 30 I.L.T.R. 156.

[70] *H.D. v. P.D.* unreported, Supreme Court, May 8, 1978 and s. 27 of the Family Law (Maintenance of Spouses and Children) Act 1976.

[71] *O.C. v. T.C.* unreported, High Court, December 9, 1981.

contribution to be required.[72] In the absence of any case law to date, it is difficult to predict how the liable relative provisions may be interpreted.

11–61 It should be noted that the operation of the equivalent U.K. legislation – the Child Support Act 1991 – has been challenged in a number of cases before the European Court and Commission on Human Rights. In particular, it has been alleged that the imposition of child support obligations under that Act – which is probably more onerous than the Irish legislation – was a breach of Article 8 (family life) of the Convention. However, the Court and Commission have to date rejected these challenges and have not found the operation of the legislation to constitute any lack of respect for the applicant's rights under Article 8 (or any other provision of the Convention).[73]

(3) Maintenance and social welfare payments

11–62 The Social Welfare Act 1989 amended the Family Law (Maintenance of Spouses and Children) Act 1976 to provide that lone parent's payments payable to the applicant should not be taken into account in assessing the amount of maintenance to be awarded. The purpose was to ensure that lone-parent families would be adequately maintained by the absent spouse or father and that the amount of maintenance would not be subsidised by payment of social welfare, there being some evidence that maintenance orders were being set at reduced levels because the applicant had a social welfare entitlement. However, as the Review notes,[74] it is not clear that this provision was applied to any extent by the family courts in practice.[75]

---

[72] *National Assistance Board v. Prisk* [1954] 1 All E.R. 400; *National Assistance Board v. Parkes* [1955] 2 All ER 1; *Hulley v. Thomson* [1981] 1 All E.R. 1128.

[73] *Logan v. United Kingdom* 22 E.H.R.R. CD 178; *Burrows v. United Kingdom*, November 27, 1996; *Stacey v. United Kingdom*, January 19, 1999.

[74] Above, n.47, p. 106.

[75] Note also that SW(C)A 1993, s. 41(2) provides that in relation to an application under the 1976 Act in relation to the payment of expenses incidental to the birth of child, the court shall not take into account the fact that the mother is entitled to maternity benefit.

CHAPTER 12

Pregnancy and Maternity Benefits

12–01 This chapter looks at the social welfare supports for women during maternity. It also discusses the position in relation to support during parental leave, for which no payment is currently made.

1. Background

12–02 The issue of social welfare provision for women during pregnancy and maternity is one of considerable importance in the overall context of the Irish social welfare system. There are around 50,000 births per year (although this has declined sharply from a peak of over 74,000 in 1980). This chapter looks at the development of social welfare provision in this area since the beginning of the century. It considers the provisions which currently exist in this area. Social welfare provisions can be broadly divided into two:

- Cash grants either at or around the time of the child's birth (hereafter maternity grants). These grants are intended in some way to reflect the additional costs arising from childbirth but generally without any clear indication as to which costs are being met or as to the extent to which the grant is intended to meet these costs (*i.e.* wholly or in part).

- Payments during maternity leave from work (hereafter maternity allowance). These payments are in recognition of the fact that women cannot, and should not be obliged to, work for a period around childbirth. They are intended to provide a wage replacement so that working women can give up work for a reasonable period at this time.

A. Development of Maternity Protection

(1) Maternity grant

12–03 Many of the friendly societies, with which workers were insured in the early 1900s, had provided a cash grant to insured women, or in respect of the spouses of insured men, on childbirth. This grant was carried over as part of the national insurance system established by the National Insurance Act 1911 and was known as maternity benefit. It was then set at a rate of £1.50 and was increased to £2 in 1920. This grant was renamed as maternity grant under the major reorganisation of the social welfare code implemented by the

Social Welfare Act 1952 and was increased to £4 in 1965. The grant was payable either on the husband's or wife's insurance record and the contribution requirements were relatively easy to satisfy. Where the woman and her husband were both insured, two grants were paid. The grant reached a relatively high proportion of mothers when one considers that social insurance did not apply to the self-employed, then a large proportion of the Irish work force. For example, in the 1930s and 1940s, maternity benefit was paid in respect of over 40 per cent of all births. The vast majority of payments at this time were paid on the father's insurance rather than on the mother's.

12–04   A proposal in the 1949 White Paper to increase substantially the maternity grant paid under the social insurance system and to pay a maternity allowance for four weeks in respect of the wives of insured persons was rejected by the then Minister for Health and Social Welfare, Dr James Ryan, on the grounds that such an increase would not benefit the self-employed and other uninsured persons.[1] The Minister stated that he preferred to introduce a means-tested grant which would benefit those not covered by social insurance who were in need of financial assistance on childbirth. Such a grant was established by the Health Act 1953 and was set at a rate of £4. However, over the subsequent period, the value of the maternity grant was allowed to decline sharply in real terms. The means-tested maternity grant was raised to a level of £8 in the Health Act 1970 and has never subsequently been increased. The social insurance maternity grant was raised to £8 in 1978 and again was never subsequently increased. It was one of the few social welfare payments to decrease rather than increase in real value from the 1950s.

(2) Maternity allowance

12–05   Although an ILO Convention of 1919 had called for maternity leave of at least 12 weeks, with maternity allowance being provided during this period, no maternity allowance existed under the Irish social welfare system until 1953. The Social Welfare Act 1952 provided for a maternity allowance which was to be paid for six weeks before and six weeks after the date of confinement. Maternity allowance was paid at a flat rate which was the same as the then rate of unemployment and disability benefit paid to men and single women (which was 33 per cent higher than the rate of disability and unemployment benefit then paid to married women). Although this payment appears to have been aimed primarily at women who had to take time off work due to pregnancy, the contribution requirements meant that it could, in fact, be claimed by women who had not worked for some time but who had kept alive their contribution record by gaining credited contributions while

---

[1]   131 *Dáil Debates* Cols 1250 *et seq.*

claiming unemployment and disability benefit. In 1973, with the introduction of the pay-related benefit scheme, a pay-related addition was paid with weekly flat-rate maternity allowance. No further substantial changes took place in maternity provisions until 1981, when a maternity allowance for women in employment was established. The Maternity (Protection of Employment) Act 1981 provided for a statutory entitlement to maternity leave of 14 weeks for most employed women. In conjunction with this development, the Social Welfare (Amendment) Act 1981 provided for a new scheme of maternity allowance. Unlike the existing scheme, this applied only to women actually in employment at the time of taking maternity leave and was intended to preserve their income at approximately the level of their take-home pay while on leave.[2] Payment was made for 14 weeks at 80 per cent of previous earnings, subject to a minimum payment. This payment was confined to those working at least 18 hours per week and also excluded women on contracts of less than 26 weeks or with less than 26 weeks left to run.

(3) The link to employment

12–06   The 1980s and early 1990s saw several important developments in maternity provision. On the one hand, there was an expansion of the scheme for those in employment to cover part-time workers. On the other hand, the proportion of mothers in employment who actually received maternity allowance declined and maternity protection for those not in employment was very much reduced. This occurred with little public debate and, perhaps surprisingly, with little public dissent. The social insurance maternity grant, first established in 1911, was abolished in 1983. The Minister for Social Welfare, Barry Desmond T.D., described the payment, which had been frozen at a rate of £8 since 1978, as "no longer of any real significance in the context of the maternity allowance scheme which was substantially improved two years ago".[3] There does not seem to have been any great opposition to this move, possibly because of the low level of the grant involved. However, the abolition of this payment was significant in policy terms since it removed the main payment aimed at "easing the financial difficulties of a family consequent upon the birth of a baby".[4] The significance of this decision can be seen in the numbers affected. In 1982, 39,055 maternity grants had been paid. In contrast, the maternity allowance, referred to by the Minister, was paid to only 18,670 women in the year from July 1983 to June 1984. Thus, many thousands of women ceased to receive assistance with maternity costs under the social insurance system. The abolition of the social insurance maternity grant did

---

[2]   327 *Dáil Debates* Col. 77.
[3]   340 *Dáil Debates* Col. 2377.
[4]   131 *Dáil Debates* Col. 1250.

not give rise to any increase in the level of the means-tested maternity grant, which remained at a level of £8.

12–07   The rate of maternity allowance was reduced to 70 per cent of previous earnings in 1984, apparently on the basis that, because of changes in the taxation system, the original formula could lead to levels of benefit much higher than originally intended.[5] The scheme of maternity allowance for women in employment was extended to include insured part-time workers earning over £25 (now €38) per week in 1991. This followed from the general expansion of employment rights to cover part-time workers under the Worker Protection (Regular Part-Time Employees) Act 1991 and the general extension of social insurance to part-time workers in that year. The contribution conditions for the general maternity allowance scheme, which had been introduced in 1952, and which had remained in place after the introduction in 1981 of the scheme for women in employment, were made significantly more onerous in 1987, leading to a sharp drop in those receiving this payment. Those affected by this change were women out of employment. The Minister for Social Welfare, Dr Michael Woods, justified this on the grounds that it was reasonable to require maternity benefit to be payable only to persons with a genuine and enduring link with the work force.[6] The Minister said that "the need for the old scheme has, to a large extent, been superseded by the introduction of the maternity allowance scheme for women in employment and I expect that henceforth the needs of women in the area will be met by this scheme".[7] The change was vigorously opposed by Deputies including Monica Barnes T.D., who pointed out that it went totally against the proposal by the Joint Committee on Women's Rights for a universal maternity allowance payable to all mothers.[8] Payment of pay-related benefit with maternity allowance was restricted and eventually abolished in 1988. Finally, the general maternity allowance payment was abolished with effect from April 1992. This now means that the only specific maternity provision for women who are not in employment is the means-tested maternity grant of £8 and payments towards maternity expenses under the exceptional needs payments of the supplementary welfare allowance scheme. However, the Minister for Social Welfare announced that women who were in receipt of unemployment and disability payments would be allowed to continue in receipt of these payments during the maternity period (although they might well not meet the statutory conditions for qualification for such payments).[9] The position outlined by the Minister

---

[5]   Joint Committee on Women's Rights, *Second Report* (Stationery Office, Dublin, 1985), p. 18.
[6]   376 *Dáil Debates* Col. 2377.
[7]   *ibid.*, 2322.
[8]   *ibid.*, 2376.
[9]   428 *Dáil Debates* Cols. 858 *et seq.*

represents an administrative practice. The Minister estimated that only about 100 women a year, who would lose out as a result of the abolition of the general scheme, would not be able to claim an alternative payment. The contribution conditions for the maternity allowance scheme for women in employment were also made more onerous in 1987. Unfortunately, separate figures for those in receipt of the two allowances were not published after 1986. However, the total number in receipt of a maternity allowance in 1986 was 19,881 (or 32 per cent of live births). This declined to 15,240 (28 per cent of live births) in 1988 and it appears that the decline was much sharper in relation to women claiming under the general scheme (*i.e.* women not in employment).

12–08 The total numbers subsequently increased again to 16,357 (31 per cent of live births) in 1991 following the extension of social insurance to part-time workers but, with the abolition of the general scheme in April 1992, the 1992 figures dropped to 14,876 (29 per cent of live births). Thus, the period from the late 1980s to the early 1990s saw a decline in the number of people who received social insurance protection during maternity, with the abolition of the maternity grant and the drop in the numbers in receipt of maternity allowance from 32 per cent of live births in 1986 to 29 per cent in 1993, despite the extension of the scope of the payment to include part-time workers and the general increase in women's participation in the labour force. The maternity allowance scheme was altered with the introduction of the new scheme in 1981, so that it applied only to those with "a genuine and enduring link with the work force". The old general maternity allowance scheme which applied to many more pregnant women has been phased out. Social insurance protection for non-working women has disappeared with the abolition of the maternity grant and the old maternity allowance schemes. There had been no move to fill this gap by the introduction of improved means-tested or universal schemes. Instead the Minister established an administrative arrangement to allow women in receipt of social welfare payments to continue to receive those payments during maternity. Thus, there is no social insurance provision at all for women who are neither in employment nor in receipt of a social welfare payment.

(4) Extending benefits

12–09 There have been a number of extensions of maternity benefit (as maternity allowance was renamed in 1993) in recent years. In 1992 an E.U. Directive on maternity leave (92/85)[10] provided that the minimum level of maternity payment be that which was normally provided to employees unable

---

[10] [1992] O.J. L348/1.

to work due to incapacity. Minor changes were made to the amount of benefit payable under the Irish scheme in 1994 as a result of the implementation of this Directive. The E.U. Directive also provides some protection for women who are unable to continue in employment due to a pregnancy or maternity related risk to health and safety. In October 1994, the Minister, in implementation of the Directive, introduced a new social insurance payment to be known as health and safety benefit. This is payable to women who are pregnant, have recently given birth or are breast feeding (up to 26 weeks) whose employment gives rise to a risk to health and safety and whose employer cannot remove the risk or move them to alternative work. It also applies to women required to do nightwork during pregnancy or in the 14 weeks after birth, where this could be a risk to their health and safety. The qualification conditions are similar to the maternity payment for women in work. This benefit is payable from the fourth week of absence from work, with the employer being required to meet the cost of the first three weeks' leave. An adoptive benefit (analogous to maternity benefit) was introduced in 1995 to assist adoptive parents during adoptive leave.

12–10   The E.U. Directive on equal treatment in self-employment (86/613)[11] provides that:

> "Member States shall undertake to examine whether, and under what conditions, female self-employed workers and the wives of self-employed workers may, during interruptions in their occupational activity owing to pregnancy or motherhood . . . be entitled to cash benefits under a social security scheme or under any other public social protection system."

Whether or not the development had anything to do with this, benefit was extended to the self-employed in 1997. Finally, a major improvement in the scheme took place when, following a review of maternity leave and benefit by the social partners, maternity leave and benefit was extended to 18 weeks (with an additional optional and unpaid eight weeks) in 2001.[12]

2. Current Situation

A. Maternity Benefit

(1) Qualification conditions

12–11   In order for a woman to qualify for maternity benefit[13]:

---

[11] [1986] O.J. L359/56.

[12] Report of the Working Group on the Review and Improvement of the Maternity Protection Legislation, (Stationery Office, Dublin, 2001).

[13] See Social Welfare (Consolidation) Act 1993 (SW(C)A 1993), ss.37–41, as amended,

(1) it must be certified by a doctor (or otherwise to the satisfaction of the Minister) that it is expected that she will be confined in a specified week;

(2) in the case of an employed person, it must be certified by her employer that she is entitled to leave under section 8 of the Maternity Protection Act 1994;[14]

(3) in the case of a self-employed person, she must have been in insurable self-employment; and

(4) she must satisfy the contribution conditions.

12–12 "Confinement" means labour resulting in the issue of a living child or labour after 24 weeks of pregnancy resulting in the issue of a child, whether alive or dead.[15]

12–13 In the event of the death of the mother within 22 weeks of the birth of a living child, the father has certain leave entitlements. Where it is certified by his employer that a man who satisfies the contribution conditions is entitled to leave under the Maternity Protection Act, then he shall be entitled to benefit similarly to a woman who was entitled to maternity leave.[16]

(2) Contribution conditions

12–14 There are slightly different contribution requirements for employed and self-employed contributors to reflect the fact that employed contributors have a weekly contribution record whereas self-employed contributors build up a contribution record on an annual basis.

12–15 An employed person must have at least 39 contributions paid in the 12 months before the "relevant day" (*i.e.* the first day in respect of which maternity benefit is claimed) and at least 39 paid or credited contributions in the last complete contribution year before the beginning of the benefit year in which the relevant day occurs, or at least 26 paid contributions in each of the last two contribution years before the beginning of the benefit year in which

---

and Social Welfare (Consolidated Payments Provisions) Regulations 1994 (S.I. No. 417 of 1994) (SW(CPP)R 1994), arts 20–25, as amended. On the health and safety benefit see SW(C)A, ss. 41A–41F inserted by the European Communities (Social Welfare) Regulations 1995 (S.I. No. 25 of 1995), and on adoptive benefit see ss. 41G–41J, inserted by SWA 1995, s.11 and substituted by Social Welfare Act 1997 (SWA 1997), s.11.

[14] SW(C)A 1993, s. 37.

[15] *ibid.*, s. 41(1)(a). See Ogus, Barendt and Wikely, *The Law of Social Security* (4th ed., Buterworths, London, 1995), pp. 271–272.

[16] SW(C)A 1993, s. 37(4) as amended by SWA 2001, s.12.

the relevant day occurs.[17] Alternatively, an employed contributor must have at least 39 paid contributions in the 12 months immediately preceding the relevant day or, having been in self-employment, she must satisfy the contribution conditions for self-employed contributors.[18]

12–16 A self-employed claimant must have 52 qualifying contributions paid in the last complete contribution year or have 52 qualifying contributions paid in the contribution year prior to the last complete contribution year. Where she was previously an employed contributor, she must have 39 contributions paid since entering insurable employment before the relevant day or at least 39 paid contributions in the 12 months preceding that date.[19]

(3) Payments

12–17 Maternity benefit is the only (partially) pay-related benefit remaining in the Irish social welfare code. The rate of benefit is an amount equal to 70 per cent of the reckonable weekly earnings of the woman in the income tax year subject to a maximum amount (currently €232.40 in 2002), or to a minimum amount (€135.60 in 2002) or the amount of disability benefit (including any increases thereof) to which the woman would otherwise be entitled whichever is greater,[20] the purpose of the setting the rate at 70 per cent was to approximate the net take-home pay. Payment of the benefit is for a maximum of 18 weeks (extended from 14 weeks in 2001). There is an optional additional eight weeks' leave under the Maternity Protection Act but benefit is not payable during this period.

(4) Disqualifications

12–18 A woman is disqualified for maternity benefit during any period for which the benefit is payable in which she engages in any occupation other than domestic duties in her own household or where she fails, without good cause, to attend for or submit to medical examination.[21] The standard imprisonment and absence from the State disqualifications also apply to maternity benefit, although the latter is subject to several exceptions.[22] Maternity benefit is payable in the following circumstances to a claimant who is absent from the State[23]:

---

[17] The latter alternative is to assist job sharers.

[18] SW(C)A 1993, s. 38 as substituted by SWA 1997, s.10 and amended by SWA 2001, s.20 and SWA 2002, s.9.

[19] SW(C)A 1993, s.38(b) as substituted by SWA 2002, s.9.

[20] *ibid.*, s.39

[21] *ibid.*, s. 40 and SW(CPP)R 1994, art. 25.

[22] *ibid.*, s. 211.

[23] See the Social Welfare (Absence from the State) Regulations 1967 (S.I. No. 97 of 1967).

(1) Where she goes abroad for the specific purpose of receiving treatment for incapacity which commenced before the person left the State.

(2) Where she is temporarily absent up to 26 weeks, or such longer period as may be allowed, having regard to the circumstances of the case, in Northern Ireland, Great Britain or the Isle of Man.

In addition, persons who are employed abroad and continue to be insured under the Social Welfare Acts are entitled to maternity benefit. Finally, maternity benefit may be paid to a claimant in other E.U. Member States in accordance with Council Regulation 1408/71.[24]

B. Other Payments

12–19 Departmental guidelines state that a person who is pregnant but who does not satisfy the contribution conditions for maternity benefit, and who is not in receipt of wages from her employer, may be considered to satisfy the conditions of being available for and genuinely seeking work during pregnancy, including confinement in hospital or at home, unless there are other factors which could call into question her general availability for work. Such persons may be paid unemployment benefit or assistance subject to satisfying the means test or contribution conditions as appropriate. Pregnancy is not considered to be an incapacity for the purposes of disability benefit. However, medical incapacity arising from pregnancy would give rise to entitlement to disability benefit.

12–20 In addition to maternity benefit, there is also an analogous adoptive benefit. Adoptive benefit is a payment to adopting parents who are either employed or self-employed to support them during a period of adoptive leave. It provides for a weekly payment to be made to persons who qualify for adoptive leave under the Adoptive Leave Act 1995.[25] Finally, there is a health and safety benefit, which is a weekly payment for women who are granted health and safety leave under the Maternity Protection Act 1994.[26] Health and safety leave is granted to an employee by her employer when the employer cannot remove a risk to the employee's health or safety during her pregnancy or whilst she is breastfeeding, or cannot assign her alternative "risk-free" duties. Under the Maternity Protection Act 1994, an employee is entitled to remuneration from her employer for the first 21 days of health and safety

---

[24] Chap 22. of Regulation 1408/71 [1971] O.J. L149/2.
[25] See SW(C)A 1993, ss. 41G–41J as inserted by SWA 1995, s.11 and substituted by SWA 1997, s.11.
[26] See SW(C)A 1993, ss. 41A–41F as inserted by S.I. No. 25 of 1995 and amended by SWA 1999, s.24 and SWA 2000, s.206.

leave, and health and safety benefit is payable for the remainder if the qualifying conditions are met.

C. Parental Leave

12–21 The Parental Leave Act 1998, which came into operation on December 3, 1998, makes provision for unpaid leave for fathers and mothers to look after young children.[27] Parental leave may be taken either as a continuous block of 14 weeks or, with the agreement of the employer, broken up over a period of time.

12–22 The Act also provides for limited paid leave (*force majeure* leave), which must not exceed three days in any 12 consecutive months, or five days in any 36 consecutive months, to enable employees to deal with family emergencies resulting from injury or illness of a family member. There is no specific social welfare payment in respect for parental leave. However, parents who take parental leave may be entitled to receive a credited contribution in respect of each week taken. This will ensure that their existing cover for social welfare benefits are fully maintained.

---

[27] See report of the Working Group on the Review of the Parental Leave Act 1998, (Stationery Office, 2002.)

CHAPTER 13

Child Support Payments

13–01 This chapter looks at the current child support payments under the social welfare system, including child benefit, increases in respect of a qualified child (also known as child dependent allowances) and orphan's payments.[1]

1. Background

13–02 Historically, the early social welfare schemes did not apply a consistent approach to child support. Some schemes included additional payments for child dependants (child dependent allowances or CDAs)[2] while others did not and payments were made at differing rates depending on the scheme. A general scheme of children's allowances was not introduced until 1944 and this initially applied only to the families with three or more children at a rate of 2 shillings 6 pence per child. The White Paper on Social Security had proposed in 1949 that child dependent allowances should be standardised for most payments, with the allowance being paid in respect of the first two children at a rate of 7 shillings (to correspond with the fact that children's allowances were then payable for the third and subsequent child), and this was implemented in the 1952 Act. However, children's allowances were extended to the second child in 1952 – mainly in compensation for the reduction in food subsidisation at that time. CDAs were extended to all children in 1960 and children's allowances were extended to the first child in 1963 – corresponding with the introduction of a new turnover tax. Thus, the original approach proposed in the White Paper of having CDAs for the first two children and children's allowance thereafter did not survive, with both payments being extended to all children by the 1960s (albeit with different qualifying ages). In addition, support for children was provided through the tax system from the earliest years of the State.[3]

---

[1] See also the domiciliary care allowance discussed in Chap. 10.

[2] The current legislation refers to "an increase in respect of a qualified child" but the term CDA is widely used in practice.

[3] F. Kennedy, *Family, Economy and Government in Ireland* (ESRI, Dublin, 1989), pp. 90–95.

13–03 There have been a wide variety of different approaches to child support policy over the decades which different governments emphasising different policy instruments from time to time. Maguire[4] shows that in the period 1952–79, children's allowances were allowed to decline significantly in relative generosity while increasing in coverage as they were extended to all children.

13–04 By the late 1970s, child income support was delivered in three main ways: first, through child tax allowances of £240 per annum; secondly, a universal child benefit of £3.50 per month in respect of the first child, and £5.50 for the second and subsequent children; and thirdly, a child dependent allowance (CDA) payable in addition to (and as part of) various social welfare payments. Over the period 1979–86, there was a significant change in this policy. Child tax allowances were first reduced in the 1979/80 tax year and reduced further in the 1980–82 period. Children's allowances were increased significantly by the Fine Gael/Labour Government in 1981, while CDAs were increased at a much lower rate. The subsequent Fianna Fáil Government also increased children's allowances significantly in 1982 in line with substantial reductions in the child tax allowance. In 1984, the Coalition Government announced in *Building on Reality* that a new unified system of child support was to be introduced through a taxable child benefit payment. In 1985, just over £400 million was being spent on child income supports, of which half went on CDAs, with 42 per cent on children's allowances and only 5 per cent on tax allowances.[5] In 1986, child tax allowances were abolished, with the resources made available being put into a significant increase in children's allowances (renamed child benefit).[6] Child benefit was not, however, made taxable, nor were child dependant additions abolished, although they were not increased in 1986.

13–05 Overall, child benefit increased significantly in real terms between 1980 and 1987 while CDAs declined slightly in value. Subsequently policy in relation to child benefit and CDAs followed a somewhat erratic pattern up to 1994. Child benefit was not increased until 1990 (a 5-per-cent increase) and then frozen until a 27-per-cent increase for the first to third child in 1993. Meanwhile, CDAs were increased incrementally up to 1994.

13–06 Comparative studies show that in the mid-1990s Ireland compared

---

[4] M. Maguire, "Components of Growth of Income Maintenance Expenditure in Ireland, 1951–1979", Economic and Social Review (2979) 15, p.75. Also, see I. Wennemo's comparative data: *Sharing the Costs of Children* (Stockholm Institute for Social Research, 1994).

[5] Kennedy, above, n.3.

[6] On this see *MhicMathuna v. Ireland* [1995] 1 I.R. 484, discussed in Chap. 8.

poorly to many other E.U. countries in terms of the level of child support.[7] In 1995, the Rainbow Government gave a significant increase in child benefit and adopted a policy of freezing CDAs and putting all investment into child benefit. While this policy was continued by the subsequent Government, increases in child benefit remained modest until 2000, when the Fianna Fáil led Government announced a major programme of investment, with £1 billion being put into child benefit over three years to almost triple the payment. In addition, this Government gave a commitment to set total child income support at 33–35 per cent of the lowest adult rate of payment.

13–07 In addition to the general child support through child benefit and child dependent allowances, specific support for "orphans" was introduced as part of the widow's pension scheme in 1935. As the number of real orphans has reduced over the years, so the definition of orphan has been broadened to include situations where a child has been "abandoned" by parents although the parents are still alive. In addition, there is a specific payment to foster parents operated by the Department of Health and Children.

2. Current Situation

A. Child Benefit

13–08 Child benefit is a universal payment (*i.e.* it is not means-tested and is not subject to payment of social insurance contributions) and legal issues about qualification rarely arise.[8] Child benefit is payable in respect of a child if:

(a) he or she is under the age of 16 (or if under 19, he or she is receiving full-time education, or is by reason of physical or mental infirmity incapable of self-support and likely to remain so for a prolonged period);

(b) he or she is ordinarily resident[9] in the State; and

(c) he or she is not detained in a reformatory or an industrial school and is not undergoing imprisonment or detention in legal custody.[10]

---

[7] J. Ditch *et al.*, *A Synthesis of National Family Policies in 1996* (European Commission, Brussels, 1998).

[8] On "ordinary residence", see *Shah v. Barnet London Borough Council* [1983] 2 A.C. 309 at 342–4.

[9] See Social Welfare (Consolidation) Act 1993 (SW(C)A 1993), ss. 192–196 and the Social Welfare (Consolidated Payments Provisions) Regulations 1994 (S.I. No. 417 of 1994) (SW(CPP)R 1994), arts 91–93, as amended.

[10] SW(C)A 1993, s. 192(1) as amended by the Social Welfare Act 1995 (SWA 1995), s.5. A child who resides with his or her parent (or other qualified person) outside the State

13–09 A child is regarded as receiving full-time education while attending on a full-time basis a course of full-time instruction by day at an institution of education. However, the following courses are excluded from the definition of a course of full-time instruction:

(1) courses provided or approved by FÁS (other than Youthreach) and in respect of which an allowance is payable;

(2) courses which form part of an employment or work experience programme;

(3) courses which arise from employment;

(4) courses which comprise, in an academic year, a period of work experience in respect of which remuneration is paid, where such period exceeds the time spent receiving instruction or tuition at an institution of education; or

(5) courses provided or approved by Teagasc, where, in an academic year such training or instruction comprises a period of work experience which exceeds the time spent receiving instruction or tuition at an institution of education.[11]

13–10 A child is regarded as continuing to receive full-time education:

(a) for periods during an academic year when that child is not attending an institution of education arising from the temporary interruption to the provision of a course of education by an institution of education; and

(b) for the period immediately following the completion by that child of part of a cycle of education, where such part finishes between May 1 and June 30 in an academic year, up to and including the next following September 30, except in relation to a child who completes the final part of a cycle of education and terminates his or her attendance at a course of full-time instruction at an institution of education.[12]

13–11 Child benefit is payable to the person with whom a qualified child normally resides.[13] Child benefit is normally payable to the mother on the basis that the child is deemed by regulation to be "normally resident" with her. This a clearly discriminatory procedure which is both eminently sensible

---

where that person is a member of the Defence Forces or the civil service and who is outside the State in the service of the Government, the State or an international organisation is deemed to be a qualified child: *ibid.*, 192(2).

[11] SW(CPP)R 1994, art. 92.

[12] ibid., art. 93

[13] SW(C)A 1993, s. 193.

and allowed by E.U. law due to the exclusion of family benefits from the scope of Directive 79/7.[14]

13–12 The detailed rules in relation to "normal residence" are set out in article 91 of the Social Welfare (Consolidated Payments Provisions) Regulations 1994. Rule 1 provides that a qualified child who is resident with more than one of the following persons – his mother, step-mother, father, or step-father – is regarded as normally residing with the person first so mentioned and with no other person. However, where the persons are resident in separate households, the child is regarded as normally residing with the person with whom he or she resides for the majority of the time.[15] Thus, if the parents are living in separate households and the child spends the majority of the time with the father, child benefit will be payable to the father rather than to the mother.

13–13 A qualified child who is resident with one only of the persons mentioned in Rule 1 is regarded as normally residing with that person and with no other person provided, where that person is the father and he is cohabiting with a woman as husband and wife, that this Rule shall not apply in respect of the child where the father so elects. On such an election, the child shall be regarded as normally residing with the woman with whom the father is cohabiting (Rule 2). A qualified child who is resident elsewhere than with a parent or a step-parent and whose mother is alive, is, where his mother is entitled to his custody, whether solely or jointly with any other person, regarded as normally residing with his mother and with no other person (Rule 3). A qualified child who is resident elsewhere than with a parent or a step-parent and whose father is alive, is, where his father is entitled to his custody, whether solely or jointly with any person other than his mother, regarded as normally residing with his father and with no other person (Rule 4). Rule 5 provides that a qualified child to whom none of the foregoing rules apply is regarded as normally residing with the woman who has care and charge of him in the household of which he is normally a member and with no other person, provided that where there is no such woman in that household he shall be regarded as normally residing with the head of that household and with no other person. Finally, Rule 6 provides that where the normal residence of a qualified child falls to be determined under Rule 3 or Rule 4 and the person with whom the child would thus be regarded as normally residing has abandoned or deserted him or her or has failed to contribute to his or her support, the relevant rule shall cease to apply in respect of that child and the

---

[14] See also the judgment in *Barber v. Secretary of State for Work and Pensions* [2002] E.W.H.C. Civ. 1915 (Admin.), in which the High Court rejected a challenge to similar U.K. provisions under the Europen Convention on Human Rights.

[15] As amended by S.I. No. 265 of 2000.

person with whom the child shall be regarded as normally residing shall be determined in accordance with Rule 5.

13–14 In summary, child benefit is normally payable to the mother (or stepmother). However, where the child is living full-time with the father (or stepfather) only, then child benefit will be payable to the father. Where the parents are residing in separate households, child benefit is payable to the parent with whom the child resides the majority of the time. If the child resides 50 per cent of the time with each parent, the mother is paid. Where the parents are dead, the child has been abandoned, or the child is fostered, child benefit is payable to the woman who has care and charge of the child in the household in which the child lives (or the head of the household where there is no such woman in the household). Finally, where a child is placed in an institution on a voluntary basis, child benefit is payable to the person who would normally get the benefit – provided that person is making adequate contributions towards the cost of the child's maintenance in the institution. Where the child is placed in an institution as a result of a court order, child benefit is only payable if the child returns home on a regular basis.

13–15 There is currently a higher and lower rate of benefit, with the lower rate being paid to the first two children and the higher to the third and subsequent child (reduced from the fifth and subsequent since 1990). Policy in relation to the relationship between the rates has varied widely. Increased payments are payable in respect of multiple births.[16] Child benefit is not taxable.

B. Increase for a Qualified Child[17]

13–16 Entitlement to an increase in respect of a "qualified child" is set out in the Act in the sections dealing with the main payment.[18] "Qualified child" is defined as a person who is ordinarily resident in the State, is not detained in a reformatory or an industrial school and, in the case of long-term payments, is under the age of 18 or is over the age of 18 and under the age of 22 and is receiving full-time education or, in the case of short-term payments, is under the age of 18 or is over 18 for the three months immediately following the completion or leaving by the person of second-level education or the completion of the Leaving Certificate.[19]

---

[16] SW(C)A 1993, s. 194 as amended by SWA 1996, s.5 and SWA 1998, s.6.

[17] Frequently referred to as child dependent allowances/increases or CDAs/CDIs.

[18] For example, entitlement to CDAs with unemployment benefit is set out in SW(C)A 1993, s.45.

[19] SW(C)A 1993, s. 2(3). During the latter three-month period, a person is disqualified for unemployment assistance so the intention is to ensure that a person does not lose

13–17 Where a person is in receipt of a social welfare payment, he or she will, in general,[20] be entitled to an increase in respect of a qualified child who "normally resides" with the person. The concept of normal residence is defined in article 7 of the Social Welfare (Consolidated Payments Provisions) Regulations 1994.

13–18 Article 7 provides that the person with whom a qualified child shall be regarded as normally residing is to be determined in accordance with the rules of priority set out in the following sub-articles:

"(3) A qualified child shall, subject to sub-articles (4) to (11), be regarded as normally residing with his parents. ['Parent' means a parent or step-parent.]

(4) A qualified child who is resident with one parent only, shall be regarded as normally residing with that parent and with no other person provided, where that parent is a member of a household, that the parent so elects.

(5) A qualified child whose parents are separated and who is not resident with either parent shall be regarded as normally residing with the parent who has custody of the child provided that that parent is contributing substantially to the child's maintenance.[21]

(6) Notwithstanding the provisions of sub-article (4), a qualified child resident with one parent who is living apart from the other parent and who is not claiming or in receipt of benefit or assistance shall be regarded as residing with the other parent if that other parent is contributing substantially to the child's maintenance.

(7) If one parent dies, a qualified child shall be regarded as normally residing with the other parent provided that that parent is maintaining the child.

(8) Where the normal residence of a qualified child falls to be determined under sub-article (6) or (7), and the person with whom the child would thus be regarded as normally residing has abandoned or deserted the child or failed to contribute substantially to the child's maintenance, sub-article (6) or (7) shall cease to apply in respect of that child and the person with whom the child shall be regarded as normally residing shall be determined in accordance with sub-article (9).

(9) A qualified child, whose normal residence does not fall to be determined under the foregoing sub-articles, shall be regarded as normally residing with the head of the household of which the child is normally a member and with no other person.

---

entitlement to a CDA while he or she is statutorily disqualified for UA. See also SWA 2002, s.7.

[20] Increases are not payable with family income supplement, death benefit by way of parent's pension under the OIB scheme, orphan's allowance and pension, and widow(er)'s (non-contributory) pension (in the latter case because widow(er)s with dependent children will be entitled to OFP).

[21] Departmental guidelines take this to mean contributing at least the equivalent of the increase in respect of a qualified child (including, where appropriate, contributions in kind).

(10) A qualified child who is a refugee within the State from another country shall be regarded as normally residing with the head of the household of which the child is for the time being a member and with no other person.

(11) Where a qualified child is resident in an institution, the child shall be regarded as normally residing only with the person (if any) who contributes towards the cost of the child's maintenance in the institution, and with whom the child would, under this article, be regarded as normally residing, if the child were not resident in an institution."

13–19 The "normal residence" rules in relation to one-parent family payment are slightly different and are set out in article 83.[22] This article provides that, for the purposes of OFP and subject to sub-article (2), a qualified child is to be regarded as normally residing with a qualified parent where: (a) the child is resident with that parent; and (b) that parent has the main care and charge of the child. Article 82(2) provides that a qualified child who is resident in an institution is regarded as normally residing with the qualified parent where that parent contributes towards the cost of the child's maintenance in the institution and with whom the child would, under sub-article (1), be regarded as normally residing if the child were not resident in an institution. Finally, article 83(3) provides that a qualified child may, in such circumstances as an officer of the Minister considers appropriate, be regarded as normally residing with the qualified parent who is resident in an institution.

13–20 "Institution" means :

(a) a hospital, convalescent home or home for persons suffering from physical or mental disability or accommodation ancillary thereto;

(b) any other similar establishment providing residence, maintenance or care for the persons therein; or

(c) any prison, place of detention or other establishment to which articles 23 and 24 of the Social Welfare (Social Assistance) Regulations 1993 (S.I. No. 364 of 1993) apply.

13–21 Increases in respect of a qualified child are currently payable at three different levels varying from €16.80 to €19.30 depending on the type of payment. The increase, unlike child benefit, is payable to the person in receipt of the payment. In the case of a couple (*i.e.* a married couple who are living together or a man and woman cohabiting as husband and wife), a half-rate increase is payable where the spouse/partner is not a qualified adult of the claimant. The increases may be taxable depending on the taxable status of the underlying payment.[23]

---

[22] As inserted by No. S.I. 426 of 1996.
[23] In *Ó Siocháin v. Neenan* [1999] 1 I.R. 533 the Supreme Court held that an increase in

13–22 Increases in respect of a qualified child are not payable where: (i) a weekly benefit or assistance (other than SWA); (ii) an increase in respect of a qualified adult; or (iii) a further increase in respect of a qualified child is payable in respect of the same child in the same period.[24] As orphan's (contributory) allowance and orphan's (non-contributory) pension come within the definition of benefit and allowance, an increase in respect of a qualified child and orphan's payments are not payable at the same time.

C. Orphan's Payments

13–23 There are two orphan's payments: orphan's (contributory) allowance and orphan's (non-contributory) pension. The term "orphan" is defined as meaning:

> "a qualified child–
>
> (a) both of whose parents are dead, or
> (b) one of whose parents is dead, has abandoned or has refused or failed to provide for the child and whose other parent–
>   (i) is unknown, or
>   (ii) has abandoned or has refused or failed to provide for the child,
>
> where that child is not normally residing with a step-parent or with a person who is married to and living with that step-parent."[25]

Thus, the definition of "orphan" goes far beyond the strict meaning of the term and includes children both of whose parents are alive where the parents have abandoned or have refused or failed to provide for the child.

13–24 The contribution condition for orphan's (contributory) allowance is that one of the following persons has qualifying contributions for not less than 26 contribution weeks:

> "(a) a parent of the orphan,
> (b) a step-parent of the orphan."[26]

13–25 Section 109 provides that orphan's (contributory) allowance is to be paid to the guardian of the orphan in respect of whom the allowance is payable. However, section 109(2) provides that an orphan's (contributory) allowance

---

respect of a qualified child payable as part of the widow's (contributory) pension was the income of the widow for income tax purposes and, as widow's (contributory) pension is taxable, therefore liable to tax.

[24] SW(C)A 1993, s. 209(2).

[25] *ibid.*, s. 2 as inserted by SWA 1995, s.20. On the meaning of "abandoned", see the Appeal Officer's decision in Social Welfare Appeals Office, *Annual Report 2001*, pp. 23–24.

[26] SW(C)A 1993, s. 107.

may, if the Minister thinks fit, be paid instead to some other person for the benefit of the orphan. It is on this basis that orphan's allowances in respect of fostered children are paid to the health authority/board on behalf of the orphan. The board/authority then make the payment to the orphan, incorporated with the foster care allowance. Where a child is legally taken into care, the health board becomes the guardian of the child. Where the fostered child is in care voluntarily, the parent(s) normally remains the legal guardian and so payment to the health board is appropriate under section 109(2).

13–26 There are analogous provisions in relation to the means-tested orphan's (non-contributory) pension.[27] Section 148 provides that, subject to a means test, an orphan's (non-contributory) pension shall be payable in respect of an orphan (as defined above).

---

[27] SW(C)A 1993, ss. 148–151.

CHAPTER 14

Scope of Social Insurance

1. Background

14–01 There are basically five main legal categories of social insurance contributor: employed contributors; occupational injuries contributors; self-employed contributors; optional contributors; and voluntary contributors. However, in practice the two latter categories only apply to very small groups of people. Conversely, the category of employed contributor is broken down into employed contributors who are fully insured for all contingencies (known as Class A contributors)[1] and "modified" contributors who are covered for only a limited range of benefits. Many of these modified groups are now closed to new entrants from April 1995, as civil and public servants recruited after that date are in Class A.

14–02 There are currently five modified categories including:
- permanent and pensionable civil servants, registered doctors and dentists employed in the civil service, and Gardaí, all of whom were recruited prior to April 6, 1995 (Class B);
- commissioned army officers and members of the Army Nursing Service, again recruited prior to April 6, 1995 (Class C);
- permanent and pensionable employees in the public service other than those mentioned in Classes B and C recruited prior to April 6, 1995 (Class D);
- ministers of Religion employed by the Church of Ireland Representative Body (Class E);
- non-commissioned officers and enlisted personnel of the Defence Forces (Class H).

14–03 Persons insured for occupational injuries benefits only (*e.g.* persons earning less than €38 per week, employees aged over 66 or people in subsidiary employment) are categorised as Class J. Self-employed contributors are categorised as Class S. Persons who were formerly insured can continue to pay contributions as voluntary contributors (not assigned any class letter for

---

[1] It should be noted the terminology of that the various classes, although widely used in social welfare literature, has no legal basis.

no apparent reason). Finally, optional contributors (*i.e.* sharefishermen or women who are classified as self-employed and are already paying Class S contributions) are also allowed to pay optional Class P contributions for additional benefits.

2. Employed Contributions

A. Insured Employments

14–04   Section 9(1) of the Social Welfare (Consolidation Act) 1993 (SW(C)A 1993) provides that:

> "(a) every person who, being over the age of 16 years and under pensionable age [currently 66], is employed in any of the employments specified in Part I of the First Schedule, not being an employment specified in Part II of that Schedule, shall, subject to paragraph (b), be an employed contributor for the purposes of this Act, and
>
> (b) every person, irrespective of age, who is employed in insurable (occupational injuries) employment shall be an employed contributor and references in this Act to an employed contributor shall be construed accordingly."

14–05   Section 9(1)(*c*) provides that every person becoming for the first time an employed contributor shall thereby become insured under the Act and shall continue throughout his or her life to be so insured.

(1) Paragraph 1

14–06   Part I of the First Schedule to the Act lists those employments fully covered by the Act. Paragraph 1, the wording of which dates back to the original National Insurance Act 1911, is the principal provision. This covers:

1. Employment in the State under any contract of service or apprenticeship, written or oral, whether expressed or implied, and whether the employed person is paid by the employer or some other person, and whether under one or more employers, and whether paid by time or by the piece or partly by time and partly by the piece, or otherwise, or without any money payment.

14–07   Thus, insurability as an employed contributor requires a person to be: (a) employed under any contract of service or apprenticeship; and (b) in the State. There is no statutory definition of "contract of service" and the general case law in relation to the distinction between a "contract of service" and a "contract for services" is relevant to insurability under the social welfare code. As is well known, a range of different tests have been applied to distinguish between the two categories of contract, including the degree of control exercised over the work of the person concerned,[2] the extent to which he or she is engaged in business on his or her own account,[3] and whether the person is an integral part of the business.[4]

14–08 In the recent case of *Henry Denny & Sons v. Minister for Social Welfare*[5] the Supreme Court considered whether a supermarket demonstrator was employed under a contract of services and thus fully insurable under the Social Welfare Acts or whether she was employed under a contract for services. The person concerned was recruited by the company and signed a 12-month contract, which was renewed over a number of years from 1991 to 1993. The 1993 contract described her as an independent contractor and purported to make her responsible for any liability to tax. When a store requested a demonstration of a product she was contacted by the company, sent to the store and carried out a demonstration. She then submitted an invoice to the company signed by the store manager and was paid at a daily rate and given a mileage allowance. She worked an average of 28 hours per week for 48 to 50 weeks per year. The demonstrations were not carried out under the direct supervision of the company, but she was provided with written instructions as to how to carry out the work and provided with the relevant materials. She required the consent of the company to sub-contact out any of the work assigned to her.

14–09 A question had arisen as to whether she was an insured person under the Acts and an appeals officer had held that she was employed under a contract of service. Having reviewed the extensive case law in this area, the Supreme Court held that in deciding whether a person was employed under a contract of service or under a contract for services, each case must be considered in the light of its particular facts and in the light of the general principles which the courts have developed. In general, the Court held that a person will be regarded as being employed under a contract of service where he or she is performing services for another person and not for himself or herself, *i.e.* where the person is not in business on his or her own account. The inference that a person is engaged in his or her own business will more readily be drawn where he or she provides the necessary premises or equipment or some other form of investment, where he or she employs others to assist in the business, and where the profit which he or she derives from the business is dependent on the efficiency with which it is conducted. The Court further held that the

---

[2] *Roche v. P. Kelly & Co.* [1969] I.R. 100.
[3] *Ó Coindealbháin v. Mooney* [1990] 1 I.R. 422, and see *Graham v. Minister for Industry and Commerce* [1933] I.R. 156.
[4] *Stephenson, Jordan and Harris Ltd v. McDonald and Evans* [1952] T.L.R. 101.
[5] [1998] 1 I.R. 34.

degree of control exercised over how the work was to be carried out was a factor to be taken into account but was not decisive.

On the basis of the facts shown in the instant case, the court held that the appeals officer was entitled to arrive at the conclusion he did.

14–10   As can be seen from the *Henry Denny* case, the question of whether or not a particular employment is or is not within the scope of the social insurance scheme can, in general, only be decided on the particular facts, although the Department obviously tries to ensure that all cases of similar employments are treated in a similar way from a social insurance point of view. The U.S. approach whereby the courts consider whether a person is an employee "as a matter of economic reality" is not in accordance with Irish law.[6] In recent decisions, the courts have held that persons delivering newspapers who owned their own delivery vehicle and were responsible for all outgoings on it were self-employed rather than employees of the newspaper distributor,[7] and that sharefishermen paid by way of a share of the profits of any catch were partners with, rather than employees of, the boat owner.[8]

14–11   In relation to the requirement that the employment be in the State, this is overruled in certain cases by E.U. law whereby persons insured under Irish law can be posted abroad and remain insured under the Irish social welfare code.[9] In addition in relation to countries outside the E.U./EEA, in accordance with the powers provided under section 25 of SW(C)A 1993, article 98 of the Social Welfare (Consolidated Contributions and Insurability) Regulations 1996[10] provides that where an insured person who is ordinarily resident in the State is temporarily employed outside the State in the service of an employer who is resident or has a place of business in the State in an employment which, but for the words "in the State" in paragraph 1 would be employment within the meaning of that paragraph, paragraph 1 shall be construed as if the words "in the State" were deleted. However, a person shall cease to be treated as temporarily employed outside the State where the period of absence exceeds 52 contribution weeks, unless the Minister otherwise decides in any particular case.

---

[6]   *Griffin v. Minister for Social, Community and Family Affairs*, unreported, High Court, October 2, 2001, Carroll J. refusing to apply *US v. Silk* 331 U.S. 704.

[7]   *McAuliffe v. Minister for Social Welfare* [1995] 2 I.R. 238. And see *McArthur v. Minister for Industry and Commerce* [1928] I.R. 555 for a similar conclusion.

[8]   *Griffin v. Minister for Social, Community and Family Affairs,* unreported, High Court, October 2, 2001, following *DPP v. McLoughlin* [1986] 1 I.R. 355.

[9]   Pennings, *Introduction to European Social Security Law* (3rd ed., Kluwer, The Hague, 2001), Chap 9. See *Kenny v. Minister for Trade and Employment* [2001] 1 I.R. 249; Case C–202/97 *Fitzwilliam Executive Search v. Bestuur van het Landelijk Instituut Sociale Versekeringen* [2000] E.C.R. I–883.

[10]   SW(CCI)R 1996 (S.I. No. 312 of 1996).

14–11A In *FÁS v. Minister for Social Welfare*, the Supreme Court considered the effect of an illegal or *ultra vires* contract.[11] The Court held that an illegal contract would not be enforced by the Courts and could not be regarded as coming within the definition of "contract of service" under the Social Welfare Acts.[12] Egan J. stated that if the Oireachtas had decided to prohibit a particular type of contract, it would be anomalous if reliance were to be placed on it for the purpose of social welfare contributions and benefits. Accordingly where a contract is found to be illegal, whether because its object was the committing of an illegal act or because it was expressly or implied prohibited by statute, it will not be recognised at law. In the case of *ultra vires* contracts, although these are void *ab initio*, it might happen in practice that the validity of the void act might become immune from challenge. This element of uncertainty means that an appeals officer should not rely on the *ultra vires* nature of a contract. It would be anomalous were the appeals officer to treat as invalid a contract that a court in its discretion might refuse to invalidate.

(2) Paragraphs 2 and 3

14–12 The First Schedule to SW(C)A 1993 also refers to a number of other types of employment which are also fully insurable. These are:

2. Employment under such a contract of service —

(a) as master or a member of the crew of—
   (i) any ship registered in the State, or
   (ii) any other ship or vessel of which the owner, or, if there is more than one owner, the managing owner or manager, resides or has his principal place of business in the State, or

(b) as captain or a member of the crew of—
   (i) any aircraft registered in the State, or
   (ii) any other aircraft of which the owner, or, if there is more than one owner, the managing owner or manager, resides or has his principal place of business in the State.

3. Employment in the civil service of the Government or the civil service of the State and employment such that the service therein of the employed person is, or is capable of being, deemed under section 24 of the Superannuation Act 1936, to be service in the civil service of the Government or the civil service of the State.

14–13 The Supreme Court held in *McLoughlin v. Minister for Social*

---

[11] Unreported, Supreme Court, May 23, 1995.

[12] *ibid.*, p. 8–9 of the judgment, albeit that this was strictly *obiter* as the Court found that neither an illegal nor *ultra vires* contract arose on the facts.

Welfare[13] that a temporary assistant solicitor employed in the Chief State Solicitor's office was employed in the civil service of the State and not that of the Government, and so was not insurable under the then provisions of the Social Welfare Act. The legislation was subsequently amended to include reference to employment in the civil service of the State. In *Murphy v. Minister for Social Welfare*[14] the High Court, applying *McLoughlin*, held that an ordinary member of the Labour Court was engaged in the civil service of the State.

(3) Paragraphs 4 and 5

14–14

4. Employment as a member of the Defence Forces.

5. Employment under any local or other public authority.

14–15 In *General Medical Services (Payments) Board v. Minister for Social Welfare*[15] the High Court held that a public authority was a board which has public or statutory duties to perform for the benefit of the public, and not for private profit.

(4) Paragraphs 6 and 7

14–16

6. Employment as a court messenger under section 4 of the Enforcement of Court Orders Act 1926.

7. Employment as a trainee midwife, student midwife, pupil midwife, probationary midwife, trainee nurse, student nurse, pupil nurse or probationary nurse. In this paragraph "nurse" includes a nursery or children's nurse.

14–17 This paragraph was inserted as a result of the High Court and Supreme Court decisions in *National Maternity Hospital v. Minster for Social Welfare*[16] and *Sister Dolores v. Minister for Social Welfare*,[17] in which it was held that the relationship between a trainee nurse and a hospital was fundamentally that of pupil and teacher and not that of master and servant nor of apprenticeship, and consequently that such employment was not insurable under the Social Welfare Acts.

---

[13] [1958] I.R. 1.
[14] [1987] 1 I.R. 295.
[15] [1976–7] I.L.R.M. 210.
[16] [1960] I.R. 74.
[17] [1962] I.R. 77.

(5) Paragraph 8

14–18

8. Employment by the Minister as manager of an employment office.

14–19   This paragraph was inserted as a result of the High Court decision in *Ó Coindealbháin v. Mooney*,[18] a tax case in which it was held that a branch manager of an employment office was employed under a contract for services.

(6) Paragraphs 9 and 10

14–20

9. Employment as a member of the Garda Síochána.

10. Employment where the employed person is a person in Holy Orders or other minister of religion or a person living in a religious community as a member thereof.

14–21   Although there does not appear to be any Irish case law directly on the point, the U.K. courts have held that a clergyman is not employed under a contract of service and it seems likely that the same would apply in this country.[19]

(7) Paragraphs 11 and 12

14–22

11. Employment by An Post as a sub-postmaster remunerated by scale payment.

12. Employment under a scheme administered by FÁS and known as Community Employment or employment under a programme known as the Part Time Job Opportunities Programme administered by or on behalf of the Conference of Religious of Ireland, where:
    (a) the said employment commences on or after April 6, 1996, or
    (b) in any other case, where, subject to such conditions and in such circumstances as may be prescribed, the person employed in either of the said employments, elects to be an employed contributor within the meaning of section 9(1)(a).[20]

---

[18] [1990] 1 I.R. 422.
[19] *Davies v. Presbyterian Church of Wales* [1986] 1 All E.R. 705. However, a cleric may be employed as, for example, a teacher: *Dolan v. K.* [1944] I.R. 460.
[20] Inserted by SWA 1996, s. 12.

14–23   As can be seen, the First Schedule covers: persons employed under a contract of service in (or linked to) the State (paras 1 and 2); civil and public servants who might not be considered to be legally employed under a contract of service but are for all practical purposes "employees" (*e.g.* paras 3, 4, 5 and 9); and a range of persons who are (probably) not employed under a contract of service at all but where it has been felt appropriate from a policy perspective to specifically include them within the scope of social insurance. In a number of these cases – including the trainee nurses and branch employment officer manager – the courts have specifically held that these persons are not employed under a contract of service. This category of cases must be under some legal doubt as a result of the decision of Blayney J. in *Griffiths v. Minister for Social Welfare*.[21] That case concerned sharefishermen who were, at that time, also included in a specific paragraph of the First Schedule. As a result of the finding that sharefishermen were not employees in *DPP v. McLoughlin*,[22] the Minister promulgated Regulations specifying the person deemed to be the employer for the purposes of the Act. However, in *Griffiths* Blayney J. held that in enacting the relevant legislation the Oireachtas did not intend to alter the traditional meaning given to the term "employment", which term necessarily implied that there be a relationship between employer and employee. Accordingly, he held that to be an employed contributor under the Act a person had to be employed by another person. In that case he held that as the relationship between the sharefisherman and the boat owner was one of partnership not employment, accordingly, the sharefisherman was not an employed contributor within the meaning of the Act. Although the case concerned only sharefishermen and the specific provisions concerning them, the logic of this decision could also apply to a number of the other paragraphs of the First Schedule where an employment relationship also does not exist. The counter-argument to this is quite simply that the decision in *Griffiths* is incorrect. The Oireachtas clearly did mean to alter the traditional meaning given to the term employment both in relation to the sharefishermen and in relation to the other non-employee groups specifically brought into insurance in the First Schedule. If the Oireachtas did not wish to do so, then its actions would be meaningless as the relevant paragraphs of the Schedule have no purpose if they are considered not to alter the meaning of the term employment.[23]

B. Excepted Employments

14–24   Part II of the First Schedule sets out a range of employments which,

---

[21] [1992] 1 I.R. 103.

[22] [1986] 1 I.R. 355.

[23] This is shown by the fact that the relevant paragraph covering sharefishermen was dropped from SW(C)A 1993 following the *Griffiths* decision as it was now otiose.

while they would otherwise be within the scope of the Act, are deemed to be excepted from insurability. Such persons are, in general, insurable for occupational injuries benefits only (Class J).

(1) Paragraph 1

14–25

1. Employment in the service of the husband or wife of the employed person.

14–25A   The purpose of the exemption appears to be to prevent the insurability of "collusive" employment relationships whereby a person employs his or her spouse at the minimum rate of pay sufficient to qualify the person for benefits. However, given that it is likely to impact disproportionately on women, it might be open to question whether this is justified under E.U. law. Where a spouse is employed under a contract of service by a partnership consisting of the spouse and another person or persons, he or she will ordinarily be regarded as employed by the partnership and not by the spouse. This will also apply where he or she is employed by a limited company in which either member of the couple is a director.

(2) Paragraph 2

14–26

2. Employment of a casual nature otherwise than for the purposes of the employer's trade or business, and otherwise than for the purposes of any game or recreation where the persons employed are engaged or paid through a club.

(3) Paragraph 3

14–27

3. Employment by a prescribed relative of the employed person, being either employment in the common home of the employer and the employed person or employment specified by regulations as corresponding to employment in the common home of the employer and the employed person.

14–27A   Again, the purpose appears to be to exclude "collusive" employment relationships. Article 93 of the Social Welfare (Consolidated Contributions and Insurability) Regulations 1996 defines this as employment, other than employment under a written contract of service or apprenticeship, by the father, mother, grandfather, grandmother, stepfather, stepmother, son, daughter, grandson, granddaughter, stepson, stepdaughter, brother, sister, half-brother or half-sister of the employed person (other than in a case where any such relative is a ward of court), where the employed person is a member of the employer's household and the employment is related to a private dwelling house or a farm in or on which both the employer and the employed person reside.

(4) Paragraph 4

14–28

4. Employment specified in Regulations as being of such a nature that it is ordinarily adopted as subsidiary employment only and not as the principal means of livelihood.

14–29 A list of subsidiary employments is specified in Schedule C of the Social Welfare (Consolidated Contributions and Insurability) Regulations 1996 as:

"Subsidiary Employment:

1. Any employment adopted by a person who is ordinarily and mainly dependent for his livelihood on another employment which is –
   (a) an excepted employment by virtue of paragraph 1 or paragraph 3 of Part II of the First Schedule to the Principal Act, or
   (b) a [modified] employment[24] ... where the person is liable to pay employment contributions at a [reduced] rate ... .
2. Employment as attendant at or in connection with examinations held by the Department of Education.
3. Employment involving occasional service only, as presiding officer or as poll clerk at Presidential elections, elections to the European Parliament, general elections, bye-elections, local elections or at referenda.
4. Employment as a member of the Defence Forces involving service in either An Foras Cosanta Áitiúil or An Slua Muirí for any period not in excess of 21 consecutive days."

(5) Paragraph 5

14–30

5. Employment specified in Regulations as being of inconsiderable extent.

14–31 Prior to 1991, employment of less than 18 hours per week was generally excluded under this heading. This excluded a significant number of

---

[24] Mentioned in SW(CCI)R 1996, arts 81(1), 82(1), 83(1) and 87(1).

part-time workers – mainly women. However, this is now defined as employment in any contribution week in one or more employments (other than systematic short-time employment) where the total amount of reckonable earnings payable to or in respect of an employee from such employment or employments is less than €38 in or in respect of that contribution week.

(6) Paragraph 6

14–32

6. Employment under a scheme administered by FÁS and known as Community Employment where the employment commenced before the 6th day of April, 1996.

C. Class A Insurability

14–33 The combined effect of the inclusion of employments in Part I of the First Schedule, the exception of employments in Part II and the modification of entitlements discussed below is to leave full-time private sector employees (aged under 66) (para. 1), civil and public service employees first employed after April 1995, and the employments listed at paragraphs 2, 6, 7, 8, 10, 11 and 12 of Part I of the First Schedule (in so far as they are not excepted by Part II) as being fully insured for all contingencies and classed administratively as Class A. There are currently about 1.75 million people in Class A.

3. Modified Employed Contributors

14–34 This group covers persons who are included in the definition of employed contributors outlined above but whose entitlements and rate of social insurance contribution are modified – generally by Regulation.

14–35 Section 11 provides that regulations may modify the insurability provisions in their application in the case of:

"(a) persons employed in any of the employments specified in paragraphs 2, 3, 4, 5, 9 and 10 of Part I of the First Schedule, or

(aa) in such cases as may be prescribed, persons employed in Bord Telecom Éireann[25], or

(b) persons employed in a statutory transport undertaking, or

(c) persons employed as teachers in comprehensive schools established by the Minister for Education, or

---

[25] Inserted by SWA 1996, s. 12.

(d) persons employed as teachers in national schools under the Rules and Regulations for National Schools, or

(e) persons employed as teachers in training colleges recognised by the Minister for Education for teachers in national schools, or

(f) persons employed as teachers in secondary schools recognised by the Minister for Education under the Rules and Programme for Secondary Schools, or

(g) persons employed as teachers in domestic science training colleges recognised by the Minister for Education, or

(h) persons employed as members of the Army Nursing Service, or

(i) persons employed in voluntary hospitals to which grants are paid from moneys provided by the Oireachtas in recoupment of revenue deficits, or

(j) persons employed by voluntary organisations which are providing district nursing services, or

(k) persons employed in an employment which is an insurable (occupational injuries) employment pursuant to section 50."

14–36 As we have seen there are five classes of modified contributor.

A. Class B

14–37 Class B consists of permanent and pensionable civil servants, registered doctors and dentists employed in the civil service and Gardaí all of whom were recruited prior to April 6, 1995.

This group is brought within the definition of employed contributor by paragraphs 3 and 9 of Part I of the First Schedule and their position is modified by the 1996 Regulations.[26] As a result they pay a reduced rate of social insurance contribution and are only entitled to widow(er)'s (contributory) pension, orphan's (contributory) allowance, limited occupational injuries benefits, bereavement grant and carer's benefit.[27] There are about 35,000 people in this group.

B. Class C

14–38 Class C consists of commissioned army officers and member of the Army Nursing Service, again recruited prior to April 6, 1995.

This group is brought within the definition of employed contributor by paragraph 4 of Part I of the First Schedule and their position is modified by the 1996 Regulations.[28] As a result they pay a reduced rate of social insurance

---

[26] SW(CCI)R 1996, art. 81 as amended by S.I. No. 85 of 1999 and S.I. No. 338 of 2000.

[27] On the basis that these groups have occupational protection against such risks, their OIB entitlements are limited. Injury benefit is not payable and they receive half-rate disablement benefit starting 26 weeks after the occupational accident or disease.

[28] SW(CCI)R 1996, art. 82 as amended by S.I. No. 85 of 1999 and S.I. No. 338 of 2000.

contribution and are only entitled to widow(er)'s (contributory) pension, orphan's (contributory) allowance, bereavement grant and carer's benefit. There are about 1,000 people in this group.

C. Class D

14–39 Class C consists of permanent and pensionable employees in the public service other than those mentioned in Classes B and C recruited prior to April 6, 1995.

In addition to persons employed (in a permanent and pensionable capacity) by local and public authorities *per se*, this group also includes certain persons employed (in a permanent and/or pensionable capacity) in a statutory transport undertaking; as a teacher in a national, comprehensive, community or secondary school, a domestic science training college, or in a teacher training college; as a doctor employed under various superannuation schemes; or persons employed in Bord Telecom Éireann.[29] This group is brought within the definition of employed contributor by paragraph 5 of Part I of the First Schedule and their position is modified by the 1996 regulations.[30] As a result they pay a reduced rate of social insurance contribution and are only entitled to widow(er)'s (contributory) pension, orphan's (contributory) allowance, occupational injuries benefits, bereavement grant and carer's benefit. There are about 110,000 people in this group.

D. Class E

14–40 Class E consists of Ministers of Religion employed by the Church of Ireland Representative Body.

This group is brought within the definition of employed contributor by paragraph 10 of Part I of the First Schedule and their position is modified by the 1996 Regulations.[31] As a result they pay a slightly reduced rate of social insurance contribution and are entitled to all social insurance benefits other than unemployment benefit and occupational injuries benefits. This treatment of one group of about 140 clergy in this way appears to arise from historical circumstances, although the legal basis for singling out one particular group of clergy must be somewhat doubtful.

---

[29] SW(CCI)R 1996, art. 83(1) and (1A) as amended by S.I. No. 416 of 1999 and S.I. No. 231 of 2001.
[30] *ibid.*, art. 83.
[31] *ibid.*, art. 86.

E. Class F

14–41 Class F consists of non-commissioned officers and enlisted personnel of the Defence Forces.

This group is brought within the definition of employed contributor by paragraph 4 of Part I of the First Schedule and their position is modified by the 1996 Regulations.[32] As a result they pay a slightly reduced rate of social insurance contribution and are entitled to all social insurance benefits. However, benefits (other than treatment benefit and widow(er)'s (contributory) pension granted in respect of widowhood arising before the current period of employment) shall not be granted while the person is serving as a member of the Defence Forces. There are about 9,000 people in this group.

4. Insurable (Occupational Injuries) Employment

14–42 The scope of insurable (occupational injuries) employment is set out in sections 49 and 50 of SW(C)A 1993. Generally speaking the scope of occupational injuries employment is broadly similar to that of Class A, except that there are no age limits. The slightly different scope of insurance is largely due to the fact that the scheme came from different origins (originally the Workmen's Compensation legislation and then the 1996 Occupational Injuries legislation) and that it has never been fully integrated into the general social insurance scheme. As we have seen, all persons insured at Class A and a number of persons in modified categories have entitlement to occupational injuries employment. In addition, there are 17,000 people who are insured only for occupational injuries benefits (*e.g.* people aged over 66). However, the self-employed are not insured for occupational injuries.

14–43 Section 49 provides that every person, irrespective of age, who is employed in insurable (occupational injuries) employment is insured against personal injury caused by accident arising out of and in the course of such employment. Insurable (occupational injuries) employment is construed to be any employment specified in Part I of the First Schedule, not being an employment specified in Part II of that Schedule (see above). In addition, the following employments are added by section 50(2) :

"(i) employment in the State in plying for hire with any vehicle, vessel, aircraft, machine or animal, the use of which is obtained under any contract of bailment (other than a hire purchase agreement) in consideration of the payment of a fixed sum or a share in the earnings or otherwise,

(ii) employment under any contract of service or apprenticeship entered into in the State (otherwise than as captain, master or a member of the crew) on

---

[32] SW(CCI)R 1996, art. 87.

board a ship or aircraft, being employment for the purpose of the ship or aircraft or of any passengers or cargo or mails carried by the ship or aircraft,[33] and

(iii) employment in the State as a member or as a person training to become a member of any such fire brigade, rescue brigade, first-aid party or salvage party at a factory, mine or works, as may be prescribed, or of any such similar organisation as may be prescribed."

14–44 Conversely, the following employments are added by section 50(3) to the excepted employments specified in Part II of the First Schedule:

"(a) employment as a member of the Defence Forces,
(b) employment, which is neither wholetime as may be defined in regulations nor under contract of service, as a member of the crew of a fishing vessel where the employed person is wholly remunerated by a share in the profits or the gross earnings of the working of the vessel,
(c) employment under any local or other public authority in the execution of any contract for services,
(d) employment, otherwise than under contract of service, specified in paragraph 10 of Part I of the First Schedule."

14–45 For the purposes of section 50, paragraph 2 of Part II of the First Schedule is to be taken as not including employment of a casual nature for the purposes of any work in or about the residence of the employer.

14–46 Section 50(6) provides that the Minister may, in relation to paragraphs 4 and 5 of Part II of the First Schedule, by Regulations provide that an employment specified as being subsidiary employment or an employment specified as being of inconsiderable extent shall be taken for the purposes of the section as not being so specified. Section 50(7) further provides that the Minister may by Regulations provide that any specified employment under any local or other public authority shall be taken for the purposes of the section as being added to Part II of the First Schedule.

14–47 Section 50(8) gives power to the Minister where it appears to him or her that the nature or other circumstances of the service rendered or the work performed in any employment which, apart from the subsection, is insurable (occupational injuries) employment and in any employment which, apart from the subsection, is not such employment are so similar as to result in anomalies in the operation of the Part, and that either:

"(i) the first-mentioned employment can conveniently be included among the excepted employments, or

---

[33] In addition, a pilot to whom the Pilotage Act 1913 applies, when employed on any ship, is deemed to be a member of the crew of that ship; see SW(C)A 1993, s. 50(5).

(ii) the second-mentioned employment can conveniently be included among the insurable (occupational injuries) employments,

the Minister may by regulations provide that the employment shall be so included."

14–48 Section 50(10) provides that a person who is unemployed shall, while in attendance at such course as may be prescribed and provided by such person as may be prescribed, be deemed to be in insurable (occupational injuries) employment and to be employed by the person by whom the course is being provided. Likewise, a person employed under a scheme administered by FÁS and known as Community Employment is deemed to be in insurable (occupational injuries) employment.[34]

14–49 It is worth noting that the Minister is empowered to provide in any given case that employment should be treated as insurable (occupational injuries) employment notwithstanding that, by reason of a contravention of or non-compliance with a statutory provision "passed for the protection of employed persons", the contract of employment was void or the insured person was not lawfully employed therein.[35] However, the general law of contract would normally mean that a person would not be entitled to occupational injuries benefits in respect of an illegal contract of employment.

5. Self-employed Contributors

14–50 The category of self-employed contributors (Class S) is really a residual category and is defined on the basis of income received rather than economic activity. There are about 270,000 people in Class S.

14–51 Section 17 of SW(C)A 1993 provides that:

"(a) every person who, being over the age of 16 years and under pensionable age (not being a person included in any of the classes of person specified in Part III of the First Schedule) who has reckonable income or reckonable emoluments shall be a self-employed contributor for the purposes of this Act, regardless of whether he is also an employed contributor."

14–52 Section 17 goes on to provide that every person becoming for the first time a self-employed contributor shall thereby become insured under the Act and shall continue throughout his or her life to be so insured, and that, in the case of a person who, not having been an employed contributor at any

---

[34] SW(C)A 1993, s. 50(11).
[35] *ibid.*, s. 52(1).

time, becomes for the first time a self-employed contributor, the first day of the contribution year in which he or she becomes a self-employed contributor shall be regarded as the date of entry into insurance.

A. Excepted Self-employed Contributors

14–53   Part III of the First Schedule lists the excepted employment as follows:

1. A prescribed relative of a self-employed contributor *not being a partner*, where he participates in the business of the self-employed contributor and performs the same tasks or ancillary tasks. Article 94 of the Social Welfare (Consolidated Contributions and Insurability) Regulation 1996 provides that the following shall be prescribed relatives: father, mother, grandfather, grandmother, stepfather, stepmother, son, daughter, grandson, granddaughter, stepson, stepdaughter, brother, sister, half-brother, half-sister, husband or wife of the self-employed contributor. Where such a person is a partner, he or she would be insurable (subject to the normal rules in this regard).

2. A self-employed contributor who is in receipt of unemployment assistance, pre-retirement allowance or farm assist.[36]

3. A person, the aggregate of whose total reckonable income, reckonable emoluments or reckonable earnings (if any) before allowable deductions under the Finance Acts is below a prescribed amount (currently €3,175).[37]

4. An employed contributor or a person who is in receipt of a pension arising from a previous employment of his or of his spouse, in the case of either of whom the income for the contribution year does not include reckonable emoluments or in the case of reckonable income, income to which Chapter II or III of Part IV of the Income Tax Act 1967 applics.

5. A person employed in any one or more of the "modified" employments specified in Regulations under section 11, being employments in respect of which the contribution payable under the said Regulations are reckoned only in relation to the grant of widow(er)'s (contributory) pension, or orphan's (contributory) allowance.

6. A person who is regarded as not resident or not ordinarily resident in the State in accordance with the provisions of the Income Tax Acts and whose reckonable income for that year does not include income to which Chapter II or III of Part IV of the Income Tax Act 1967 applies.

---

[36] As amended by SWA 1999, s. 17.
[37] SW(CCI)R 1996, art. 92.

6. Voluntary Contributions

14–54   The purpose of voluntary contributions was more relevant in the past, when a wide range of employments (including self-employment) was not covered by social insurance. The intention was to allow a person with a record of compulsory insurance who fell outside the scope of social insurance (*e.g.* due to a change of job) to keep up his or her insurance record. Voluntary contributions are now of limited relevance given the wide scope of compulsory insurance (and credited contributions) other than, perhaps, to persons leaving the workforce due to family responsibilities who will not be covered by insurance.[38] There are currently only about 1,600 voluntary contributors.

14–55   Section 21 of SW(C)A 1993 provides that where a person ceases to be an employed or self-employed contributor, other than by reaching pension age and has qualifying contributions in respect of not less than 156 contribution weeks, he or she shall, on making application in the prescribed manner and within the prescribed period, be entitled to become an insured person paying contributions under this Act voluntarily. Article 28 of the Social Welfare (Consolidated Contributions and Insurability) Regulations 1996 provides that application must be made in writing to the Minister within 12 months of the end of the contribution year in which the person ceased to be an employed or self-employed contributor or in which a contribution was last credited to the person, or such longer period as the Minister, having regard to the circumstances may allow. In practice, extensive backdating of contributions is not allowed, as this would allow persons, with the benefit of hindsight, to "top up" their contribution record to maximise entitlements at minimal cost.

14–56   The occupational injuries insurance of any person is disregarded in determining his or her right to become, or to continue to be, a voluntary contributor and the rate of voluntary contribution payable in any case shall not be affected by such insurance. A voluntary contributor who becomes an employed or self-employed contributor ceases to be a voluntary contributor.[39] Voluntary contributors are generally entitled only to widow(er)'s (contributory) pension, orphan's (contributory) allowance and bereavement grant.

7. Optional Contributors

14–57   As we have seen, the High Court held in *DPP v. McLoughlin*[40] that

---

[38] In practice, such persons rarely avail of voluntary insurance.
[39] Except in so far as is provided in SW(C)A 1996, s. 22(2).
[40] [1986] I.R. 355. In *McLoughlin* the Court highlighted three main factors indicating a

sharefishermen remunerated by a share of the profits from the catch were partners of, rather than employees of, the boat owner. A subsequent attempt by the Minister/Department to deem the owner of the boat to be the employer was struck down by the High Court in *Griffiths v. Minister for Social Welfare.*[41] Subsequently the Department attempted to approach the issue on a case-by-case basis, but in a recent case the High Court has upheld the *McLoughlin* decision that fishermen paid by share are partners.[42] The effect of this decision appears to be that any fisherman remunerated by share rather than by a set payment is to be considered not to be an employee. While this may appear not to be in line with the economic realities of the situation, it would appear to be settled law in the absence of legislative reform.[43] Subsequent to the *Griffiths* decision, the Oireachtas introduced a new category of optional contributors, whereby self-employed sharefishermen who were already paying Class S insurance could pay an additional contribution to gain entitlement to limited unemployment benefit, limited disability benefit and treatment benefit.[44] This has not proved to be an attractive option and a minimal number of people are ensured at Class P.

8. Credited Contributions

14–58 In conclusion, it should be noted that where persons who have built up a record of social insurance contributions are unable to continue to pay insurance due to the occurrence of a recognised contingency (such as unemployment or disability), they may be grated "credited contributions" which will help to qualify them for future benefits. Generally credited contributions count only for the "second" contributions requirement, *i.e.* the requirement that a person has a certain number of contributions in a recent year or a yearly average of a certain number of contributions. Credited contributions are also granted to persons entering insurance for the first time to assist them in qualifying for short-term benefits should the need arise.[45]

---

partnership: (1) each voyage was a separate venture; (2) payment was by share rather than wages; and (3) the rate of remuneration was determined partly by custom and partly by agreement.

[41] [1992] I.L.R.M. 44. I have suggested that this decision is incorrect: see Cousins, "Social Welfare – Persons engaged in sharefishing: employees or self-employed" (1994) 16 D.U.L.J. 207.

[42] *Griffin v. Minister for Social, Community and Family Affairs*, unreported, High Court, October 2, 2001.

[43] See contrary the old case of *Donnelly v. Hanlon* (1893) 27 I.L.T.R. 73.

[44] See SW(C)A 1993, ss. 24A–24C.

[45] For an excellent overview of the policy issues involved see Department of Social, Community and Family Affairs, *Review of Credited Contributions* (1999).

14–59   Section 27 provides that Regulations may provide for:

"(a) making exceptions from the liability to pay contributions for any specified periods, and

(b) crediting contributions to insured persons for any specified periods, including, in particular—
   (i)   periods for which there is an exception from the liability to pay contributions by virtue of paragraph (a), and
   (ii) the period between the beginning of the contribution year last preceding that in which they become insured persons and their entry into insurance, and
   (iii) periods ... in which they become or cease to be a homemaker ..."[46]

14–60   Article 56 of the Socail Welfare (Consolidated Contributions and Insurability) Regulations 1996 provides that an employment contribution (known as *pre-entry credits*) shall be credited to an insured person (other than a person insured for occupational injuries benefits only) in respect of each complete contribution week from the beginning of the second-last contribution year preceding that in which his or her entry into insurance as an employed contributor occurred up to the date of such entry into insurance.

14–61   Articles 58, 59, 59A,[47] 60, 61, 62, 63A,[48] 63B[49] and 64 provide that an employment contribution shall be credited to an insured person:

(a) in respect of a day of duly notified incapacity for work or of proven unemployment[50] in any contribution year;

(b) in respect of any week in which an insured person is in receipt of maternity benefit, health and safety benefit, adoptive benefit, invalidity pension, retirement pension, carer's allowance or benefit, disability allowance, and pre-retirement allowance;[51]

(c) in respect of any week in which an insured person is in receipt of carer's allowance or lone parent's allowance where immediately prior to claiming the said allowance the insured person was entitled to be credited with employment contributions by virtue of paragraph (a) or (b);

(d) for any week during the whole or part of which he or she attends a course of training provided or approved of by FÁS, CERT Limited, Teagasc or Bord Iascaigh Mhara;

---

[46] As inserted by SWA1996, s. 24.
[47] As inserted by S.I. No. 292 of 1997.
[48] As inserted by S.I. No. 569 of 1998.
[49] As inserted by S.I. No. 76 of 2001.
[50] Note that it is not necessary for a person to prove that they are genuinely seeking work.
[51] As amended by S.I. No. 338 of 2000.

(e) for any contribution week during the whole or part of which he or she is employed under a scheme administered by FÁS and known as Community Employment;

(f) in respect of any week during the whole or part of which he or she is participating in the Back to Education Allowance scheme, the Vocational Training Opportunities Scheme, or any other course of education or training approved of by the Minister;

(g) in respect of each contribution week during which he or she avails of parental leave or *force majeure* leave under Part II of the Parental Leave Act 1998 or unpaid additional maternity leave under the Maternity Protection Act 1994;

(h) for any week in the contribution year in which a person becomes or ceases to be a homemaker from the relevant date.

14–62 Clearly, where an employed contribution is payable in respect of any week no credited contributions are granted. In addition, where there are no employment contributions paid or credited in respect of an insured person for any two complete consecutive contribution years, then an employment contribution is *not* generally credited to that person unless, since the end of the second of the contribution years, 26 employment contributions have been paid in respect of such person.[52]

9. Conclusion

14–63 The scope of social insurance in Ireland is now quite extensive. In contrast to the position at the time of the Commission on Social Welfare, self-employed persons are covered (albeit for a limited range of benefits) as are the vast majority of part-time workers and persons employed under "community employment" type work. Only employees earning less than €38 per week or self-employed persons earning below €3,175 per annum are excluded and at these earnings levels occupational income is clearly not the person's main source of income. In addition, assisting spouses and relatives are, in general excluded but this group continues to fall in size and such persons can be employed in such a manner as to be insurable if this is so desired.

14–64 As can be seen, the question of whether and how a person is insured under the Social Welfare Acts is, in general, reasonably clear, although there are complicated legal issues in relation to some cases – particularly those at the margins between employment and self-employment (or partnership).

---

[52] SW(CCI)R 1996, art. 57.

Indeed, this has always been the case and the law reports since the establishment of the precursor schemes are full of cases involving disputes as to whether or not particular employments fell within the scope of insurance (or indeed of the workmen's compensation scheme).

14–65   As we have seen, those employed under a contract of service are fully insured and the legislative tendency has been to add specific groups of workers who were not so employed rather than to attempt to broaden the general definition for insurability. Indeed, it is difficult to see that any one definition could cover the full range of employments currently within the scope of the Acts. However, consideration might be given to a general statutory broadening of the "contract of service" test as applies in the case of a number of employment protection statutes. This might assist in including workers who are in economic reality dependent on the "employer" although they may, in strict law, be employed under a contract for services.

14–66   Some concern in this regard has recently been expressed by the Social Partners and a group was established under the Programme for Prosperity and Fairness to examine the issue. The group was, in particular, concerned that an increasing number of people may be categorised as self-employed even though the reality is that employment status would be more appropriate to them. The group, however, did not come to any very definite conclusions and simply issued a code of practice which would be monitored by the group.[53]

---

[53] Report of the Employment Status Group, 2001.

CHAPTER 15

General Legal Provisions

15–01 In this chapter we look at a range of legal provisions which apply to the generality of social welfare payments.

1. Making a Claim

15–02 Section 205(1) of the Social Welfare (Consolidation) Act 1993 provides that it shall be a condition of any person's right to any benefit (*i.e.* any social insurance benefit listed in section 30(1), assistance listed in section 118(1), child benefit, family income supplement or continued payment for qualified children) that he or she makes a claim therefor in the prescribed manner.[1] Section 205(2) provides that where a person fails to make a claim for benefit within the prescribed time, he or she shall be disqualified for payment for specific period (see below).[2] The detailed provisions in relation to claims are set out in the Social Welfare (Consolidated Payments Provisions) Regulations 1994 as amended. The Regulations provide that every claim for benefit must be made in the form approved by the Minister or in such other manner as the Minister may accept as sufficient.[3] The usual requirement is that the claimant must complete and sign the appropriate application form and ensure that it is submitted to the Department within the prescribed time.

15–03 Article 100 of S.I. 417 of 1994 allows the Minister discretion in regard to what may be accepted as constituting a valid claim. The Minister may accept a letter, or other suitable form of notification, as satisfying the requirement of making a claim within the prescribed time. In practice this

---

[1] As amended by Social Welfare Act 1996 (SWA 1996), s. 37. The fact that the individual sections of the Act dealing with entitlement to specific payments are stated to be "subject to this Act" indicates that a claim is a necessary precondition for entitlement, unlike the position in the U.K., where the House of Lords held that a valid claim was not a precondition of entitlement as opposed to the right to payment: *Insurance Officer v. McCaffrey* [1985] 1 All E.R. 5. The U.K. legislation was subsequently amended.

[2] As substituted by SWA 1997, s. 32 and amended by SWA 1998, s, 21, SWA 1999, ss. 17 and 19 and SWA 2000, ss. 11 and 14.

[3] Social Welfare (Consolidation Payments Provisions) Regulations 1994 (S.I. No. 417 of 1994) (SW(CPP)R 1994), art. 100.

discretion is applied administratively by officers within each scheme. Such a decision is not subject to appeal to a social welfare appeals officer as it is a ministerial rather than a deciding officer function. A dissatisfied claimant may, however, request the decision to be reviewed, and the review will be carried out by an officer of higher rank. In practice a claim for any social welfare payment will normally be accepted as a claim for a related social welfare payment and a claim for a non-contributory payment will be accepted as a claim for the equivalent contributory benefit. In addition to making a claim, the person is required by article 101 to provide necessary certificates, documents or information for the purpose of deciding the claim, and he or she may be required to attend at an office or other place in order to establish eligibility.

15–04 Section 205(4) provides that any claim or notice made or sent by post or by any other method shall be deemed to have been made or given on the date of receipt of such claim or notice by an officer of the Minister.

2. Time for Claiming and Late Claims

15–05 The "prescribed time" for making a claim is specified in article 102 of S.I. No. 417 of 1994. Where a claim is made after the prescribed time, a statutory disqualification is incurred, and payment cannot be made for the period of disqualification. The period of disqualification is prescribed in section 205 (as substituted by section 32 of the Act of 1997).[4] The prescribed time for making a claim and the period of disqualification for late claims are set out below.

Prescribed time for making a claim and period of disqualification for late claims

Type of claim	Prescribed time for making claim	Disqualification for periods prior to
Adoptive Benefit	First date of entitlement	Date of claim
Bereavement Grant	Within three months of death of deceased	Date of claim
Blind Pension	First date of entitlement	Date of claim
Carer's Allowance	First date of entitlement	Date of claim

---

[4] And amended by SWA 1998, s. 21, SWA 1999, ss. 17 and 19 and SWA 2000, ss. 11 and 14.

Type of claim	Prescribed time for making claim	Disqualification for periods prior to
Child Benefit	Within six months of first date of entitlement	Date of claim
Constant Attendance Allowance (OIB)	Within three months of first date of entitlement	Three months before date of claim
Death Benefit (OIB)	Within three months of death of deceased	Three months before date of claim
Disability Allowance	Within seven days of first entitlement	Seven days before date of claim
Disability Benefit	Within seven days of becoming unable to work	Seven days before date of claim
Disablement Benefi (OIB)	Within three months of first date of entitlement	Three months before date of claim
Family Income Supplement	First date of entitlement	Date of claim
Farm Assist	First date of entitlement	Date of claim
Health And Safety Benefit	First date of entitlement	Date of claim
Invalidity Pension	Within three months of first entitlement	Six months before date of claim
Occupational Injury Benefit (OIB)	Within 21 days of first day of incapacity	Date of claim
Old Age (Contributory) Pension	Within three months of first entitlement	12 months before date of claim
Old Age (non-contributory) Pension	First date of entitlement	Date of claim
One-Parent Family Payment	Within three months of first entitlement	Date of claim
Orphan's (Contributory) Allowance	Within three months of first entitlement	12 months before date of claim
Orphan's (non-contributory) Pension	Within three months of first entitlement	Date of claim
Pre-Retirement Allowance	First date of entitlement	Date of claim
Retirement Pension	Within three months of first entitlement	12 months before date of claim
Unemployability Supplement (OIB)	Within three months of first entitlement	Three months before date of claim
Unemployment Assistance	First date of entitlement	Date of claim
Unemployment Benefit	First date of entitlement	Date of claim
Widow's (Contributory) Pension	Within three months of first entitlement	12 months before date of claim
Widower's (Contributory) Pension	Within three months of first entitlement	12 months before date of claim

Type of claim	Prescribed time for making claim	Disqualification for periods prior to
Widow's (non-contributory) Pension	Within three months of first entitlement	Date of claim
Widower's (non-contributory) Pension	Within three months of first entitlement	Date of claim

15–06 Section 205(2D),[5] however, provides that the period specified in section 205(2) may be extended by a deciding officer or appeals office in prescribed circumstances and conditions. These are outlined below.

A. "Good Cause"

15–07 Article 105 of S.I. No. 417 of 1994 allows for the backdating of claims in the case of most payments where the delay can be shown to be for "good cause".[6] "Good cause" is not generally defined in legislation[7] and the departmental guidelines state that it must be assessed by deciding officers by applying common sense principles to the contentions put forward by the claimant and by evaluating the evidence available to support those contentions. However, in the case of occupational injuries benefit, good cause is stated to include delay in claiming for a period of up to 13 weeks while the person is an in-patient in a hospital as a result of the accident and for a period of up to three weeks following discharge from hospital if this also falls within the 13-week period.[8]

15–08 Departmental guidelines suggest that lack of knowledge by itself is not regarded as a sufficient reason for not claiming in time. It is stated that:

> "The Deciding Officer must consider what is a reasonable level of knowledge to be expected in the particular case. If, for example, legislation extends entitlement to a particular scheme a plea of ignorance of the change may be reasonable. Similarly particular circumstances may arise where the Deciding Officer is satisfied that it was reasonable for the person to believe that he or she had no entitlement, or that there was nothing to enquire about."

15–09 The guidelines also state that the receipt of incorrect advice or

---

[5] As inserted by SWA 1007, s. 32.

[6] Social Welfare (Consolidation) Act 1993 (SW(C) 1993), s. 205(2A) makes provision in this regard for child benefit claims.

[7] On the extensive U.K. caselaw see Ogus, Barendt and Wikely, *The Law of Social Security* (4th ed., Butterworths, London, 1995), pp. 641–644 and M. Partington, *Claim in Time* (Legal Action Group, 1994).

[8] Social Welfare (Claims and Payments) (Amendment) Regulations 1967 (S.I. No. 85 of 1967), art. 9.

information from any person other than a person employed by the Department is not normally regarded as good cause for failure to claim at the correct time. However, the deciding officer should have regard to whether the person believed that the source of advice was authorised by the Department and therefore whether it was reasonable for the person to rely on this advice rather than make further enquiries of the Department. This may apply in relation to state or semi-state offices where claim forms and information leaflets are officially made available to the public on behalf of the Department. The legislation limits the period for which payments may be backdated under this clause to six months prior to the date the claim is actually made.[9] Entitlement throughout the period must also be proven to the satisfaction of the deciding or appeals officer.

15–10 Where a delay in making the claim resulted from information given by an officer of the Department to the person concerned or to a person appointed to act on his or her behalf, the claim may be backdated to the date of commencement of entitlement if subsequent to the date the information was given or (if entitlement already existed) the date on which that information was given, plus any period in respect of which a disqualification would not have been imposed if the claim had been made on that date.[10]

15–11 Where the delay arose because the person was incapacitated to such an extent that he or she was unable to make a claim or appoint a person to act on his or her behalf, backdating of the claim may be considered.[11] The guidelines state that an illness that, though disabling, would not by its nature cause the claimant's mental faculties to diminish significantly will not be regarded as sufficient reason for the failure to make a claim in time. In these circumstances, the claim may be backdated to the date of initial entitlement where such incapacity existed at that time or, in other cases, to the date the person became so incapacitated, plus any period in respect of which a disqualification would not have been imposed if the claim had been made on that date, provided that the claim must be made within 12 months of the person ceasing to be so incapacitated.

B. "Force Majeure"

15–12 Claims may also be backdated where "force majeure" delays the making of a claim (other than in the case of unemployment benefit and

---

[9] Other than in the case of child benefit, where the claim may be backdated to the date when entitlement would have first existed.

[10] SW(CPP)R 1994, art. 104A(2) as inserted by S.I. No. 159 of 2000.

[11] *ibid.*, art. 104A(3) as inserted by S.I. No. 159 of 2000.

assistance and supplementary welfare allowance).[12] "Force majeure" means events or actions which by their nature were so intense as to render it impossible for a claimant to satisfy the requirement of making a claim. Where the circumstances constituted "force majeure" no longer continue, a claim must then be made before the expiry of the normal period for making the relevant claim, in order that backdating may be considered under this provision. The inability to claim must be the direct result of the "force majeure" itself. In these circumstances, the claim may be backdated to the date of initial entitlement if the "force majeure" then existed, or the date of the commencement of the "force majeure", plus any period in respect of which a disqualification would not have been imposed if the claim had been made on that date.

(1) Financial hardship

15–13   A claim may also be backdated where the person has a current level of financial indebtedness which cannot reasonably be financed from current income, or the disposal of current assets, or any combination of these.[13] Where financial hardship is shown to exist, backdating may be made to the date of entitlement, or whatever date after the date of entitlement is considered appropriate by the deciding or appeals officer.

C. Proportionate Arrears for Long-term Pensions

15–14   In addition to the general rules in relation to backdating payments set out above, a further proportion of benefits may be payable in relation to late claims of old age contributory pension, orphan's contributory allowance, retirement pension or widow(er)'s (contributory) pension.[14] Basically the period for which payment is made is extended by a percentage of the total amount which would be due had the claim been made in time. This percentage decreases as the period from the date of entitlement to the actual date the claim was made increases. Thus, where the gap from entitlement to claim exceeds one year but not two years, a person will be paid 50 per cent of the number of weeks exceeding one year from the date the claim was made (in addition to the full arrears for the first year). The proportion of arrears which will be paid declines progressively over time, so that where the gap exceeds five years, a person is paid only 10 per cent of the number of weeks exceeding five years from the date the claim was made plus 73 weeks (arrears being paid in respect of the 73 weeks).

---

[12] SW(CPP)R 1994, art. 104A(4) as inserted by S.I. No. 159 of 2000.

[13] *ibid.*, art. 104A(5) as inserted by S.I. No. 159 of 2000.

[14] *ibid.*, as inserted by S.I. No 55 of 1998.

D. Departmental Delay and Compensation

15–15 Where a person makes a claim under section 205 and payment is delayed for a period exceeding 12 months due solely or mainly to circumstances within the control of the Department and the person has not contributed to such delay, additional payment will be in respect of the loss of purchasing power and in respect of prescribed costs actually and necessarily incurred by the person.[15]

3. Overlapping Provisions

15–16 Section 209(1) provides that where more than one benefit (other than death benefit, bereavement grant or widowed parent grant), any assistance (other than supplementary welfare allowance or widowed parent grant) or infectious diseases maintenance allowance would be payable, only one benefit or allowance shall be payable.[16] In addition, where benefit, assistance, infectious diseases maintenance allowance (IDMA), an increase in respect of a qualified adult, or an increase in respect of a qualified child would be payable to or in respect of a qualified child, only one shall be payable.[17] Notwithstanding these provisions, the Minister may make Regulations enabling more than one payment to be made to a person. Thus the legislation sets out a general ban on double payment which may be relaxed by regulation.[18] In general terms only one social welfare income maintenance payment is payable at a time, although it is, of course, possible to receive an income maintenance payment (such as unemployment benefit) and a child support payment such as child benefit.

15–17 The Social Welfare (Consolidated Payments Provisions) Regulations 1994 provide that a person shall receive concurrently:

(1) disablement benefit and any social assistance or social insurance payment[19];

---

[15] SW(C)A 1993, s. 206A as inserted by SWA 1998, s. 11 and S.I. No. 160 of 2000.

[16] As amended by SWA 1999, s. 17 and SWA 2000, s. 14.

[17] SW(C)A 1993, s. 209(2).

[18] The legislation now allows the Minister to specify those situations in which double payment is allowed. This replaces the previous arrangements whereby the Minister *disallowed* double payment by regulation, a procedure which was found to be so illogical, arbitrary or unfair as to be *ultra vires* the Act by the Supreme Court in *McHugh v. Minister for Social Welfare* [1994] 2 I.R. 139. McCarthy J. stated that it would seem more desirable that restrictions on entitlement, itself determined by primary legislation, should be provided for in similar fashion, [1994] 2 I.R. 139 at 156. See M. Cousins, "Note" (1992) 14 D.U.L.J. 193.

[19] SW(CPP)R 1994, art. 125(1).

(2) widow(er)'s pensions, death benefit by way of widow's, widower's or parents pension or one parent family payment and *half* the personal rate of one of the following payments:
- disability benefit;
- injury benefit;
- unemployment benefit;
- unemployability supplement; or
- maternity benefit.[20]

Payment of disability benefit or unemployability supplement is limited to 390 days. More than half the personal rate of the benefits may be payable, where the rate of pension in payment is reduced due to the application of a means test or contribution test.

(3) blind pensions where the recipient is under 66 or orphan's pension or allowance payable to a person and one of the following:
- adoptive benefit;
- death benefit by way of widow's, widower's or parent's pension;
- disability benefit;
- health and safety benefit;
- injury benefit;
- one parent family payment;
- maternity benefit,
- unemployment benefit;
- unemployability supplement;
- widow's or widower's pension.[21]

In addition, family income supplement, for a period of up to six weeks, and disability benefit are payable concurrently, where a person who is working and claiming FIS becomes incapable of work.[22]

4. Absence from the State

15–18 Section 211(1) and (2) provides that a person is disqualified from receiving any benefit while that person is absent from the State and from receiving any increase of benefit in respect of the person's spouse for any period during which that spouse is absent from the State.[23] However, the Minister is enabled by section 211(2) to make Regulations allowing such

---

[20] SW(CPP)R 1994, art. 127(1).
[21] *ibid.*, art. 128.
[22] SW(C)A 1993, s. 209(7).
[23] The definition of "qualified child" set out in s. 2(3) provides that the child must be "ordinarily resident in the State".

payments in prescribed circumstances. In addition, section 211 is subject to the overriding provisions of E.U. law where these are relevant.

15–19 Regulations provide that the following schemes, mainly contributory pensions and long-term benefits, are all payable while the recipient is absent from the State[22]:

- widow(er)'s (contributory) pension;
- orphan's (contributory) allowance;
- old age (contributory) pension;
- bereavement grant;
- death benefits (including an increase thereof) under the occupational injury benefit scheme;
- disablement benefit[25];
- retirement pension[26];
- invalidity pension.[27]

Increases may also continue to be paid where it is the qualified adult or child who is absent from the State.[28]

15–20 In addition, regulations allow for payment abroad or in respect of a period abroad in certain limited situations (including temporary absences) in respect of the following schemes:

- disability benefit[29];
- maternity benefit[30];
- injury benefit[31];
- unemployment benefit (in particular where the person is on holidays for up to two weeks or representing Ireland in an international sporting event).[32]

15–21 Section 204 provides that in Part VI of the Act (which includes section 211), the word "benefit", except where otherwise provided, includes assistance

---

[24] Social Welfare (Absence from the State) Regulations 1967 (S.I. No. 97 of 1967), art. 4(1)(d) (SW(AS)R 1967).
[25] *ibid.*, art. 4(1)(e) of S.I. No. 97 of 1967.
[26] *ibid.*, art. 4(1)(f) as amended by S.I. No. 220 of 1970.
[27] *ibid.*, art. 4(1)(g) as amended by S.I. No. 220 of 1970.
[28] *ibid.*, arts 4(2) and 5.
[29] *ibid.*, art. 4(1)(a).
[30] *ibid.*
[31] *ibid.*, art. 4(1)(c).
[32] Social Welfare (Absence from the State) Regulations 1988 (S.I. No. 154 of 1988) and see SW(AS)R 1967, art. 4(1)(bb) as inserted by S.I. No. 229 of 1967.

payments. However, in addition to the general ban on the payment of "benefits" outside the State set out in section 211(1), there are a number of further provision in relation to social assistance payments to persons "absent from" or "resident outside the State". This is obviously the result of an incomplete consolidation of earlier provisions but it does create some duplication and lack of clarity in relation to the legal position.[33] The specific provisions provide that:

(1) A person is disqualified for receiving unemployment assistance (UA) and pre-retirement allowance (PRETA), disability allowance (DA) or farm assitance while he or she is resident, whether temporarily or permanently, outside the State.[34]

(2) Old age (non-contributory) pension and blind pension is not payable to any person absent from the State except where a person takes up residence in Northern Ireland, where payment may continue for a period of five years or until the person receives a payment from the Northern Ireland authorities.[35]

(3) A widow's (non-contributory) pension and an orphan's (non-contributory) pension are not to be granted to or in respect of a person resident outside the State.[36]

(4) A person is disqualified for receiving one-parent family payment, deserted wife's allowance and prisoner's wife's allowance while he or she is resident, whether temporarily or permanently, outside the State.[37]

(5) Finally, section 211(15) provides that child benefit shall only be paid in the State.[38] However, this provision is frequently overruled by E.U. Regulations on social security law, as discussed in Chapter 17.[39]

15–22 The EU Regulations on social security only apply to those payments within their scope (see Chapter 17). It is arguable that some of the "absence from the State" provisions may fall foul of E.U. law on the right to travel to avail of services. At present, Irish law would, in theory, disqualify claimants

---

[33] On "temporary absence" see *Chief Adjudication Officer v. Baker*, reported in R(S)1/96.

[34] SW(C)A 1993, s. 211(6) substituted by SWA 1999, s. 17.

[35] *ibid.*, s. 211(7) and (8).

[36] *ibid.*, s. 211(13).

[37] *ibid.*, s. 211(14).

[38] See also SW(C)A 1993s. 192, which defines qualified child as for the purposes of child benefit as being a child "ordinarily resident in the State" except in the case of children of members of the Defence Forces or the civil service working outside the state for the Government, the State or an international organisation.

[39] Pennings, *Introduction to European Social Security Law* (3rd ed., Kluwer, The Hague, 2001), Chap. 16.

of several social assistance schemes for receipt of payment if the claimant is absent from the State. Thus, such a person could be disqualified if, for example, he or she went on holidays to another Member State although he or she would be entitled to go on holidays anywhere in Ireland. Such persons can be within the scope of E.U. law.[40] Article 2 of Directive 73/148 on the abolition of restrictions on movement and residence within the E.U. with regard to establishment and provisions provides that Member States must allow persons wishing to go to another Member State as recipients of services to leave their territory. It is arguable that the disqualification of a social welfare claimant for receipt of his or her only income is an effective denial of the right to leave the territory and that it is therefore in breach of E.U. law.[41] In practice, however, under administrative arrangements, most social assistance claimants are allowed to take holidays abroad for two to three weeks without affecting their right to payment.

5. Imprisonment

15–23 Section 211(1) provides that a person is disqualified from receiving any benefit while that person is undergoing penal servitude, imprisonment or detention in legal custody, and that a person is disqualified from receiving any increase of benefit in respect of the person's spouse for any period during which that spouse is undergoing penal servitude, imprisonment or detention in legal custody.[42] However, the Minister is enabled by section 211(2) to make Regulations enabling such payments in prescribed circumstances. The terms "penal servitude, imprisonment and detention in legal custody" are not statutorily defined, but in the U.K. it has been held that the equivalent disqualification apples only to detention connected with the criminal law. In a number of cases, the U.K. adjudication authorities have held that a person who is interned or who is committed to prison for failure to pay a maintenance order is not disqualified for benefit.[43] As the leading U.K. authority points

---

[40] Joined cases 286/82 and 26/83 *Luisi v. Ministerio del Tesoro* [1984] E.C.R. 377 and Case 186/87 *Cowan v. Tresor public* [1989] E.C.R. 195.

[41] Van der Woude and Meade, "Free Movement of the Tourist in Community Law" (1988) 25 C.M.L.Rev. 117; Weatherill, "Casenote on *Cowan v. Tresor public*" (1989) 26 C.M.L. Rev. 563.

[42] The definition of "qualified child" set out in s. 2(3) provides that the child must be "ordinarily resident in the state".

[43] *R. (O'Neill) v. National Insurance Commissioner* [1974] N.I. 76 and Ogus and Barendt, *The Law of Social Security* (3rd ed., Butterworths, London, 1988), pp. 368–370. In *Chief Adjudication Officer v. Carr*, reported in R(IS) 20/95, the Court of Appeal held that a person on "home leave" from prison was not detained in custody. The reference to penal servitude is now otiose, it having been abolished by the Criminal Law Act 1997, s.11. Specific provisions are set out in the Social Welfare (General Benefit) Regulations 1953 (S.I. No. 16 of 1953) (SW(GB)R 1953) as amended regarding social

out, this appears to be a narrower reading of the law than is required by the plain wording, and it is not clear what view an Irish court would take. The Social Welfare Regulations in a number of cases imply that detention in custody for non-criminal reasons is covered by the disqualification. The European Commission of Human Rights has held that the suspension of entitlement to benefits while a person is in prison is not in breach of the European Convention on Human Rights.[44]

15–24 Regulations provide that the following schemes are wholly exempt from the imprisonment disqualification:

- death benefits under the occupational injury benefit scheme;
- disablement gratuity[45]; or
- bereavement grant.[46]

In addition, there are specific exemptions in relation to social insurance payments where the detention is in respect of a criminal offence and the charge is subsequently dropped or the person is acquitted, where imprisonment is undergone in lieu of paying a fine, or where the detention is for the treatment of mental or infectious disease (other than a "criminal lunatic").[47]

15–25 Section 204 provides that in Part VI of the Act, which includes section 211, "benefit", except where otherwise provided, includes assistance payments. However, in addition to the general ban on "benefits" payable to persons in legal detention set out in section 211(1), there are a number of additional provision in relation to social assistance payments payable to person in legal detention. As in the case of the "absence from the State" provisions, this is obviously the result of an incomplete consolidation of earlier provisions, but it again creates some duplication and lack of clarity in relation to the legal position. The specific provisions provide that:

(1) A person is disqualified for receiving UA, PRETA, DA and farm assist

---

insurance benefits; Social Welfare (Social Assistance) Regulations 1993 (S.I. No. 364 of 1993), arts 23 and 24 (SW(SA)R 1993) regarding widow's non-contributory pensions and allied payments; Social Welfare (Occupational Injuries) Regulations 1967 (S.I. No. 77 of 1967), arts 12 and 13 (SW(OI)R 1967) regarding occupational injury benefit claims; and SW(CPP)R 1994, art. 7(11) regarding child dependants.

[44] *Szrabjer v. United Kingdom* [1998] P.L.R. 281; *Carlin v. United Kingdom* (1998) 25 E.H.R.R. CD 73.

[45] SW(OI)R 1967, art. 12(4)(a).

[46] SW(GB)R 1953, art. 5(3) as amended by S.I. No. 219 of 1970.

[47] *ibid.*, art. 5 and SW(OI)R 1967, art. 12. A "criminal lunatic" is defined in SW(GB)R 1953, art. 3 as a person who, in pursuance of an order of the Minister for Justice, is removed to an detained in a district mental hospital within the meaning of the Mental Treatment Act 1945 or the Dundrum Central Criminal Lunatic Asylum.

while he or she is undergoing penal servitude, imprisonment or detention in legal custody.[48]

(2) A person is disqualified for old age (non-contributory) pension and blind pension where he or she has been convicted of any offence and ordered to be imprisoned without the option of a fine or to suffer any greater punishment while he is detained in prison in consequence of the order.[49]

(3) A person is disqualified for receiving one-parent family payment, widow's (non-contributory) pension, deserted wife's allowance and prisoner's wife's allowance for any period during which she is undergoing penal servitude, imprisonment or detention in legal custody (except where Regulations provide otherwise).[50]

15–26 The disqualification does not apply to the latter group of payments where the detention is in respect of a criminal offence and the charge is subsequently dropped or the person is acquitted of the charge or where the imprisonment is undergone in lieu of paying a fine.[51] In addition, notwithstanding that a person is disqualified by virtue of section 211(10) from receiving OFP, by reason of undergoing a period of penal servitude, imprisonment or detention in legal custody, the increase of the payment shall be paid to any person appointed by the Minister for the benefit of the child in respect of whom the increase is payable.[52]

15–27 It is important to note that, in general, even where a person is excepted from disqualification, payment of benefit or allowance is normally suspended while the person is detained and is paid at the end of the period of detention. Alternatively, it may be paid during the period of detention to a person appointed by the Minister to deal with the money on behalf of the person or dependant.[53]

15–28 Finally, section 192 defines "qualified child" for the purposes of child benefit in such a way as to exclude a child detained in a reformatory or in an industrial school or undergoing imprisonment or detention in legal custody.

15–29 The European Court of Justice has held that a Member State is not necessarily required under E.U. law to treat imprisonment in another E.U.

---

[48] SW(C)A 1993, s. 211(6) substituted by SWA 1999, s. 17.
[49] *ibid.*, s. 211(9).
[50] *ibid.*, s. 211(10).
[51] SW(SA)R 1993, art. 23 of S.I. No. 364 of 1993.
[52] *ibid.*, art. 24.
[53] SW(GB)R 1953, art. 6, SW(OI)R 1967, art. 13, and SW(SA)R 1993, art. 24.

Member State as equivalent to imprisonment in the competent State.[54] In that case, an Irish national resided in the U.K. On a visit to Ireland he was imprisoned and, while in prison, became ill. On his return to the U.K., he claimed sickness benefit. U.K. law provides that imprisonment is a bar to entitlement to benefit but it appeared that judicial interpretation confined this to imprisonment in the U.K. The Court of Justice was asked whether Regulation 1408/71 allowed imprisonment in another E.U. country to be treated as equivalent to imprisonment in the competent State. While this might appear to lead to a more co-ordinated application of national provisions, it was argued that there was considerable variation between the rules in relation to detention in legal custody in the Member States. The Court held that the prohibition on discrimination in Regulation 1408/71 did not apply to possible differences in treatment resulting from the differences between the laws of Member States, provided that these laws were based on objective criteria and did not take into account the nationality of the person concerned. Thus, whether or not detention in legal custody in another E.U. Member State (or indeed in any foreign country) operates as a disqualification would depend on whether or not as a matter of legal interpretation such detention falls within the definition of "undergoing penal servitude, imprisonment or detention in legal custody" set out in section 211 (having regard to the non-discrimination principle in cases covered by E.U. law).[55]

6.   Overpayments and Repayments

15–30   The law in relation to overpayment of social welfare and the recovery thereof is set out in Part VIII of the Act.[56] However, as liability to repay is in many cases determined by the revision of a deciding officer's decision, regard must also be had to sections 248 and 249.[57]

15–31   Section 248 provides that a deciding officer may, at any time, revise any decision of a deciding officer if it appears that the original decision was erroneous in the light of new evidence or of new facts which have been brought to his notice since the original decision or by reason of some mistake having been made in relation to the law or the facts or if it appears that there was a relevant change of circumstances. Section 249 provides that:

---

[54] *Kenny v. Insurance Officer* [1978] E.C.R. 1489.

[55] In the U.K., it was eventually held after protracted litigation that the disqualifcatory provision in U.K. law did apply to periods of detention abroad; Ogus and Barendt, *The Law of Social Security* (2nd. ed., Butterworths, London, 1982), p. 401.

[56] SW(C)A 1993, ss. 277–283.

[57] The position concerning pre-termination procedures is discussed in Chap. 18.

"A revised decision ... shall take effect as follows–

(a) where ... the revised decision is given owing to the original decision having been given, or having continued in effect, by reason of any statement or representation (whether written or verbal) which was to the knowledge of the person making it false or misleading in a material respect or by reason of the wilful concealment of any material fact, it shall take effect from the date on which the original decision took effect but the original decision may, in the discretion of the deciding officer, continue to apply in any period covered by the original decision to which such false or misleading statement or representation or such wilful concealment of any material fact does not relate;

(b) where ... the revised decision is given in the light of new evidence of new facts (relating to periods prior to and subsequent to the commencement of this Act) which have been brought to the notice of the deciding officer since the original decision was made, it shall take effect from such date as the deciding officer shall determine having regard to the new facts or new evidence,

(c) in any other case, it shall take effect as from the date considered appropriate by the deciding officer having regard to the circumstances of the case."

15–32 Thus, in summary, where the original decision arose from any statement or representation (whether written or verbal) which was to the knowledge of the person making it false or misleading in a material respect or by reason of the wilful concealment of any material fact, the revised decision will apply *ab initio* and an overpayment will be incurred in accordance with section 278.[58] In any other case, the decision will apply from such date as the deciding officer shall determine or consider appropriate and an overpayment may or may not arise.

15–33 The legislation does not provide any guidance as to how this discretion should be operated. However, departmental guidelines suggest that section 249(b) should be applied with retrospective effect if:

---

[58] In *State (Hoolahan) v. Minister for Social Welfare*, unreported, High Court, July 23, 1986, the Court held that prior to a finding of fraud, the rules of natural justice required that this allegation be put to the claimant to allow him or her the opportunity to respond. The U.S. Supreme Court has held that under U.S. law there is no constitutional requirement that a oral hearing be held in relation to the assessment of an overpayment of social security benefits. However, the Court held that the legislation required that an oral hearing be held where a claimant requested a waiver of the overpayment or the basis that the overpayment arose without any fault of their part or that it would be, *inter alia*, inequitable to recover the moneys. While the later decision was on the basis of a purposive reading of the legislation, the strong implication was that the Court would have, if necessary, found that this was also a constitutional requirement: *Califano v. Yamaski* 442 U.S. 682.

- new facts have occurred since the person claimed the social welfare payment in question, or if new evidence has come to light which was not available at claim stage and the person was aware of the new facts or evidence but failed to report this information to the Department; or
- it is not possible for the deciding officer to establish that the person wilfully concealed the facts on a previous interview or enquiry but the deciding officer is satisfied that the person could reasonably have been expected to be aware of the new facts (or evidence) and their relevance.

15–34 Circumstances where it suggested it would be appropriate to revise a decision under section 249(b) with effect from a current date include cases where the deciding officer is satisfied that:

- the person could not reasonably have been expected to know the relevance of the new fact; or
- the person was not aware of the undisclosed evidence at the point when he or she made the claim or subsequently; or
- the evidence on which the decision was based was defective in a material respect through no fault of the person concerned, *e.g.* arithmetical error in means report.

15–35 Section 278 provides that where, in accordance with the provisions of sections 249, 264 (revised decision by appeals officer) or 269 (revised determination by health board official concerning SWA), a decision or determination is varied or revised by a deciding officer, an appeals officer or an officer of the health board (as the case may be) so as to disallow or reduce any benefit, assistance, child benefit or family income supplement paid or payable to a person:

(a) any benefit paid in pursuance of the original decision shall be repayable to the Social Insurance Fund to the extent to which it would not have been payable if the decision on the appeal or revision had been given in the first instance and such person and any other person to whom the benefit was pad on behalf of such person, or the personal representative of such person, shall be liable to pay to the said Fund, on demand made in that behalf by an officer of the Minister, the sum so repayable;

(b) any assistance (other than supplementary welfare allowance under Part III), child benefit or family income supplement paid in pursuance of the original decision shall be repayable to the Minister to the extent to which it would not have been payable if the decision on the appeal or revision had been given in the first instance and such person and any other person to whom the said assistance, child benefit or family income supplement (as the case may be) was paid on behalf of such person, or the personal representative of such person, shall be liable to pay to the said Fund, on demand made in that behalf by an officer of the Minister, the sum so repayable;

(c) any supplementary welfare allowance paid in pursuance of the original decision shall be repayable to the health board to the extent to which it would not have been payable if the revised determination had been given in the first instance and such person and any other person to whom the supplementary welfare allowance was paid on behalf of such person, or the personal representative of such person, shall be liable to pay to the said Fund, on demand made in that behalf by an officer of the health board, the sum so repayable.

15–36 Further, section 279 provides that where, in any case *other than a case involving a revised decision or determination*, a person has been in receipt of any benefit, assistance, child benefit or family income supplement for any period during which he or she was not entitled to it or was in receipt of a higher rate that that to which he or she was entitled, that person (and any other person to whom it was paid on behalf of such person or his or her personal representative) is liable to pay to the social insurance Fund, the Minister or the health board (as the case may be) on demand the amount of the overpayment. This section establishes a right to recover a repayment made due to an administrative error.

15–37 Section 279A (as inserted by the Social Welfare Act 1997) provides that where a person is convicted of an offence under section 32 of the Larceny Act 1916 by virtue of having received any benefit, assistance, child benefit or family income supplement which he or she was not entitled to receive, that person shall be liable to pay a sum not exceeding the amount of such benefit, assistance, child benefit or family income supplement to which the conviction applies to the Fund, the Minster or the health board (as the case may be).

15–38 Finally, section 279B (as inserted by the Social Welfare Act 1998) copper-fastens sections 279 and 279A by providing that where a person has received moneys from the Department to which he or she was not entitled, the person shall be liable to repay that money on demand. The intention of this section is to cover situations such as impersonation, where a person other than the person entitled to the payment receives money from the Department.

15–39 The cumulative effect of these provisions is that once a decision is made to disallow or reduce any payment, or where a person receives benefit to which he or she is not entitled or at a higher rate than that to which he or she was entitled, the amount of the overpayment is repayable to the Fund, the Minister or the health board as the case may be. Unlike earlier legislation, it is no longer necessary for the Department to show (in certain cases) that the overpayment arose due to a false or misleading statement or wilful concealment of a material fact by the person concerned.[59] Indeed it would appear that the obligation to repay can apply even where the overpayment arose though the fault of the Department. This is, however, tempered in practice by the operation of a code of practice established under section 282.

15–40   Section 281 provides that all sums due to the Social Insurance Fund, the Minister or the health board, other than in accordance with section 279 (*i.e.* due to an administrative overpayment), shall be recoverable as debts due to the State and, without prejudice to any other remedy, may be recovered by the Minister or the health board as a debt under statute or a simple contract debt in any court of competent jurisdiction, *i.e.* the District Court for sums up to €6,348.69 and the Circuit Court for sums up to €38,092.14. Proceedings for the recovery of any sum due to the Fund by way of employment contributions under section 10(1) or self-employment contributions under section 18(1) may be brought at any time, so the normal limitation periods do not apply.

15–41   The relevant provisions have recently been considered by the Supreme Court in *Minister for Social, Community and Family Affairs v. Scanlon.*[60] In that case, the defendant had been in receipt of disability benefit from 1985 to 1994. This was revised by a deciding officer in 1994 and subsequently by an appeals officer, on the basis that the defendant had worked between those dates and was therefore not entitled to disability benefit. The appeals officer, unlike the deciding officer, was "not fully satisfied" that Mr Scanlon knowingly made false or misleading statements but, based on the new evidence that he was working, was satisfied that benefit was not payable and should be refunded. The Minister sought to recover a sum of £43,000 from the defendant.

15–42   The Supreme Court, in a judgment delivered by Fennelly J., held that the current provisions, which originally came into force between 1991 and 1993, had retrospective effect and that the Minister was entitled to recover payment made in the period 1985 to 1991 even though they would not have been recoverable at the time as no false or misleading statement had been found by the appeals officer. The Court, which took a different view on this issue than had Laffoy J. in the High Court, held that the rule against retrospective legislation was designed to guard against injustice, in the sense that new burdens should not be imposed in respect of past actions. However, as a rule of construction and not of law, it amounted to a presumption which might be displaced by the clear words of a statute and, perhaps surprisingly,

---

[59] The legislation was adopted in its current form in 1993. On the earlier legislation, see *Scanlon,* below, n. 60.
[60] [2001] 1 I.R. 64.

held that the wording of section 249(b) was sufficiently clear to require retrospective effect.

15–43 In addition, the Court held that while a formal demand was required by section 278, the letter conveying the decision of the deciding officer constituted a demand. The Act did not envisage that any new demand be made after the confirmation of the decision of the deciding officer by an appeals officer and the claim could proceed on foot of the claim based on the original decision including the demand made on foot thereof. Thus the Court has given a broad, purposive interpretation of the overpayment provisions.

15–44 Any benefit, assistance or family income supplement repayable under sections 278 or 279, 279A or 279B may without prejudice to any other method of recovery be recovered by deduction from any benefit or assistance (except supplementary welfare allowance) or family income supplement to which the person is or becomes entitled.[61] Any child benefit repayable under sections 278 or 279, 279A or 279B shall be recoverable from any payment of child benefit to which the person is or becomes entitled. So general benefit or assistance overpayments may be recovered from any benefit or assistance entitlement other than SWA but not CB. CB overpayments may only be recovered from CB entitlements (without prejudice obviously to civil action to recover the debt).

15–45 Section 282 provides that, notwithstanding anything to the contrary, an authorised officer of the Minister or an officer of the health board may, in accordance with a code of practice, suspend, reduce or cancel repayment of any amount due to be repaid. The code of practice referred to in section 282 is contained in the Social Welfare (Code of Practice on the Recovery of Overpayments) Regulations (S.I. No 227 of 1996).

15–46 The Code states that due account shall be taken of the interests of taxpayers and social insurance contributors, including employers who finance the various social welfare payments, as well as the ability of the person concerned to repay. In accordance with natural justice, the Code requires that where an overpayment has been assessed against a person, he or she shall be:

(a) advised of the factors which gave rise to the overpayment;

(b) advised of the amount of overpayment involved;

(c) advised of the proposed method of recovery;

---

[61] SW(C)A 1993, s.281(6) as amended by SWA 1996, s. 7, SWA 1997, s. 30 and SWA 1998, s. 20.

(d) afforded an opportunity to bring to the notice of the Department or health board:

(1) any views he or she wishes to offer on the assessment of the over-payment;

(2) his or her views on the proposed method of repayment; and

(3) any facts or circumstances which he or she considers relevant to the repayment of the overpayment.[62]

15–47 Having considered the person's response (if any), the authorised officer will make a determination in relation to the recovery of the overpayment (*e.g.* the weekly amount to be repaid). There is no appeal from this determination as it is not a deciding officer function. It can, however, be reviewed by another authorised officer. The Code states that every effort should be made to recover payments in full. However, it also provides that the amount of repayment shall not reduce a person's weekly income below that of his or her basic needs. A person's basic needs shall be taken to mean the weekly rate of supplementary welfare allowance appropriate to his or her family circumstances. In addition, repayment may be deferred, suspended or reduced where the person liable to repay is unable to do so at the time. The period of deferral, suspension or reduction is to have regard to the circumstances which prevent the person making repayment, and the circumstances which gave rise to the deferral, suspension or reduction are to be reviewed from time to time to ensure that repayment commences (or increases) as soon as the person concerned is in a position to do so. The repayment of an overpayment may be cancelled where there is no reasonable prospect of securing repayment in whole or in part.

15–48 Finally, the repayment of an overpayment assessed against a person may be reduced or cancelled where it arose because of the failure by the Department or health board to act within a reasonable period on information which was provided by or on behalf of the person concerned, or an error by the Department or health board of which the person concerned could not reasonably have been expected to be aware.

15–49 In conclusion, it should be noted that section 280A (as inserted by the Social Welfare Act 2001) provides that where sums are due to the Minister or the Fund in accordance with sections 279 or 279B because the person dies before the payment intended for him or her was paid into his or her account in a financial institution, the payment may be recovered directly from the institution on written notice being given to the institution by the Minister.

---

[62] See *State (Hoolahan) v. Minister for Social Welfare*, unreported, High Court, July 23, 1986.

Given the increasing use of electronic fund transfer by social welfare claimants, there is also an increasing incidence of payments being made in the period between the death of the person and notification of death reaching the Department. The intention of this section is to allow the Minister to recover such moneys directly from the financial institution without having to seek recovery from the estate.

7. Distribution of Assets

15–50 The Social Welfare Acts impose various obligation on the personal representative of a deceased person who was in receipt of a social assistance payment (and, by implication, on the lawyers acting on behalf of such personal representatives). This has particular relevance to older persons in receipt of an old age (non-contributory) pension or widow's (non-contributory) pension. The purpose of the legislation is to establish the means of a person at the time of his or her death, to compare this with the means as disclosed to the Department, and to recover any overpayment from the estate. This is a provision which is commonly applied.

15–51 Section 280(1) requires a personal representative of a person "who was at any time in receipt of assistance" to inform the Minister in writing of his or her intention to distribute the assets of that person not less than three months before commencing to distribute them and to provide the Minister with a schedule of the assets of the estate. The wording of this section is extremely broad and it would, in practice, be difficult for a personal representative to know if a deceased person had been in receipt of any social assistance payment at any time. As departmental guidelines accept, the provision are applied mainly in the case of old age and widow's (non-contributory) pensions, as these are the groups of claimants where deaths mostly occur. It should be noted that the Department computer-match details of all probates extracted in a year against departmental records of social welfare claimants. Cases in which probate was granted but the Department has not been notified are further investigated. On receipt of the relevant information, the Department will compare the schedule of assets with its own record of the claimant's means. If there is no discrepancy, the personal representative will be notified that he or she may proceed to distribute the assets. If, however, there is a discrepancy, the personal representative will be notified of this. If requested by the Minister within three months of providing the information, the personal representative must ensure that sufficient assets are retained to repay any sum which may be determined to be due to the Minister or that State in respect of payment of assistance to the person when the person was not entitled thereto, or payment in excess of the amount to which the person was entitled. For the purposes of determining the sum due to the Minister, the means of the deceased person for the period in respect of which assistance was paid to him, shall, in the absence of evidence to the contrary, be calculated on the basis that his or her assets at the time of death belonged to him or her for that entire period.

15–52   A personal representative who contravenes section 280(1) and distributes the assets without payment of the sum due to the Minister shall be *personally* liable to repay this amount to the Minister.[63] Finally, any proceedings to recover assistance due to the Minister as a debt due to the State under section 281(3) must be brought against the estate of a deceased person within six years, commencing on the date on which the notice or schedule of assets is received by the Minister.[64]

---

[63] SW(C)A 1993, s.280(3).
[64] *ibid.*, s. 280(4) as amended by SWA 1996, s. 41.

CHAPTER 16

Payments On or After Death

16–01 This chapter looks at the three main payments on or after death: bereavement grant; widowed parent's grant; and the "payments after death" arrangements whereby social welfare payments continue in payment for a period after the death of the claimant or beneficiary. It should also be noted that payments in respect of funeral arrangements may be made under the supplementary welfare allowance scheme and that the health boards have, in certain circumstances, the power to provide for burials (see Chapter 7). In addition, certain death benefits are payable under the occupational injuries scheme where the death arises from an occupational accident or disease (see Chapter 5).

1. Background

16–02 Benefit on death had long been provided by the friendly societies and commercial insurance companies which preceded social insurance. Perhaps because of this fact the initial social insurance schemes did not provide for specific death benefits. The 1949 White Paper proposed the introduction of a social insurance death benefit of £20 on the basis that this would be possible at rates which would be cheaper than those through private commercial agencies. However, this was dropped from the Social Welfare Act 1952.[1] It was not until 1970 that a death grant was actually introduced. However, this was subsequently allowed to decline in real value until 1999, when it was increased significantly to £500 (€635). In addition, a widowed parent's grant was introduced the following year to provide financial support to widow(er)s with dependent children at the time of the spouse's death.

16–03 The issue of proof of death rarely gives rise to legal issues. In the case of the bereavement grant, for example, a copy of the death certificate and funeral bill is normally all that is required. At one time the law, following medical science, treated death as marked by the cessation of breathing or of heartbeat. At present the law appears to treats death as meaning brain stem death. In *Airedale N.H.S. Trust v. Bland*, Lord Browne-Wilkinson stated that:

---

[1] See M. Cousins, *The Birth of Social Welfare* (Four Courts Press, Dublin, 2002).

"Until recently there was no doubt what was life and what was death. A man was dead if he stopped breathing and his heart stopped beating. There was no artificial means of sustaining these indications of life for more than a short while. Death in the traditional sense was beyond human control. Apart from cases of unlawful homicide, death occurred automatically in the course of nature when the natural functions of the body failed to sustain the lungs and the heart.

"Recent developments in medical science have fundamentally affected these previous certainties. In medicine, the cessation of breathing or of heartbeat is no longer death. By the use of a ventilator, lungs which in the unaided course of nature would have stopped breathing, can be made to breathe, thereby sustaining the heartbeat. Those ... who would previously have died through inability to swallow food can be kept alive by artificial feeding. This has led the medical profession to redefine death in terms of brain stem death, *i.e.*, the death of that part of the brain without which the body cannot function at all without assistance. In some cases it is now apparently possible, with the use of the ventilator, to sustain a beating heart even though the brain stem, and therefore in medical terms the patient, is dead: 'the ventilated corpse'."[2]

In certain circumstances the courts may presume death if someone has not been heard of for at least seven years.[3]

2. Current Situation

A. Bereavement Grant

16–04   A bereavement grant is a once-off social insurance payment which is payable on the death of certain persons.

(1) Qualification conditions

16–05   A bereavement grant is payable on the death[4] of:

(a) a pensioner, a qualified adult of a pensioner, a spouse of a pensioner, a qualified child in respect of whom an increase in contributory pension was being paid at the time of death, an orphan, or a person to whom an orphan's (contributory) pension is payable under section 109; or

(b) an insured person, the spouse of an insured person, the widow or widower of a deceased insured person, or a qualified child (as above).[5]

---

[2] [1993] A.C. 789 at 878.
[3] *Chard v. Chard* [1956] P 259.
[4] On legal issues in relation to death, see para. 16–03.
[5] Social Welfare (Consolidation) Act 1993 (SW(C)A 1993), s. 114 as substituted by Social Welfare Act 1999 (SWA 1999), s.19.

16–06 "Pensioner" is defined as a person who, at the time of his or her death, was in receipt of an old age (contributory) pension, retirement pension, invalidity pension, widow(er)'s (contributory) pension, or deserted wife's benefit, or who would have been in receipt of one of these payments but for receipt of an old age (non-contributory) pension, a blind pension, a widow(er)'s (non-contributory) pension or carer's allowance at a higher rate (*i.e.* where the person would have been entitled to a reduced contributory pension and was therefore better off on a mean-tested payment). A qualified adult will also qualify where an increase would have been payable but for receipt of one of the mean-tested payments.

"Orphan" means a person in respect of whom an orphan's (contributory) allowance is payable.

16–07 While the detailed qualification conditions set out above are somewhat complicated, their effect is quite broad so that, basically, a bereavement grant is payable on the death of:

• an insured person;

• the wife or husband of an insured person;

• the widow or widower of an insured person;

• a contributory pensioner (or spouse of a contributory pensioner);

• a child under age 18, or under age 22 if in full-time education (where either parent or the person that the child normally lives with satisfies the contribution conditions);

• the qualified adult of a contributory pensioner, including those who would be qualified but are in receipt of another social welfare payment;

• a qualified child;

• an orphan or a person to whom an orphan's (contributory) allowance is payable.

Only one bereavement grant is payable in respect of any one death.[6]

(2) Contribution conditions

16–08 The "relevant insured person" must have at least: (a) 156 paid contributions since his or her entry into insurance; or (b) 26 paid contributions *and* either 39 contributions paid, credited or voluntary in the relevant contribution year, *or* a yearly average of 39 contributions paid, credited or voluntary over the three or five contribution years before the death occurred or pension age was reached (age 66 at present), whichever occurs first, *or* a

---

[6] SW(C)A 1993, s. 114.

yearly average of 26 weeks' contributions paid, credited or voluntary since 1979 (or since entry into insurance if later) and the end of the contribution year before the death occurred or pension age was reached, *or* a yearly average of 26 weeks' contributions paid, credited or voluntary since October 1, 1970 (or since entry into insurance if later) and the end of the contribution year before the death occurred or pension age was reached.

16–09 "Relevant insured person" is defined as:

(a) where the deceased person was a qualified child (i) the father or mother of such deceased person, (ii) the person with whom the deceased person was normally residing at the date of death (or would be so residing if he or she had not been committed to a reformatory or industrial school), or (iii) the spouse of that person; or

(b) in any other case, the deceased person or his or her spouse.

Again, these are very flexible contribution requirements and the bulk of persons should be able to qualify.

(3) Payments

16–10 Bereavement grant is a once-off lump sum, currently €635.[7]

(4) Disqualifications

16–11 The normal disqualifications where the claimant is undergoing penal servitude, imprisonment or detention in legal custody or is absent from the State do not apply to bereavement grant.[8]

B. Widowed Parent Grant

16–12 A widowed parent grant is a once-off payment to assist with the income support needs of a widow or widower with dependent children immediately following the death of her or his spouse.

(1) Qualification conditions

16–13 In order to qualify, the person must be a widow or widower in receipt of one of a range of qualifying social welfare payments and have child dependants.

---

[7] SW(C)A 1993, Pt V of Second Sched., as amended by SWA 1999, s.4.
[8] *ibid.*, s. 211. See Chap. 15.

16–14 "Widowed parent" is defined a widow or widower who:

(a) has at least one qualified child who normally resides with him or her; and

(b) (i) is entitled to or in receipt of bereavement grant; or
   (ii) is entitled to or in receipt of:
   - death benefit under section 60 of the Social Welfare (Consolidation) Act 1993, *i.e.* by way of widow(er)'s pension under the occupational injuries scheme; or
   - widow(er)'s contributory pension; or
   - widow(er)'s contributory pension under E.U. Regulation 1408/71 or by virtue of a reciprocal agreement between Ireland and another country under section 238 of the 1993 Act; or
   - one-parent family payment,

which includes an increase in respect of a qualified child.

16–15 "Widow(er)" includes a man or woman who would otherwise be a widow(er) but for the fact that his or her marriage has been validly dissolved.[9]

16–16 As entitlement is based on receipt of one of a range of other social welfare payments; there are no additional contribution or means-test conditions for widowed parent grant.

(2) Payments

16–17 Widowed parent grant is a once-off lump sum, currently €2,500.[10]

C. Payments after Death

16–18 Section 210 of the 1993 Act as amended provides for continued payment of social welfare in respect of a claimant with a qualified adult or a qualified child for a period of six weeks after the death of the claimant, adult or child, as the case may be.

16–19 The legislative provisions are complicated but basically provide that:

(a) where a person who is in receipt of a benefit or allowance which includes an increase in respect of a qualified adult, or which would include such an increase but for the receipt by that person's spouse of certain other social welfare payments in his or her own right, dies, payment of the

---

[9] SW(C)A 1993, s. 116A as inserted by SWA 2000, s.13. For general issues relation to the definition of a widow or widower see Chap. 3.
[10] *ibid.*, s. 116A(1) as amended by SWA 2002, s.4.

benefit or allowance shall continue to be made for a period of six weeks after the date of death and shall, during that period, be made to such person and subject to such conditions as may be prescribed; and

(b) where a qualified child, in respect of whom an increase of a benefit or allowance is being paid, dies, the amount of such increase shall continue to be made for a period of six weeks after the date of death; and

(c) where a qualified adult in respect of whom an increase of a benefit or allowance is being paid, or in respect of whom such an increase would be payable but for the receipt by the qualified adult of certain social welfare payments in his or her own right, dies, payment of such increase shall continue to be made for a period of six weeks after the date of death.

Section 210 sets out specific provisions in relation to individual social welfare payments to broadly the same effect as that set out above in the general provisions.[11]

---

[11] See the Department of Social and Family Affairs Guidelines on "Payment Related Issues" for a detailed summary of the current position in relation to entitlement.

CHAPTER 17

The E.U. Social Security Regulations

17–01 This chapter will examine the E.U. Regulations concerning the social security rights of persons moving within the Union.[1] We look first at the relevant E.U. legislation and at its implementation in Irish law and administrative procedures. The chapter goes on to consider the personal and material scope of the E.U. Regulations. It then provides a brief outline of the substantive legislation in a number of important areas which illustrate the different approaches taken in relation to different types of benefits. The E.U. rules also apply in the countries which make up the European Economic Area, *i.e.* Iceland, Liechtenstein, Norway and Switzerland. It should be noted that the E.U. Commission has relatively recently published major proposals for reform and simplification of the Regulations.[2] These are currently under discussion by the Council of Ministers. It should also be noted that Ireland has bilateral agreements with a number of non-E.U. countries, including Australia, Canada, New Zealand and the United States, which cover long-term payments such as old age, widow(er)'s and invalidity pensions.

1. E.U. Law on Free Movement of Workers

17–02 Article 39 of the E.C. Treaty provides for the right of free movement for workers and the abolition of discrimination against migrant workers. This Article has direct effect in Irish law, *i.e.* it creates legal rights which can be relied on by individuals before the national authorities.[3] If there is a conflict between E.U. law and national law, E.U. law must, of course, take precedence.[4] Article 39 is implemented, *inter alia*, by Council Regulation 1612/68 on freedom of movement of workers within the Union.[5] Article 7(2) of that

---

[1] For a detailed consideration of the Social Security Regulations, see F. Pennings, *Introduction to European Social Security Law* (3rd ed., Kluwer, The Hague, 2001).

[2] The various proposals are discussed in detail in Pennings, above, n.1.

[3] Case 41/74 *Van Duyn v. Home Office* [1974] E.C.R. 1337; Case 167/73 *Commission v. France* [1974] E.C.R. 359.

[4] Case 106/77 *Amministrazione delle Finanze dello Stato v. Simmenthal* [1978] E.C.R. 629.

[5] Council Regulation 1612/68 of October 15, 1968 (O.J. Spec. Ed. 475) as amended by Council Regulation 312/76 of February 9, 1976 [1976] O.J. L392.

Regulation provides that migrant workers are entitled to the same social advantages as other workers. The concept of social advantage has been defined broadly by the European Court of Justice, which has stated that it includes all those advantages:

> "... which, whether or not linked to a contract of employment, are generally granted to national workers primarily because of their objective status as workers or by virtue of the mere fact of their residence on the national territory and whose extension to workers who are nationals of other Member States therefore seem likely to facilitate the mobility of such workers within the Union."

The Court also stated that this concept:

> "... encompasses not only the benefit accorded by virtue of a right but also those granted on a discretionary basis."[6]

Social advantage has been defined by the Court as including various social assistance (or means-tested) payments in several Member States.[7]

17–03   In recognition of the importance of social security in ensuring free movement of workers, Article 42 of the E.C. Treaty declared that the Council should adopt such measures in the field of social security as would be necessary to provide freedom of movement for workers. Council Regulation 1408/71 on the application of social security schemes to employed and self-employed persons and their families moving within the Union was adopted in accordance with this objective.[8]

17–04   The basic purpose of Regulation 1408/71 is to co-ordinate the various national social welfare systems. It provides that a migrant worker must be treated in the same way as a national of any E.U. Member State and that such workers will not lose benefits to which they are entitled even if they go to live in a different Member State. It also provides for the *aggregation* of contributions paid in other Member States as though such contributions were paid in the state where the claim for benefit is made. In other words, if, having worked in at least two Member States of the E.U./EEA, one claims a social security benefit in one Member State, the social insurance contributions paid

---

[6]   Case 65/81 *Reina v. Landeskreditbank Baden-Württemberg* [1982] E.C.R. 33.

[7]   For a more detailed consideration of the effects of this Regulation on the Irish social welfare code, see G. Whyte, "The Impact in Ireland of EC Law on the Social Security Rights of Migrant Workers" in *Free Movement of Persons* (ICEL, Dublin, 1990).

[8]   Regulation 1408/71 has been amended on numerous occasions. The amended version of the Regulation is published in the *Compendium of Community Provisions on Social Security* (Luxembourg, 1995). This version has itself subsequently been amended on several occasions, most recently by Regulations 410/2002. The E.U. Commission proposed substantial reform and simplification of the Regulations in 1998 and this is currently under ongoing discussion by the Council of Ministers: COM (1998) 779.

in other Member State(s) may be taken into account in deciding if one is entitled to a payment. Generally speaking, the Member State in which one last worked is responsible for the payment of short-term benefits, *e.g.* unemployment or maternity benefits. In the case of long-term payments, *e.g.* old age pension, the responsibility for making payments is shared pro rata amongst all the Member States in which the claimant worked (subject to entitlements under national law).

2. The Implementation of the Regulations in Ireland

17–05 The Regulations with which we are mainly concerned in this chapter are Regulation 1408/71 on Social security schemes for migrant workers and its implementing Regulation 574/72. As E.U. Regulations, these provisions are directly applicable in the Irish legal system and create legal rights without any need for implementing measures.

17–06 In contrast to the situation in several other Member States, the Irish social welfare code did not, at the time of Ireland's entry to the E.U., contain any discrimination on the basis of nationality. This is perhaps due to Ireland's geographic position and the fact that the number of non-Irish social welfare claimants was always extremely low. Thus, there was no need to remove any existing discriminatory provisions in regard to nationality. Conditions requiring a claimant to have completed a period of residence in Ireland in order to qualify for a payment existed in the case of the old age (non-contributory) pension and certain payments to lone parents at the time of Ireland's entry into the E.U.[9] Such conditions have since been removed.

17–07 Prior to Ireland's accession to the E.U., the only bilateral social security Conventions which existed were with the United Kingdom.[10] In accordance with Article 6 and Article 7 of Regulation 1408/71 and Annex III thereof, the only provision of these Conventions which remains in force is

---

[9] The ECJ has recently held that by maintaining a condition relating to the duration of residence in its territory for the grant of the guaranteed minimum income, Luxembourg was in breach of article 7(2) of Regulation 1612/68: C–299/01 *Commission v. Luxembourg*, June 20, 2002, not yet reported.

[10] The relevant Conventions were implemented in Irish law in the following provisions: Social Welfare (Great Britain Reciprocal Arrangements) Order 1960 (S.I. No. 96 of 1960); Social Welfare (Northern Ireland Reciprocal Arrangements) Order 1964 (S .I. No. 213 of 1964); Social Welfare (United Kingdom Reciprocal Arrangements) Order 1966 (S.I. No. 67 of 1966); Social Welfare (United Kingdom Reciprocal Arrangements) Order 1968 (S.I. No. 218 of 1968); Social Welfare (United Kingdom Reciprocal Arrangements) Order 1971 (S.I. No. 270 of 1971).

Article 8 of the agreement of September 14, 1971.[11] Therefore these conventions are now largely defunct (only applying to the Channel Islands and the Isle of Man, which are not part of the E.U.) and their provisions have been overtaken by the provisions of the E.U. Regulations. In addition, an agreement was signed with Austria prior to its accession to the E.U., but again this is largely (if not totally) superseded by E.U. law.

17–08 Claims made for social security payments under E.U. law are dealt with by the same decision-making system as applies to the general social welfare payments. Decisions in relation to entitlement to payments are made by deciding officers (see Chapter 18). Any person who is dissatisfied with the decision of a deciding officer may appeal against this to an independent officer known as an appeals officer. To date, an appeals officer has not referred any case to the European Court of Justice for a preliminary ruling under Article 234 of the Treaty. The Court in *Vaassen-Göbbels*[12] decided that a Dutch social security tribunal was entitled to refer a question to the Court in accordance with Article 234 of the Treaty. It is arguable that the appeals officers of the Social Welfare Appeals Office also have the power to make such a reference.

3. Scope of the Regulations

17–09 In this part we look at the personal and material scope of the social security Regulations and, in particular, at how these are applied in Ireland.

A. Personal Scope

17–10 The Regulations apply to employed or self-employed persons who are or have been subject to the legislation of one or more Member States and who are E.U. or EEA nationals (or refugees or stateless persons residing within the territory of one of the Member States).[13] The Regulations also apply to members of their families and their survivors (irrespective of their

---

[11] S.I. No. 270 of 1971. Although the decision of the ECJ in Case C–277/89 *Ronfeldt v. Bundesversicherungsanstalt für Angstellte* [1991] E.C.R. I–323 would suggest that pension rights acquired under agreements not continued in force by Regulation 1408/71 may still have effect in some circumstances. The Regulations still apply to persons from the Channel Islands and the Isle of Man and others not covered by the E.U. Regulations. Negotiations with the U.K. authorities to amend these agreements are ongoing and a revised agreement is expected to be ratified shortly.

[12] Case 61/65 *Vaassen-Göbbels v. Beambtenfonds voor het Mijnbedrif* [1966] E.C.R. 261.

[13] Regulation 1408/71, art. 2(1). Proposals to extend cover to third-country nationals have been agreed by the Council of Ministers and are currently under discussion in the European Parliament.

nationality).[14] The Regulations apply to the survivors of employed or self-employed persons who have been subject to the legislation of one or more Member States, irrespective of the nationality of the employed or self-employed persons where the survivors are E.U. or EEA nationals (or refugees or stateless persons).[15]

17–11 In relation to employed persons Annex I of Regulation 1408/71 states that:

"Any person who is compulsorily or voluntarily insured pursuant to the provisions of Sections 9, 21 and 49 of the Social Welfare (Consolidation) Act 1993 shall be considered an employed person within the meaning of Article 1(a)(ii) of the Regulations."[16]

17–12 In relation to self-employed persons the Annex states that:

"Any person who is compulsorily or voluntarily insured pursuant to the provisions of Sections 17 and 21 of the Social Welfare (Consolidation) Act 1993 shall be considered to be a self-employed person within the meaning of Article 1(a)(ii) of the Regulation."

17–13 These provisions indicate that the Irish social welfare system is considered to be "a social security scheme for all residents or for the whole working population" under Article 1(a)(ii). Section 9 of the Social Welfare (Consolidation) Act 1993 relates to insurance for the main social security risks, such as unemployment, disability, retirement, old age, and widowhood. Section 17 refers to insurance for the self-employed and section 21 to voluntary insurance, while section 49 refers to insurance for occupational injuries only. As outlined in Chapter 14, the Irish social insurance code is quite complicated and currently contains a number of different categories of insured persons. The provision in Annex I ensures that all persons who are compulsorily or voluntarily insured under the Irish social insurance scheme, even if only for one contingency, *e.g.* occupational injuries, are considered to be employed or self-employed persons (as the case may be) for the purposes of the Regulation in relation to the benefits insured against.[17]

17–14 In *Walsh v. National Insurance Officer*,[18] the Court of Justice ruled that Regulations 1408/71 and 574/72 must be interpreted as meaning that a person who is entitled under the legislation of a Member State to benefits

---

[14] Regulation 1408/71, art. 2(1). "Member of family" and "survivor" are defined in Art. 1.
[15] *ibid.*, art. 2(2).
[16] As amended by Regulation 1223/98.
[17] The Court has given a similar general interpretation in Case 71/93 *Van Poucke v. Rijksinstituut voor de Sociale Verzekeringen der Zelfstandigen* [1994] E.C.R. I–1101.
[18] Case 143/79 *Walsh v. National Insurance Officer* [1980] E.C.R. 1639.

covered by Regulation 1408/71 by virtue of contributions previously paid compulsorily does not lose his status as a "worker" within the meaning of the Regulations by reason only of the fact that at the time when the contingency occurred he was no longer paying contributions and was not bound to do so. Thus, under E.U. law, it is not necessary that a person be in employment or paying contributions at the time when a contingency arises in order to rely on the Social Security Regulations. In addition, sections 9 and 17 of the Act state that every person becoming for the first time an employed or self-employed contributor shall thereby become insured under the Act and shall thereafter continue throughout his or her life to be so insured. It is not generally possible under E.U. law for a person to be compulsorily insured under two different legislations at the same time, and so it is submitted that where a person insured under Irish legislation subsequently becomes insured under the legislation of another Member State, the Irish insurance must be deemed to be suspended under E.U. law. However, should the insurance under the social security scheme of the other Member State subsequently lapse, it is arguable that the person becomes again insured under the Irish legislation, if he or she is resident in Ireland.[19] Thus a person could remain insured under the Irish legislation and consequently be considered to be an employed person within the meaning of the E.U. Regulations even where the criteria set out in the *Walsh* case were not satisfied, *i.e.* even where the person concerned was not "entitled under the legislation of a Member State to benefits covered by Regulation 1408/71 by virtue of contributions previously paid". Since it is a matter for the Member States to define the scope of their legislation, there is nothing inconsistent with E.U. law in Irish legislation giving a very broad definition to the personal scope of the Regulation (subject, of course, to the provisions of articles 13 to 17a of Regulation 1408/71).

17–15 Since May 1995, students (who would not otherwise come within the scope of the Regulations as employed or self-employed persons) come within the scope of the Regulation, but only to a limited extent.[20] From October 1998, civil servants also come within the scope of the Regulation.[21]

B. Material Scope

17–16 The E.U. Regulations apply to all legislation concerning the following branches of social security: sickness and maternity, invalidity benefits, old

---

[19] Regulation 1408/71, art. 13(2)(f) provides that a person to whom the legislation of a Member State ceases to apply without that of another Member State becoming applicable shall be subject to the legislation of the Member State in which he or she resides in accordance with the provisions of that legislation.

[20] Regulation 307/99; see Pennings, above, n.1, pp. 38–39.

[21] Regulation 1606/98; see Pennings, above, n.1, p. 39.

age benefits, survivor benefits, benefits in respect of accidents at work and occupational diseases, death grants, unemployment benefits and family benefits.[22] Article 4(2) of Regulation 1408/71 states that the Regulations apply to all general and special social security schemes, whether contributory or non-contributory.[23] The Regulations do not, in accordance with article 4(4), apply to "social and medical assistance'. Benefits for victims of war are also excluded from the scope of the Regulation. The Regulation now also applies to special non-contributory benefits which are provided under legislation or schemes other than those referred to in article 4(1) or excluded by article 4(4) where such benefits are intended either to provide supplementary, substitute or ancillary cover against the risks covered by the branches of social security referred to in article 4(1) or solely as specified protection for the disabled.

17–17 The background to this somewhat confusing categorisation is that, in line with the social-insurance-based systems of the original EEC Member States, the Regulation originally was intended to apply only to social security. This was initially interpreted as meaning that only social insurance payments (and child benefit) were covered by the Regulation and that all social assistance (*i.e.* means-tested) payments were not covered.[24] However, the case law of the Court of Justice held that payments cannot simply be divided into those payable on the basis of contributions and those payable on the basis of a means test, with the latter being outside the scope of the Regulation. The Court of Justice ruled in several cases that means-tested payments are within the scope of Regulation 1408/71. The Court stated that:

> "The distinction between benefits which are excluded from the scope of Regulation 1408/71 and benefits which come within it rests entirely on the factors relating to each benefit, in particular its purpose and the conditions for its grant, and not on whether the national legislation describes that benefit as a social security benefit or not."[25]

17–18 Following the case law of the Court, two criteria had to be satisfied if a payment was to be considered within the scope of the Regulation.[26]

1. The legislation under which the benefit is granted must place claimants in a legally defined position as a result of which they have a clear right to benefit as opposed to a discretionary entitlement.

---

[22] Regulation 1408/71, art. 4(1).

[23] *ibid.*, art. 4(2).

[24] See the list of benefits declared to come within the scope of art. 4(1), *Compendium*, p. 250.

[25] Case 249/83 *Hoeckx v. Openbaar Centrum voor Maatschappelijk Welzijn, Kalmthout* [1985] E.C.R. 973.

[26] See P. Watson, "Minimum Income Benefits: Social Security or Social Assistance" (1986) 11 E.L.Rev. 335.

2.   The benefit must cover one of the risks set out in article 4 of Regulation 1408/71.[27]

17–19   It was arguable that several payments under the Irish social welfare system that were not considered to be covered by the E.U. Regulations were in fact legally within their scope. However, the Council of Ministers adopted an amending Regulation in 1992 to clarify the situation in relation to which payments are and are not covered by the Regulation.[28] The Regulation now applies to non-contributory benefits where such benefits are intended to provide supplementary, substitute or ancillary cover against risks covered by the branches of social security referred to in the Regulation or where they are intended solely as specific protection for the disabled. These non-contributory benefits must be specified in declarations by the Member States and are listed in a new Annex IIa. Ireland has included most social assistance payments that might be within the scope of the Regulations. The Regulation inserted a new Article 10a, which provides that the special non-contributory cash benefits are to be granted "exclusively in the territory of the Member State" in which the claimant resides in accordance with the legislation of that State. Member States under whose legislation entitlement to such a non-contributory benefit is subject to conditions of employment, self-employment or residence must regard such periods completed in another Member State as though completed in their own territory. Where payment of a non-contributory supplement is subject to receipt of a particular benefit, receipt of any corresponding benefit under the legislation of another Member State must be treated as sufficient.

17–20   It now appears that there are four categories into which a payment may fall:

1.   social security benefits (article 4(1) & (2));

2.   special non-contributory benefits declared by the Member States which supplement, substitute or provide ancillary cover under one of the social security branches or where they are intended solely as specific protection for the disabled (these benefits are not exportable (article 4(2a)));

3.   non-contributory benefits to which the Regulation does not apply (article 4(2b))[29];

4.   social and medical assistance (article 4(4)).

17–21   This amendment has provided a legal basis for the existing

---

[27] Thus "minimum income" payments that did not relate to a specific contingency listed in art. 4(1) were not covered.

[28] Council Regulation 1247/92 of April 30, 1992 [1992] O.J. L136/1.

[29] There are no such Irish benefits.

interpretation of the scope of the Regulations. However, recent E.U. case law has again reopened the question of the material scope of the Regulation. In recent cases the ECJ held that a care payment in Austria and a maternity payment in Luxembourg were exportable despite being listed in Annex IIa. However, neither case is really surprising on its own facts. In *Jauch*[30] the ECJ, following its decision in relation to a similar German payment in *Molenaar*,[31] held that the care payment, which was payable as a legally defined right and aimed to improve the state of health and quality of life of persons reliant on care, was to be regarded as a sickness benefit. The Court also held that it was contributory in character. In *Leclere*, the maternity allowance in question was clearly a family benefit and accordingly could not be regarded as "special".[32] In themselves the decisions are unobjectionable, as while Regulation 1247/92 was designed to allow the creation of a category of hybrid benefits, it was not intended to allow Member States to classify benefits that were clearly social security as hybrid.

17–22 The strict approach taken by the ECJ has led the Commission to re-examine the benefits listed at Annex IIa and to reconsider whether the benefits listed, including 12 benefits listed by Ireland, are entitled to be there. In the Irish case, the benefits are all non-contributory and no issue should arise on this point. Equally, all are payable as of right (with the possible exception of some health payments) and again no issue should arise. However, in the light of *Jauch*, the question arises as to whether they are "special". The ECJ's consideration of the meaning of "special" benefits in both recent cases has been quite short and obviously related to the characteristics of the benefits under consideration. The decisive point in *Jauch* was that the ECJ had previously held that a similar German benefit was a sickness benefit (in *Molenaar*) and clearly felt unable to come to a different conclusion in the Austrian case.

17–23 Given the very different nature of the Irish benefits, it would be premature to conclude that re-categorisation is required. The key issue is whether the Irish benefits are "special" benefits where such benefits are intended "to provide supplementary, substitute or ancillary cover against the risks covered by the branches referred to in article 4" or are intended solely for the protection of disabled persons. It is suggested that the word "special" needs to be interpreted in the light of the phrase "intended to provide

---

[30] Case C–215/99 *Jauch v. Pensionsversicherungsanstalt der Arbeiter* [2001] E.C.R. I–1901.

[31] Case C–160/96 *Molenaar v. Allgemeine Ortskrankenkasse Baden-Württemberg* [1998] E.C.R. I–843.

[32] Case C–43/99 *Leclere v. Caisse nationale des prestations familiales* [2001] E.C.R. I–4265 at para. 36.

supplementary, substitute or ancillary cover". In the Irish case, it is arguable that almost all the listed benefits are intended to guarantee a minimum income level and to provide supplementary, substitute or ancillary cover, *i.e.* they are special. However, the Commission's current approach would appear to suggest that most benefits that fall within one of the contingencies listed at article 4(1) of Regulation 1408/71 are, therefore, not special and come fully within the scope of the Regulation. This clearly was not the original intention of Regulation 1247/92, nor is it clear that the ECJ decisions require this approach. Ultimately a further ECJ decision on a more relevant payment may be necessary to clarify the position.

4. Rules for Specific Benefits

17–24   In this section we look briefly at the specific rules in relation to a number of different types of benefit.

A. Pensions

17–25   The field of pensions is one of the most important in practice for social security entitlements throughout the E.U.. Extensive case law has built up on this issue, although there do not appear to have been any issues raised in relation to the Irish application of Regulation 1408/71. It is only possible here to give a general overview of the operation of E.U. law in relation to pensions.[34] The rules in relation to old age pensions are set out in Chapter 3 of Title III of Regulation 1408/71. In the Irish context, old age pensions refer to the old age (contributory) and retirement pension.[34]

(1) Aggregation and apportionment

17–26   The two basic principles of aggregation and apportionment apply. This means that a person who has worked in more than one E.U. country and who claims pension entitlements under E.U. law will be entitled to have periods of insurance in one Member State taken into account in another. In addition, subject to national entitlements, the cost of the pension is apportioned pro-rata amongst all the E.U. countries in which the person has worked in proportion to the period during which he or she was affiliated to the social insurance scheme of each country. Thus in satisfying the qualifying conditions for pensions, Irish social insurance contributions and periods of social

---

[33] See Pennings, above, n.1, Chap. 15.

[34] A similar approach is applied in relation to widow(er)'s (contributory) pensions. Old age (non-contributory) and widow(er)'s (non-contributory) pension are listed in Annex IIa.

insurance in another E.U./EEA country or countries can be combined. However, there must be at least 52 contributions in the relevant country.[35] In a number of E.U. countries, entitlement to a pension is based on periods of work or residence rather than insurance contributions *per se*, but the E.U. Regulation requires that all these periods be aggregated for the purposes of acquiring entitlement to a pension.

(2) Calculation of benefits

17–27   The rate of pension, where insurance contributions in another country are being combined with Irish contributions, is calculated as follows.[36]

1.   The *notional* or theoretical pension is calculated. Notional pension is that which would be payable if all social insurance contributions, both full-rate Irish and non-Irish, were treated as Irish contributions. The full-rate Irish and non-Irish reckonable contributions are therefore added together and the total is then divided by the number of years to get the yearly average number of contributions. This calculation is carried out by each Member State where a person has been insured (for at least 52 weeks).

2.   The following formula is then used to calculate the pro-rata benefit

$$A \times B / C$$

where
A = the notional rate of pension
B = the number of Irish contributions
C = the total number of contributions (Irish + other E.U. or bilateral)

In other words, the person receives that proportion of the notional rate of pension which relates to his or her period of insurance in Ireland. So if, for example, a person has spent half his insured working life in Ireland, he will receive 50 per cent of the notional amount from Ireland.

While the increase for a qualified adult and the age 80 allowance are subject to the pro-rata calculation, the other allowances (increases for qualified children and living alone allowance) are payable at the standard domestic rate. Increases in respect of qualified children (where applicable) is payable in one country only.

3.   The pro-rata pension is then compared with the pension to which the person would be entitled under Irish law alone. If a person is entitled to a higher pension under national law alone, this will be paid to the person,

---

[35] Regulation 1408/71, art. 14.
[36] *ibid.*, art. 46.

as the E.U. rules in this area do not operate as rules against overlapping of pension entitlements.[37]

B. Unemployment Payments

17–28   The rules in relation to unemployment benefits are set out in Chapter 6 of Title III. The term unemployment benefits is not defined.[38] The only Irish payment that has been declared by the Department to be fully covered by the Regulation is unemployment benefit. Unemployment assistance is listed in Annex IIa. In *Campana*,[39] the Court of Justice held that benefits which take the form of assistance with vocational training could also come within the scope of Regulation 1408/71 as unemployment benefits. Several such schemes exist in Ireland (*e.g.* the Vocational Training Opportunities Scheme). However, these schemes are all based on administrative schemes rather than on legislation, and it is arguable that they would not fall within the scope of Regulation 1408/71.

(1) Aggregation of periods of insurance

17–29   The Regulation provides that the social security authorities of all Member States are to take into account insurance periods completed in another Member State to the extent necessary, as though they were periods completed under their own legislation (article 67(1)). Other than in exceptional cases, for aggregation to apply, the person concerned must have last been insured with the social security authorities to whom the claim is made. In other words, if a person last worked in Ireland and becomes unemployed there, he or she can claim unemployment benefits from Ireland and have insurance periods in any other Member State taken into account in order to qualify for benefit. However, if that person, having become unemployed in Ireland, moves to another Member State, he or she will not (subject to the exceptions set out below) be able to rely on the insurance periods in Ireland or any third Member States to qualify for unemployment benefits.

17–30   Thus, one must generally claim unemployment benefits in the country

---

[37] Pennings, above, n.1, pp. 159–167. The original intention of Regulation 1408/71 was that a pensioner would not receive a larger total pension than the notional or theoretical amount. However, the ECJ held in a number of cases that E.C. legislation could not reduce the benefits which a person might claim under national law. In practice in Ireland, where there is an entitlement under national law, it is normally higher than the E.U. entitlement, so that the national person if normally payable.

[38] Although see Case 375/85 *Campana v. Bundesanstalt für Arbeit* [1987] E.C.R. 2387 ; Case 39/76 *Bestuur der Bedrijfsvereniging voor de Metallnijverheid v. Mouthaan* [1976] E.C.R. 1901.

[39] Case 375/85 *Campana v. Bundesanstalt für Arbeit* [1987] E.C.R. 2387

where one last worked. Most Member States have traditionally applied a very restrictive approach to paying unemployment benefits outside their own country. There has been a fear that claimants may abuse the right to claim benefits if they are in another country and not subject to the control procedures of the paying State. In addition, there has been a fear that unemployed persons from less well-off countries will go to those countries with more generous social protection systems to claim benefits – a concept know as social tourism – leading to unfair financial burdens on such countries. The E.U. rules concerning free movement of unemployed persons are therefore much more restrictive than those applying to workers and most other categories of social security claimants, *e.g.* disabled or retired persons.[40]

(2) Export of benefits

17–31 Article 69 of the Regulation provides for a relaxation of the strict territorial rules concerning unemployment payments referred to above. This allows a claimant of unemployment benefits to go to another Member State to look for work and to continue to claim benefit for a period of three months. However, in order to do so, one must first have been registered as unemployed for a period of at least four weeks (although this can be reduced by the social security authorities). A claimant must register with the employment services of the Member State to which he or she goes within seven days of leaving the first Member State. The claimant must, for the period of his or her stay, comply with the control procedures of that country. This procedure can be used only once between two periods of employment.

17–32 Point G9 in Annex VI of the Regulation provides that:

> "An unemployed person returning to Ireland at the end of the period of three months for which he continued to receive benefits under the legislation of Ireland in application of Article 69(1) of the Regulation shall be entitled to apply for unemployment benefits notwithstanding Article 69(2) if he satisfies the conditions laid down in the aforementioned legislation."

17–33 This favourable provision avoids the difficulties encountered by the strict interpretation of the Court of Justice of article 69(2)[41] of the Regulation and ensures that a person returning to Ireland after the expiry of the three-month period retains his entitlement to unemployment benefits under Irish legislation (in so far as this exists under Irish law).

---

[40] Case 20/75 *D'Amico v. Landesversicherungsanstalt Rheinland-Pfalz* [1975] E.C.R. 891; Joined Cases 41,121 and 796/79, *Testa v. Bundesanstalt für Arbeit* [1980] E.C.R. 1979.
[41] Joined Cases 41, 121 and 769/79 *Testa v. Bundesanstalt für Arbeit* [1980] E.C.R. 1979.

(3) Frontier workers

17-34 A frontier worker is defined as a person who pursues his or her occupation in the territory of a Member State and resides in another Member State to which he or she returns as a rule daily or at least once a week (article 1(b)). A frontier worker can retain this status for a period not exceeding four months even if he or she cannot return daily or weekly to the place or residence, for example, if the worker is posted elsewhere for a short period.[42] In accordance with article 71(1)(a), a frontier worker who is partially or intermittently unemployed is entitled to claim benefit in accordance with the laws of the State where he or she works. However, if he or she is wholly unemployed, the claim must be made to the authorities of the State of residence. In *Miethe*,[43] the Court of Justice ruled that these provisions set out exclusive rules and that a wholly unemployed frontier worker was only entitled to claim benefits from the Member State where he resided even though he was entitled to benefits under the national law of the Member State where he worked. This decision must be treated with some caution, however. Together with two other decisions given around the same time by a three-judge chamber of the Court[44] that interpreted E.U. law so as to have the effect of extinguishing entitlement to benefits under national law, it appears to be contrary to the previous case law of the Court, which had held that E.U. law did not disentitle a claimant to benefits gained solely under national law.[45] The basic principle behind these rules is that workers should receive unemployment benefits in the conditions most favourable to the search for new employment. Accordingly, in some exceptional cases where a wholly unemployed "atypical" frontier worker has a better chance of finding work in the Member State in which he was last employed, he or she may claim benefit from that Member State.[46]

(4) Persons other than frontier workers working outside the country of residence

17-35 Article 71(1)(b) provides particular rules for persons, other than frontier workers, who have temporarily gone abroad to work in another Member State. Such a worker who becomes partially or intermittently unemployed is entitled to benefits from the Member State where he or she works. However, a wholly unemployed person can receive benefits either

---

[42] Case 236/87 *Bergemann v. Bundesanstalt für Arbeit* [1988] E.C.R. 5125.
[43] Case 1/85 *Miethe v. Bundesanstalt für Arbeit* [1986] E.C.R. 1837.
[44] Case 302/84 *Ten Holder v. Nieuwe Algemene Bedrijfsvereniging* [1986] E.C.R. 1821; Case 60/85 *Luijten v. Raad van Arbeid* [1986] E.C.R. 2365.
[45] Case 92/63 *Moebs v. Bestuur der Sociale Verzekeringsbank* [1964] E.C.R. 281; Case 27/75 *Bonnafini v. INPS* [1975] E.C.R. 971; Case 69/79 *Jordens-Vosters v. Bestuur van de Bedrijfsvereniging voor de Leder-en Lederverwerkende Industrie* [1980] E.C.R. 75.
[46] Case 1/85 *Miethe v. Bundesanstalt für Arbeit* [1986] E.C.R. 1837.

from the Member State where he or she worked or from the Member State of residence as though he or she had been last employed there (provided he or she makes him or herself available to the employment services of that Member State).[47] It would appear that the provisions of article 71(1)(b) might be of particular relevance to many Irish workers. This article, in relevant part, provides that:

"An employed person, other than a frontier worker, who is wholly unemployed and who makes himself available for work to the employment services in the territory of the Member State in which he resides, or who returned to that territory, shall receive benefits in accordance with the legislation of that State as if he had last been employed there; the institution of the place of residence shall provide such benefits at its own expense."

17–36 This provision would seem to be relevant to Irish persons who, while retaining their residence in Ireland, go abroad temporarily, in particular to the U.K., to take up employment. A person who had gone to work temporarily in the U.K. while maintaining his or her residence in Ireland could, on becoming unemployed, opt to return to Ireland and claim unemployment benefit, and have the insurance periods completed in the U.K. taken into account to qualify for benefit.

17–37 The concept of residence has been considered by the Court of Justice in several cases, in particular in *Di Paolo*.[48] In that case the Court held that in coming to a decision as to the Member State of residence of the claimant:

"... account should be taken of the length and continuity of residence before the person concerned moved, the length and purpose of his absence, the nature of the occupation found in the other Member State and the intention of the person concerned as it appears from all the circumstances."

17–38 The Court also said that:

"... the fact that the worker has left his family in the said State constitutes evidence that he has retained his residence there, but is not of itself sufficient to allow him the benefit of the exception laid down in Article 71(1)(b)(ii). In fact, whenever a worker has a stable employment in a Member State there is a presumption that he resides there, even if he has left his family in another State. Accordingly it is not only the family situation of the worker that should be taken into account, but also the reasons which have led him to move, and the nature of the work."

---

[47] For unusual applications of these provisions see Case 236/87 *Bergemann* [1986] E.C.R. 1837 and Case 1/85 *Miethe* [1986] E.C.R. 1837.
[48] Case 76/76 *Di Paolo v. Office National de l'Emploi* [1977] E.C.R. 315.

17–39   It is clear from the case law that a person may be abroad for a considerable period of time and yet can retain his or her residence in Ireland. For example, in a case before the U.K. authorities[49] a U.K. claimant went to West Germany and worked there under a succession of fixed-term contracts for two years. It appears that the claimant was working for the same company but was employed through a succession of different employment agencies. The U.K. Social Security Commissioner considered that in all the circumstances of the case the claimant had retained his residence in the U.K. In a case before the Court of Justice,[50] the Court stated that there was no specific time limit on article 71(1)(b) and that this provision could apply to a German claimant who had worked in the U.K. on a temporary basis for 21 months.

17–40   The EC Commission put forward proposals to liberalise the rules in relation to unemployment benefits as long ago as 1980.[51] However, the Council of Ministers has not yet agreed on any proposals. Reform in this area is given added importance by the fact that the Court of Justice has held that unemployed persons are entitled to go to another EC country to look for work and may remain there for six months, or longer in some cases.[52]

C. Family Benefits and Allowances

17–41   The rules in relation to family benefits are set out in Chapter 7 of Title III of Regulation1408/71. "Family benefits" are defined as all benefits in kind or in cash intended to meet family expenses.[53] "Family allowances" are defined, more narrowly, as periodical cash benefits granted exclusively by reference to the number and, where appropriate, the age of members of the family.

17–42   A number of issues have arisen in Ireland in relation to the scope of family payments. The only benefit declared as a family benefit is child benefit.[54]

---

[49] *R(U)7/85.*

[50] Case C–216/89, *Reibold v. Bundesanstalt für Arbeit* [1990] E.C.R. I–4163.

[51] Proposal for a Council Regulation amending, for the benefit of unemployed workers, Regulation 1408/71 on the application of social security schemes to employed persons and their families moving within the Community [1980] O.J. C169/22.

[52] Case C–292/89 *R. v. Immigration Appeal Tribunal, ex parte Antonissen* [1991] E.C.R. I–745.

[53] Regulation 1408/71, art. 1(u)(i).

[54] In addition, child benefit and dependent increases in respect of retirement pension, old age (contributory) pensions and invalidity pension are declared to be benefits referred to in art. 77, while child benefit, orphan's (contributory) allowance and child-dependent increases in respect of widow's (contributory) pension are declared to be benefits referred to in art. 78. There are special rules for family allowances for pensioners (Art. 77) and orphans, see Pennings, above, n.1, pp. 181–188.

It is clear from the *Lenoir* case that "family allowances" are included within the category of family benefits.[55] Thus all increases in respect of a qualified child payable with Irish social security payments are family benefits. The ECJ has held that the U.K. family credit is a family benefit for the purposes of the Regulation.[56] This would imply that the Irish family income supplement (which is very similar to family credit) is also within the material scope of the Regulation. Deserted wife's benefit (now abolished for new claims) was not originally considered to be with the scope of the Regulation, as it is a payment unique to Ireland. However, it was a social insurance payment and was paid as a legal right. The only question in relation to deserted wife's benefit was whether the payment fell within the definition of "family benefits" as defined above. It was subsequently held by an appeals officer that deserted wife's benefit (for persons with qualified children) is intended to meet family expenses and therefore is within the definition of family benefits.[57]

(1) Entitlement to family benefits

17–43 The rules in relation to family benefits are set out in Chapter 7 of Title III of the E.U. Regulation. As child benefit in Ireland (and the U.K.) is granted on the basis of residence rather than being an insurance-based payment, issues in relation to aggregation of insurance periods do not apply in this area in the Irish case. The main issue which does arise is in relation to the country (or countries) which are responsible for the payment of family benefits where the person is working in one State but his or her children are living in a different Member State. Article 73 provides that an employed or self-employed person subjected to the legislation of a Member State shall be entitled to the family benefits provided by the legislation of that Member State for members of his or her family as if they were residing in that State. Thus the primary rule of priority is the *law of the place of employment* and, therefore, a person working (in insurable employment) in Ireland is entitled to child benefit for his or her children although they are living in another E.U. country.

17–44 However, it may happen that both parents are working in different E.U. countries and are both entitled to family benefits or, alternatively, that one parent is working in two E.U. countries and is entitled to benefits from

---

[55] Case 313/86, *Lenoir v. Caisse d'allocations familiales des Alpes-Maritimes* [1988] E.C.R. 5391.

[56] Case C–78/91 *Hughes v. Chief Adjudication Officer* [1992] E.C.R. I–4839.

[57] The decision of the ECJ in Joined Cases C–245/94 and C–312/94 *Hoever v. Land Nordrhein-Westfalen* [1996] E.C.R. I–4895, in which the Court held that a child-raising allowance intended to meet family expenses and remunerate the service of bringing up a child was within the scope of the Regulation, would also suggest that OFP might be considered to be a family benefit although it is declared by Ireland to be a special non-contributory benefit under Annex IIa.

both. In many E.U. countries (unlike Ireland and the U.K.) family benefits *are* linked to employment. Accordingly, article 76 of the Regulation provides that entitlement to family benefits under article 73 is suspended if, by reason of carrying on an occupation, family benefits are also payable under the legislation of the Member State where the members of the family are residing. Thus, if there is a conflict between two places of employment, the second order of priority is the *law of the place of residence*. A similar rule was introduced in article 10 of Regulation 574/72 for those countries in which entitlement is not based on employment. This provides that entitlement to family benefits or allowances under the legislation of a Member State where such benefits are not subject to conditions of insurance is suspended where benefit are due under the laws of another Member State. However, where the parent is carrying out an occupational activity in the first Member State, that Member State is responsible for the payment of family benefits. In other words, if a person from Ireland with children living here works in the U.K. he or she is entitled to child benefit for his or her children living here under U.K. legislation in accordance Article 73 (law of the place of employment). Any entitlement to child benefit under Irish law is suspended under article 10(1)(a) of Regulation 574/72. However, if his or her spouse works in Ireland, then Article 10(1)(b) means that the law of the place of residence takes precedence and the spouse is entitled to child benefit, while the person's entitlements under U.K. legislation are suspended. The drafters of the E.U. legislation originally intended that such suspension would operate so as to stop any payment of child benefit from the first country of employment in such a situation. However, the Court of Justice interpreted this provision to mean that only the amount of child benefit up to that paid in the country of residence was suspended.[58] The E.U. legislation has now been amended to reflect that interpretation.

17–45 While the position in principle is quite straightforward, there has been extensive case law in relation to particular situation, such as persons who are divorced, and the legislation has been amended on a number of occasions to reflect the developing case law.[59]

---

[58] Case 100/78 *Rossi v. Caisse de compensation pour allocations familiales des régions de Charleroi et Namur* [1979] E.C.R. 831. It should be noted that the approach taken here is different to that which the ECJ took in relation to overlapping of benefits, In the case of pensions, the right to full national pension is allowed, whereas in the case of child benefit only that amount up to the highest benefit is payable.

[59] Pennings, above, n.1, Chap. 16.

CHAPTER 18

Social Welfare Decisions and Appeals

18–01 This chapter looks at the social welfare decisions and appeals system. Over 1,400,000 persons currently benefit from social welfare payments and over a million new claims are lodged each year. These claims are adjudicated on, in most cases, by deciding officers of the Department and, in the case of supplementary welfare allowance (SWA), by superintendent community welfare officers. There are two main social welfare appeals systems: the Social Welfare Appeals Office, which deals with most appeals for payments administered by the Department, and a separate appeals systems operated by the regional health boards/authorities for payments under the SWA scheme.[1] The Social Welfare Appeals Office dealt with 16,500 appeals in 2001. The SWA appeal system deals with approximately 5,500 appeals per year.[2] This chapter outlines the operation of the social welfare decision and appeals system. It goes on to look at the operation of the SWA appeal system. We begin with a brief look at the rules of fair procedures as they apply to welfare appeals.

1. Decisions, Appeals and Fair Procedures[3]

18–02 The constitutional right to fair procedures applies in relation to all appeals, whether there is a formal appeals system or not.[4] The right to fair procedures means that the claimant is entitled to know the information upon which a decision has been made in relation to his or her case,[5] to see and comment on any reports or other documentation which may be relied on in coming to a decision on the case,[6] and to know the reasons for a decision to refuse the claim under appeal.[7] In coming to a decision on an appeal, the

---

[1] On the historical development of these systems see M. Cousins, "Social Welfare Adjudication, 1847–1995" (1993–1995) XXVIII–XXX Ir. Jur. 361.

[2] 517 *Dáil Debates* Col. 1174 (April 6, 2000).

[3] See generally Hogan and Morgan, *Administrative Law in Ireland* (3rd ed., Round Hall Sweet and Maxwell, 1998).

[4] *Kiely v. Minister for Social Welfare (No. 2)* [1977] I.R. 267; *Duffy v. Eastern Health Board,* unreported, High Court, March 14, 1988, see Whyte, "Social Welfare Law 1987/88: The Year in Review" (1988) 7 *J.I.S.L.L.* 82 at 103.

[5] *Kiely v. Minister for Social Welfare* [1971] I.R. 21; *State (Williams) v. Army Pension Board* [1983] I.R. 308.

[6] *Kiely v. Minister for Social Welfare* [1971] I.R. 21.

[7] *State (Creedon) v. Criminal Injuries Compensation Tribunal* [1989] I.L.R.M. 104.

adjudicating officer must come to a decision based on the evidence before him or her.[8] The officer must not take into account irrelevant matters[9] nor must the officer allow a set rule or policy or another official or organisation to dictate the outcome of the appeal.[10] It is also arguable that in some cases where there is a clear conflict of evidence the claimant should be entitled to an oral hearing of the case so that the claimant can present the evidence in person and can question any person who is giving evidence that is contrary to the claimant's case.[11] However, the Irish courts have not, to date, held that there is a constitutional right to an oral hearing.[12] It also appears that appeals officers are required to give reasons for their decisions, at least where that decision is being challenged.[13]

18–03   The European Court of Human Rights has held that the provisions of Article 6(1) of the European Convention on Human Rights apply to social welfare payments – both in relation to contributory and occupational injury benefits and also to non-contributory benefits where there is a legal right to payment.[14] However, the provisions of the ECHR to not apply to initial decisions. Article 6(1) provides that:

> "In the determination of his civil rights and obligations . . . everyone is entitled to a fair and public hearing within a reasonable time by the independent and impartial tribunal established by law. . . ."

18–04   The Court has, for example, held that failure to allow an appellant to submit her views or to afford her or her representative the oppurtunity to consult medical reports in relation to her case was in breach of the Convention.[15] Failure to decide a social welfare appeal within a "reasonable time" is in breach of the Convention.[16]

---

[8]   And not material of which the claimant has no notice; *Kiely (No. 2)* [1977] I.R. 267.

[9]   *State (Keller) v. Galway County Council* [1958] I.R. 142.

[10]   *State (Kershaw) v. Eastern Health Board* [[1985] I.L.R.M. 235; *State (McLoughlin) v. Eastern Health Board* [1986] I.R. 416; *Galvin v. Chief Appeals Officer* [1997] 3 I.R. 240.

[11]   See *Goldberg v. Kelly* 397 U.S. 254.

[12]   In relation to many appeals to the Social Welfare Appeals Office, the appellant will be entitled to an oral hearing in accordance with the statutory provisions (see below).

[13]   *State (Creedon) v. Criminal Injuries Compensation Tribunal* [1989] I.L.R.M. 104. Again, there are specific legislative provisions under the social welfare code (see below).

[14]   *Feldbrugge v. The Netherlands* 8 E.H.R.R. 425; *Deumeland v. Germany* 8 E.H.R.R. 448; *Salesi v. Italy* 26 E.H.R.R. 187; *Schuler-Zgraggen v. Switzerland* 16 E.H.R.R. 405; *Mennitto v. Italy*, October 5, 2000. See S. Jones, "The Human Rights Act 1998 and the Appeals Service" (2000) 7 *J.S.S.L.* 134 at 146-152 and *idem*, "Case digest" (2000) 7 J.S.S.L. D117.

[15]   *Feldbrugge v. The Netherlands* 8 E.H.R.R. 425 at para 44.

[16]   *Deumeland* 8 E.H.R.R. 448 at paras 77–90; *Mennitto v.Italy* October 5, 2000 at para 30.

18–05 The Court has held that failure to hold an oral hearing in a social welfare appeal is not necessarily a breach of the ECHR.[17] The Court stated that the public character of court hearings constitutes a fundamental principle enshrined in Article 6(1). It accepted that neither the letter nor the spirit of this provision prevented a person from waiving of his or her own free will, either expressly or tacitly, the entitlement to have the case heard in public; but it held any such waiver must be made in an unequivocal manner and must not run counter to any important public interest. In the instant case the Court held that it might reasonably be considered that the appellant had unequivocally waived her right to a public hearing. However, severely modifying its earlier broad statement of the importance of an oral hearing, the Court went on to say that:

> "Above all, it does not appear that the dispute raised issues of public importance such as to make a hearing necessary. Since it was highly technical, it was better dealt with in writing than in oral argument; furthermore, its private, medical nature would no doubt have deterred the applicant from seeking to have the public present. Lastly, it is understandable that in this sphere the national authorities should have regard to the demands of efficiency and economy. Systematically holding hearings could be an obstacle to 'the particular diligence required in social-security cases'… and could ultimately prevent compliance with the 'reasonable time' requirement of Article 6(1)…"

The Court held that there had accordingly been no breach of Article 6(1) in respect of the oral and public nature of the proceedings.

18–05A As the provisions of the European Convention on Human Rights are taken into account in interpreting E.C. law, it is arguable that this guarantee of a fair hearing applies in all appeals involving claims under E.C. law, *i.e.* in relation to Regulation 1408/71 on the social security rights of migrant workers and the Directive 86/378 on equal treatment in social security.[18]

2. Social Welfare Decision and the Social Appeals Office

A. Decisions

18–06 Decisions relating to entitlement to social welfare payments and to insurability of employment are made by "deciding officers" appointed by the Minister.[19] Section 247 of the Social Welfare (Consolidation) Act 1993

---

[17] *Schuler-Zgraggen v. Switzerland* 16 E.H.R.R. 405.
[18] Case 222/84 *Johnston v. Chief Constable of the RUC.* [1986] E.C.R. 1651; Case 222/86 *UNECTEF v. Heylens* [1987] E.C.R. 4097.
[19] Social Welfare (Consolidation) Act 1993 (SW(C)A 1993), ss. 246 and 247.

provides that every question to which it applies, save where the context otherwise requires, shall be decided by a deciding officer. Section 247(2) specifies that this involves every question arising under:

"(a) Part II (social insurance) being a question—
  (i) in relation to a claim for benefit,
 (ii) as to whether a person is or was disqualified for benefit,
 (iii) as to the period of any disqualification for benefit,
 (iv) as to whether an employment is or was insurable employment or insurable (occupational injuries) employment,
 (v)   as to whether a person is or was employed in an insurable employment or insurable (occupational injuries) employment,
 (vi) as to what rate of employment contribution is or was payable by an employer in respect of an employed contributor,
 (vii) as to who is or was the employer of an employed contributor,
(viii) as to whether a person is or was entitled to become a voluntary contributor,
 (ix) on any such other matter relating to Part II as may be prescribed,
 (x)   as to whether an employment is or was an insurable self-employment,
 (xi) as to whether a person is or was in insurable self-employment, or
 (xii) as to what rate of self-employment contribution is or was payable by a self-employed contributor,
(b) Part III (social assistance) other than Chapter 11 (supplementary welfare allowance) [excluding supplementary welfare allowance other than such categories of claims as may be prescribed under subsection (2B)];
(c) Part IV (child benefit);
(d) Part V (family income supplement); and
(e) Part VA (continued payment for qualified children);
(f) Part VI (general provisions relating to social insurance, social assistance and insurability);
(g) Part IX (liability to maintain family)."[20]

18–07   Thus deciding officers make all decisions concerning claims for and disqualification for all social insurance benefits and also decide all questions concerning entitlement to social assistance payments (except SWA, which, as we have seen, is dealt with under a separate system) and child benefit.[21] They also decide questions relating to whether an employment (including self-employment) is insurable under the Social Welfare Acts (*i.e.* whether a PRSI contribution is payable or not), what rate of contribution is payable, who the insured persons's employer is, and whether a person is entitled to become a voluntary contributor. A deciding officer may refer a question to an

---

[20] As amended by Social Wefare Act 1998 (SWA 1998), s.24 and Social Welfare Act 2000, s.30.
[21] In a very limited number of cases involving decisions concerning persons who are the subject of investigation by the Criminal Assets Bureau, decisions are made by deciding officers who are members of the Bureau. See SWA 1999, s. 30.

appeals officer rather than deciding the question himself or herself.[22] Deciding officers are "required to be free and unrestricted in discharging their functions."[23]

18–08 Administrative decisions, *e.g.* which day the claimant signs on or the time at which the claimant signs, are not decided by deciding officers but by other social welfare officers. Decisions relating to social welfare schemes that are not provided for in the Social Welfare Acts are not made by deciding officers, *e.g.* the Household Benefits and the fuel allowance. Other exclusions are questions concerning the granting of credited contributions and decisions to suspend payments. Such decisions are therefore not subject to appeal to an appeals officer.

18–09 When the deciding officer makes a decision, it must be given in writing and, where the decision is not in favour of the claimant, the deciding officer must set out the reasons for the decision and a memorandum of this must be issued to the person as soon as may be after the making of the decision.[24] Decisions in relation to the insurability of employment and the reasons therefore are given to all parties who are subject to the decision. Deciding officers are told that, while not legally necessary, it may be appropriate to give reasons for favourable decision in certain circumstances.

18–10 In *Murphy v. Minister for Social Welfare*,[25] a case involving a dispute as to the insurability of the applicant, Blayney J. held that the deciding officer only had jurisdiction in relation to the question specifically before him, in that case as to the appropriate rate of contribution payable by the applicant. He held that the deciding officer did not have jurisdiction to decide that the applicant was not in insurable employment at all. It is submitted that this interpretation is excessively legalistic and is not justified by the broad terms of section 247.[26]

B. Revision of Decisions

18–11 A deciding officer may revise a decision at any time if the original decision was erroneous in the light of new evidence or new facts which came to light since the original decision; or by reason of some a mistake having been made in relation to the law or the facts; or if there has been a relevant

---

[22] SW(C)A 1993, s. 250.

[23] *McLoughlin v. Minister for Social Welfare* [1958] I.R. 1 at 27.

[24] Social Welfare (Consolidated Payments Provisions) Regulations 1994 (S.I. No. 417 of 1994), art. 107A as inserted by S.I. 139 of 1999.

[25] [1987] I.R. 295.

[26] See G. Whyte, *Social Inclusion and the Legal System* (IPA, Dublin, 2002), p. 132.

change of circumstances since the decision was given.[27] An appeal can be made against a revision of a decision in the same way as an appeal against the original decision. A deciding officer cannot revise a decision that is under appeal unless the revision would be favourable to the claimant.[28] In any other case, a deciding officer can revise a decision in a way which will be unfavourable to the claimant, *e.g.* if he or she feels that the claimant is no longer entitled to the payment. However, before a deciding officer comes to a decision that the claimant who has been in receipt of a social welfare payment should have a continuing payment disallowed, the courts have held that the rules of natural justice require a pre-termination procedure.[29] In particular, the deciding officer "should inform the person concerned that the position is being reviewed by him; the grounds upon which he is considering disallowing further payment; and the person concerned should be given an opportunity to answer the case made against him."[30] This need not involve an oral hearing and the deciding officer may inform the person either in person or by letter.[31]

18–12   Decisions may be revised on receipt of notification that the claimant has submitted an appeal, although there is no statutory framework for such a process. Deciding officers are advised that the arguments put forward by the appellant should be carefully examined to see whether the decision should be revised, wholly or in part, or whether it should stand. In practice almost all appeals in which there is a dispute about medical incapacity or disablement are referred by the Department for a further medical opinion from the Department's medical referees. If a more favourable medical decision is given, the deciding officer will revise the decision in favour of the claimant. In an appeal where there is a dispute about means, the Department may arrange for a further investigation by a social welfare officer. If the deciding officer decides to revise the decision by allowing the case *in part only*, the person will be asked whether he or she is satisfied with the revised decision or whether he or she wishes to pursue the appeal.

---

[27] SW(C)A 1993, s. 248. On "change of circumstance", see *Adjudication Officer v. McKiernan*, reported in R(1) 2/94.

[28] *ibid.*, s. 248(2).

[29] *Thompson v. Minister for Social Welfare* [1989] I.R. 618. In *State (Hoolahan) v. Minister for Social Welfare*, unreported, High Court, July 23, 1986, Barron J. stated that the claimant "should know fully the extent of the case being made against her and that no decision should be made until she has been given proper opportunity to deal fully with a case". See also *Goldberg v. Kelly* 397 U.S. 254; *Mathews v. Eldridge* 424 U.S. 319.

[30] *Thompson* [1989] I.R. 618 at 621.

[31] In the United States, the Supreme Court held that the constitutional guarantee of due process required that an oral hearing be held prior to termination of "welfare" payments: *Goldberg v. Kelly* 397 U.S. 254. However, the Court subsequently distinguished *Kelly* (arguably on somewhat unconvincing grounds) to hold that an oral hearing was not required prior to termination of disability benefits: *Mathews v. Eldridge* 424 U.S. 319. And see *Richardson v. Wright* 405 U.S. 208.

C. Appeals[32]

18–13 The Social Welfare Appeals Office was established in 1990 as an independent executive office with its own separate premises and staff. The Chief Appeals Officer is responsible for the distribution of appeals to the appeals officers and, ultimately, for the overall operation of the Social Welfare Appeals Office. There are currently 18 appeals officers in addition to the Chief Appeals Officer and Deputy Chief Appeals Officer. All appeals officers are departmental officials and are appointed by the Minister. Appeals officers are quasi-judicial officers and are "required to be free and unrestricted in discharging their functions".[33] However, the Supreme Court has also held that decisions by appeals officers (and deciding officers) are "inherently administrative" and that the fact that such officers are bound to act judicially does not alter the character of their functions.[34]

18–14 Any person who is dissatisfied with a decision given by the deciding officer may appeal to an appeals officer by giving notice of appeal to the Chief Appeals Officer within the time laid down.[35] Therefore, any claimant who is dissatisfied with a decision can appeal against that decision. An employer who is dissatisfied with a decision regarding, for example, insurability or rate of contributions, can also appeal against a decision. To appeal, the claimant must give notice, in writing, to the Chief Appeals Officer within 21 days from the date on which the claimant received notification of the decision.[36] However, notice of appeal given outside this time can be accepted with the consent of the Chief Appeals Officer.[37] The notice of appeal should contain a statement of the facts and the contentions upon which the claimant intends to rely, *i.e.* the grounds of the appeal. Any written evidence, *e.g.* medical reports, etc., should be submitted with the notice of appeal.[38] If written evidence is not available when the appeal is being submitted, it can be submitted at a later date or at the appeal itself. The appeals officer does have the power to look for further details of the grounds of the appeal, although

---

[32] The provisions concerning appeals are set out in Chap. 2 of Pt VII of SW(C)A 1993, ss. 251–265 (as amended), and in the Social Welfare (Appeals) Regulations 1998 (S.I. 108 of 1998) (SW(A)R 1998).

[33] *McLoughlin v. Minister for Social Welfare* [1958] I.R. 1.

[34] *Minister for Social, Community and Family Affairs v. Scanlon* [2001] 1. I.R. 64 at 87.

[35] SW(C)A 1993, s. 257. Where the Chief Appeals Officer certifies that the ordinary appeals procedures are inadequate to secure the effective processing of an appeal, the appeal is submitted to the Circuit Court: s. 253A as inserted by SWA 1997 and amended by SWA 1999. This relates to Criminal Assets Bureau cases.

[36] SW(A)R 1998, art. 9.

[37] *ibid.*, art. 9(2).

[38] *ibid.*, art. 9(4).

this is rarely done.[39] The appeals officer also has the power to allow the claimant to raise matters at the appeal that were not mentioned in the appeal notice. Any person who wishes to withdraw an appeal can do so by sending a notice of withdrawal to the Chief Appeals Officer.[40]

18–15   When the Chief Appeals Officer receives a notice of appeals he or she must send it to the Department, which is required to send back:

1.   a statement from the deciding officer setting out to what extent the claimant's facts or arguments are admitted or disputed, and

2.   any information, document or item that the deciding officer has that is relevant to the appeal.[41]

D. Hearings

18–16   About 60 per cent of appeals are heard orally, mainly in areas such as carers, disability, occupational injury and unemployment appeals. Questions concerning the means test are more often dealt with summarily. Oral hearings are held in private.[42] The appeals officer has a discretion as to whether to grant an oral hearing or not, but this is not an unlimited discretion.[43] The basic rule is that the claimant should be given an oral hearing unless the case can properly determined without one. The Supreme Court has stated that:

> "an oral hearing is mandatory unless the case is of such a nature that it can be determined without an oral hearing, that is, summarily. An appeal is of such a nature that it can be determined summarily if a determination of the claim can fairly be made on a consideration of the documentary evidence. If however, there are unresolved conflicts in the documentary evidence, as to any matter essential to a ruling of the claim, the intention of the Regulations is that those conflicts shall be resolved by an oral hearing."[44]

18–17   In *Galvin v. Chief Appeals Officer*,[45] a case concerning a dispute as to whether social insurance contributions had been paid in the past by the applicant, Costello P. held that:

---

[39] SW(A)R 1998, art. 12.

[40] *ibid.*, art. 9(5).

[41] *ibid.*, art. 10.

[42] *Quaere* this position in the light of Art. 6(1) of the European Convention on Human Rights. However, the European Court of Human Rights has appeared to be prepared to accept private hearings, and indeed non-oral hearings, in several social security cases (*supra* at 18–04).

[43] SW(A)R 1998, arts 13 and 14.

[44] *Kiely v. Minister for Social Welfare (No. 2)* [1977] I.R. 267 at 278.

[45] [1997] 3 I.R. 240.

"there are no hard and fast rules to guide an Appeals Officer … as to when the dictates of fairness require the holding of an oral hearing. The case (like others) must be decided on the circumstances pertaining, the nature of the inquiry being undertaken by the decision-maker, the rules under which the decision-maker is acting, and the subject matter with which he is dealing and account should also be taken as to whether an oral hearing was requested."

18–18 In the instant case, the Court came to the conclusion that an oral hearing was necessary, as otherwise it would be extremely difficult if not impossible to arrive at a true judgment on the issues because of a range of factors, including of the distant time period to which the dispute referred (between 36 and 50 years previously) and departmental errors in relation to the contribution record.

E. Assessors

18–19 Assessors are appointed by the Chief Appeals Officer on the nomination of the trade unions and employer organisations.[46] They are asked to serve on a rota basis and do so about twice a year. Two assessors are called to oral hearings involving unemployment assistance or unemployment benefit claims (except for means-test appeals), one from the employers' panel and the other from the trade union panel. If either or both assessors are not present, the appeals officer must get the claimant's consent before the appeal can go ahead. If the claimant does not wish to consent to this, the appeal cannot go ahead and must be adjourned.[47] It is quite usual for either or both of the assessors to be absent. The assessors do not decide the appeal and do not have any say in the appeals officer's decision. Their function is simply to assist the appeals officer with their local knowledge of the employment situation. The Supreme Court has interpreted the role of assessor very narrowly and has held, in the case of a medical assessor, that the assessor should not take an active part in the appeal or ask questions directly of the claimant.[48] This decision, based on case law under the Workman's Compensation Act 1934,[49] is arguably not appropriate to the very different role which an assessor should play in unemployment appeals. Such assessors should, and frequently do in practice, take a sufficiently active part in the appeal to allow them to properly assist the appeals officer with their expert knowledge.

---

[46] SW(C)A 1993, s. 255.

[47] *ibid.*, s. 260 and see *Thompson v. Minister for Social Welfare* [1989] I.R. 618.

[48] *Kiely (No. 2)* [1977] I.R. 267. For decisions in other jurisdictions, see *R. v. Deputy Industrial Injuries Commissioner ex p. Jones* [1962] 2 All E.R. 430 and *Richardson v. Perales* 402 U.S. 389.

[49] *Delaney v. Valentine* [1945] I.R. 1.

F. Representation

18–20   If an oral hearing is granted, the claimant may appear in person. If public transport is available, the appeals office will provide the claimant with travel vouchers to and from the appeal. Otherwise, the appeals officer can award the claimant travelling expenses. The appeals officer may also award any other expenses that the claimant incurs in attending the appeal, *e.g.* if the claimant has to take time off work.[50] A claimant may, with the permission of the appeals officer, be represented by a member of family or by any other person [51] In practice, the appeals officer will almost always give this permission.[52] The Government-funded Legal Aid Board cannot represent the claimant at a social welfare appeal because such appeals are excluded from the scope of the Civil Legal Aid Scheme. In *Corcoran v. Minister for Social Welfare*,[53] Murphy J. held that there was no authority for the proposition that a lay tribunal exercising a quasi-judicial function must afford to the parties an opportunity to procure legal advice and be represented by lawyers or that the State should be bound to pay for such assistance. If a solicitor or other representative appears at the appeal, the Appeals Officer can award expenses only in respect of that person's actual attendance.[54] The deciding officer may appear at the appeal, although it is less usual for this to happen, or he or she may be represented by another officer of the Department or any other person appointed by the Minister. Any other person who in the opinion of the appeals officer should be heard may also appear at the hearing, *e.g.* an employer in a question involving a dismissal from work.[55]

G. Evidence, Witnesses and Procedure

18–21   In dealing with an appeal, the appeals officer is not confined to the grounds on which the deciding officer decided the case and may decide the

---

[50] SW(C)A 1993, s. 261.

[51] SW(A)R 1998, art. 15.

[52] In *Corcoran v. Minister for Social Welfare* [1991] 1 I.R. 175, Murphy J. expressed the view that a solicitor could not, as a matter of right, attend a hearing, although it would have been "churlish" if the appeals officer had refused to hear a solicitor.

[53] [1991] 1 I.R. 175.

[54] SW(C)A 1993, s. 261 (as amended by SWA 1996, s.34) provides that in relation to appeals, an appeals officer may make an award to a person appearing before the officer towards the person's expenses. "Expenses" means (i) expenses necessarily incurred by the appellant or a witness in respect of his or her travel and subsistence or loss of remuneration, and (ii) in the case of a person appearing before an appeals officer in a representative capacity, an amount only in respect of that person's actual attendance. This is a legislative reversal of *O'Sullivan v. Minister for Social Welfare* unreported, High Court, May 9, 1995, Barron J.

[55] SW(A)R 1998, art. 15.

question as if it were being deciding for the first time.[56] The procedure at the hearing is determined by the appeals officer.[57] In practice, the procedure is very informal and the appeal usually takes the form of a question-and-answer session between the appeals officer and the claimant. Thus, given the frequent absence of any departmental representative, the hearing normally assumes an investigative rather than the adversarial approach, with the appeals officer explaining the background to the case and the reasons for the Department's decision and then clarifying the claimant's case by questioning him or her and any relevant witnesses.[58] The appeals officer can hear evidence from any person concerned in the appeal or any person who the appeals officer feels should be heard. The appeals officer may also admit any duly authenticated written statement as prime facie evidence if he or she thinks that it is appropriate to do so.[59] However, it appears that written evidence should be outweighed if a witness can give credible oral evidence contradicting the written statement.[60] For example, the appeals officer can admit a report from the Department's medical referee stating that, in the medical referee's opinion, the appellant is capable of work as evidence of that fact. However, if the appellant's doctor attends the appeal and gives evidence which contradicts the written report, this should usually outweigh the medical referee's evidence.[61] Therefore, it is very important for the claimant to make sure that any witnesses attend the appeal. In the case of a medical appeal, the appeals officer can award expenses to the claimant's doctor if he or she attends as a witness.

18–22 The appeals officer has the power to take evidence on oath and may administer oaths to people who attend as witnesses at hearing.[62] The appeals officer also has the power to require any person to attend to give evidence or to produce any documents relating to the appeal.[63] A notice requiring a person's

---

[56] SW(C)A 1993, s.257(3).

[57] SW(A)R 1998, art. 18.

[58] The Supreme Court in *Kiely (No. 2)* [1977] I.R. 267 seemed to be of the opinion that appeals were intended to operate on an adversarial basis, with a representative of the Department attending to argue its case. This certainly does not happen in practice and, in the author's opinion, it is questionable if such an approach would be in the claimant's best interests.

[59] SW(A)R 1998, art. 18(3).

[60] *Kiely v. Minister for Social Welfare* [1971] I.R. 21.

[61] In practice, a rigid interpretation of *Kiely* might require the Department to have its medical referees available to give evidence in each appeal in case conflicting oral evidence was given. This could give rise to great practical difficulties. See the very similar U.S. case of *Richardson v. Perales* 402 U.S. 389, in which the Supreme Court held that written reports by doctors who had examined a claimant for disability benefits did constitute "substantial evidence" supporting a finding of nondisability, despite the absence of cross-examination and the opposing testimony of the claimant and his medical witness.

[62] SW(C)A 1993, s. 258.

[63] *ibid.*, s. 259.

attendance must be either given to him or her in person or sent by registered post to the address at which the person ordinarily resides or to his or her place of business.[64] A person who has received such a notice and who refuses or willfully neglects to attend or to give evidence or to produce documents is guilty of an offence and will be liable, on summary conviction, to a fine not exceeding €1,270.[65] Where a person required to attend to give evidence or to produce documents fails to do so, the appeals officer may, on serving notice on that person, apply to the District Court for an order directing the person to attend or to produce the documents.[66] If, once notice of the hearing has been given, the claimant or any other party fails to attend, the appeals officer may take such steps as he or she thinks appropriate, including deciding the appeal in the claimant's absence.[67] The appeals officer may postpone or adjourn the appeal from time to time.[68] If the claimant is unable to attend the appeal, an adjournment may be requested by contacting the appeals office. This will normally be allowed if there is a legitimate reason for asking for adjournment.

H. Appeal Decision

18–23 If an oral hearing is held, the appeals officer normally does not give a decision there and then. The appeals officer sends the decision as soon as possible to the Chief Appeals Officer, who then notifies the claimant of the decision. Where the decision is not in the claimant's favour, the appeals officer must give a note of the reasons for the decision and this will also be sent to the claimant.[69] The reasons should make clear to the unsuccessful appellant in "general and broad terms" the grounds of the decision [70]

I. Criminal Assets Cases

18–24 Section 253A[71] provides that where an appeal has been made and where the Chief Appeals Officer certifies that the ordinary appeals procedures are inadequate to secure the effective processing of the appeal, the Chief Appeals Officer may direct the appellant to submit the appeal to the Circuit Court. This is basically intended to cover cases involving investigations by the Criminal Assets Bureau.[72] The Circuit Court may affirm or substitute the

---

[64] SW(C)A 1993, s. 259(2).
[65] *ibid.*, s. 259(3).
[66] *ibid.*, s. 259(4).
[67] SW(A)R 1998, art. 16.
[68] *ibid.*, art. 18(2).
[69] *ibid.*, art. 9.
[70] *State (Creedon) v. Criminal Injuries Compensation Tribunal* [1989] I.L.R.M. 104; *Crake v. Supplementary Benefits Commission* [1982] 1 All E.R. 498.
[71] As inserted by SWA 1997, s.34 and amended by SWA 1999, s.29.
[72] See *McGinley v. Deciding Officer, Criminal Assets Bureau*, unreported, Circuit Court, May 30, 2001.

deciding officer's decision on the same evidence as would otherwise be available to the appeals officer. There is no appeal from the decision of the Circuit Court.

2. Further Appeal

18–25   The appeals officer's decision is stated to be final and conclusive[73] but there are several ways in which such a decision can be challenged.

A. Revision of the Decision by an Appeals Officer

18–26   An appeals officer may, at any time and from time to time, revise any decision of an appeals officer if the original decision appears to be wrong in the light of new evidence or new facts which came to light since the original decision was made or if there has been a relevant change of circumstances.[74] There is no set procedure for asking for a revision of a decision and one should simply write to the appeals office asking that the decision be revised and setting out the new facts, new evidence or change of circumstances which would justify a revised decision.

B. Revision by the Chief Appeals Officer

18–27   The Chief Appeals Officer may, at any time and from time to time, revise the decision of an appeals officer if it appears that the decision was wrong because of a mistake in relation to the law or to the facts.[75] Therefore, the claimant does not need to show new facts or new evidence to have a decision revised. Again, there is no set procedure. The Chief Appeals Officer may refuse to revise the decision, he or she may allow the claim, or he or she may set aside the appeals officer's decision and arrange a new hearing before a different appeals officer. The Chief Appeals Officer will normally only revise an appeals officer's decision if it is clearly wrong and one which no reasonable appeals officer would have come to, or if a serious mistake was made in hearing the appeal.

C. Revision of the Decision by a Deciding Officer

18–28   A deciding officer may revise a decision of an appeals officer if it appears that there has been a relevant change of circumstances which has

---

[73] SW(C)A 1993, s. 265.
[74] *ibid.*, s. 262.
[75] *ibid.*, s. 263.

come to notice since the decision was given.[76] This provision reverses the High Court decisions in *Lundy v. Minister for Social Welfare* and *O'Connor v. Minister for Social Welfare*, in which the Court held that there was no such power of revision under the legislation as it stood at that time.[77] The purpose was to clarify that deciding officers can revise a decision where there has been a change of circumstances and to avoid the administrative burden which would otherwise be imposed on appeals officers.

D. Appeal to the High Court

18–29   There is a specific right of appeal to the High Court on a point of law from an appeals officer's decision set out in the Social Welfare Acts.[78] Section 271 of the 1993 Act provides that any person who is dissatisfied with the decision of an appeals officer or the revised decision of the Chief Appeals Officer, on any question other than a question to which section 265 applies, may appeal that decision or revised decision to the High Court on any question of law. Section 265, in turn, provides that:

> "The decision of an appeals officer on any question
>
> (a) specified in section 247(2)(a)(i), (ii) or (iii), other than a question arising under Chapter 10 of Part II as to whether an accident arose out of and in the course of employment, and
>
> (b) arising under Part III, IV, V, VI, VIII or this Part, shall, subject to sections 248(1)(b), 262, 263 and 271, be final and conclusive."

18–30   This might suggest that the right of appeal is limited to a narrow range of issues not referred to in section 265. However, in *Kinghan v. Minister for Social Welfare*[79] Lynch J. took a broad view of the High Court's jurisdiction in hearing such appeals, stating that the legislation excluding the right of appeal should be construed narrowly so as not to oust the jurisdiction of the High Court, save where such ouster was clear. He held that:

> "It would be strange if the High Court were not to be allowed to assist in resolving [a question in relation to the true construction of the statutes and Regulations] although in a wide sense it could be said to be a question arising in relation to a claim for benefit. I think that I have jurisdiction to deal with the question …"[80]

18–31   The effect of this decision appears to be that an appeal lies on a point

---

[76] SW(C)A 1993, s. 248(1)(b).

[77] *Lundy v. Minister for Social Welfare* [1993] 1 I.R. 406; *O'Connor v. Minister for Social Welfare* unreported, High Court, April 30, 1993.

[78] SW(C)A 1993, s. 271.

[79] Unreported, High Court, November 25, 1985.

[80] *ibid.*, at p. 4.

of law in respect of all decisions of an appeals officer. Order 90 of the Rules of the Superior Courts sets out the procedures for appeals under section 271. The rules provide that costs shall not be allowed in such proceedings except by special order of the court. The deciding officers and appeals officers are also subject to the general power of the High Court to judicially review any administrative decision. In addition, the Chief Appeals Officer may, where he considers it appropriate, refer a question to the High Court for a decision.[81]

18–32 In *Henry Denny*,[82] a case brought under section 271, Hamilton C.J. expressed the view that:

> "the courts should be slow to interfere with the decisions of expert administrative tribunals. Where conclusions are based upon an identifiable error of law or an unsustainable finding of fact by a tribunal such conclusions must be corrected. Otherwise it should be recognised that tribunals which have been given statutory tasks to perform and exercise their functions, as is now usually the case, with a high degree of expertise and provide coherent and balanced judgments on the evidence and arguments heard by them it should not be necessary for the courts to review their decisions by way of appeal or judicial review."

18–33 Keane J. followed the Supreme Court decision in *Mara (Inspector of Taxes) v Hummingbird Ltd*,[83] a case concerning income tax appeals, in which Kenny J., speaking for the Court, said:

> "A case stated consists in part of findings on questions of primary fact . . . These findings on primary facts should not be set aside by the courts unless there was no evidence whatever to support them. The commissioner then goes on in the case stated to give his conclusions or inferences from these primary facts. These are mixed questions of fact and law and the court should approach these in a different way. If they are based on the interpretation of documents, the court should reverse them if they are incorrect for it is in as good a position to determine the meaning of documents as is the commissioner. If the conclusions from the primary facts are ones which no reasonable commissioner could draw, the court should set aside his findings on the ground that he must be assumed to have misdirected himself as to the law or made a mistake in reasoning. Finally, if his conclusions show that he has adopted a wrong view of the law, they should be set aside. If however they are not based on a mistaken view of the law or a wrong interpretation of documents, they should not be set aside unless the inferences which he made from the primary facts were ones that no reasonable commissioner could draw."

---

[81] SW(C)A 1993, s. 253.
[82] *Henry Denny & Sons (Ireland) Ltd v. Minister for Social Welfare* [1998] 1 I.R. 37.
[83] [1982] 2 I.L.R.M. 421.

E. Ombudsman

18–34   The Ombudsman may review the actions of the Appeals Officer.[84]

F. Reference to the European Court of Justice

18–35   In accordance with Article 234 of the E.C. Treaty, where any question concerning the interpretation of E.C. law is raised before any court or tribunal of a Member State, the court or tribunal may, if it considers that a decision on the question is necessary to enable it to give judgment, request the European Court of Justice to give a ruling on that question. The Court of Justice has considered the question as to which national bodies are to be considered to be tribunals for this purpose and therefore to have the power to refer a question to the Court. The Court has taken a broad interpretation of the concept of what constitutes a tribunal for this purpose.[85] The Court decided that a tribunal of a Dutch social security fund was entitled to refer a question to the Court. The Court of Justice noted that the tribunal was set up under public law, its rules had to be approved by a Dutch Minister of State, the members of the tribunal were appointed by the responsible Minister, and the tribunal was bound to apply the rule of law in disputes coming before it. Similarly, the position of appeals officer is set up under the Social Welfare Acts, the Regulations relating to appeals are made by the Minister who also appoints the appeals officers, and an appeals officer must apply the law in coming to a decision on an appeal. The decision of an appeals officer is legally binding. Therefore it is arguable that the position of appeals officer comes within the definition of a tribunal for the purpose of Article 234 of the E.C. Treaty and that an appeals officer has the power to refer a question involving an interpretation of E.U. law in relation to an appeal to the Court of Justice. References to the Court of Justice are frequently made by the social security appeals bodies in other Member States, including the Social Security Commissioners in the United Kingdom.

3. The Supplementary Welfare Allowance Appeal System

18–36   As we have seen, the Supplementary Welfare Allowance (SWA) Scheme is administered by the regional health boards/authorities on behalf of the Department. Each health board is subdivided into community care areas. Decisions on entitlement to supplementary welfare allowance are made by the Superintendent Community Welfare Officer (SCWO) for the community

---

[84] See Hogan and Morgan, above, n.3, Chap 8.
[85] Case 61/65 *Vaassen-Göbbels* [1966] E.C.R. 261.

care area in which the claimant lives. A SCWO may, at any time and from time to time, revise any decision if it appears that the original decision was wrong in the light of new facts or new evidence which have been brought to his or her notice since the original decision was given or if there has been a relevant change in circumstances.[86]

18–37 Section 267 of the Social Welfare (Consolidation) Act 1993 provides that where a person is dissatisfied with the determination by an officer of a health board of a claim for supplementary welfare allowance, an appeal shall lie against such determination to a person (being either another officer of the health board or a person not such an officer) appointed or designated by the Minister. In practice, the functions of an appeals officer are normally carried out as part of a range of other functions, but specific appeals officers have been appointed in some health board areas.

18–38 Sections 267(2) and 273A[87] provide that the Minister may by Regulations specify the procedures to be followed in making determinations on SWA and provide for the making and determination of appeals. The Social Welfare (Consolidated Supplementary Welfare Allowance) (Amendment) (Determination and Appeals) Regulations 1998 (S.I. No. 107 of 1998) set out the rules in this regard.

18–39 Article 35 of the Regulations provides that a determination by any officer of a health board on a claim to supplementary welfare allowance is to be in writing and that if a determination is not in favour of the person, it must include a note of the reasons for the determination. Article 36 provides that any person who is dissatisfied with the determination by a health board of a claim for supplementary welfare allowance and wishes to appeal against such determination must give notice in that behalf, in writing, to an officer of the health board appointed or designated by the Minister under section 267 of the 1993 Act to determine such appeal. An appeal must be made within 21 days from the date of the notification of the determination to the appellant; but notice of appeal given after the end of that period may, with the approval of the designated officer, be accepted. The notice of appeal should contain a statement of the facts and contentions upon which the appellant intends to rely and the appellant should include with the notice of appeal any documentary evidence in support of the appeal.

18–40 The designated officer then sends the notice of appeal the health board, which returns to the designated officer: (a) a statement showing the

---

[86] SW(C)A 1993, s. 268.
[87] The latter inserted by the SWA 1996.

extent to which the facts and contentions advanced by the appellant in relation to his or her appeal are admitted or disputed; and (b) any information, document or item in the power and control of the health board that is relevant to the appeal.[88] The designated officer may seek further details on the appeal from the appellant or the health board. He or she may allow the amendment of any notice of appeal, statement or particulars at any stage of the proceedings.[89]

18–41 The SWA Appeal Regulations do not make any reference to oral hearings and it is rare for an oral hearing to be given under the SWA scheme at first instance. Article 39 provides that the appeal determination must be in writing and that in any case where the determination is not in favour of the appellant, it must include a note of the reasons for the decision. The health board then notifies the appellant of the determination and (where relevant) of the reasons therefor.

18–42 All decisions regarding eligibility for SWA are subject to judicial review by the High Court and they can also be investigated by the Ombudsman.

18–43 The Social Welfare Act 1996 provided that appeals in relation to SWA could be brought to the Social Welfare Appeals Office following exhaustion of the health board appeals system.[90] Section 257A of the 1993 Act now provides that where a person is dissatisfied with the determination of an appeal by him or her under section 267 in relation to a claim for supplementary welfare allowance, the question shall, on notice of appeal being given to the health board within the prescribed time, be forwarded by the board to the Chief Appeals Officer for referral to an appeals officer. This section has been commenced in relation to supplementary welfare allowance payable under sections 177, 178 and 179 (*i.e.* basic SWA payments and weekly supplements).[91] It was not extended to exceptional needs payments because of their discretionary nature. Appeals in relation to SWA are dealt with in the same manner as general social welfare appeals (as outlined above) once submitted to the SWAO.[92]

---

[88] Social Welfare (Consolidated Supplementary Welfare Allowance) Regulations 1995 (S.I. No. 382 of 1995), art. 37.

[89] *ibid.*, art. 38.

[90] SW(C)A 1993, s. 257A as inserted by SWA 1996, s.30.

[91] Social Welfare Act 1996 (Section 30) (Commencement) Order 1998 (S.I. No. 106 of 1998).

[92] The provision of the Social Welfare (Appeals) Regulations 1998 (S.I. No. 106 of 1998) apply to SWA appeals before the SWAO.

Index

References are to paragraph numbers.